IN THE PSYCHIATRIST'S CHAIR III

ANTHONY CLARE

Chatto & Windus
LONDON

Published in 1998

2 4 6 8 10 9 7 5 3 1

Copyright © Anthony Clare 1998

Anthony Clare has asserted his right
under the Copyright, Designs and Patents Act 1988
to be identified as the author of this work

First published in Great Britain in 1998 by Chatto & Windus
Random House, 20 Vauxhall Bridge Road,
London SW1V 2SA

Random House Australia (Pty) Limited
20 Alfred Street, Milsons Point, Sydney,
New South Wales 2061, Australia

Random House New Zealand Limited
18 Poland Road, Glenfield,
Auckland 10, New Zealand

Random House South Africa (Pty) Limited
Endulini, 5A Jubilee Road, Parktown 2193, South Africa

Random House UK Limited Reg. No. 954009

A CIP catalogue record for this book
is available from the British Library

ISBN 0 7011 6723 8

Papers used by Random House UK Limited are natural,
recyclable products made from wood grown in sustainable forests.
The manufacturing processes conform to the environmental
regulations of the country of origin.

Typeset by Deltatype
Printed and bound in Great Britain by
Mackays of Chatham PLC.

To my children – Rachel, Simon, Eleanor, Peter, Sophie, Justine and Sebastian – from whom I have learned so much

Acknowledgements

I am indebted once more to my friend and colleague Michael Ember, whose legendary professional skills as producer and editor of BBC Radio 4's *In the Psychiatrist's Chair* are in large part the basis of its success over the past sixteen years. Liz Ember's unfailing administrative skills have ensured that the logistics of coping with the needs of busy interviewees and my own somewhat chaotic life-style were always superbly organised. I am grateful to the BBC for their belief in the programme. Eugenie Boyd has provided first-class editorial support. I must thank Penny Hoare who has been throughout the consummate editor, firm, encouraging and wise. Lastly, there are the twelve subjects of this book who provided me with so much to think about and who gave generously of their time and reflections.

Contents

Martin Bell

In 1980 the term 'post-traumatic stress disorder' was introduced into the influential American classificatory system of disease, the Diagnostic and Statistical Manual, 3rd edition, (so-called DSM-111). It reflected widespread acknowledgement of the psychological distress experienced by veterans of the Vietnam War, although recognition of post-traumatic symptoms has a much longer history. It has been shown, for example, that not only the symptom profile of what we call PTSD but also its profound personal and social consequences can be found in accounts of the Trojan War. Samuel Pepys documented it after the Great Fire of London when he had difficulty sleeping after the disaster, while Charles Dickens reported symptoms after surviving a serious train crash at Staplehurst in Kent in 1865. Conditions such as 'irritable heart' described in US Civil War soldiers, and cardiac neurosis, combat fatigue and shell shock in soldiers fighting in the two world wars and the Korean War strongly resemble current notions of post-traumatic stress. Yet, surprisingly perhaps, the issue of post-traumatic stress remained relatively neglected until the DSM-111 initiative. Since then there has been a veritable epidemic. A sophisticated community study in the US suggests that one in 14 people will suffer from the syndrome at some stage in their lifetime and it has been reported and studied in a wide variety of groups and settings, including Australian fire-fighters, Armenian earthquake survivors, casualties of the Piper Alpha oil-rig explosion, inhabitants of Lockerbie, concentration camp survivors, victims of torture and everyday victims of such crimes as rape, assault, stalking, mugging and terrorist bombings.

Symptoms include the persistent remembering or reliving of the stressful event in intrusive flashbacks, vivid memories and/or recurring dreams, avoidance of circumstances resembling or associated with the stressful event, and a variety of other distressing experiences including irritability, memory difficulties, emotional outbursts, sleep disturbances, marked anxiety and depression.

One of the commonest beliefs, both lay and professional, is that talking through traumatic or stressful experiences is crucial to the long-term recovery of those who have suffered the physical and psychological effects of trauma. The belief originated in the work of British military doctors in World War One in the study and treatment of so-called 'shell shock'. These psychiatrists pioneered the principles of 'forward psychiatry' whereby traumatised soldiers were debriefed immediately and close to the front lines and, on recovery, quickly returned to their units. The condition was readily accepted as a genuine psychological disorder with a good prognosis. In post-war Germany, in contrast, physicians and psychiatrists questioned whether traumatic neurosis was a genuine illness and preferred instead to see affected veterans as unstable personalities seeking, consciously or unconsciously, to gain compensation, financial or otherwise, from their illness. These two contrasting attitudes to PTSD exist to this day and colour our attempts to understand and treat it.

In general, however, post-traumatic counselling and so-called 'debriefing' programmes have proliferated. Scarcely has the dust settled on a major public tragedy or disaster before an army of counsellors and psychotherapists is on hand to encourage and assist victims and emergency workers to ventilate their feelings and relive their experiences. The development undoubtedly reflects the widespread public view, encouraged by psychiatrists and psychologists, that this is the most appropriate response to the therapeutic needs of workers in emergency services, victims of disasters and those who have been affected by trauma and violence in society at large. There is a large and growing literature which in general does indeed testify to the effectiveness of such post-traumatic debriefing, although recently voices have been heard questioning whether debriefing invariably has a positive effect on recovery, and raising the possibility that in some instances it actually may make matters worse.

One group of people exposed to traumatic events is journalists who report on war, revolution and civil unrest. Martin Bell, once referred to by his journalist colleague Simon Jenkins as 'the BBC's star war reporter', has seen more than his fair share of military and civilian slaughters and is well placed to discuss the impact of such witness on his own and other people's mental stability. In addition to reporting such 'theatres of war' as Vietnam, Biafra, the Gulf, Central America, Northern Ireland and Bosnia, he has himself been injured in the line of fire when, on camera, he was hit in the groin by a fragment of a shellburst in Sarajevo in 1992. He is frankly sceptical of psychiatry and resolutely insists that while he accepts the reality and the legitimacy of PTSD he has never suffered it and certainly has had no need of debriefing. He does not appear to have suffered any untoward physical or psychological consequences of the sniper's bullet and is, in this interview as elsewhere, well-nigh contemptuous of the well-meaning suggestion of his employers, the BBC, that he should avail himself of counselling on his return from Sarajevo.

Does that mean that a career reporting at close quarters on man's inhumanity to man leaves no mark whatsoever on the personality of the reporter, and brings about no change in his beliefs and attitudes? Is it just another job? At first glance Martin Bell would appear to believe so. But what makes him singularly interesting to interview is the fact that he is undoubtedly a highly complex man, exceedingly suspicious of anything that smacks of self-analysis. He is also more than a little contradictory. On the one hand, he hankers after what he calls in the interview the 'old school of BBC reporting ... distant, dispassionate, objective'. He aspires to a cool, laconic, self-deprecatory, unheroic persona for whom 'understatement is more eloquent'. He distrusts feelings, and at one point rebukes me pointing out 'I'm paid to be a witness. I'm not paid to tell people what to think or feel.' The job of a reporter is to tell it as it is without frills, fancies or opinion. But what of feelings? 'It's not my business,' he observes flatly, 'to parade my emotions.'

And yet he has written a book about Bosnia, *In Harm's Way*, which oozes anger, frustration and distress. In a celebrated and notorious film which he made for *Panorama*, he stepped outside the confines of the detached war reporter when, overwhelmed by the ethnic cleansing and the carnage, the indifference of the politicians and the impotence of the peacekeepers, he passionately demanded that the Western world 'do something to stop the slaughter' and actively intervene. He had moved a long way from the reporter merely telling it as it is.

Martin Bell is an intriguing single-case study in the argument over whether exposure to violence desensitises or arouses. He has seen and described terrible things, some of the most terrible to have taken place in this blood-soaked and murderous century. His experiences as a war reporter, particularly in the Balkans, do appear to have changed him. In this interview he says as much. He is more passionate, more committed, more involved. It has led him to exchange the relatively passive role of reporter for the seemingly more active role of politician, although the transition, which occurred after this interview was recorded, owes more to another expression of his passionate feelings, in this case relating to allegations against Neil Hamilton of political sleaze.

But was Martin Bell truly changed by Bosnia? Was it a case of a man with relatively few feelings and all of these kept carefully under wraps moved to action by feelings of anger, frustration and despair provoked by the awful events occurring around him? Or did witness of such atrocities finally enable him to express feelings always present but always constrained, feelings for which hitherto he had had a certain suspicion and English fastidiousness? On the occasions when I have met him, and there have been several, I have always been struck by the intensity of his feelings which cohabit a trifle uneasily and revealingly with his intellectual insistence on the need, at all times, for emotional control. When, near the end of the interview, we discuss the issue of debriefing in relation to his own traumatic experience in Sarajevo, he is abruptly dismissive, preferring to put his faith in the recuperative powers of 'blokedom'. He does not and never did suffer post-traumatic stress syndrome. He has no need of external support. He fears the counsellor turning into a crutch. He will do it his way.

Early in the interview Martin Bell anticipates that I will be disappointed to discover he had a happy childhood and family life. Why? Because, as he puts it, 'if you're in the psychiatry business you want to go back to all sorts of traumas that must have afflicted me when I was young and none did, you know'. He makes a good case for an absence of trauma. He had a good start in life – a sound and supportive relationship with his parents and his sister. He was afforded a good education and availed himself of it, obtaining a superb degree at Cambridge. He developed in adolescence and early adult life a resilience and an aptitude for coping with challenge and change which was to stand him in good stead in Bosnia and Biafra, Belfast and the Basra Road. I am not at all disappointed. Rather I believe that Martin Bell's fortunate beginnings are not unconnected with the fact that he has subsequently shown such emotional strength and resilience in his adult life coping with the traumatic experiences and sights which were a feature of his career as a reporter.

John Simpson, another of his journalistic colleagues, once wrote that perhaps the motivational well-spring of the good reporter lies in him or her 'being an outsider: uncommitted, frank, unimpressed'. Martin Bell appears to have been all of these. The good reporter needs a secure sense of himself and a sound assessment of his strengths and weaknesses. In the studies on debriefing, evidence is beginning to emerge that people with strong, well-developed personalities, a mature sense of their ability and worth and a belief in themselves, characteristics seen to a greater extent in individuals who have had relatively stable family backgrounds, cope with traumatic situations better and do not need debriefing. In contrast, people particularly prone to develop post-traumatic stress syndrome and in need of systematic and professional debriefing and counselling are more likely to include those who have had family disruption, parental conflict, difficulties in personal development earlier in their lives. Martin Bell believes that he is a changed man and that Bosnia helped change him. He has in addition changed his profession. But, if he is right, his early childhood and family life, which he expected would disappoint me by virtue of their stability, will as assuredly help him cope with the vicissitudes of life at Westminster as it has helped him survive the horrors of Sarajevo.

CLARE: Famous for his lucky white suit and the terse yet impassioned delivery of his television news reports, Martin Bell is the doyen of British war correspondents. Born in 1938, he was educated at The Leys School and, after two years of National Service, King's College, Cambridge, which he left with a double first in English. He joined the BBC as a trainee news assistant and since his first foreign assignment in 1966, he has reported from 80 countries and covered 11 wars, including Vietnam, the Middle East, the Gulf War and for the last four years, the Bosnian conflict. He has been voted twice Television Reporter of the Year by the Royal Television Society, and he was awarded an OBE in 1992.

Martin Bell has been married twice and has two grown-up daughters. In his recently published biographical account of his experiences in Bosnia, *In Harm's Way*, he quotes Bell's Law number one, which states, 'the worst that can happen will happen'.

Martin Bell, what do you think, looking back, is the worst that has happened to you?

BELL: Well, first of all, Bell's Law in Bosnia has just been confounded because the worst that could happen didn't happen and more hopeful things started to happen. The worst that has happened to me is the same as the best that has happened to me. I've been exposed to so much human suffering in these past four, three and a half years, that's hard to deal with, and yet, I know it's changed me. It's not really for me to judge, but I don't think it's changed me for the worst. It's made me understand what's going on in the world rather better and be less distant from it, perhaps, than I used to be.

CLARE: You feel that this last three or four years changed you – in a way that your previous exposure to many conflict situations hadn't changed you?

BELL: I think I felt something a little bit like this way back in 1966, which was really my first exposure to foreign conflict. It was a massacre of Ibos in Northern Nigeria by Hausas. It was essentially a tribal conflict and I saw some terrible things. It was actually the origin of the Biafran war. But I think I was too young and inexperienced to cope with it and too much consumed with the logistics of reporting and broadcasting, which can hijack the whole enterprise. It was what would now be called an ethnic cleansing and I remember being deeply moved at the time. But, of course, what I've seen since April '92 in Bosnia I suppose makes that pale a little bit because I had never been so close to the suffering of people. Day in day out, week in week out, month in month out, and it does change your view of things, yes.

CLARE: In what way?

BELL: It changes your view of things. I was brought up in another tradition. The old school of BBC reporting, shall we say, which was distant, dispassionate, objective. Having been what I'd been through, you can't be distant and dispassionate if somebody beside you is being shot. Some totally innocent person. On a number of levels you respond. One is, your armoured vehicle becomes an ambulance and you take the guy to hospital. I think it's affected me in, in other ways too. I mean this is really quite extraordinary. It's been the first war in Europe in 50 years, the first genocide in Europe in 50 years and I suppose what I've moved to is what I refer to in my book as a journalism of attachment. A journalism that cares as well as knows. And I don't mean crusading journalism. I'm as far from the John Pilger type of journalist as it is possible to be because my doubt about crusading journalism, which often works in print but it doesn't on television, is that you find what you're looking for and you go deeper and deeper down some road, often without a lot of collateral facts to support you.

CLARE: Would you have said that, when you started out you were a somewhat detached and, if you like, uncommitted sort of person?

BELL: I think so. There was a culture in those days of war reporters. I started with some of the really famous ones.

CLARE: I meant even before that. In other words, it fitted you with what was needed then. That was the sort of person that you were – detached, observing, not emotionally involved?

BELL: Rather shy, I think, too. I had no idea what I was getting into. Nobody sets out to become a war correspondent. Becoming a war correspondent is something that just happens to you.

CLARE: How did it happen to you?

BELL: I think all newspapers, all news organisations, run a kind of a taxi system. They have a team of young reporters and they line up nearest the door and it could be a small bank robbery in Wood Green; it can be a traffic accident in Southwark; it can be a ferry going down in the English Channel and one day it's a war. And you go and do it. And if you survive it and you come back with a reputation of at least not having been totally scooped and your camera crew likes you, which is very important because you're actually leading a team, you'll probably be asked to do it again and then again and again and again, until you discover, rather too late, that it's all you're asked to do.

CLARE: There must be some people who, having done a war say, 'Well, I don't think really that's for me, I'll do something else'?

BELL: There are a lot. It's been very interesting. A lot of the hot shot American reporters in Bosnia, one of them got as far as Split, one got as far as Belgrade, another actually reached Lucavista Barracks and was unwilling to cross the airport under fire, which I entirely understand.

CLARE: But you weren't like that?

BELL: No, but you never know about these things until you're in it. And it's not a moral quality, is it? It's like having a long nose or a short nose. You can stand up reasonably under hazardous conditions or you can't. You're not necessarily a better person because you can, you're just lucky.

CLARE: Yes, although you might be temperamentally suited. It might suit you, the fact that you can take it, that you can remain cool. You're quite right, I'm not suggesting it's moral or immoral, I'm merely wondering the extent to which people find their niche, niches find their people, and that it calls for a certain kind of coolness, detachment, objectivity. And then, over the last four years, that starts to change for reasons we'll come back to. But I'm talking about those early days when you really were carving out that niche for yourself.

BELL: I think that's a good point. But there are two dimensions of coolness here. There's coolness under fire, which is feeling fear, using fear, because fear keeps you alive, but not succumbing to panic, because under panic you take disastrous decisions and panic can kill you. Then there's another kind of coolness which is really saying, 'Oh, this is another war, I'll go and do it and then when it's over, it won't mean anything to me.' And that's

8

the kind of coolness that I didn't have, and I don't have. It means a lot to me.

CLARE: For example, would people have said of you in your ordinary daily life that you're cool, observing sort of person, detached, cool, not easily given to emotional displays?

BELL: I don't really know what people think of me, to be quite honest. One of the reasons I like talking to people, and it's probably one of the reasons I've come on this programme, is that I find other people's perceptions more interesting than mine because I can never be surprised by mine.

CLARE: Perceptions of you?

BELL: Oh no, of life in general, of anything.

CLARE: What about their perceptions of you?

BELL: Well, I'm not sure what their perceptions are. I do tell you that when I was shot I was absolutely appalled, one of the interviews called me burly. I never thought of myself as burly before. You know – suave, svelt, lissom perhaps, burly never!

CLARE: What about people who are close to you, your daughters, for instance. Would they see you as cool? The image that comes across of you as a war correspondent is what you've said really. I'm not saying uninvolved, I've never used that word, but cool, observing, detached, not given to emotion, though it's there, because I've read your book.

BELL: It's there but it's controlled, I think.

CLARE: Very controlled.

BELL: Yes, I think the girls, they're 21 and 23 and they've never really understood very much about what I do or why I do it. Partly because for 12 years they were, I was, we were all in the United States and, of course, they didn't see British television and they've both lived abroad a lot since. But I think they like the idea of somebody who's in control. It's better to have a father that's in control than not but they've never really understood what I do and I know in later years they've been a bit worried by it.

CLARE: Would you know what they make of you?

BELL: I have no idea. They say very nice things. When I wrote that book my younger child, Catherine, who's now 21, wrote me the most beautiful letter, the most wonderful letter I've ever

9

received, about how she now understood me and what made me tick. And I realised that perhaps I may have been to her a rather remote, paternal figure in the sense that, that my father was to me. But because in this book I actually wrote things down and, unusually, I expressed quite explicitly some things that I felt, that helped her and I think it's drawn us closer.

CLARE: You would agree that it's unusual that you express some things you feel?

BELL: For sure, for sure. It's not my business to parade my emotions. It's really not what I'm about. It's certainly not what I'm paid for by the BBC. I don't think I'd last very long if I went into some emotional rant at what I saw.

CLARE: But we're talking about a book in which, in addition to you talking about what you saw and what you did, you are really for the first time talking a little bit about you, Martin Bell. That was what was interesting about the book and what emerges is that there is a lot of emotion there.

BELL: It was actually one of the reasons for writing it. It collects the mind. You can think of what's mattered to you and what hasn't mattered to you. Look, I work in the most ephemeral branch of communications journalism known to man. It just disappears into the ether every evening in a minute and 42 seconds on the News so it made sense to write some of this down, not really so much for anybody else's benefit as for mine. What is it – emotion recollected in tranquillity, I suppose.

CLARE: I know you'll say to me, well, it wasn't that kind of book and that's fair enough, but there is nothing really about your background in the book. Hardly anything about the double first in Cambridge, your school, your background. I've no idea whether you have many brothers and sisters or none at all. I don't know what your father did. I can't get any feeling of where this man Martin Bell came from.

BELL: Well, you see this is where I'm going to disappoint you deeply because I know nobody who had a happier childhood than I did or came from a happier marriage.

CLARE: Why do you think that will disappoint me?

BELL: Because, clearly, if you're in the psychiatry business, you want to go back to all sorts of traumas that must have afflicted me when I was young, and none did, you know.

CLARE: But I don't!

BELL: You don't?

CLARE: No, I'm as interested to know how people survive as how they collapse. And that's why, I make no bones about it, I'm interested in you because you've seen terrible things and you appear to have survived and I'm interested to know what makes that happen. Can you think of what would happen to some of the people I see if they were exposed to a tenth, a hundredth, of the visual images you've seen? They would suffer terribly, they just would not be able to manage. You do it. You've done it night after night in places all over the world. I don't buy for a minute that it hasn't touched you. I accept it has touched you. What I'm interested in, therefore, is to know what it is that makes this man able to do this kind of thing and retain, as you clearly do in your book, your compassion. So, if you tell me it was a happy childhood, I want to hear more, particularly since I hear so little about happy childhoods. You did say, however, that your father was a detached man. Or, no, he was unemotional, I think you said?

BELL: We can break new ground here. Maybe it's been easier for me to deal with the scenes I've been through because I do come from a background of great stability. In those days fathers were not New Age fathers, were they? He was an author, he wrote the first *Times* crossword puzzle ever. A really remarkable man and I'm deeply proud of him. His books are still widely read in East Anglia and beyond. They were country novels.

CLARE: And what was he like temperamentally?

BELL: Very clever, very, very calm.

CLARE: Calm?

BELL: Full of ideas and a great, a great talker and a thinker who could actually describe more eloquently and expressively what he found in the pond in his backyard than I could from a battlefield in Vietnam. I envied his power of words enormously.

CLARE: Did he mistrust emotion?

BELL: I've no idea. I've never asked him.

CLARE: Did he express much?

BELL: No, I think in his books, probably. But he had a great love of tranquillity and order in life and very much regretted the passing of the old order. He wrote a wonderful chronicle of the change in British agriculture. He lived through the Depression. He worked as a farmer through the Depression and he expressed it very well. But I think he would express it. With him as with me, you will find much more emotion in the words than in the man, if you met the man.

CLARE: What was he like with you?

BELL: He's the only father I ever had so you see I cannot really compare him to other fathers.

CLARE: Was he ambitious for you?

BELL: To the extent that both my mother and father sacrificed enormously. They had very little money and what little they had they spent all on the education of their children. They never had a holiday of any kind for 20 years so, yes, I suppose that's the quiet ambition, yes.

CLARE: What was your mother like?

BELL: Very loyal, a wonderful woman, really deeply loved, who devoted her entire life to him, to us. There was no career, there was no thought of a career. She was a secretary when she met him and she was everything. She helped him write his book. She helped him compose his crossword puzzles. She brought up his children. And then I think when he died, she was kind of angry because, you know, having given everything of her life, you know, she was suddenly off on her own for a while. She collected herself but it was very, very difficult, I know. I don't know anybody who was more immediately affected by widowhood than my mother.

CLARE: When did that happen?

BELL: He died 16 years ago.

CLARE: And your mother?

BELL: Five years ago.

CLARE: And how many of you were there?

BELL: I have a twin sister who lives in Canada. She married a clergyman. He was the head of the Faculty of Divinity at Toronto University. My older sister, who's two and a half years older than I am, is a very wonderful woman. She's the English translator of Asterix, the French cartoon character. She's made a wonderful career for herself. She also translated Willi Brandt's memoirs. She translates out of French and German into English.

CLARE: You say it was a happy childhood, do you remember yourself having any particular ambitions of what you wanted to do with your life?

BELL: Yes, I did, because my father's father, my grandfather on that side, was a Scottish journalist who came south, first to the *Yorkshire Post* then to the *Observer*. The *Observer* at that time had a rather famous grandee editor, Garvin, who clearly took the wrong side in a lot of the controversies, but he used to hang out in the country houses and have his ear bent by the great and the mighty and somebody had to put out the newspaper. And the London *Observer* then was I think really in its heyday, and that was my grandfather, Robert Bell. And I remember, I talked to him a lot up to the time I was 11 and 12 in our vicarage in Redisham in Suffolk. And I remember thinking to myself, this would be a nice way to earn a living. So, certainly from the age of 12, I was determined to be a journalist.

CLARE: What did your father make of that?

BELL: Well, he perfectly understood it because I think he would have been too if he hadn't been subject to migraines once a month. Very severe ones, which constricted him and this is why, well, he always wanted to be a farmer. He got into farming. He wrote about farming and he supplemented his living by writing these crossword puzzles which, since a lot of people bought *The Times* for them, I suppose you could think it was kind of journalism.

CLARE: Was it a very ordered, steady, stable kind of childhood? Did things just roll around?

BELL: I'm sorry, this is not going to interest you at all, it really was. It was. It was round the seasons as, if you're in a farming family, they will be. No holidays, no trips. All three of us were at boarding schools. We got together in the holidays, yes, very ordered.

CLARE: It encouraged self-reliance?

BELL: I think so, except you were part of a very close family and could therefore also depend on each other.

CLARE: How were you seen? Did people see you as very bright? When you say they sacrificed, was that because you were seen to be someone who would reward the sacrifice? You were going to go places?

BELL: No, they sacrificed because they were sacrificing kind of people. If I'd had the intelligence of the village idiot they would have sacrificed just as much or probably more. I mean that's the kind of people they were.

CLARE: And at school, what were you like there?

BELL: I think I was impressionable. I didn't mind going away to boarding school. It was deemed to be natural. I believe my mother cried. I just didn't want her to be seen crying in public. You know how it is. I was probably more than most boys reclusive. I will absolutely admit to having been quite shy, and this was a real problem when it came to being a journalist. I had to fight this shyness for years and years and years.

CLARE: Why?

BELL: You know, going up to strangers and talking to them because in our very unitary and cohesive family I didn't have to talk to a lot of strangers. And there wasn't the sort of money to go travelling so very much we lived within the hedges and walls of this house at Redisham in Suffolk for a long time.

CLARE: And then there was National Service.

BELL: National Service was terrific for me because that broke the mould. I spent two years in the Suffolk Regiment which no longer exists.

CLARE: When you say broke the mould?

BELL: It broke the mould of just being a very quiet, rather retiring somewhat shy, if I suppose, cleverish boy. I actually had to meet real people and because, blessedly, I failed my officer selection board, I went on meeting real people for two years, the kind of people who lived across the hedge and down the village were now my mates in the tent. And this did me a lot of good because initially I was classed as a college boy, you see. College boys were clever and were singled out for extra trench digging.

CLARE: Why did you fail the officer selection test, do you know?

BELL: Yes, I do know, because one of my favourite brigadiers, who I met in Bosnia nearly 40 years later, was sent from there to preside over exactly the ritual that I'd failed and he dug out my records from all those years previously and it turned out I was so nervous, I had to sit my intelligence test twice and it went to a kind of appeals procedure, you know, whether this man was officer material or not. You had to do strange things with planks and poles and cross imaginary rivers and radioactive dumps and things, and I'm not very clever with my hands, or in that sense with my brain, and so I failed that catastrophically and I got nervous. I think they said in the report that I was too aggressive. Well, maybe I'm just a natural other rank, you know, and that was terrific because I got to meet real people for two years.

CLARE: What does 'natural other rank' mean? Do you mean bolshie?

BELL: Not born to command. I think, sort of independent and critical of authority. I don't think that's bad in a journalist. I think that's useful in a journalist. If you're too deferential, heaven help you.

CLARE: Why were you nervous? Where did that come from?

BELL: Because it was the first test I'd ever, ever had.

CLARE: No, I don't mean just in that. I noticed you said that you were shy, nervous in school.

BELL: I think if you've led a protected life, as I really had, then your first encounters with the outside world, you really don't quite know how to deal with it. So I was shy at school and a certain shyness remained through the two years of National Service and I never really broke it until much later in life, because I had to. There's not much of a living to be made by reclusive journalists, is there.

CLARE: What about Cambridge, what was that like?

BELL: Cambridge, I don't think I got the most out of Cambridge. It was a wonderful college, King's, and because my parents had sacrificed so much to get me there, and they went on paying a lot of money while I was there, I felt I really had to come out of there with a good degree to reward them. I probably worked too hard and didn't do enough in an extra-curricular way which I should have done.

CLARE: You were a serious person?

BELL: Yes, serious I think would just about sum it up. More serious than you should be at the age of 21 I guess, yes.

CLARE: Were there girls or booze or . . .

BELL: Not at the sort of scale that prevails at universities today or for that matter at Cambridge in those days. Moderate amounts of both I would say.

CLARE: What about politics? It was the late 1950s so it would have been between Suez and Harold Wilson. Would you have been active or interested in politics?

BELL: I do remember that I was the only member of my college, I think, who wasn't a Marxist and I actually joined the Marxist Society in order to argue with them. Brian Pollit was there at the time, the son of Harry Pollit, the then Communist Party leader and the kind of opinions I had I think were sort of deeply unfashionable, but I enjoyed that.

CLARE: You did. You do?

BELL: I still enjoy being deeply unfashionable, yes.

CLARE: Go on, why? Why do you enjoy being deeply unfashionable?

BELL: Because I like to question the received opinions. I'm fairly critical in my book, and in my life, of political correctness and all its manifestations. I just like to think things through for myself, and you're not encouraged as a BBC reporter to inflict political opinions on anybody and I don't have very, very strong ones. Although I do now have quite strong feelings about things.

CLARE: You do have strong feelings about things. Sometimes you give the impression that you don't have strong feelings about things. Almost as if feelings, strong feelings about things is a bit ...

BELL: A bit over the top? There are ways of expressing them. There are ways of getting them over on television. I think I mentioned earlier, in print you can be a crusading journalist all over the front page. You can't crusade on television because the pictures make the case for you. I mean all you do is to supply a few words.

CLARE: But sometimes you feel the need to add more than a few words. Sometimes it was all so appalling. I sense that in the book, that sometimes you feel the need to shake the audience. There's a quote where you say 'It is not a question so much of "I can't say it, you can't understand it," as it's that "You won't listen to what I say."'

BELL: Well, this comes from my contact with genocide, which has had a profound impression on me. And, as I read back, one of my great heroes is Eli Wiesel who, of course, is the most eloquent survivor of the earlier and arithmetically yet more terrible holocaust, I listen to what he had to say and how he dealt with it and one of the points he makes is that the culpability not only lies with the hatred that makes it happen, but with the indifference that lets it happen. And he also talks, which speaks to what I've been through, about the difficulty of communicating this. His actual words are engraved on my heart. He says, 'It is not because I cannot explain that you won't understand, it is because you won't understand that I cannot explain.' That's the difficulty, that's the difficulty in television . . .

CLARE: What interests me, though, about you is that I sense that kind of war goes on inside you. That you want to be dispassionate, I don't just mean in your reporting, dispassionate, detached, cool, in control, but you know that there are great passions inside you. You worry about being a crusading journalist because you could be one?

BELL: I could be . . .

CLARE: That you have that kind of passion and you do get moved. There are some journalists that don't get moved, presumably. You can tell me if I'm wrong but I sense that.

BELL: No there are people, there are people for whom it's just another war and they move on.

CLARE: So isn't that the problem?

BELL: No, it's not a problem, it's a solution. If I become too emotional and parade my feelings and make a case I'm much less effective.

CLARE: Why do people, particularly English people, talk about parading their feelings, but exhibiting their rationality? Why do we say that? Why, time and again you say 'parade your feelings' as if you're going to overwhelm me with passion, whereas in fact I'm not really . . .

BELL: Because I'm paid to be a witness. I'm not paid to tell people what to think or feel.

CLARE: But you'll only influence them in so far as you feel?

BELL: Yes, but the influence is so much greater with understatement. It's in the nature of television. Look what Michael Buerk did with the Ethiopian famine.

CLARE: Ah, but it's you too, it's you too.

BELL: Yes, I do it too.

CLARE: No, I meant irrespective of television. We're not on television now and you're still doing it. You prefer understatement.

BELL: Because understatement is much more eloquent.

CLARE: Because you fear emotion.

BELL: No, because it's technically the good way to do it.

CLARE: No, I meant in terms of ordinary everyday relationships.

BELL: Not really, no, I deny it completely. I don't fear emotion but I don't like emotion out of control. Look, in television a lot of the time I just shut up because the pictures are so powerful and the sounds that go with them. I call it the art of writing silence. It's much more effective than ranting away and it gets the message over. I talk to you, we seem to be having a fairly friendly and amicable discussion but if I suddenly burst into a rant, you would think, 'What's gone wrong with this guy, he's lost it,' wouldn't you?

CLARE: Yes, but you present a dichotomy of extremes. I'm not asking you to burst into a rant, and I'm sure you wouldn't anyway. I'm saying that the extent to which one expresses emotion, that of course has to be regulated, but when I discuss emotion at all, your instinct is to see it as a parading of emotion, whereas I'm just thinking of the manifesting of it. And I sense that's a kind of tension in you. It came to a head, if you like, with the Bosnian conflict because detached reporting didn't seem even to you to be enough.

BELL: I'll accept that. I'm a more emotional man than I used to be. I think everybody's probably got one book in them and one speech in them. I've got one speech which I'm not going to expose you to tonight but it's much more emotional than the minute and 42 seconds on the evening news.

CLARE: What about in your personal life? I asked you about your children. You had two wives. Would they have seen you as a person who kept his emotions under wraps?

BELL: I can hardly talk about my second wife because it was a very strange experience. I married an American. It just didn't work and the relationship was odd. My first wife, Helen, the mother of my children, yes, she used to. I used to come home from

Angola or somewhere and she'd burst into a wonderful speech about all the things that happened in my absence, you know, not things that had gone wrong, things that had gone right. And then she'd say, 'Well, why's he saying so little?' It's because I suppose I didn't want to give her a broadcast about my experiences in Angola which I didn't think would be of enormous interest to her. A lot of the soldiers coming back from Bosnia have the same problem, you know. They want to talk about Bosnia and the family's eyes glaze over. I've said all I've got to say professionally. It's just really nice to be home.

CLARE: What about something that you referred to in the book, the problem that when you are working as you have been against this kind of canvas, how can the minutiae of life in Willesden or Hampstead or Bootle, the everyday ordinary preoccupations of people, about *Coronation Street* or the Test Match or who's going to win a by-election, how can it matter?

BELL: It works on two levels. It is wonderful to be back in a completely different world. I live in a tiny little cottage in North London which I just adore. It's the perfect refuge for somebody who earns his living in a war zone. In one of these studios in the BBC, I was invited to take part in a Radio 5 Live talk-in with the great and good of British journalism and they were discussing the big issues of the day and the big moral issue of the day, this was at the height of the Bosnian war. And the big moral issue of the day was whether the winner of the National Lottery was entitled to anonymity. And I said, you know, is this my country, is it my planet? A lot of soldiers have felt the same. They're just amazed. They come home to some village in Wiltshire and the whole village is up in arms about some question about a right of way over a field. And I think the, the intelligent way to look at this is that there is nothing wrong with a country, there's nothing deeply or seriously wrong with a country if that's what people are getting worked up about.

CLARE: But it wasn't easy when you came home from Angola or the Middle East or the Gulf or whatever, when you came home to people who you were involved with, that this was their world, even though you understood it as you've just said, but your world was so different.

BELL: I think it was a little bit of a difficulty. It was as if they were separate worlds and for a time I just slipped out of one into another before going back again. It was like living in different boxes. I think it's different now because obviously the Bosnian war has had a deep impression on me and I want to talk about it in a way that I didn't want to talk about other wars that didn't have such a deep impression on me.

CLARE: What sort of impression did they have? When you look back, what's your explanation for the fact that you stayed in this particular niche, that you stayed being a war correspondent and that you covered so many wars?

BELL: I think looking at it as dispassionately as I can, I was good at it. The camera crews liked working with me because I was getting older and they like working with old people because it's a bit like an old u-boat captain isn't it; I mean the guy's obviously lucky and they felt I wouldn't be trying to make my name at their expense. You know, I didn't want to be the reporter most shot at because, you know, that's how people make their names very often in television and I'm cautious. I also wasn't actually offered anything else and maybe there was an element of excitement. I don't mean in the head-banging sense that I enjoyed being shot at, only a fool enjoys being shot at, but in a sense of living and working beyond the rim of the civilised world, of having a grandstand seat in the making of history or, in the Bosnian case, so often the remaking of history. And if news is the first draft of history – this is the first time that television has been part of the first draft – so that was very sort of professionally gratifying. And in the Bosnian case even more so because it was so dangerous, very few of us worked there consistently from the start.

CLARE: And the tension between recording, observing, describing, and then actually affecting or influencing – there's a passage in your book which you describe yourself, there are these two Croatian refugees, an old lady and her granddaughter, and you yourself say, we shouldn't have really been recording this, we should have been helping them. But you state it as a dilemma. I'm not sure what your resolution of it is?

BELL: I don't have a resolution of it but I think that it behoves us to be critical of ourselves and the way we do business.

CLARE: Let me share something with you. You're in my living room. You come across and you describe to me a terrible thing going in Europe, and I belong to Europe, I'm sitting there in my house in West Dublin, and I feel a bit like you feel. You're there telling me it and you haven't done anything about it either but you feel, 'If I tell them about it, something might happen.' But I watch this and I feel there's nothing I can do about this either. I can turn it off but I'll watch it, but maybe I shouldn't just be watching it, maybe I should be doing something, but what can I do? Other than, I presume, talk to someone else who's watched it. What I'm wondering about is that – are we totally distracted by all of this? Has this got anything to do with how life is actually lived? You and I are engaged, you telling me and I listening to you, it's a process and it has to be gone through because life has got to be told. But neither of us are going to have really any impact because we're impotent.

BELL: No, no, we are not impotent, here I would quarrel with you. If the story is told straight and responsibly, there at least spreads through the whole community, in London, in Dublin or whatever, an awareness of what is going on in the world around us.

CLARE: Even if it's as basic an awareness as 'This is awful, it must stop.'

BELL: Anthony, we live in a political community. We have political leaders. The political leaders respond to what voters are telling them.

CLARE: But, you know this better than anyone, you know that it is precisely the power of the visual image to show something terrible, but the complexity? Even now, many years and many articles and many television programmes later, the complexity of the Balkan situation overwhelms. You've lived in it and are steeped in it but as I read your book at times I had to check back and say to myself, well now, hang on a minute, and who's this? The ultimate horror came across in a television communication but my problem, the dilemma you stated in your book, of the journalist on the spot not knowing whether to describe or to do something, is a shared dilemma by the viewer, who's not sure whether to watch or to do something?

BELL: That's probably true up to a point, but there's complexity and there's simplicity. I don't see a great deal of complexity in 3,000 people being taken out in groups of ten from various places and executed.

CLARE: The complexity is to stop it.

BELL: Yes, but you can't stop it unless you're first aware of it and, for all my faults, I'm the instrument of your awareness.

CLARE: It struck me as I read through the book, I thought you, Martin Bell, could be one of those very remarkable soldiers that you've described from time to time, Colonel Bob, for example, the characteristics you admired in some of these men were curiously enough the mixture that you seem to have yourself – solid professionalism, coolness under fire.

BELL: And they care don't they?

CLARE: Not wanting to risk themselves, but the difference was that of course they were soldiers, they were doing something. I wondered as I read the book about this evolution, that what is happening to Martin Bell is that he is moving from a position of being the detached observer which suits the BBC, if you like, down to the ground, to being someone who actually is certainly drawn to being much more involved.

BELL: A mover and a shaker.

CLARE: As they were in their way, small limited ways because of course they, the soldiers, the best of them in Bosnia, had their own problems and had very little perhaps long-term influence. But, none the less, there were moments which you describe very powerfully in the book when somebody gives a command and at last the Coldstream Guards move out and go along and they clear a barricade that should have been cleared months ago and I got the sense from the way you wrote it that at last something was being done.

BELL: And something was done, wasn't it?

CLARE: This was written by a man who hitherto would have said, 'My job is to objectively describe.' Now I sense that you felt more and more, 'This is in its own way a bit crazy. We've got to do something.'

BELL: I plead absolutely guilty to that and to being a founder member of the something-must-be-done club. If I didn't, your men in little white coats should come and carry me away, shouldn't they?

CLARE: Would you have liked to have been a soldier?

BELL: No, I tried being a soldier.

CLARE: I know that.

BELL: I did not enjoy it.

CLARE: That was their problem.

BELL: I did not enjoy it. I do not like being ordered about.

CLARE: But do you enjoy being a war correspondent?

BELL: I think in a way the experiences are similar. We are witnesses to the same things. I have more freedom. I have an amazing amount of freedom. More than I had when I started in Vietnam. Much more. And a lot of responsibility, more than the soldiers have. They have brigadiers and generals on top of them who are second guessing them all the time. My editors are pretty liberal people and they let me get on with it.

CLARE: Right. There's the freedom and you prize that. There's the independence, but there's a desire to do something. That's the paradox, isn't it, that the more you want to do something the more you get emeshed in organisations. You're not an organisation man.

BELL: Not at all, but it's hard to be exposed to what I've seen and really say, this is none of my business. And if for instance we were to have a foreign policy which was based entirely on a calculation of national interest, well, there's no national interest in stopping 3,000 people being executed in Srebrenica. But you rewind history, you go back down 50 years and you can see the destination of that argument with a chilling clarity. It is that Buchenwald was none of our business and Auschwitz was none of our business.

CLARE: I accept that. I accept that the reasons any of us do anything are complex and multiple and you've identified part of the reasons that you do what you do, but to go on doing it, there must be an addition to that kind of moral justification. There must be, you used the word 'enjoy' and I wondered, as you describe it, how much you enjoyed the excitement?

BELL: Not the danger, not the danger at all. The only thing I will admit to in that regard is this wonderful phrase of Winston

Churchill's who was an early practitioner of this art in the Boer War, who described the exhilaration of being shot at without result. If you come through a dangerous day, there's a feeling of achievement in just having survived but I think that's all it is. There are other recompenses for this daft way of earning a living. Look, you're not just in at the making and remaking of history, but you are also the witness not just to cruelty but to the most incredible heroism.

CLARE: But when you go with your little team out of the hotel and down the street, that is risky?

BELL: When the stuff's flying, it's quite hard to psyche yourself up, to get out of the hotel in the first place. I remember a moment last May when I got down to the garage of the Holiday Inn and all the hacks were gathered there because everything was coming in and one vehicle had just gone out and been shot at. I said, 'OK, let's go and do it,' and we went out and we kind of broke the invisible barrier and it was all right.

CLARE: Have you ever had the equivalent of say, stage fright, of just not being able to go out?

BELL: I've had times I've said, 'I'm not going to do this thing.' The most scary situations are always the unknown. It's a road you haven't been up before. You don't know if it's mined, you don't know if it's not mined, you don't know if there's an ambush. I very often have not done that and I've often reproached myself in the past because I must have missed some. I've surely missed a lot of stuff and so many things went on that we didn't know, but there's not much point in reporting a war in which you can't survive, is there?

CLARE: And the day you got shot, did that change you?

BELL: Yes, it changed me in a lot of ways. First of all, it made me understand that I truly was not immortal.

CLARE: Did you think you might be?

BELL: Oh, you have to. If you ever talk to soldiers in dangerous situations. I mean suppose you'd been in the trenches of the Somme? You have to believe that you're not going to be hit because it's the way you keep going. And I suppose I succumbed a little bit to that illusion but after August '92 I didn't. It changed me in a way that after that I was much more cautious because I realised this was real stuff and I was lucky that they hit me and not my team because I'm responsible for everybody. And it changed me in other ways because I became a pretty sunny optimist after that. I realised that, after that, every day I was living, I wouldn't say borrowed time but given time. It's as if every day was the first day of the rest of my life after that. It gave me a different perspective on things, yes.

CLARE: Would you say you'd been a pessimist before that?

BELL: Compared to what I was after it, yes, probably, yes. You really do see the dark side of human nature. You are aware of good and evil not as abstractions but as realities in the world.

CLARE: Would you have ever, during your life, despaired, for either personal reasons or arising out of things you'd seen and things you'd seen people do to other people? Have you ever felt, 'This is too much, more than I can bear?'

BELL: Yes, there's a despair. I've quite often felt this sense of despair because I had not realised I think until this last war that evil was such an active force in the world. But I think the dangerous thing is when you get angry.

CLARE: Why?

BELL: Because in a journalist I think indignation is fine, indignation can inspire you to kick down the doors behind which truth lies hidden. But anger blinds the mind, anger skews the judgement.

CLARE: That's as a journalist. What, what's it like, I don't know, as a father or as a husband, were you angry then?

BELL: Well, I'm the least angry man you've ever interviewed. I don't get angry. I believe it's probably the most culpable of the seven deadly sins actually.

CLARE: So what do you do?

BELL: If I get angry?

CLARE: No. What do you do in a situation that would make somebody like me get angry?

BELL: I don't get angry. I don't know if I can use this expression on your programme, but shit happens, that's what I think. It doesn't particularly bother me.

CLARE: And what do other people make of that? I mean in a family situation, here's a man who doesn't get angry!

BELL: Look this is, I come from a family that never got angry. Never.

CLARE: Good God!

BELL: I'm sorry to disappoint you.

CLARE: No, no, it intrigues me!

BELL: My mother and father, if they ever had a row it was certainly well out of sight of the kids. I think my mother once cried when she was tired. That was a real shock to us.

CLARE: Both of them were cool?

BELL: I prefer the word serene because it reflects an inner strength which they both had. Cool is almost as if they don't care about things. They cared deeply. They were serene people and they just met and loved each other.

CLARE: Right, but unless you were a saintly little boy there must have been things you did that they didn't much like.

BELL: I don't remember much chiding. I never remember a voice raised in anger.

CLARE: Or a profound disagreement?

BELL: I suppose at the age of 12, I was not allowed to go on a bus to Carrow Road, and watch Norwich City in action. That's the worst it ever got, you know, so I went into a deep gloom and sulked for 12 hours. But it would be hard as a psychiatrist to draw large conclusions from that wouldn't it?

CLARE: Did you marry a woman that had the same kind of temperament as your parents had and you had?

BELL: No, I think Helen was a little bit more, more fiery. She was always under control but . . .

CLARE: What did she make of this temperament?

BELL: I think she rather liked it. She is truly a wonderful woman.

CLARE: Why didn't it work?

BELL: I don't know, it was probably my fault. I probably grew apart. I always think she married me because she rather liked the company of the English. She's French and she didn't like hanging out with French people very much and she very much valued this extraordinarily stable background that I came from. Hers was much less so and she just adored my mother and she just liked the whole set-up. It was a rooted, secure place.

CLARE: And what happened?

BELL: What happened? I made a mess of it, didn't I. I can blame my job or anything but it's hard to know if something happened on account of that or happened after that, what the connection is. It's a long time ago now and it turned out OK. We're friends, we're good friends and that's very important for the children. I know marriages which are together which are much less strong than ours which is apart and it's important for the girls.

CLARE: Would the work have been a factor?

BELL: It's an easy alibi isn't it? It's a great alibi.

CLARE: You don't think it is?

BELL: I think it's an alibi. But of course a lot of apartness doesn't help. I don't know anybody who does the job I do in print, in television, in any of these things, travelling through war zones, who leads what I would call a stable emotional life at home and has done for a consistent period of time. It just doesn't go together. Though whether this is the kind of job that those people attract is another question. You can argue either way.

CLARE: Well, what interests me and it really does, there's no hidden agenda, is as we talk, something takes shape in relation to this, well, conflict may be too strong a word, but to this balance between rationality and emotion.

BELL: Well, that's human nature isn't it? We have reason and emotion.

CLARE: Yes, and what is very interesting about you is that you come from a background in which hardly a voice is raised, there is no great conflict, yet your work has taken you to situations and places where great emotions are certainly generated. I'm interested, therefore, in the sense in which that which is useful in a war correspondent, a sense of detachment, in the best sense of the word, could itself be a problem in personal relationships which involve the expression of a great deal of emotion?

BELL: Well, I think it's rather the other way round, because I live and work in these rather bizarre situations and am deeply moved by them, sometimes lately to anger. I need to recreate in my own home the kind of serenity I enjoyed as a child, if you like, and I do. It is a very serene background. There is no conflict between the commotion at one end of my life and the serenity at the other but it is the one that makes the other necessary.

CLARE: Which makes which necessary?

BELL: I think it's the commotion that makes the serenity necessary.

I have not been driven out to do this by a need to do exciting things.

CLARE: How do you know that?

BELL: I just feel it in me. It's just something that happened, because I never asked to become a war correspondent. I never said, 'Send me to do this and send me to do that.' I just did what came along.

CLARE: Oh, but come on, you didn't come back and say, 'God, I don't want to do this any more!'

BELL: No, maybe the serenity at home made it much easier to go back. But no, I enjoy what I do. I don't deny that.

CLARE: But it's a fascinating juxtaposition, isn't it? Bosnia is a magnificent example of it, if I'm allowed to use that adjective. That's to say, it is a charnel house of unreconstructed visceral emotion. That's what you're seeing. You're seeing the very belly of Europe throw up the most appalling, primitive, emotional impulses. Reason is suspended. And if you wanted to write a novel you couldn't think of a juxtaposition of such stark contrasts. Your own background, as you've described it yourself, where hardly a voice was raised, where you can hardly remember a conflict, where you proceeded through your childhood and adolescence serenely, the battlegrounds of the patients in my professional life, you proceeded through them unshelled, unmarked.

BELL: Well, of course, it makes it easier in the other world. And just imagine if I came out of the war zones of Bosnia to hit a war zone at home, how intolerable that would be?

CLARE: But aren't you intrigued by what is released? Aren't you intrigued by this power, this emotional power? Aren't you actually yourself in a sense struggling to harness it constructively?

BELL: I'm struggling to ...

CLARE: Can you live without that kind of emotional power?

BELL: No, I'm struggling to understand it and express it and this has happened.

CLARE: I meant in your own emotional power.

BELL: You mean inside myself?

CLARE: Yes, yes.

BELL: I don't know I have any emotional power.

CLARE: You've enormous emotional power. Even here you are tremendously intent on keeping it under control. You use words like 'I'm not going to parade my emotions' as if I'm asking you to abreact here. But I read your book very carefully, *In Harm's Way*, and it's full of passion. There's a piece for instance which I adore where you suddenly have a go at our mutual employer, the BBC. And you write that the BBC issues us with a stopwatch and takes away our right to hold opinions, still less to express them. Then, when the time comes to leave after 30 years and more before the colours, the men in the Giorgio Armani suits, our leaders, take time off from the 16 concurrent seminars they're holding in a country-house hotel into the future of broadcasting in the year 2004, and they form themselves into a hollow square and hand us back our right to hold opinions. They also retrieve their stopwatch. It may be different these days when reporters are hired not for life but for a year at a time, but the ethos is the same. That is passion. That just is a bit of good old-fashioned anger. And I happen to share the sentiments, but that's beside the point. The point is that there's a considerable amount of passion here and I sense that you are keen to control these emotions, not because you don't have them but because you feel that, when expressed, they are dangerous.

BELL: I don't think they're dangerous. They're better expressed controlled than uncontrolled.

CLARE: Yes. Better expressed controlled than not expressed at all.

BELL: The reason I wrote the book was to express them. I had things I wanted to say.

CLARE: But you agree you wouldn't have written that book but for Bosnia. You'd seen so many wars, you'd seen the Gulf and the Middle East, you'd seen Northern Ireland, you'd seen Cambodia, do you think looking back that you paid a price for being so ably in control of your emotions, that it took Bosnia to shake you out of it?

BELL: It's done things to me which were probably useful. I've found emotions in myself which I've expressed and controlled in expressing them because they're better controlled like that. If you'd interviewed me five years ago, I'd have probably given you an extremely boring diatribe about army press relations. I've been much made aware of the moral dimensions of things, including journalism.

CLARE: Let me ask you something the other way around. How easy are you for someone to express emotions to?

BELL: Oh I'm a good listener, I'm a good listener.

CLARE: Feelings. To other people's emotions?

BELL: I don't deal well with other people's anger because I have a particular problem with anger. Otherwise, carry on, express emotion to me.

CLARE: So what do you do with other people's anger?

BELL: I tend to switch off a bit. I regard it as a very dangerous emotion. I've seen the effects of anger. Anger is lethal. Anger kills people.

CLARE: You knew that before you went to Bosnia, and yet you'd never seen much of it at home? How did you learn that?

BELL: Well, I learnt it by seeing it.

CLARE: Ah, you were worried about emotions long before Bosnia?

BELL: Was I?

CLARE: Yes, you didn't express anger as a child and as an adolescent in the early years because you hadn't seen it. Now you don't express it because you've seen it.

BELL: But I do, I do. There's a certain amount of anger in there. You haven't heard my stump speech which ...

CLARE: No, no. You said it yourself, you said to me just now, express any emotions, but anger I have a thing about anger. Now Bosnia casts a particular light on it, but the thing about anger is, it is there quite a while back.

BELL: It surfaced in Bosnia, it surfaced in Bosnia from April 1992.

CLARE: But where did it come from? Is it possible that, because it wasn't expressed when you were growing up, it was just an emotion that you weren't familiar with?

BELL: Now I can see where you're leading now, I had too happy a childhood, didn't I? It's not sufficiently interesting for you because there was no anger, there were no voices raised, there was no abuse. I'm really the worst subject you ever had on your programme!

CLARE: But it was you who said, 'I have a thing about anger,' not me.

BELL: But because I have later come upon it in life, I have later seen the expressions of it, and I don't like it when I find it in myself because it does not consort with useful journalism, and I think the fundamental reason I now want to leave Bosnia behind me is that I found this anger in me which is not useful. It stops me being a good journalist, so I want to leave and go and do something else.

CLARE: What do you want to do?

BELL: I can do some more of the same because I know how to survive in nasty places and this is something that you learn over a period of years. I would love to go back to Belfast where I spent some of my formative years as a journalist. I find that absolutely fascinating. I wrote a thousand-word piece in *The Times* which wasn't much more than a job application you know, saying, angling even, for a job covering the next election campaign. I would find that interesting. I used to do politics and I wouldn't mind doing it again. I'd just like to diversify a little bit.

CLARE: Do you think you'd miss the world of war?

BELL: I would and I wouldn't. There are physical elements of this. It's really unique. To be a war reporter you need I think an old man's head on a young man's body because you've got to be pretty fit for that life-saving sprint across open ground. It's the extra half second it takes you under 26 lbs of body armour. That's lethal, can be lethal. So it's a young man's job in many ways. So there's a physical side of this as well.

CLARE: When you talk in your book about your various superstitions, I wasn't sure whether that was for somebody like me, you were pulling a leg a bit or whether in fact those superstitions are all . . .

BELL: No, believe me, please believe me, Anthony.

CLARE: Well, tell me about them then. What ones do you have?

BELL: Well, you must be familiar with superstitions. I wear a white suit, I have green socks. I have in my travelling bag a collection of little items that people gave me. There are silver crosses and St Christophers and a brass pixie and . . .

CLARE: Would you check that they were there?

BELL: Oh every time I leave, they're there.

CLARE: You'd go through an inventory?

BELL: Yes, I know what should be there. I know what is there because I never take them out. And if people send me these things I always keep them rather than discard them because you never are going to know what works and what doesn't.

CLARE: And what ... you carry them around in a little bag or something?

BELL: Yes, I have a shoulder bag and they go in there.

CLARE: What if you lost one, would you be upset?

BELL: Deeply.

CLARE: Would it make you uneasy?

BELL: No, I'd be troubled. But I think this is normal, this is really normal. I got a letter from a survivor of a bomber crew in World War Two who'd been there from the first and I don't know what their life expectation was but it wasn't, I think, more than a couple of weeks, and he put huge store by the superstitions he had, so he understood immediately. I think people who work routinely in dangerous situations rather than just rock into them and are out of them and say, 'Phew! that's over,' would understand exactly what I'm about there. You must have met it before.

CLARE: And would the superstition be linked with a particular experience? If something happened and you survived it and got through it, might you pair that with a pair of socks that you were wearing at the time, a tie or something that somebody had given you? In other words, how did they develop?

BELL: They developed from the start of the war in Slovenia, which was a very short war, only ten days, because I happened to be wearing a white suit and green socks and it was much more dangerous than I expected and I came to identify what I was wearing with my survival somewhat against the odds. And in the Croatian war which was much more dangerous, this became something of an obsession and I began to see that – I mean it doesn't sound very rational does it, but it made sense to me and that's all it has to do because I'm not asking anyone else to believe this stuff and it's not harmful. It gives me a feeling of more security to be quite honest in extremely dangerous situations.

CLARE: How would something like entering buildings at the same time through the same unconventional ways, sometimes the main door is bad luck. Do you remember how that developed?

BELL: This happened at a particularly dangerous time in June 1992, when the Holiday Inn had just opened its doors. It had been severely war damaged in April and the whole side entrance was shattered. I took a room there although we were living elsewhere, mostly for the gossip so I could pick stuff up from other journalists and share the rumours of the day. And I always went in through this particular shattered window and I always walked the long way round. I always walked a clockwise role and anticlockwise round the corridor and if you had understood the amount of stuff that was flying through the air at the time, anything that could give you this extra feeling of reassurance that you'd seen the sun rise and you were going to see the same sun set, you go for it.

CLARE: And are they all linked with your war zone work? Do you take any of these back into your peacetime life, to your life in Britain?

BELL: Only if I'm doing something potentially hazardous like appearing *In the Psychiatrist's Chair*, for instance. I definitely wore the white suit for this one, you bet!

CLARE: Seriously, it's in war situations?

BELL: It's in war situations.

CLARE: And it would be related to particular locations so that, for instance, the Holiday Inn in Sarajevo you would go through the side entrance but you wouldn't go through the unconventional entrance of some other hotel?

BELL: Oh no, no, no. That relates to a particular place and particular dangers. But if I go back to a war zone somewhere else, the white suit and the green socks will be there because they have worked for me. I don't expect to convince anybody else of this, I'm only to convince me.

CLARE: Would you get very fearful? How frightened would you have got?

BELL: Oh, very, but I have a theory about this which I learnt from my friends in the army, not when I was doing National Service but much, much later, that fear is useful, fear keeps you alive, I mean fear is on your side.

CLARE: Unless presumably you're paralysed by it?

BELL: Ah well, fear is knowing that if you poke your head up over that parapet it's going to be blown away so you don't. I've seen enough people who didn't feel fear and they scare me. There are a few people, I don't think so much reporters but photo journalists, what we call snappers, who are really fearless, fearless, and there's one guy works for, did work for ITN, who was totally fearless, and he really scared me. Not because he was the kind of competition I didn't want, because I don't want to compete with people who feel no fear, it's a very competitive business, but just because he really did survive everything. I mean he led a charmed life, but those people are scary.

CLARE: And they are scary because?

BELL: They're scary because this can be infectious. You too can think you can walk unscathed through the incoming shell fire and you can't. Or they are also scary for practical reasons that maybe they're wrong and one day they will be hit and they're going to be out there exposed and wounded and in open ground and then you've got to go and help them.

CLARE: Is there much macho stuff going on? When you've got a team going and one of them adopts a position of relative indifference to the actual seriousness of the danger, is there a danger there that other people will do things they mightn't ordinarily do?

BELL: For sure, this is the competitive pressure, this is why, when the war began in 1992 I, I held a meeting, I hate meetings but we actually got everyone together and said this is crazy, if there's a battle going on in one street corner, on one particular front line, why do we have three or four of us there instead of just one? And, for the first time ever in my experience, we formed a voluntary pool in which we helped each other and shared our images and there were no scoops, but I'm convinced it saved lives. And that prevailed for more than three years. I'm proud of that.

CLARE: You know a lot about all the stuff about post-traumatic stress and people who have been exposed to dreadful situations having all sorts of symptoms afterwards, nightmares, withdrawal symptoms, reliving experiences. Have you ever had that happen to you?

BELL: The most that I have had is, on returning to this very small house in North London, I can't sleep because it's too quiet. But I think that's it. The silence keeps me awake. I think it's no secret, that the BBC often wishes to pressure us into having therapy and counselling and . . .

CLARE: Debriefing?

BELL: You bet, but I don't need it. I have seen shell shock and there is such a condition as shell shock, I've seen it in colleagues, I've seen it in soldiers. I've never suffered from it, I think it's a medical condition. Such people have to be withdrawn from the front line. But the way we do it, which is not greatly fashionable with BBC management, is to talk it out among ourselves. Because if you give me some stress counsellor, they don't know what it's like. They've never been there. I can't relate to them but I talk it out with my mates. I think this is denounced by the political correctness of the day as 'blokedom'. Well, I'm in favour of 'blokedom' and some of the best blokes I know actually are the women in the business.

CLARE: Why is it politically incorrect?

BELL: Because we're supposed to need counselling when we go back and they want to give it to us and it makes them feel good. But you know, we really do sort this out ourselves. It's much better. I've talked to my army friends about this. This is where the padre comes in. If a soldier gets hit, the padre is a member of the regiment and he's been hanging around and they know him and he knows what they've been under and it's one of the great uses of padres. And when you've taken a hit, when you've lost somebody, there is a natural healing process which takes time.

CLARE: When you were hit, did you have any kind of immediate reaction to the trauma of the place and the time?

BELL: Well, only to try and calm the people down all around me and say this was no big deal. I don't know how they reacted to it because I was spirited away, but I didn't want them to be unduly worried because I knew it was a nasty incident but it was no big deal.

CLARE: This is I know a matter of balance. I was intrigued that in your own book you quoted General Rose who, in 1994, said, 'You cannot expose yourself to that sort of predicament where

35

you're living daily with appalling death and destruction without it affecting you as a human being.' And I remember the only other time you and I talked about this, I was aware myself of this. You couldn't win. If I talk to this journalist and he says, 'No, it hasn't touched me at all,' then that's interesting. If he tells me, 'Yes, it has touched me indeed,' then of course I'm also interested because I want to know in what way. Now having read the book I know that Bosnia has affected you. But what I don't know is, if I'd met you five or six years ago, had the Middle East or the Gulf or whatever, had it affected you?

BELL: Not in the same way at all.

CLARE: Though you would have seen some terrible things in some of those wars?

BELL: Not in the Gulf strangely, apart from the Basra Road.

CLARE: Well the Basra Road itself was pretty horrible.

BELL: It was horrible, it was horrible.

CLARE: Vietnam?

BELL: I was too young and inexperienced to head off in the right direction.

CLARE: Is it possible you've changed?

BELL: Sure I've changed.

CLARE: That your changing coincided with Bosnia but that over the years you were changing?

BELL: Over the years everybody changes.

CLARE: Ah yes, but in relation to this?

BELL: Yes, Bosnia was a catalyst for my changing. Without Bosnia I might not have changed. I'd be a different person, I may be a better person or a worse person, I'd be a different person. But what's happened has clearly changed me more than the other wars.

CLARE: You wouldn't say for the better?

BELL: I hope so. I think it's made me a better journalist because it's made me care more and it's made me much more aware of the moral dimensions of what I do. The same as with the soldiers. It's a funny thing about soldiers. They don't like to be seen to have too strong a sense of right and wrong, especially the senior officers, because then the generals think they're unsound. Bad thing for a soldier to be unsound. But my goodness, they do.

They've been exposed to the same things we've been exposed to. Read Bob Stewart's book, it's all in there, you know.

CLARE: And in a sense the same of journalists, that if they show feelings, they might be unsound?

BELL: We might be unsound too.

CLARE: You don't like the prettifying of war, pictures, you don't like the glamorisation of war. You feel, look, you've got to see it. But if you want to have a real impact on me, you have to move me. I'm unashamedly saying there is a role for emotion but the difficulty is getting it right. As you say, if it is over emotional it is a rant. It's highly politicised, it's ideologically committed or it's contaminated in some way. But if you take the pictures away, because people might get too upset, or you make the commentary bland, because otherwise people might accuse you of taking sides, then it has no effect at all. So that, you and I are caught in the same dilemma. How do you balance a rational argument with an emotional power?

BELL: Because the medium is itself emotional and the medium conveys the emotion.

CLARE: But do you have the same worry about that emotion as you have about your own emotion? Do you worry that the net effect of all these people sitting in their drawing rooms, watching, watching these pictures, that, that it might have the same effect on them as uncontrolled anger. That they just might be roused to a sort of incoherent response?

BELL: I think people are very moral. I think in some ways they are ahead of their politicians. They know the things that move them. They are aware of what's going on in the world.

CLARE: But it will be emotional won't it. It will be almost overwhelmingly emotional. The rationality of the argument pales beside the sight of butchered bodies.

BELL: It's a powerful medium. I think I can argue this both ways. Sometimes I think that I've seen all this and I've lived through all this and I'm supposed to be a kind of a hot shot reporter with a way with words, working in the most powerful medium in history on the first war in Europe in 50 years and it's had no effect at all. And then the other half is that I don't think there would have been any UN there because there would have been no call from the electorates for the UN to be there and, finally, there would have been no IFOR there and an effective intervention which we now have without the power principally of television. So something has moved there as a result of the television images. Sometimes when I'm feeling particularly as if I really haven't achieved anything, I'll say this has been a waste. I think I'm right in saying that Maggie O'Kane of the *Guardian*, who wrote some wonderful pieces about Bosnia in the early days, gave it up because she felt nobody's paying any attention. I sometimes feel that and I sometimes feel, well, they are paying attention but I also feel that actually, it's not really that much, it's not my business to set the British government's agenda for it. If people, politicians, really don't know, if they don't know, don't care very much, then there's a vacuum and that's when television has an effect. That's what Kofi Annan, the chief peacekeeper of the United Nations, says. And I quote Lord Carrington who, in one of his interviews, was asked if the British government policy was not being blown off course by television, replied in that rather dry aristocratic manner of his, 'Well, it always depends if there's a course to be blown off, doesn't it!'

CLARE: When you're not working are you very self-reliant. Do you spend a lot of your time with yourself?

BELL: Yes, I always have since I was a child in this rather serene background. I hope that's not a culpable offence!

CLARE: You and your twin – were you close?

BELL: I was very, very close as twins are. Then of course she went off to Canada and married this clergyman. Whenever I'm in the States I go up and see her but that old closeness is no longer there.

CLARE: You wouldn't see her that much?

BELL: No, probably once a year at the most.

CLARE: So you would be used to spending a lot of your time in your own company, so to speak?

BELL: Well, yes, but I've got much more sociable as I've grown older, I have to say. I just like being with people.

CLARE: Reading you and other war correspondents, it seems to me that the job really does call for a certain kind of independent, self-reliant person who can live with themselves and can do without too close a personal relationship for quite a long time.

BELL: I would agree with that. I think you have to be, as the French say, comfortable in your own skin. If you're continually questioning yourself, in a state of personal turmoil, it ain't going to work.

CLARE: What makes you angry?

BELL: I will tell you that the Srebrenica thing made me angry because only in 1996 were the worst fears confirmed, in March and April. We now know what happened and that it was inevitable that it was going to happen.

CLARE: What else makes you angry?

BELL: I can't think of anything else that makes me angry. I don't get angry in traffic jams. I'm the most serene guy in traffic jams in the world because I think, 'Look, I'm alive in this traffic jam.' No, I'm not easily angered.

CLARE: Are you a religious man?

BELL: Only in the sense that I have more than ever a deep sense of good and evil as active forces in the world. I find it very difficult to believe in a benevolent deity. I think at the best He's been a bit of an absentee landlord in recent years.

CLARE: And death for you?

BELL: Well, I've had brushes with it. I don't look forward to it because I enjoy life far too much. It's been a companion, real or potential, for a long time and I don't think it bothers me too much.

CLARE: How do you feel talking about yourself?

BELL: I'm not comfortable talking about myself. I don't like talking about myself.

CLARE: Why?

BELL: I explained at the beginning, I'm so much more interested in the opinions of others because I can't be surprised by my own. I know what I think, I know who I am, I don't find myself a terribly interesting person. I would find you a much more interesting person because I don't understand psychiatrists. I don't understand what moves you. I don't understand why on earth you went into this strange profession in the first place. I think if I needed you as my psychiatrist, I would then come to depend on you. You would be my crutch and I would get so addicted to this crutch that I would walk with a limp for the rest of my life and I would tend to look inside, I look inside myself for the solutions to my problems. I am, as you correctly charge me, self-reliant. I think there has to be such a thing as sorting yourself out. I don't know if it's a concept in psychiatry but it certainly is in common sense. I would be really scared to rely on even the best and most urbane psychiatrist such as yourself, because I would have felt I'd have lost a certain control, wouldn't I?

CLARE: Martin Bell, thank you very much indeed.

BELL: Pleasure, sir!

Tony Benn

In 1984 a tabloid newspaper carried a piece about Labour politician, Tony Benn, allegedly written by an unnamed American psychiatrist which declared that Benn was greedy for power, 'would do anything to satisfy his hunger' and concluded that he was 'a man driven by his own self-interest and thinking himself as God-like'. It was not an isolated but fairly typical piece of denigration of the time. Anthony Wedgwood Benn, who first entered Parliament in 1950, and who had successfully renounced his inherited title of Viscount Stansgate in the early 1960s after a massive battle, had steadily evolved into the most powerful left winger in the Labour Party and the politician most hated by the Tories since Aneurin Bevan. He was portrayed by his many critics as eccentric, unstable, even mad, a diagnosis based not only on his radical political opinions but on a cluster of harmless but well-publicised idiosyncrasies, including teetotalism, vegetarianism, republicanism and an obsessional predilection for the meticulous and painstaking recording, transcribing and storing of a record of his every daily activity.

Yet it is precisely the lack of any inner turmoil, emotional tension or personal conflict – rather than any hint of significant psychological instability – that is so striking in this encounter with Tony Benn. In his seventies, he exudes a calm, genial, donnish charm. He welcomes the opportunity to talk to a psychiatrist with all the confidence of someone who believes that if anyone is out of step, and clearly he feels many are, he certainly is not one of them. From the outset, he enmeshes me enthusiastically within the lineage of his extraordinary family tree, a tree where the foliage is

41

rich with religion and politics, both densely intertwined. There is no rebellion within the Benn family psychology. There is no dissent within the extended Benn family. In the classic Freudian canon, fathers are there to be overthrown by their sons. But the young Tony Benn is no Stephen Fry or Paul Theroux. His father is not confronted, let alone overthrown. He remains powerful, admirable, venerated and to be emulated.

Within minutes of the start of the interview, we hear the first of Tony Benn's many positive references to the impact and influence of his father. It is to the fact that his father joined the Labour Party a year after Tony Benn's birth. The party and the son are intertwined. Benn's father's politics become his politics. And any rebellious feelings about an elderly, powerful and awesomely impressive father are quickly and effectively directed outwards by way of the very politico-religious philosophy which he had taken from him. His socialism, Benn tells me, had deepened 'the sense of anger at the way people are treated, the realisation that what's wrong is wrong at the top and not at the bottom of society'. There is reverberating through the interview the strongest of identifications with his father – his memories of his father taking him to hear Oswald Mosley rant, to meet Gandhi in 1931, to see Ramsay MacDonald at the Trooping of the Colour, his father's advice, aphorisms, last words to him on his death-bed. There is no sense of any filial resentment at paternal control, authority, dominance. Tony Benn, later in the interview, confesses to 'a deep suspicion of being bullied and lectured and harassed and so on by people who claim to have some authority over you' but none of that suspicion, consciously at any rate, appears ever to have been focused on his father. Much of it, however, was to be directed at father figures including teachers, political leaders, senior churchmen, powerful figures in business and industry.

His father's age, nearly 50 at the time of Tony Benn's birth, almost certainly militated against any easy identification of son with father. The normal stages of personal growth – admiration, identification, rebellion, adult relationship – do not seem to have occurred. Benn remains the dutiful, respectful son, born to carry on the family tradition of radical Christian socialism. The death of his admired and admirable older brother seems to have intensified this filial role. Again and again, in descriptions about Benn, the adjective 'boyish' crops up. I interviewed him when he was 71 years of age and there is indeed a perceptible and engaging youthfulness, a scarcely concealed adolescent delight in being unpredictable, a conspiratorial desire to remain outrageous, still clinging to him. But if the adult Benn appears perennially youthful, the child Benn appears precociously mature. His thank-you speech aged three at a tea party with Mosley, the exchange with Miss Babcock, his teacher, when he is all of five years of age, his visit at six to Gandhi – the crucial dynamic is that of a father old enough to be his grandfather and a child who, from the outset, is treated as an adult son.

It is this powerful amalgam of religion and politics within the very personality of Tony Benn that fuels the talk of madness. He does, with all his certainty and unshakeable, serene reasonable conviction, come across at times like some latter-day nineteenth-century evangelist, one not so much promising salvation in the next life as a civilised existence in this one. And of course there is his familial (or could it be genetic?) religious sectarianism. His maternal great-grandfather was a member of a sect of the Plymouth Brethren, his maternal great-grandmother became a Congregationalist, Cromwell's communion, and Benn himself talks of the family and extended family in terms suggestive of a great, embattled and supportive religious commune. His politico-religious sect is one that provides this member at any rate with the answers to all of life's great mysteries, political and religious.

What is his faith – to challenge power. But what happens when you gain power, when you are in power? He is, after all, in politics which is all about the seizing and the wielding of power. He has been a cabinet minister in two Labour governments and chairman of the party in the 1970s. But there is that highly revealing remark, 'I've been very ambitious for influence, but not for office,' and the strange, maddening contradiction that others have identified in Benn's political behaviour whereby, even when inside a party, inside a cabinet, he seems to behave as if he is not of it but is in opposition to it. In enumerating the people he admires who wielded influence, none of them, Galileo, Darwin, Freud, Marx, was a politician. All of them were assailed for their views. 'Dare to be a Daniel, dare to stand alone.' I am tempted to wonder whether that exhortation to the young, impressionable Benn made, inevitably, by his father, explains Benn's seeming preference to be in opposition, in a minority, than in actual power.

There is in Tony Benn's fusion of religion and politics a whiff of that messianic identification which so worried the anonymous American tabloid psychiatrist. But profoundly religious people in politics, as Americans are particularly well placed to know, are almost invariably messianic. They possess the reassuring certainty that defeat is always temporary and indeed to be expected, the final victory, come what may, is ultimately theirs. Benn knows that no matter whether outvoted, nor how often, being in an unpopular minority is the definitive Christian position. One way to be sure you are in the right is to be crucified or, as he puts it, 'I'm a socialist and am hammered into the ground like most people who believe in anything very seriously nowadays but it helps me very much, gives me a map of the territory through which we are passing.'

There is a curious lack of adventure, of risk-taking about him. A radical politician he may have seen himself to be but in all other matters he remains a deeply conservative figure. Richard Crossman wrote of Benn that he 'has at times a kind of mechanical non-conformist self-righteousness about him!' But for Benn religion and politics are indivisible – no wonder a largely secular establishment thought him mad! His religion is prosaic, pragmatic, practical. There is not the merest whiff of the supernatural or the mystical. His references are to Genesis, the Acts of the Apostles, the Reverend John Ball and the Peasants' Revolt in 1381, to Thomas More's *Utopia*.

I greatly enjoyed my meeting with Tony Benn. I have little doubt he must have been a maddening colleague at times but of his own sanity I have little doubt. Earlier and elsewhere he has written of his grief at the loss of his brother and of the doubts and uncertainties that assailed him during his professional life. Now, in the Indian summer of his remarkable life, he has that peace and acceptance that age brings to those who have few doubts. *Free at Last* is to be the title of the seventh and final volume of his memoirs and in an engaging vision he imagines himself writing,

'Not feeling very well today' as his last entry. I hope very much he makes it to Thursday, April 3rd, 2025, his hundredth birthday and that I am there to interview him.

CLARE: The second of three brothers, Anthony Wedgwood Benn was born on the 3rd April, 1925. Both his grandfathers and his father, who later became the first Viscount Stansgate were Members of Parliament. Realising his childhood ambition, he himself became an MP at the age of 25 after Westminster School, New College Oxford, two years in the RAF and a spell as a magazine salesman and a BBC producer.

Following the death of his father in 1960, he became a household name during his acrimonious and, after three years, eventually successful battle to renounce his inherited title. He is now the longest-serving parliamentarian with Edward Heath, having been elected 15 times and served 11 years as a minister of cabinet rank in Labour governments of the 1960s and 1970s. Several times he was close to becoming either leader or deputy leader of his party and was its chairman in the early 1970s.

Still at Oxford, he proposed to an American student, Caroline De Camp, nine days after meeting her. They have now been married for 46 years and have four grown-up children.

Tony Benn is a famously teetotal, vegetarian, pipe-smoking, tea-drinking socialist and, most famously, controversial. At various times in his career, he was vilified and ridiculed by the press as a bogey man and 'loony Benn', was a target for death threats and the Secret Service's attention and, even within his own party, often referred to almost in Biblical terms – 'self-righteous with a halo of martyrdom', 'evangelical reformer', 'beardless prophet who thinks he alone speaks the gospel'. But what no one has ever questioned is his courage and fundamental integrity.

Tony Benn, your personality has been a source of endless fascination for other people, so I wonder whether, from time to time, it intrigues you?

BENN: Not my personality, but the life I've had. You see, I'm a great believer that the only teacher is experience, that's what really shapes you, experience when you're young. You know more about it than I do, what you experience in life, right up to today. People ring you and they come to see you and rather like you, I do my surgeries every week, six hours, people come and talk to me on the train and on the street, and I think that to learn from that and to convey it is interesting. But not specially about myself, although everyone is interesting.

CLARE: What immediately interests me is that while you say, experience of life, the fact remains that the core elements of your life, for example, your socialism, that has not only never wavered but you once said, 'I never became a socialist, I was one,' so there's a sense in which ...

BENN: Well, yes, I was born into a Labour household. My dad had been a radical Liberal, joined the Labour Party a year after I was born, and so in a sense the socialist politics was the politics of home, but of course, as I've got older my socialism has deepened, the sense of anger at the way people are treated, the realisation that what's wrong is wrong at the top and not at the bottom of society.

CLARE: Well, let me ask you again because I think somewhere I've read, it may not have been attributed to you, the observation that as men grow older they tend to move from the left to the centre and indeed, sometimes to the right, through age and disillusion. I think it's been attributed to you but it has not happened to you.

BENN: No, it's quite the opposite and my father, you see, began as a Liberal, as a radical Liberal, ended up as a left-wing socialist.

CLARE: So what's the explanation do you think for that?

BENN: Well, I think the explanation is experience. I was always Labour and remember, in the thirties Fascism was the great threat. I went out in the streets one Sunday in 1935 and I saw Oswald Mosley and the Blackshirts go by and it frightened me. I went to a meeting with my dad in the East End of London and it was broken up by the fascists, we had to escape. I heard the voice of Hitler on the radio from Nuremberg. I couldn't understand a word of German but you knew that this was going to end in conflict and I remember the Spanish Civil War, I met Mr Gandhi when he came to London in 1931 and so my whole ...

46

CLARE: You were five.

BENN: Just six and my father, who was secretary of state for India, took me to see him. I don't remember anything he said to me, I don't remember anything I said to him but what I do remember, something that you would remember, this great man, sitting on the floor, devoted his whole attention to this little boy of six and my older brother. Now not many adults do that, they pat you on the head and talk to your dad. And so, in a sense, that was the framework of my thought. But then, as I got older, particularly when I became a minister, particularly when I had this nonsense over the peerage, you began to see that the whole system needed to be changed. And so, like Mr Gladstone, who began as a Conservative and ended up as a very radical man, I moved to the left and I think it's the only logical thing to do truthfully. I'm not criticising anybody else but ...

CLARE: No, no, I understand that and it makes a coherent picture of how it happened to you but what is striking is that it is the exception, and I'm interested in you in that sense, as the exception. I mean there are others, I don't want to make it out that it's unique but it is an exception, that you have, as you say, deepened your socialism when so many others, with age, seem to water it down?

BENN: Well, I wouldn't want to comment on the motives of others but there are lots of temptations you know in politics.

CLARE: Well, say something about those.

BENN: I thought I'd overcome most of them. The final one is this kindly old gentleman who's quite harmless, if you see what I mean. Well I'm not, I may be kindly and I may be old and I could possibly be a gentleman, but I'm not harmless! And so, at every stage, there are ways of winning you over to the Establishment point of view, which is very, very powerful. And, of course, a career usually depends on pleasing a leader, in this society of ours corrupted by patronage. But I'm not criticising other people because there are lots of reasons for changing your opinion but some people began reading Marx as students and ended up in the House of Lords and I suppose you could argue I did it the other way around. But the basis of it is my experience, of what I've seen, the people I've met, what's happened to people, the rising tide of anger against injustice and that's what's done it to me.

CLARE: Well, what, what about your genes? Let me just for my own purposes summarise what really is, by any standards, a remarkable genetic inheritance of politics. I've read back through, through your life: your paternal great-grandfather, he was a pastor in Wapping and your maternal great-grandfather was a provost in Paisley. Your paternal grandfather was an MP for Tower Hamlets, he started out as a Liberal home ruler, as you say, he became, if anything, more left and ended up in the Labour Party. Your maternal grandfather, he was an MP for Govern. You say of him 'not a politician, more a scholar' and I'll come back to that in a moment. Then there's your father, who was a Liberal MP for Leith wasn't he, and Labour MP for Gorton and your mother was herself very political, I mean religious and political so that it's really like I was interviewing someone for whom politics was their experience right through three or four generations. This is a political family, the Benn family. It extends back through three generations.

BENN: Well, it does and I think that makes you familiar with the subject. One of the advantages of being born in a Labour home was that my political awareness began much younger. I met Oswald Mosley when he was a Labour Member of Parliament in 1928, and I remember it. The first speech I ever made.

CLARE: You remember it? You were three!

BENN: I was three. I stood up after tea in his house in Smith Square and I said, 'Boys and girls and sailors, thank you for the nice tea.' I don't know why I said it but he was then a Labour MP and then he became a Labour Minister and then he became a fascist. I saw him on the streets of London. So, I mean, it gives you a certain familiarity with the movement of people. He had been a Conservative before, of course, and then he joined the Labour Party and then went fascist. And I met Ramsay MacDonald in 1930 when I was five at the Trooping of the Colour. So all that because of the opportunities I had, plus what I drew from my grandparents. I never met my father's father because he died just before I was born, but he began as an office boy working in London at the age of eleven and went to work in his mother's boots, but he became a founder member of the London County Council and was a sort of Ken Livingstone or Herbert Morrison of his day and, as you mentioned, he stood as a home ruler, defeated a Tory minister who said, 'If you give Ireland home rule there'll be anarchy and terrorism,' and that was in 1892. And my father fought against the Black and Tans, you see, so, the support for the Irish National Movement is in my bloodstream. But then it wasn't just that, it was what was discussed at home. You see, my mother's father, I don't know how far you want to pursue this, but my mother's grandfather was a very, very sectarian Scot, from Irvine. He was a member of what was called the Irvine Brethren. They wouldn't accept that they were the Plymouth Brethren, but the Irvine Brethren, and it turned my grandfather into an atheist, and my mother was so upset that her father told her that there was no God she felt that she was born in an orphanage. So, at the age of eight, she went to church on her own. A little girl of eight went to the local Church of Scotland and became a Christian. But her dissenting tradition was such that she left the Church of England in the end and became a Congregationalist and therefore, in a way, in religious terms, joined up with my father's religion, which was Congregationalist, and that's the dissenting tradition. You challenge power, you believe in the priesthood of all believers. You don't believe in bishops, popes, kings, so that is all in my recesses of my mind and it's very, very helpful.

CLARE: Right, now what I'm interested in is that the dissenting is in terms of ideas, whereas in my clinical work I see a lot of dissent in terms of actual family relationships – sons turning away from fathers, embarking on a very different route. Apart from that maternal grandfather who became an atheist, perhaps in reaction to a much sterner and sectarian father, that seems to have been the sum total. There is very little internal dissent within the Benns.

BENN: No, I'm afraid you'd have to probe a long time to find anything. My father was 20 years older than my mother so, in a way, was my grandfather. He was born in 1877 and my grandfather was born in 1850. You see, my father's father was born in 1850.

CLARE: So he was nearly 50 when you were born.

BENN: He was nearly 50 when I was born and my mother was 20 years younger so the family relationship was an interesting one. My father was in politics, my mother was very, very deeply interested in theology and I was brought up on the Bible. Now, when I was young I was told a lot of things by my mother and my father which I thought went in one ear and came out the other and I find now, at my age, that they've lodged there. For example, my father used to say to me, 'Dare to be a Daniel, dare to stand alone, dare to have a purpose firm, dare to let it known.' My mother used to say when I learnt to fly, she would remind me of 'underneath of the everlasting arms'. Now these are very, very strong and powerful influences. She used to tuck me up at night and say, 'Goodnight darling, another happy day tomorrow.' Now that fed my optimism, we might have had a flaming row but tomorrow would be a happy day. Father was full of aphorisms ... 'never wrestle with a chimney sweep,' he said. Well, I wasn't likely to but I didn't realise what he was saying. If somebody plays dirty with you, don't play dirty with them or you'll get dirty too. Now these were childhood influences which, far from leading me to revolt against my parents, led me to appreciate the experience they brought to bear. I mean it must be as common as having a row with your parents, but I don't know. Certainly in my case I followed and admired and respected them.

CLARE: What was he like, your father? He's had an enormous influence on you.

BENN: Well, he did, yes. He was a radical you see, too. He was thrown out of the window at University College, London, because he opposed the Boer War and he was a great admirer of Campbell-Bannerman ...

CLARE: And he'd tell you about this would he?

BENN: Oh yes, of course. Well, he was a great talker, he was a very amusing man, extremely entertaining man. And he was very boyish in his character. Although he was much older, very nearly 50, I mean he really was a sort of companion. He made lots of jokes and never, never rebuked us in any way. So he did have a big influence politically particularly because we discussed all the politics of the thirties. I remember the Spanish Civil War. He'd had a meeting recently in Stoke-on-Trent on the International Brigade. I wrote an essay in my schoolbook about the Spanish Civil War, attacking Franco in 1937, when I was 12 and the teacher said, 'Disgusting' because he supported Franco. And so, do you see what I mean, it's been a continuing theme? The one advantage of that is it's given me a political memory of a man of 90; maybe therefore you are not so easily pushed off your opinion because you've seen it all happen. It isn't an opinion formed from a headline or a public opinion poll or a prospect of promotion. You think you understand it from experience and that is something enormously powerful.

CLARE: And there is the sense that it will, one day, come right.

BENN: Well, I wouldn't say that because, I mean, there are grounds for pessimism and sometimes I get very depressed. I conceal it as far as I can from the public because I think morale is 90 per cent of every victory and I don't want to tell people when I'm very, very depressed about the political situation. I am, too, on occasions. I mean this victory of the American right, and Yeltsin who's a thug and all that, I find that very depressing.

CLARE: Those are the things that would depress you?

BENN: Yes, really. There was a programme on the BBC earlier this year about whether we should bring the stocks back and shame criminals and I can imagine the BBC having a quite serious programme about the case for public executions. And all these ideas. So you feel you have to resist them. On the other hand, underneath, where all change begins, there is more radical stirring in the mid-90s than I remember since the 1930s. Animal Rights, the campaign against the poll tax, the campaigns of pensioners, nurses and so on. I identify myself with them but obviously you have to be realistic. Things are still shifting to the right because fear is the great instrument of popular control and if you can frighten people then they'll do what you tell them. I try to give people the confidence in themselves.

CLARE: The political and the religious in you – somewhere you said they're indistinguishable?

BENN: Yes, I think Church and State should be separate but that religion and politics are the same thing. You see there are some socialists in the Labour Party and there are some Christians in the churches and all organisations begin with a flame of faith. Then when a structure is set up, then the flame is used to burn heretics. I find the inquisitions in the Labour Party against the left, for example, very similar to the inquisitions that occurred against dissenting Christians. My socialism comes out of the book of Genesis I suppose – 'Am I my brother's keeper?' When Cain killed Abel and the Lord had a word with him about it, Cain said, 'Am I my brother's keeper?' Now, that is the question: 'Am I my brother's keeper?'; 'An injury to one is an injury to all'; 'United we stand, divided we fall'; 'You do not cross a picketline.' That didn't come from the Kremlin, that came from the book of Genesis and these ideas of solidarity are very deeply entrenched in me through my mother's teaching and then reinforced by what I've seen. The way the miners were treated was disgraceful.

CLARE: So to say to you that, you could have been a preacher, you could have been a pastor, it would not be regarded by you as a term of rejection?

BENN: Well, Wilson said I was a beardless prophet, but then for Harold Wilson the greatest term of abuse he could use was to say 'that's a theological argument' as if theology was self-evidently nonsensical. But it is interesting. You see, I do a lot of talks on Christianity and socialism. Mind you, my Christianity is an ethical Christianity now. I find the mysteries of religion not very helpful. But I did a meeting with the bishop of Gloucester and all his priests not long ago, about socialism and Christianity, and at the end an evangelical got up and said to me he was getting very impatient with me. He said, 'Do you believe that Christ is our Lord?' and I said, 'Well, I'm a republican, I don't believe in lords.' And then he said, 'Do you believe in the kingdom of Heaven?' So I said, 'Well, as I say, I'm a republican. If you say, "Do you accept Jesus as your teacher, or shop steward? Do you believe in the commonwealth of humanity?" it's fine. But the patriarchal, hierarchical language of the Church puts me off. I do believe in the priesthood of all believers. That's to say, everybody has a hotline to the Almighty, whatever that may mean, but you don't need a priest or a bishop or a cardinal or pope to tell you what you ought to believe.' Now that is the heart of the whole dissenting religious and political tradition.

CLARE: Your psychology doesn't need the more metaphysical side of religion, if you like, the emotional, the charismatic?

BENN: Well, I mean, religious practice is part of the culture of society. I love hearing hymns and going to church and listening to church music. That's part of the cultural inheritance but if you ask me whether the mysteries of religion are either helpful to me or very relevant, I have to say now, not. But I must counter that with saying something else. I have a great respect for people who have any faith because we live in a society where there is no faith, where God has been replaced by Mammon in Canterbury Cathedral and I don't believe in the worship of Mammon and we've all been told to do that. So I have a respect for people who retain their faith, even though, as I say, the, the theological aspects of it and the mysteries of it don't actually help me very much or play a very large part in my interpretation of the Christian message.

CLARE: What did you mean when you said God has been replaced by Mammon in Canterbury Cathedral?

BENN: Well, I think that the choice is between God and Mammon and we are a nation now that worships Mammon. We're told to worship Mammon and the City of London and the Dow Jones Industrial Average has replaced the Ten Commandments and that I find deeply offensive because it's a virus that's infected everybody, including the Labour Party. They call it modernisation in the Labour Party but actually it's the acceptance that Mammon will run the world. Now I know I'm using theological language but that's because I do see it in that way.

CLARE: But in your family, religion and politics were very enmeshed. Your mother was a highly religious woman.

BENN: Oh very much so, yes. And, you see, she came to religion in an interesting way. She didn't believe. She wrote a book called *My Exit Visa*, which was a marvellous title for a book, just before she died. She didn't believe that Jesus was God Incarnate. She believed that Jesus embodied the creator. Now the idea of embodiment as distinct from the idea of incarnation is a very interesting distinction. Here was a man who, in his life, embodied what the creator wished but wasn't actually God incarnate. Now, I know only theological students will understand the differentiation between the two but it's very important. The ethics of Christianity, the teachings of Jesus seem to me to be enormously helpful but the mystery set up by the Church about the risen Christ, as I say, I don't find very helpful. Anyway, they were all developed after the crucifixion.

CLARE: Just pursuing it for a minute, this identification which you've described as an ethical, religious foundation for your politics – I noticed quite early on that people were struck by this in your oratory. I came across a reference, I think, to a speech you gave in Bath very early on describing you: 'He almost sounded like a young lay preacher preaching the socialist faith.' Now, you've often made those kind of statements and they're interesting statements in a country which is predominantly secular in the way it formulates things. I wondered what your colleagues early on made of this?

BENN: Well, they'll have to tell you that.

CLARE: What do you think?

BENN: Well, I don't know. Lots of people would give an explanation. But as I've got older I've studied the past in order to understand where we came from. For example, there'd be a big debate in the Labour Party in 1995 about Common Ownership. Well, the Acts of the Apostles, if you read them, which I did – all things in common and people were rewarded according to their needs. If you look at the Reverend John Ball and the Peasants' Revolt in 1381, he said, 'Things will not go well in England until all property is held in common.' Look at Thomas More's *Utopia*, he said the same. If you look at the Levellers at the time of the English Revolution, they said, 'The earth is a common treasury, it is a crime to buy and sell the earth for private gain.' Now that was long before Karl Marx began studying capitalism. I've always regarded Karl Marx as the last of the Old Testament prophets. He was an old Jew who studied capitalism, was horrified by its injustice and so socialism is a faith as well as a form of analysis and so on and so on. And I'm proud of that. I'm a socialist and am hammered into the ground like most people who believe in anything very seriously nowadays but it helps me very much, gives me a map of the territory through which we're passing.

CLARE: One of the interesting things about religious leaders is that they're often lonely. They lead. Of course a politician is not always taking the soundings and then deciding where to go. He has occasionally to lead and that's a very religious idea, the prophet with the idea who is leading. Of course, there is the extent to which a prophet is, by definition, never really acknowledged until some time later. It's a lonely existence.

BENN: Well, I wouldn't say that really. But, certainly, if I ask myself who has really had the greatest influence, it's very rarely the people who held high office. If I could remember all the chancellors of the exchequer backwards from now to the war, which with a bit of effort I could, how many of them have left any footprints in the sands of time. If you take Galileo, who has only recently been acquitted of blasphemy by the pope – I was very glad because up to then I wasn't absolutely sure whether to believe what Galileo said – but Galileo studied the world and explained it. Darwin studied the world and explained it. Freud studied the world and explained it. Marx studied the world and explained it. And these are the people who've had an influence. Now I've been very ambitious for influence, but not for office and I think that that's probably puzzled people. They think, 'Oh well, the man must be saying that because he wants to get on.' Well, truthfully, if I had wanted to get on in the traditional way I wouldn't have said 90 per cent of the things I've said. So, in that sense, it's not really lonely. And as to leadership, I've got a quote. You may have heard me use it before. It's Lao-tzu the Chinese philosopher who I like very much. He said, 'As to the best leaders, the people do not notice their existence, the next best the people honour and praise, the next best the people hate, the next best the people fear but when the best leader's work is done, the people say, we did it ourselves.' Now that is my definition of leadership. You encourage people to have confidence in themselves and not in you. And it's very different from the normal way in which politics is conducted but it's not lonely because there are lots of people who are glad you said it, you know.

CLARE: None the less, as you've described it, it sounds very selfless.

BENN: No no, no, no.

CLARE: No? So what are the rewards?

BENN: You have to live with yourself, don't you? People talk a lot about images but my image is what I shave in the morning. I can't change it and I don't believe in all the spin doctors and imagers.

CLARE: What is your image?

BENN: I think the point is you have to live with yourself.

CLARE: What is your image?

BENN: Well, my image is what I say and do and so on. It's all open to the public to be seen by those who want to study it. But I don't think that it's goody goody because the comfort in the end of the day in knowing that you really said what you thought to the best of your ability, that's the real reward isn't it? You may be wrong, I've been wrong a million times. I was wrong on nuclear power, the Cold War, lots of things, but, at least what I said was based on my interpretation of what was going on. Now that's a huge thing. There are some things that people do, and I've done them myself, you're utterly ashamed of and so that's rather different. It is true nobody honours a prophet in his own country and all that stuff but I've had all the rewards, you know, really, I can't complain. I've been in Parliament and cabinet and so on. I haven't really been in a wilderness although there are some people who like to put you there. So you mustn't make me look as if I've been extremely selfless and all that. I've just tried to say, no, no, you know, I'm a very ordinary guy! [Laughter.]

CLARE: No, not for a minute. Nor do I buy this image of you as a sort of holier than thou, righteous, religious freak. Quite the contrary. I'm interested, however, that there are certain things clearly you don't derive all that much pleasure from. Alcohol is one – you're a teetotaller. You smoke and you drink tea and we know about that. You are a man who gets an enormous amount of satisfaction out of ideas and out of influence and out of teaching and listening to people. The question I ask you is – there are things that give you the kind of buzz that other people get from drink or drugs or maybe sex or whatever. I've watched you speaking, sometimes, in so far as one ever sees Tony Benn possessed, intoxicated, it is when you are in full flow. Is that how it feels?

BENN: Not really, no. I try not to speak from a text. I try to think about what I'm going to say.

CLARE: But you are passionate.

BENN: If you want to know what moves me it is what happens to me. I'm not a trained observer of the human mind but six hours a week I sit and listen to people with the most horrific problems. If I didn't have a good stamina I'd burst into tears at what I'm told. I get 20,000 letters a year roughly and I try to read them all and learn from them and that makes me very angry. Not in a personal sense and therefore when you get an opportunity to talk you try to convey that and at the same time give people the greater confidence in themselves. The word possession does sound slightly obsessive. It isn't really that. It's an attempt to communicate what you feel to other people in a way they will understand. I don't know whether that looks like possession. It doesn't feel like it.

CLARE: No. I'll explain it because I didn't mean it to have any negative or positive connotations. What I really was trying to get at was that you've been for many, many years a very powerful speaker. It goes right back. You've talked about giving a speech at the age of three. Clearly the use ...

BENN: It didn't do Oswald Mosley much good, did it? [Laughter.]

CLARE: No! But clearly, very early on, you must have realised, that you had a power. You could move an audience.

BENN: Well, I think of it as communication.

CLARE: I know that, I know that, but I'm pushing you. I know you do.

BENN: Well, I mean if it's successful ... some people can write and some people can draw and some people can do other things, but I suppose having done, I think in the Miners' Strike I did 299 public meetings in a year for the miners, now, clearly when you've done that you do get a sort of feel for it and you begin developing arguments that you know register with people, and so you use them. But whether that's manipulative or some special oratorical skill? You see, some of the best speeches I have ever heard in my life, and I hear lots, were made by women in the Women's Support Groups in the Miners' Strike. And when afterwards you spoke to them, they'd never spoken before in their lives but an experience had welled up in them and they were able to communicate what had happened in their pit village to their husbands, to their children, and the poverty they'd experienced and so on. So, I don't really believe that public speaking is a skill.

CLARE: What do you think it is?

BENN: I think it's something that comes out of you through your mind and mouth into the hearts of other people, and that is communication. I mean that's what everybody tries to do. I suppose in conversation you try to explain to people, just as I'm trying to do to you now, what I really feel. I don't know whether that's exactly manipulative or a special skill. I don't know.

CLARE: Presumably it can be but it needn't be. But, there is this passion, there is this anger.

BENN: Well there is and, and that's what moved me to the left.

CLARE: Does it ever surprise you, the intensity of it?

BENN: Well, I don't know really. I'm more fired up now than I was a few years ago because I see the horrors of what's happening and this is where my childhood comes in, you see. I know that mass unemployment produces fascism and scapegoatism because I've seen it and so when I see 20,000,000 unemployed in the European Union, 20,000,000 unemployed, I remember it was 6,000,000 unemployed in Germany that brought Hitler to power. So, in a sense, as you get older and you can tap your own experience over a longer period, you're fired by so many things that you didn't perhaps realise were there. It's a mixture of experience and probably the grounding I had because my mother taught me a great deal about justice and a lot of other things. I was taken out of Bible class when I was five. Miss Babcock once said in Bible class that God was angry and I said, 'God is love' so she removed me and rang up my mother and said, 'I'm afraid Mrs Benn that when I begin he begins.' So, during Bible class I had to sit and read on my own in a room while she continued to teach her very fundamentalist religion. It was very funny. That was when I was about five or six I was then, you see. So, it does go back a bit. It is not just absolutely new. I wasn't prepared to have Miss Babcock tell me that God was angry because I didn't really believe that that was exactly how God interacted with people. It's strange this. It's very interesting, of course, because it shows why you can't be blown off course by a critical leading article in the *Guardian*.

CLARE: It is a striking self-confidence, this little boy with this . . .

BENN: Well, it's not in yourself but it's in the ideas, really, isn't it?

CLARE: Or isn't it in yourself, isn't it in yourself?

BENN: Well, I don't know, I don't know. You could say that, I suppose you could say that. You, a psychiatrist, you must have learned from your own experience that when you handle certain sorts of people you know enough about them to know you can be helpful. Now, is that any different, that self-confidence based on your experience, than feeling a certain confidence? Although I do think that the political problems facing this country are so difficult, so challenging, so interesting, and I contrast them with the shallow, abusive, the type of political discourse which I detest.

CLARE: Well, I'm going right back, because very honestly you give me the picture not of Benn in the twenties and thirties and forties of his life, but right back. That little boy with his formidable fundamentalist religious teacher, he has that confidence. He says, 'God is love'; she says, 'God is angry.' This is you nearly 70 years ago! Now, it's a characteristic that 70 years on people say of you, they say you are not daunted.

BENN: Well, yes, partly, I mean that's one way of putting it.

CLARE: Well, yes, it is.

BENN: But I think it was a dissenting tradition, you see. I think you mustn't mistake dissent for self-confidence because like everybody else I worry all the time, 'Am I doing and saying what I should be doing?' Because I've a very strong sense of right and wrong you see, and very often the little conscience on my shoulder tells me, do something and I don't, so you mustn't think it's that type of self-confidence.

CLARE: No, but that's different.

BENN: But it is a deep suspicion of being bullied and lectured and harassed and so on by people who claim to have some authority over you. I don't know whether that's quite self-confidence or just being obstinate.

CLARE: It's courage. OK, well, maybe that's it then.

BENN: I don't know. You know more about it, you've seen lots of patients and I'm a ...

CLARE: Yes, I know, but I think you take for granted that remarkable strength. Many little boys would like to say, 'God is love' but they just wouldn't have the nerve or the confidence.

BENN: Well, I got it from my mother, you see. You must be fair, it was mother who had said God is love and Miss Babcock said He was angry so I felt it was an obligation to point out to Miss Babcock that she'd got it wrong. The fact that I was five is of no particular relevance to that.

CLARE: Only in the sense that you've been at it ever since. [Laughter.] Yet behind the seeming self-confidence of many politicians is a considerable feeling of insecurity and doubt.

BENN: Well, not so much insecurity, because I haven't that. But doubt, anxiety, are you doing the right thing, what should you do? I'll give you an example now – the Cold War in retrospect was a total fraud. It was all designed to make out that if you opposed the government you were an agent of the KGB and so on and so on and so on. We wasted billions and billions and billions of pounds. I suspected at the time, I feel I now know it for certain. Now I see the war against Islam building up, Willie Clunes, the new secretary-general of NATO, said, 'Now the communists are defeated.' Now, I know much less about Islam, I'm not going to have another crusade imposed on us. So, in a way, although you have all sorts of doubts because obviously some of the Islamic practices I don't like, their attitude to women maybe and so on, but I'm not being told now that we've got to have nuclear weapons to deal with the Arab world and Islam. So that in a sense, it comes out of the moments of doubt and what should you do and then, in the end, when your view forms, you have to express it and then if it's wrong you have to adjust it.

CLARE: Some of the politicians I've met, they're very powerfully motivated by a desire to be liked. They get uneasy if they're unpopular.

BENN: Well, that's very understandable.

CLARE: Oh indeed, indeed, but it's a characteristic I don't detect in you?

BENN: Well, I wouldn't say that. I mean you like to be liked. I'd love to open the *Guardian* one morning and read the leading article saying, 'In another wise address to the nation, Mr Benn properly reminded us ...' but of course, I know it won't happen. But then I know ...

CLARE: But you don't do it to make it happen?

BENN: Well no. The one remaining corruption, when you get into your seventies that I mentioned, that you're a kindly old gentleman, that's the way they win you over in the end. But you have to go on, otherwise I wouldn't want to be in public life, I wouldn't want to be in politics if I was really dancing to somebody else's tune. And anyway, who are the people who like you? A tiny minority of people like you. The people are powerful people who think you are no longer a threat. But if you're talking about popularity, whatever that may mean, I'm sustained all the time by the letters, by the people who write to me, the people who come up to me and so on. So, you mustn't think that because you're unpopular with Fleet Street or the City of London or MI5, that means you're really unpopular.

CLARE: Or even your political colleagues?

BENN: Yeah, exactly, your political colleagues. The House of Commons is an ice box. I get in the train for Chesterfield and all of a sudden I feel a free man you see. So it's a different view of the whole political process. It's what happens at the bottom that matters.

CLARE: Can I ask you about that? There are politicians of all political persuasions who love the House of Commons. They talk about it in comradely ways, they see it as a club. It's a tremendous support, an emotional haven in a way. But I don't sense that of you. It's indeed very interesting, you called it an ice box.

BENN: I mean, the political atmosphere. Mind you it's not as bad as it was for me a few years ago, but the House of Commons is a club. We don't live in a democracy. We don't elect our president as Mary Robinson is elected in Ireland. We don't elect our second chamber as they do in the United States. We have a very limited democracy. Parliament has been going for 700 years and only in the last 70 years have men and women had the vote at the same age. I was born in 1925 and women didn't get the vote at 21 until I was three years old, 1928. And so democracy is very, very shallow and, and now it's gone, probably, within the European Union where laws are made that you don't vote for yourself. So, I mean we're in a different position and I think Parliament is a sort of mini platform really.

CLARE: And how do you feel there when you are there?

BENN: Well, I mean, I'm an old hand at it and I try and say in the House of Commons, make the same speech that I would make in public. And, indeed, I have a very simple test of personal integrity. If I meet somebody I want to know, does he say, or does she say, that in cabinet, in Parliament, in the constituency, at the party conference and at home? And it's a self-policing system that and I've known some people who've sounded quite different at the party conference than they did in the cabinet. And so, in a way, I see Parliament as a platform.

CLARE: But isn't a lot of politics people manifesting a number of different kinds of appearances, negotiating with different kinds of interests? Isn't a lot of politics the art of compromise?

BENN: Well, yes. Having been in the Labour Party for 53 years you know that very well but I think you have to argue your case. If you're outvoted, I've never found that very difficult, being outvoted, I was outvoted in the cabinet very often as a member of the Labour Party, we've been outvoted the last four general elections, I don't find defeat difficult to cope with, but what I think would be disreputable would be if you said what you didn't believe in order to get some advantage. The arguments in the cabinet were very, very strong and powerful and I would have been ashamed if I hadn't put my view in the cabinet, but then, if in the end, the cabinet decided to do something else you'd say, 'Well, the cabinet discussed this and decided to do that and that's the position.' So, I think there's a difference between compromise and facing the fact that you may have a longer struggle.

CLARE: Well, was it difficult for you, for example, in a party system, to find yourself voting for certain things that you didn't much agree with?

BENN: I think the problem of resignation is quite a difficult one. I faced it many, many times – should I resign from the cabinet? And I used to go to my local party and say, 'What shall I do, shall I resign?' I don't think any other cabinet minister would do that, and the local party usually said, indeed always said, 'Stay and fight your corner.' If you do resign from a cabinet, there's a vote of confidence that afternoon in the House of Commons and you then vote for the cabinet you've resigned from and if the government falls, do you then vote for the re-election of the government from which you've resigned? I have done it several times in my life. I resigned from the front bench in 1958 over nuclear weapons. I resigned from the National Executive in 1960 and so on. But I think that resignation is probably only appropriate if you come to the conclusion that the party of which you are a member is no longer the lesser of two evils. I've agonised over this many, many times. The important thing is to go on saying what you believe and trying to win your argument.

CLARE: But that's how you would see a political party, as the lesser of two evils?

BENN: Well, that's how it is in a way. You know, all political parties are coalitions of different forces. After all I sat in the cabinet with people I knew perfectly well weren't Labour like David Owen, Roy Jenkins. Reg Prentice left the cabinet and became a Tory back bencher and Tory minister. I knew he wasn't Labour. But you have to see, and I see the Labour Party as an instrument created by the British working-class movement to improve its conditions and that's why I could never leave it. And I try to persuade it to certain views and then try to persuade people to put it in power and it seems to me to be reputable, but of course, it's very difficult but it's not exactly tightrope walking. You know it's a bit different from that. You argue your case, you lose, you come back and try and win it again, and that seems to me to be a reputable thing to do. But of course compromise is a part of the business of being in any organisation.

CLARE: I was thinking that it was the difference between, if you like, a religious leader and a political leader. A religious leader has a message and you go forth with it and you give that message and people take it or they don't take it. A political leader is involved much more in the practical implementation, the day-to-day application of power and how power is exercised.

BENN: Oh yes, well you have to be competent. If you're a minister, and I was responsible for nuclear power for years, I thought it was cheap, safe and peaceful. It took me years of office to realise that it wasn't cheap, it was three times the cost of coal, it wasn't safe and it was all about the atom bomb. I made a big mistake but I learned, but while I was there I tried to do a proper job and I worked very hard and stayed up late at night reading all the papers and I tried to be a competent minister. But when the big political choices came up in the cabinet about whether we should have nuclear weapons, what we should do about the economic policy, should we make cuts to please the bankers, then I was able to present a political view which wasn't exactly an administrative position, it was my own convictions and sometimes I lost and sometimes I won. But you do have to argue your case. There's nothing disreputable about that. But then compromise is a funny word. It suggests that you've sort of abandoned something. The way I see it, is having to accept defeat and I've never found defeat, funnily enough, difficult. I've been defeated so many times it would be difficult for me to have taken any other view. But defeat is an experience from which you learn and after all, life is learning from your experience.

CLARE: And what do you learn from defeat?

BENN: Well, you learn all sorts of things. First of all, if you're a minister and you're defeated you go out of office back into the real world, and that's very helpful. I remember in 1970 we were defeated, I'd been a minister for six years, saying to myself, 'What do I do now?' And I thought, well, you defend the people whom you represent. Then I said, 'Well why didn't we do that when we were in government?' It was a very simple thing that came like a bolt from the blue and I realised what was wrong with the Labour government, we hadn't defended the people who'd elected us. So I find the learning process is fascinating. I really enjoy it and every night that's why I do my diary, I go over the experience and say, 'What have I learnt today? What lessons are there, what might be done?' and so on. That is, I think, what makes politics so interesting.

CLARE: Every night you do it?

BENN: Yes, I do, yes.

CLARE: How long does it take you?

BENN: Well, sometimes three or four in the morning before I finish. Once I went to sleep while I was dictating my diary in Tokyo and when I woke up my machine had switched itself off and I went back to that little bit of rubbish that comes just before you doze off.

CLARE: And when you say you might finish at three or four in the morning, when would you have started?

BENN: Well, if we had meetings that went to two in the morning, I'd come home and spend an hour dictating. If there was an interesting cabinet, I'd miss my lunch and dictate from memory while it was fresh, what happened in the cabinet. And I think that's partly also religious. Because time is very important to me. My father read a book called *How To Make Twenty-four Hours Out of Every Day* and he had a time chart and his theory was that work and sleep should equal 24, which meant conversation, holidays, everything else was a waste of time. And I had a time chart for years.

CLARE: Did you?

BENN: It is a feeling that you're somewhere at the throne of the Heavenly Grace, or perhaps even *In The Psychiatrist's Chair*, you're accountable for what you've done in your life. And so a diary is a sort of record for that as well as being a record of experience.

CLARE: But at the same time you don't believe that any more, do you?

BENN: Well, but you know what I mean, you are responsible.

CLARE: You've got that sense of responsibility?

BENN: I think so, yes. You may say that's goody goody too but it isn't really. I find it very difficult to go to bed if I haven't done my diary. Tonight, I'll be doing it before I go to bed.

CLARE: When you say you find it very difficult, you mean physically?

BENN: Oh yes, you're very tired.

CLARE: But you'd find it very difficult not to?

BENN: There are many times I get home and I've finished my red boxes at one, or two, in the morning, then you've got to do your diary and I find it extremely difficult to let a night go by without doing it. Sometimes on holiday I miss a day or two.

CLARE: And if you do, how do you feel?

BENN: Well, I don't think you call it an addiction or duty or something but it, it, it worries me if I haven't made a record of that day's activities and when I mentioned the throne of the Heavenly Grace I was using the old theological language, the Day of Judgement, you've got to explain what you've done with your life and I think that it may be odd but it's explicable to me anyway.

CLARE: You mention work and sleep as those two cardinal elements; is there much time in your life for doing other things?

BENN: Well, people think politics is all about sort of hack party campaigning but politics is life really. Everything that happens impinges in some way or another on the political system. I've got children and grandchildren and I'm very happy with them and it is true and I do find that life is so interesting and life in some ways impinges. I get letters from all over the world. I had a letter recently from a man who'd been reprieved in Jamaica and he thanked me because I'd written to the high commissioner in London. I don't know whether it played any part, but anyway he thought it worth writing. And that was very satisfying. And all sorts of people come and my surgeries I do find absolutely riveting because I've done it for 45 years now and I find it interesting. And yet the problems brought to me are not particularly political. One man came to me on crutches and said he wanted to prosecute his son about something his son had done, I think he accused him of stealing or something. And, in the end, after about half an hour I said to him, 'Could it be you're disabled and your son's young and that you're a bit jealous of him?' And he said, 'Mr Benn, I believe you're right.' And he walked out. Now I felt I was moving into your territory really but it just occurred to me that something was so odd about this man on crutches wanting to prosecute his son. I get lots of stuff like that and that is very interesting. I mean, in a way, it's as interesting as yours.

CLARE: You are enormously curious about the world.

BENN: Yes, I am, yes. And I learn from everybody I meet. The cab driver brought me here, training up, he told me, to try and become an Olympic rower, sculling. Told me all about it. Yesterday, it was a cab driver taking me somewhere else who told me he was a lighterman. He told me about the watermen, the stevedores, the dockers, and I put it all in my diary because I think the illumination and explanation and account of what you've learned is so interesting. It's not about me, it's really what people tell me.

CLARE: And again, you'll dictate that on to a machine?

BENN: Oh, yes, absolutely.

CLARE: And the task of saying what the day is, what the week is?

BENN: Well, I have a diary going forward over a year ahead and then all the engagements and then I try and type them up.

CLARE: And you'd be responsible for filing them?

BENN: Well, I've got people helping in the office.

CLARE: But when you started out?

BENN: No, I didn't. Well, I only started the dictated diary in 1966. Before that I used to dictate it to a secretary.

CLARE: But that's nearly 30 years ago!

BENN: Oh yes, yes. The diary goes back to 1934 I think, my first diary was when I was nine.

CLARE: What do your family make of it? What does your wife make of the fact?

BENN: Some of them keep diaries. But they're all very busy, you see, themselves. Everyone of my family are involved in some way in politics, in education and one in trade union work and so on. So, it's an interest really.

CLARE: Which must be enormously satisfying?

BENN: Well, it is. They don't all agree with it all but they were brought up, you see, in very difficult circumstances. The family was under siege, journalists outside the door every night, banging on the door, shouting at the children on the way to school in the hope they'd reply and so on. So they all had to be trained to cope with this and I think they suffered terribly, but they're all involved in one way or another.

CLARE: How did you cope with that?

BENN: Well, it wasn't very pleasant. I didn't like it very much. I used sometimes to have to come down after you'd been harassed by journalists and lie down on the bed and literally recover from it and you were frightened of going out in the mornings because they'd all be there and so on. And then you got all the death threats. I don't talk about it very much but it was very unpleasant and that has subsided a bit now.

CLARE: A bit? It doesn't still happen?

BENN: Oh well, more than a bit. It doesn't happen any more now. But the capacity to drive people, to frighten people into silence, of the British Establishment and its cohorts, is something to be experienced. I mean, if you haven't experienced it, what it's really like – 'You're mad,' 'You're dangerous,' 'You're a communist,' 'You're incompetent' – and so on and all these things poured out and very, very threatening it can be too. It really is threatening. The British press at its worst is a sort of terror squad, if you know what I mean, to frighten you into stopping and I wasn't prepared to budge on that, but I didn't like it a bit.

CLARE: And one of the common ways of doing it was in fact to suggest your rationality was questionable, that you were mad.

BENN: Yes, yes. I did realise after a time that they'd created their own image and they were firing at somebody who wasn't me and so that was a bit of comfort. That they had made it up and therefore I didn't believe it. But to begin with I didn't quite understand why they should say such absurd things. But mind you, other people, Arthur Scargill, was accused of financial corruption which was an outrage, or Frank Cousins, a lot of people have suffered much more than I have. But I did have a very rough time and that was because of what I said and when I realised it was because of what I was saying and not for the reasons they gave, then you were able to survive. You walked across the battlefield knowing they weren't really shooting at you, they were shooting at somebody else that they had invented. But I must admit it was very unpleasant.

CLARE: Did you ever, at any stage, lose heart, feel you couldn't go on?

BENN: No, not really. No, not really. If you were to give up you would have to give up everything really. I don't want to make out to be too courageous, you know, it just wasn't pleasant. It was like being shouted at, jeered at, not by the populace but by the paid hacks of Fleet Street. But I don't want to make too much of it. It was a nasty period in my life and I realise what other people have had to put up with, particularly the miners' leaders in the strike. That's why I've had such huge sympathy for Arthur Scargill. I remember being with him in Derby when a big man jumped on the platform and struck him in the stomach with an iron bar and then the BBC said it was a dissatisfied working miner. It wasn't at all. It was a policeman, or retired policeman, who had struck him and the lies that are told about people are quite unbelievable really. Still, that's by the way. That's the price you pay but it's not as bad as being in South Africa.

CLARE: And it doesn't shake your faith?

BENN: No, I think on the whole it gives you an idea of who your friends are and who are not. No, I don't think so.

CLARE: Can you conceive of yourself as having been anything other than a politician?

BENN: Well, I started life as a journalist, in the BBC. I was a salesman and then a journalist.

CLARE: But you always wanted to be a politician?

BENN: I did always want to be in politics, yes, I did. And the war, you see, radicalised me because I went to a public school where you had absolutely no knowledge of the world at all and two or three years in the air force as a trainee pilot, as an aircraftsman, I learned a hell of a lot.

CLARE: Did you learn anything in public school?

BENN: Well, I'm not sure really. I'm not sure.

CLARE: Did you enjoy it?

BENN: Not really no, not really very much. I suppose being a boy and an optimistic person I threw myself with enthusiasm into everything, including the debating society and moving motions condemning the Munich Settlement and all that sort of stuff in 1938. But my education has come subsequent to school and university. Even at university I think I was supposed to be studying modern civilisation, no reference was made to Marx except, I think, one professor said casually, 'He was wrong.' Well, since Marx has been one of the greatest influences in the human story, just to dismiss him like that . . .

CLARE: Would you have made any friends from schooldays?

BENN: Oh yes, I have a few people that I knew but I'm afraid the nature of the lives you lead does tend to keep your nose to the grindstone and that is a price you pay. The family paid and others paid. But of course I keep in touch with a few people.

CLARE: Yes, can I ask you about that. The extent to which it is difficult to make close friendships in politics. Reading the biography of you, reading your own diaries, that first volume, I was struck by how many political heavyweights, the things they say about each other. It's a tough arena. It must be very difficult in the end to know who your friends are?

BENN: Well, you have to remember about the Labour Party it's a bit like a family. You get massive abuse and then at the end they'll all join round and be very friendly. Because you know them very well. Even the people that I've argued with and who've been most offensive about me or perhaps the other way around, you know them and you've known them over 30, 40 and in my case nearly 50 years.

CLARE: And what does that mean?

BENN: Well, it means that your relationship with them isn't quite as violent as the political commentators would make out. It's not, again, it's not a goody goody view but people are interested in how their problems will be solved. They're not terribly interested in yah-boo. But the Labour Party is a funny, it is a sort of family really, it's the only way you could describe it. And with all the sort of tension and also the bonhomie of a family and I'm very fond of it.

CLARE: But it wasn't like your family?

BENN: No no, not really, no. Although you had rows in the family too. You know, every family has rows. You mustn't think that because I was much influenced by my parents and I loved my brother who was killed and my other brother who is still alive, that there weren't moments of great tension, there were. I've got a copy of *Mein Kampf* which I bought when I was 13, I think, and I had a fight with my brother and he tore it in half and I had to glue it together and I've still got it on the shelf.

CLARE: This is Michael?

BENN: My brother Michael and I had a fight over something and he tore up *Mein Kampf*, which is a very important book to read because fascism is coming back again, do you see what I mean? So there is a book, which symbolises the political interest of the family, and the family row and the sticking it together and the current use of the same book.

CLARE: And was it, in that sense, a fiery family? Was there great political argument?

BENN: There was political discussion but not major disagreements, no. My brother and I corresponded a great deal, before he was killed during the war, about religion and politics. He wanted to go into the Church, you see. He would like to have been a Christian minister and he would have been very good at it. And there were a lot of discussions but never rows about that, but there were rows about everything there are rows about in families, who started it and all that stuff. But never to damage the fabric at all of the family.

CLARE: Was it competitive between you and Michael and your younger brother?

BENN: Well, no, not particularly, not that I'm aware of. I wasn't aware of that.

CLARE: Your mother would have been the strength of the two parents, would she? You described your father as more detached.

BENN: Well, she was in a way, yes. I think that's true but then mothers usually are aren't they?

CLARE: What was she like?

BENN: Well, she was a remarkable woman really. Her father being a school teacher he never sent her to school. She didn't go to school until she was eight. So when she went to school she had to sit in a tiny little desk for five year olds and she couldn't read so she had this passion for self education and she went and studied theology after she got married and she was a very scholarly person but without any formal education. In the end she was made an honorary doctor of the university, which gave her great pleasure.

CLARE: Was she physically very affectionate?

BENN: Well, she was very warm and when you used to say, 'Who's your favourite?' she'd say, 'Well I love you in the Michael way, and you in the Anthony way and you in the David way.' No, it wasn't in that sense, no, but it was a very warm family. But she was very busy too. And my father was very busy and the household was a very busy household and then the war came and father went into the war and mother looked after the constituency and we were away and we were in the war and we corresponded and so on but it's always been a very close family.

CLARE: So the passion comes from both?

BENN: My father's understanding of the world and mother's commitment to religion and father's dissenting radical socialist ideas and mother's belief in the prophetic. I was always taught to support the prophets against the kings and I think the conflict between the kings and the prophets, you referred to it earlier, is a very interesting one. The kings exercise power and the prophets preach righteousness and in that sense I've more of the prophetic than the kingly side.

CLARE: Indeed, you're a little suspicious, more than a little suspicious of kings.

BENN: Oh gosh yes, absolutely. I think anyone who has got power should be looked at most sceptically and I have developed, others may have heard it, my five little democratic questions when you meet a powerful person: what power have you got? Where did you get it from? In whose interest do you exercise it? To whom are you accountable? And how could we get rid of you? Now, that last question, how can we get rid of you, is a democratic question and if people who govern you can't answer that question, whatever merits they have, you don't live in a democracy. I think the suspicion of power is absolutely correct, so long as it isn't motivated by personal ambition.

CLARE: And does that mean that psychologically you might have felt just a little bit more at ease out of power, more at ease now?

BENN: Well, no, if you have got a job as a minister, you've got to do a proper job. It's like any job. You've got to think about it and I spent hours and hours agonising over the motor industry and British Leyland and the shipbuilding industry and so on but I think you ought to be the same in and out of office. You ought to argue your case and one of the things that annoyed my colleagues was that I used to put papers into the cabinet about the work of other departments. Now that was quite intolerable. The chancellor was the only man who was allowed to say anything about economics and then I'd put a paper in on economic policy. And that was trying to perform that function. But, of course, when you're not bogged down by a lot of ministerial detail you have more time to travel, you meet more people and you have more time to think and to that extent I've never been unhappy in opposition, except at the thought that somebody else was in power, which meant they were doing damage to the people I represented. But, personally, I can't say office has attracted me enormously. It is a bit different perhaps from other people's view of it all but there you are.

CLARE: It is quite different isn't it?

BENN: That's why I'm so happy at 70.

CLARE: You are?

BENN: Yes, if I'd known what fun it was I'd have become 70 years ago, if you know what I mean.

CLARE: Why is it better?

BENN: Well, it's better because you've learned more, you're free. The last volume of my diaries, the seventh volume, is going to be called *Free at Last*.

CLARE: Free of what?

BENN: Well, free of all the sort of temptations, I suppose. I don't know what, but ...

CLARE: Go on, what?

BENN: Well, when you get older you're free, aren't you? You're not tempted to say something to get on, or whatever it is. You're absolutely free to tap your own experience. I won't be at the launch party of the last volume because the last day will be in my tape recorder at St Thomas's Hospital and 'Not feeling very well today' will be the last entry.

CLARE: And you're not joking I sense?

BENN: Well, maybe I'm not if I'm fit enough to do it. I sat with my father when he died and, very interesting, he died in Westminster Hospital and he was 83. He'd had his time but he took my finger with his hand and wrote with it, as if it was a pencil. And he described his father, he said how hard he worked, he used to come home at night and had to go out and do lecturing to earn money and so on. And the death, it doesn't scare me at all. My mother used to quote her mother who said, 'The great thing about death is it's the last journey and you don't have to pack.' And there's another quotation of my mother's – that 'Death is God's last and greatest gift to the living.' Now I find that very comforting, that in the end, death comes as a release. It depends what sort of death you have but I'm not at all afraid of death. I don't like the thought of having to leave, but death itself doesn't particularly worry me.

CLARE: And afterwards?

BENN: Well, you don't know do you really? You just don't know. I think probably immortality is something that comes through what you leave behind you really, by the children or ideas and so on. I remember my father quoting his father saying, 'A life is like a pebble dropped into a pool and the ripples go out and back and out and back and even though you can't see them they go on for ever.' Now that was a very calming thing to say and so I can't say I'm worried about it but I don't want to go, don't misunderstand me. My hundredth birthday is on Thursday, 3rd April, 2025 and Thursday is always a Polling Day so I can't entirely guarantee that I won't be a candidate!

CLARE: And when you look back at your life, the 70 years, I'm not anticipating this as an obituary, what are the things that you feel are the particular ripples that you will have left?

BENN: Well, I don't think I would necessarily want to be remembered by the legislation I have pioneered. I changed the postage stamps, changed the British Constitution on peerage law and helped to get the first referendum, brought North Sea Oil into public ownership, set up the Giro. These are the sort of ordinary achievements that would be in your obituary. No, I think what I'd like to be remembered for is the extent to which what I said illuminated the problems facing people and gave them confidence to tackle them. If I had an epitaph I'd like it to be that 'He encouraged us'. In a way, you can't judge a political career by how far you got up the slippery pole. I didn't get very far. I got some way but I wouldn't regard not having become leader or deputy leader in any sense a failure. The thing is, even if you've been there, could you have done a lot? You'd want to be judged by the extent to which you've helped people to understand. And one of the nice things about getting older, as you will probably realise, is that when you're young your span of thought is so short. I remember my fifth birthday very well, walking along the street saying how silly I was when I was four. I remember that, and I couldn't hardly remember my fourth birthday, I couldn't imagine my sixth birthday. But now, I can go back over centuries and understand what the arguments were about. And you know, 1850, my grandfather was born, his father was born in 1830 and now that means that the whole of the nineteenth and twentieth centuries are well within my comprehension. You understand what Gladstone, Disraeli were arguing about. You understand about the politics of that period and that gives you a huge advantage over people who are younger. I don't mean that they've not, probably, got it right, but at least you could move with ease over time, go back and imagine the arguments at any period of history. Now that's what's nice about getting older.

CLARE: Are you interested in the arts?

BENN: Well yes, I am but I'm not musical. One of my great complaints about school, I don't know if it's still true, is that the right to do something badly was never accepted. Why are you only judged whether you can do something well. I might have learned a bit of music but I was never any good at it. The only prize I ever won was a prize for an essay I wrote on the prophets of Israel and my brother said that I helped mother quite a bit with it. [Laughter.]

CLARE: Do you go to the cinema?

BENN: I watch a lot of television. I see a lot of it, when I have the opportunity. I love some of the programmes and I occasionally go to the movies, not very often. But I think the arts interest me now in a way as the carriers of political messages. For example, there's a retired professor called Roy Bailey from Sheffield who sings radical folk music. I met him in 1976 in the Burford Church when we were celebrating the Levellers. I gave a talk on the Levellers and he played his guitar about the English

Revolution. And he and I now go round the country, about three or four times a year. I read revolutionary statements over the last 500 years from a book I edited called *Writings on the Wall* and he sings about them. And it's tremendously powerful. His songs are much more powerful than my readings but that is the use of the arts for the purpose of giving people confidence in themselves. Other members of my family are very musical and very talented and I'm not. And postage stamps, I changed the postage stamps because I thought minuscule art, the one bit of art that everybody has, is the postage stamp, so I changed them all.

CLARE: Yes, yes . . .

BENN: And my father was very artistic and so was my grandfather, so I picked up a little bit of it from that but I have no talent.

CLARE: Yes, there is a wonderful story, isn't there, of you taking them to Her Majesty the Queen and laying them out on the floor and you peering at them.

BENN: I did, and I introduced children. I got the first children's stamps designed by children. And so in that sense, I encouraged the arts but I have no talent at all, I'm afraid.

CLARE: You said you are a happy man.

BENN: Yes, I'm a very happy man.

CLARE: I have to tell you that it is very rare indeed that somebody will say that. That doesn't mean that they aren't, I am just saying it's very rare that people will say it. And I'm interested in what your understanding of being happy is? What constitutes happiness and what do you think explains it?

BENN: Well, I suppose I don't want anything. Do you know what I mean? I'd like to be in Parliament, I've just been re-selected and so if I'm endorsed as a candidate and then elected I shall complete 50 years in Parliament. The year 2000 is my fiftieth so I mean to that extent I mustn't pretend I don't very much want to continue my present work. But, which religion is it, is it the Buddhists who believe that not wanting anything makes you happy. I don't want anything. I enjoy my work. I've got vitality. I've got reasonably good health. And what more could you ask than that? And so I'm surprised you say it's rare. I would have thought probably old age, except for those who have ill health or some terrible tragedy, old age was probably a very satisfying period of life. I think if I retired I'd be dead in a week, of boredom. But that wouldn't necessarily be the same as being out of Parliament because there's all the work to be done, whether you're in Parliament or not and I would still do meetings and write and so on.

CLARE: You've always been physically fit, though you had a brush with the Guillain-Barre syndrome – post-infective polyneuropathy?

BENN: Yes I did. It was very funny that. It was described in the tabloids as a nervous disease. Actually it's the sensory nerves so that you couldn't stand up because your feet didn't tell you which way to move and so on. That was a handicap but of all the diseases you could have ...

CLARE: Did you, did it scare you, do you worry about physical disease?

BENN: No, not really. I think I probably worried more when I was young when I was flying – would I kill myself and all that. I didn't terribly want to go at that age, no. I've been very lucky. To be in good health and strength at my age and still doing the job you like to do and looking forward confidently to be able to do it for a bit longer, I mean, what more could you ask really?

CLARE: You sleep well?

BENN: Oh yes, I go out like a light. I go to bed at 25 to one and if I go to bed before 25 to one I feel guilty. If I go to bed much later than that I feel I should have and I get up at five to seven and that's my pattern. And then sometimes, like recently, I had 14 hours in bed and felt much better for it. But I travel a lot and I sleep on the train. I've got little pillows I blow up and I sleep on the train. I can sleep almost anywhere. I'm very lucky, I think if I couldn't sleep that would probably be awful.

CLARE: Do you dream?

BENN: I suppose I do, yes, I do. I dream all sorts of funny dreams. If this were a programme of dream interpretation I expect you could have a lot of fun. But some of them are, are political dreams [laughter] believe it or not! [Laughter.] I don't know how you would interpret a dream involving the public sector borrowing requirement and the international monetary fund but given five minutes, I am sure you would. [Laughter.]

CLARE: Tell me more. I am fascinated by the way you describe the order, the control really, bed at 25 to one, getting up at five to seven. What other features of your life . . .

BENN: Well, I'll tell you a funny thing about my father, and this has had a very adverse effect on my life. His father, who was a local councillor, was once taken to court because he said the Conservatives had voted against school milk for children and the court said all they voted against was *free* school milk for children, so he was faced with bankruptcy. And my father was terribly worried about money. And at home, I had a penny a week pocket money for existing, another penny a week for going to school and a third penny a week if I submitted my accounts, how I'd spent the three pennies to Miss Triggs, his secretary, every week. And I've still got all these account books. I remember once, when I was very keen on carpentry, I went to Woolworths and bought a little vice for sixpence and I put 'vice: sixpence', and Miss Triggs queried it. What vice you could have got for sixpence when you were five or six, I don't know. But, as a result of this, I can't pay in cheques. I can't pay bills. I've got an absolute hangup about that. Now that's a consequence, really, of father's absolute obsession with bankruptcy. He always thought we were going bust and that was the result of his childhood, do you see what I mean, and it has had a very bad effect on me. So that was very orderly. My teetotalism was never a discipline at all. Father used to tell a lovely story about his parents – his father was born in Hackney, his mother was born in Stepney – about drunkenness in the East End of London. And he said they used to sing an old temperance hymn without realising its double meaning: 'The good ship *Temperance* is heading for the port' and they had no idea it could have meant anything else. So temperance and tea and accounts and time have been very much a part of the framework of my life. And, anyway, once you've got all that straight you are free to get on with your life. You're not worried about these things.

CLARE: It's a structure.

BENN: It's a structure, that's the word I was trying to find, framework or structure, within which you live. And if you have too many decisions to make about your daily life every day then you are a bit diverted, I think, from whatever it is you really ought to be doing. So it's quite comforting to have a reasonable structure. I find it so anyway.

CLARE: And it's a kind of control, it keeps you disciplined.

BENN: A sort of control, yes, it is a sort of control. If I go to bed very, very late, which I sometimes do, sometimes two or three in the morning, then that puts you out a little bit but I try to correct it the following day by a nap, and so on. But I'm not complaining. You mustn't think I'm in some sort of a self-imposed prison, because I'm not.

CLARE: No.

BENN: That lovely prayer, is it – 'whose service is perfect freedom'. Now, I forget which prayer it is, but the idea that service is a perfect freedom is a very interesting idea. Didn't Mandela, when he was in Robben Island prison, say to his gaolers, 'You're imprisoned, I'm free.' Now that struck me as a most interesting way of turning the tables on them.

CLARE: The extent to which the control is perceived as something you take on yourself as distinct from something that's imposed, that distinguishes surely the extent to which it's neurotic from the extent to which it is healthy. The kind of detail that you describe, the attention to time, the attention to order, the attention to detail, that could in some people become a crippling burden, just meeting it. But you don't seem to feel that. Going to bed at night, you said, 'Well, I might feel a bit guilty if I didn't do it,' or a bit uneasy, you'd do it the next day.

BENN: Oh yes, but only you could tell me what my mental condition is. I've had so much advice from others!

CLARE: Indeed you have and diagnosis!

BENN: So I would accept a diagnosis from you. But it just means that you're free, I think, to get on with the job. Mind you, remember this, I'm very very lucky, unlike most people, that I am free to do what I want to do. I've got to get through my work but I don't have to clock on in the morning and clock off at night and although I work very, very long hours and seven days a week I determine what I do and that is compared to being a miner or being a railwayman or being in your profession, you've got to start and so on. That is really marvellous. You are the master of your own diary and so it's much easier than you'd think. I mean most people are absolutely controlled by the lunch hour, the commuter train and so on, and I'm not. This means that I can work longer but still it's my own work and not somebody telling me what to do on a particular hour of the day.

CLARE: Regrets?

BENN: Well, I wish I'd learned what I think I now know much earlier really. I think that's the one regret you are bound to have. I think life is a progression and you look back. No, not really, no. I've done things I wish I hadn't done. I've left undone those things I ought to have done and done those things I ought not to have done and there is no health in me, to quote the Confession, but I've had a very, very satisfying life. It couldn't have been richer in terms of experience and comradeship and a sense sometimes of usefulness. Though there are moments when I think I've never done anything useful in my life and other days when on a hype you feel that you've got a greater contribution to make than probably you really have, and you go up and down like that. There's a bit of that in life inevitably.

CLARE: Tony Benn, thank you very much.

Sir Kenneth Dover

According to the critics, Sir Kenneth Dover is probably the outstanding expert on Ancient Greece and the Greeks of our time. His keen intelligence and sharp analytic mind have produced one of the finest commentaries on a play of Aristophanes, the best introduction to Aristophanic comedy, one of the most admired contributions to the study of Thucydides and a definitive study of homosexuality in Ancient Greece. He has had a distinguished administrative career too – a fellow of Balliol College, professor of Greek and later chancellor at St Andrews University – a professor of classics and a classic academic don.

But it was during his period as president of Corpus Christi College, Oxford, that an event occurred which, in the eyes of many commentators and critics, suggested that Dover represented a typical example of one of the great stereotypes, some might say caricatures of our time, that of the coldly rational, supremely intellectual university don with the emotions of a laptop computer. Trevor Aston, a brilliant but seriously disturbed historian and colleague at Corpus Christi and editor of the official history of Oxford University, was found dead in his room in October 1985 after a furious row with Sir Kenneth. The college president had warned him in a letter about his drunken and abusive behaviour. Aston was an exceedingly difficult man, who waged interminable wars with his colleagues over everything from accommodation to library facilities, drank abusively, harangued guests at 'high table', the nightly dining ritual at Oxbridge colleges, and drove his wife to distraction and separation. Worst of all he appeared absolutely impervious to criticism or reason.

However, despite pressure from Sir Kenneth and a number of other dons, Dr Aston showed no sign of changing his behaviour. Sir Kenneth faced a dilemma: if he tolerated Aston's behaviour he risked damage to the reputation and standing of his ancient and beloved institution but if he tried to get rid of Aston, whom he considered a pest and an embarrassment, he risked contributing to his death. In his autobiography, *Marginal Comment*, published a decade later, Sir Kenneth writes with supreme clinical detachment: 'But it was clear to me by now that Trevor and the college must somehow be separated. My problem was one which I feel compelled to define with brutal candour: how to kill him without getting into trouble!'

Dover knew of Aston's long and troubled psychiatric history. He knew too, because Aston's psychiatrists had told him, that the man had a very precarious hold on life and were he to be dismissed from his beloved Oxford he could well kill himself. The college president then sent a carefully worded letter reminding Aston how much his academic energies, imagination and ambitions were admired but that his behaviour just could not any longer be tolerated. 'We all want,' Sir Kenneth wrote, 'to see the good Trevor all of the time and the appalling Trevor none of the time.' At first Aston appeared unmoved. Then he took issue with the accuracy of some of the comments and challenged Dover: 'You're trying to push me out of the college.' Dover pointedly said nothing and Aston left. Several days later he killed himself with a combination of medication and alcohol, shortly after receiving a notice of the date of divorce proceedings and after writing a letter of farewell to his wife.

Critics, including many of those closely involved in the problems Aston had caused, admitted being shocked by the chilly detachment of Dover's account of what was a terrible personal tragedy for Aston and his family. Particularly disturbing was Sir Kenneth's frank admission of a certain feeling of relief after Aston's death: 'Next morning,' he writes in his autobiography, 'I got up from a long sound sleep and looked out of the window across the fellows' garden. I can't say for sure that the sun was shining but I certainly felt it was. I said to myself, slowly, "Day One of Year One of the Post-Astonian Era." For a little while I even regretted my decision to retire the following year.'

Before I met Sir Kenneth I read his autobiography. I read too of attempts by some, such as Lord Monkswill, to have him charged with murder, or at least manslaughter, and of support from others, such as history fellow Brian Harrison, who compared Dover's desire to see Aston dead to Henry II willing the death of the turbulent priest, Thomas à Becket. I assumed that when I met Sir Kenneth I would be confronted by the archetypal hyper-rational don who would place an inordinate emphasis on reason and intellect, who would relegate the needs of the individual to those of the community and who would display an insensitivity to emotion.

The term 'schizoid' is often used to describe individuals who manifest an obvious split or divorce between the emotional and intellectual functions. The schizoid individual is a quiet, undemon-strative, analytic person who shows little emotion, has a poorly developed ability to empathise with others, is usually unsociable and indulges in excessive private fantasy. Sometimes the term refers to an exterior mask of detachment, indifference even, which conceals turbulent, often aggressive feelings. There is a harshness and a lack of spontaneity, a preference for solitariness and an avoidance of close, personal, intimate relationships. Not uncommonly, such individuals take a jaundiced view of the worth of human life and appear much more at home and secure inhabiting the world of ideas.

Reading the media reactions to Dover's revelation of his murderous impulses towards Aston fuelled, to an extent at least, my expectation that Sir Kenneth would indeed turn out to be such a cold, calculating, clever man with a firm grip on powerful internal feelings. Initially the interview began to yield support for such a formulation. There is Sir Kenneth's personal revelation of a deformity, not a psychological but a physical one – the condition known as funnel chest. He speculates on the extent to which this embarrassing skeletal deformity contributed over the years to his profound sense of being on the margin rather than at the centre of life, an observer rather than a participant. (In this regard, incidentally, he anticipates some of the regret and irritation Ann Widdecombe expresses at the way people with disabilities and deformities are still made to feel freakish in our supposedly liberated and tolerant modern world.) Then there is the fact that his father had a mercurial temperament and a terrible temper leading Sir Kenneth to experience a deeply unhappy childhood and to cultivate in adolescence an outward mask of stoical indifference enabling him to appear, outwardly at least, calm, unmoved, impassive. 'I associated emotion,' he declares, 'particularly with bad emotion, with anger, hatred and so on rather than with compassion, love.' The interview quickly centres on the extent to which this external mask of calculation and control is taken for the real man. Sir Kenneth's view: 'my actual hostile emotional reactions, instantaneous reactions, are in fact quite strong. But I don't give them away, I swallow them.' An only child in a bookish house, as an adolescent, according to his own description, he was something of a 'pretty cold fish'.

It is interesting how often, when talking to men, the issue of emotions and unease concerning their expression comes up. Martin Bell spoke disparagingly of 'parading' his emotions. Sir Kenneth struggles hard to manifest an unemotional persona but reveals that not far underneath is an irritable, potentially aggressive individual, who hints at quite violent fantasies, which he experiences in the setting of a struggle between his sense of order and rationality and the dangers of unfettered emotions and impulses. In the conflict between the individual and the institution, between Trevor Aston and Corpus Christi, he opts predictably for the institution. The Times suggested in a provocative editorial, entitled 'Death in the Cloister', that Dover's 'merciless subordination of individual to group interest' derived from 'the mentality and ethical code of the era he studies', only to be accused in turn in a letter from a Cambridge academic of 'a fearful ignorance of the ethics of the classical world'. Most of us have thought and many have said 'I wish him/her dead' and few of us are students of ancient classical societies. Sir Kenneth's rationality, much prized in the modern world of humanist and scientific scholarship, is clearly manifest in his sombre analysis of Aston's fate – 'Is there any way in which I could bring about a situation in which this man is dead?' but in this instance at least his rational, intellectual, detached analysis is closely allied to deep, emotional impulses. Aston was the kind of hostile, mercurial, emotionally incontinent individual that he, Dover, is most allergic to – and at the most primitive level of feeling Dover wanted him dead. A less honest, less cerebral man than Sir Kenneth would never admit such a thing and indeed he did struggle at times to avoid admitting it to me. On at least one occasion, while denying he ever would have done it, he appeared to suggest that what primarily deterred him was not the fact that murder is wrong as that it is illegal! On another occasion he insists that had Aston telephoned him and revealed he had taken an overdose he would have helped him. Both these expressions of intent seem to me to be true though somewhat contradictory.

But Sir Kenneth did not come across, to me at any rate, as a particularly cold, detached or callous man. He seemed aware of the power of his feelings, frightened by them, intent on keeping them firmly under control. However, he has inherited from his mother an unwavering commitment to speaking his mind and, as a result, while he censors his feelings, he lets his thoughts run surprisingly freely. 'I have to accept the statements of others that I am unusual in revealing so much about myself,' he observes towards the end of the interview, 'but whether I'm unusual in having these things to reveal, I cannot know.'

CLARE: Sir Kenneth Dover is one of the world's leading classical scholars, the author of numerous books, papers and articles on Ancient Greece, fellow of Balliol College, Oxford, professor of Greek at St Andrews, president of Corpus Christi College, Oxford from 1976 to 1986, chancellor of St Andrews University, these are amongst his academic achievements. His highly acclaimed works on Ancient Greece, Greek homosexuality, Greek popular morality and Greek world order are read by students worldwide. He also inspired and presented television programmes on the BBC dealing with Greece and the Grecian legacy. In 1977 he was knighted for his services to scholarship.

He was born on March 11th, 1920 in London, the only son of a civil servant; he was by all accounts a precocious child. He was reading by the age of three, won a scholarship to St Paul's and later to Balliol College. He saw action during World War Two as an artillery officer in the Western Desert and in Italy and he was mentioned in dispatches.

In 1994, the publication of his autobiography entitled *Marginal Comment* startled both the academic world and the general public with what the critics described as its 'robust frankness and brutal candour'. Particularly compelling was the revelation that Sir Kenneth, while president of Corpus Christi College, contemplated killing, for the good of the college, Trevor Aston, a troublesome and troubled fellow academic. When Aston, a manic depressive and alcoholic, committed suicide, Sir Kenneth received the news with a sense of relief.

Sir Kenneth, you have said that you've had this feeling that, 'I have been masquerading as a human being all my life.' I wondered quite what you meant by that?

DOVER: Well, in the context I'm talking about the deformation of my chest, you see, because I became aware of this suddenly in 1932. I'd somehow or other not been aware of it before then and I suddenly realised that I had a worse formed body than anyone I knew and this has been with me, you know, all the time, it's worried me. And perhaps it's putting it strongly to say 'masquerading as a human being' but I felt that because I was the wrong shape I was somehow below the level of humanity. As I've said in the book, there are people who have much worse deformities and disabilities but I also know a hell of a lot who don't have any.

CLARE: And this chest deformity, when you realised that that's what it was, was this because others had pointed it out to you?

DOVER: Oh yes, yes.

CLARE: Little boys?

DOVER: Yes.

CLARE: You were 12 at the time?

DOVER: It was in the changing room almost my first day at St Paul's when my friend exclaimed at the sight of my chest and then, in a matter of seconds, I realised that I was the only one in sight in a changing room full of naked boys, with that deformity.

CLARE: And prior to that, your mother had never said anything about it?

DOVER: Well, not that I remember you see. And I'm pretty sure that I wasn't aware of it although, since then of course, I've seen photographs of myself at the seaside at the age of about eight and it's pretty obvious then but nevertheless, I suppose, this is some kind of vast scotoma.

CLARE: And the deformity actually takes the shape of what?

DOVER: Well, it's a hollow in the middle you see and the ribs at the side sticking out.

CLARE: And it's called in fact a funnel chest?

DOVER: Yes.

CLARE: You say that feeling stayed with you?

DOVER: Well the feeling about it has stayed with me and it means I don't take my shirt off in public.

CLARE: Never?

DOVER: No. I don't go on the beach or anything like that or if I do it's somewhere lonely.

CLARE: And did it affect your behaviour at school?

DOVER: Well yes, I think it did affect me in the sense that I didn't take any part, any more part in sports than a day boy at St Paul's needed to, and that wasn't a great deal. And that's something I very much regret because I would have liked to, particularly in track sports. I was quite a fast runner at my first school and I might have been some good at long jump and so on, but what I was afraid of was the changing room and not the sports field.

CLARE: Do you think it's affected you in other ways?

DOVER: Yes, I think it probably has given me a feeling quite a lot of standing aside and watching the rest of the world, and that's one reason why I called the book *Marginal Comment* because of this. Well, I suppose nowadays we call it marginalisation. And, of course, in late adolescence, it certainly affected me sexually in the sense that I didn't think a girl would ever look at me seriously. About that I was wrong but for a time that was depressing.

CLARE: How long?

DOVER: Well, it's rather curious really. The first girl, first woman who appeared to me to be genuinely sympathetic about it was a Turkish prostitute in Cairo who was a very nice girl. But then later on when I fell in love with my wife I found that she didn't give a damn about it and never has worried.

CLARE: And when you say you feel it's contributed to that sense of being an observer and somewhat on the margin, this wouldn't have been the only factor would it? I'm struck by the fact that you're an only child and there appears from your autobiography to have been quite a considerable amount of discord in your family, as you grew up?

DOVER: Yes, yes.

CLARE: Was that something again in which you would have been, if you like, the observer, or were you actually drawn in and part of that discourse?

DOVER: Well, by the time I was 15, I realised that my father and I were perhaps on a sort of collision course. You see my father was basically a very unreasonable man with a very bad temper and my mother was basically a very reasonable person so I naturally tended to side with her. Although my father on good days was extraordinarily witty and imaginative and so on. He'd be tremendous fun when he was OK but then I think, perhaps I always found that recollection of bad experiences was much more powerful than recollection of good ones. Anyway, by the time I was about 15, as I say, we seemed to me to be on a sort of collision course, and that I was going to just blow up. And I thought, 'Well, this won't do. I can't let this happen.' So I had to try then to cultivate a sort of stoicism, a sort of indifference to my surroundings and feel that whatever happened I'd somehow or other manage and that is the other thing perhaps that contributed to perhaps for some time an exaggerated stoicism which I gradually fed. I think when I was about 17, 18, 19, I was what you might call hyper-rational. I associated emotion particularly with bad emotion, with anger, hatred and so on rather than with compassion, love. But from that time onwards I suppose I gradually humanised myself, if you like.

CLARE: It's interesting how often in descriptions of you people remark on this, almost as if it's a conflict still going on. That there's this man, Sir Kenneth Dover, who certainly prizes rationality and control and reason ...

DOVER: Yes.

CLARE: But people who know you might notice that underneath this man is quite an emotional man. People who don't know you say, 'Oh, he's a cold clinical, inhuman man,' so there must still be a residue of that early stoical decision, that you still come across to some people initially as hyper-rational?

DOVER: Well plainly I do, and far more so than I realise because since the publication of my book some of my former colleagues at Corpus Christi have spoken of me as a cold, calculating super-rational person and so on, which in a way I found a little bit comic because it was my passionate desire to act in the interests of the college which led me to contemplate the possibility of causing Trevor Aston's death. I don't see how rational calculation could have caused me to want his death. Rational calculation obviously would come in if I were going to do something about it because if one doesn't use reason over the means to an end, one is not likely to realise the end. But it was essentially I think a sort of passionate desire to fulfil an obligation to the college for which I felt responsible that led me to think, 'Is there any way I can cause this man's death?' But the only other thing is that one or two people, former colleagues for some of whom I have an enormous regard, once they've got this idea of my excessive rationality in their minds, they push it rather far. One of them, Valentine Cunningham, in a piece in the *Times Higher Educational Supplement*, spoke of my logic chopping in presenting an issue to a college meeting. Well, as far as I can see, what he didn't like was dividing up a problem into its essential components. Because what I was trying to do was to cause the governing body to take decisions about things in an order which would result in a real decision and I don't call that logic chopping myself.

CLARE: Is it possible do you think that your early exposure to emotion in the shape of your father has meant that while you're still an emotional man yourself, that you are so sensitive to and sensitised to displays of emotion that you react badly to them?

DOVER: Well, I don't react badly to all displays of emotion. I wouldn't react badly to displays of good emotion but I certainly react with very hostile feelings to displays of bad temper.

CLARE: Anger?

DOVER: Well, unreasonable, well, no not quite anger because if one is angry, as I use the word, one is angry with something, against something for some reason, whereas bad temper is a state that one is in in which almost anything that happens can provoke an adverse reaction. My mother was perfectly capable of anger but not of bad temper, whereas my father often had long periods of bad temper in which things made him angry when one couldn't see what on earth there was to be angry about. But it's quite true, I do have, I think I have had all my life, a very unfriendly reaction to bad temper.

CLARE: And your father, do you know, looking back, what was the fuel for this kind of periodic irritability and bad temper and all-round abrasiveness?

DOVER: I don't know, quite honestly. If one goes back to his own childhood, his mother, of course, was a very irrational person. Unlike him, she was also stupid. He was very jealous of his younger sister, I know that, and she also was a very emotional person in all kinds of emotions and also, I think, rather stupid. So that wasn't too good a start. But also, of course, he did have music in him and in an ideal world he should have been a professional pianist but he was terribly afraid of financial insecurity. He had a safe job in the lower reaches of the Civil Service. He couldn't really lose the job except through some delinquency, a safe pension at the end of it, and he simply didn't dare to cut loose for that and really try to be a musician. And this, I think, was a considerable stress. Now, of course, I wasn't aware of this in my childhood but, looking back, I think there was probably a fair amount of sexual discontent because my mother certainly lost her looks pretty early on and she got varicose veins and things like that. She looked much older than she was. Certainly that was true when I was a little bit older and I think my father had a pretty high libido and maybe he'd have just have liked a harem, I don't know!

CLARE: Were there other women?

DOVER: No, never, never no.

CLARE: But he was verbally very hostile to your mother?

DOVER: A lot of the time, yes.

CLARE: When you were growing up?

DOVER: Well, not when I was in the room, at least usually not when I was in the room, or not when anybody else was present.

CLARE: You would hear it?

DOVER: Well sometimes I heard it and the hostility was tangible really. You know what sort of atmosphere somebody with a bad temper can create and later on, after my father had retired, as I mentioned in the book, my mother did confide to me, this must have been when I was in my forties, that she was afraid he might murder her. But, at other times, of course, he was extravagantly affectionate and he was immensely grieved when she died. And I suppose he did swing from one extreme to another. He was one sort of person one day and quite a different sort the next day.

CLARE: What did he want of you?

DOVER: Success. He was very proud of my academic success.

CLARE: He was?

DOVER: Of course he was. He was immensely proud of my getting the presidency of Corpus and of getting a knighthood and things like that. He gave me the impression that he sort of basked in that, you know, simply from the way he'd introduce me to other people. He'd say things like 'This is my son, Sir Kenneth Dover' with a bit of an emphasis on the 'Sir' which made me curl up but I couldn't stop him doing it.

CLARE: Did you ever in later life talk to him about the early displays of bad temper?

DOVER: Well not after, I think it was 1946, when he was getting invalided out of the Civil Service. He did then talk to me more frankly about himself and his life than he'd ever done before and more frankly than he ever did subsequently. That was the only period I think, namely the summer of 1946, when I could say that I talked to him but I never felt on other occasions that it served any useful purpose to bring up what life had been like when I was a small child. Because among other things, you see, perhaps a curious thing, I never hated him after I was a small child. I think as a small child perhaps I did hate him but after the age of 15, no, I didn't want to hurt him. I didn't want revenge or anything like that, so there wasn't any point in my sort of laying into him saying, 'You did this and that and the other' you see. I would have found that rather painful.

CLARE: And you had no sense of your mother's anxiety before she told you about it when you were in your forties?

DOVER: No.

CLARE: You didn't sense that there was any danger?

DOVER: No and I don't think there was. I think she was wrong because he would have been terrified, I think, of doing anything which would have become known outside the home. He was immensely afraid of what people would think, you see, and anxious to put on a good show and so on and so I think whatever he said to her, it was all verbal. I didn't myself believe that she was in any danger. I certainly don't believe he ever struck her at any time in their lives.

CLARE: You describe your mother as unfailingly reasonable. So they were really quite a contrast?

DOVER: Oh yes.

CLARE: Because this man was, if not unfailingly unreasonable, he was pretty regularly unreasonable?

DOVER: Yes, yes.

CLARE: There is a very striking split. He would have been all uncontrolled emotion from time to time. She would always have been reasonably in control.

DOVER: Well, unless she had something really to be angry about which other people too would have been angry about. She never got into a bad mood or anything like that. As I say, she was certainly capable of being angry with me or with my father or with other people for a reason. But they were in some ways, I suppose you could say, complementary in a way that a couple sometimes can be. Provided neither of them is bad tempered! Clearly a couple can be complementary in all kinds of ways but what brought them together of course was music because my mother was, to begin with, quite a good pianist and they used to play duets and my father used to in fact transcribe orchestral works as piano duets and so on. But my mother didn't really have a chance to keep it up after I was born so she didn't progress beyond a certain point. She didn't get any further with the piano.

CLARE: You quoted her in relation to an interesting thing in that she never said, 'Oh, what a dreadful thing to say' or 'You shouldn't think that' and I was interested in that in the context of your autobiography. Because one of the very candid aspects of your autobiography is that you often say things that people actually do think but they don't always reveal. That was important to her, was it, the notion that if you thought things you thought them, if you said things, you said them, that there weren't controls necessarily?

DOVER: What I think is even more important is that one should never judge the truth or falsity of a statement by how one felt about the person who said it. In other words, it didn't matter who said a thing, what mattered was whether it was true or not, whether it rested on evidence or not, and, and that was something that increasingly I became aware of, I think, in my teens and it's something that I valued enormously.

CLARE: When you look at yourself, when you look at these two people, I wonder which of them you identify with the more? Do you think there's more of him or her in you?

DOVER: I think there's more of her. But there's certainly more of him than I would have liked to admit earlier in me.

CLARE: Like what?

DOVER: Well, my actual hostile emotional reactions, instantaneous reactions, are in fact quite strong. But I don't give them away, I swallow them.

CLARE: But you feel them inside?

DOVER: Oh yes, yes, I have a sort of bad-tempered reaction but it's a matter of seconds and I keep it down.

CLARE: But you are conscious of it?

DOVER: Oh I'm conscious of it.

CLARE: Of having to keep it down?

DOVER: Yes.

CLARE: And does it ever emerge?

DOVER: I hope not.

CLARE: Yes, you hope not. But I wondered did it, or does it?

DOVER: I'm trying to think of an example.

CLARE: At home?

DOVER: Yes, I think when my children were small, I would sometimes feel a sort of surge of anger against something my son did when he was about three or four, say. Certainly, there are occasions when I have a sort of violent reaction against something my wife does or says. But, again, it's a matter of seconds, because we, we don't bear each other grudges. For example, we can go into town from where we are either by bus or we can take the car. To catch the bus you have to walk along to a fork in the road and pick up the bus there and two days running, my wife missed the bus, through not getting there soon enough. And it does irritate me if she's not on time for things. But this is a sort of surge that lasts for a second or two. It doesn't cast a shadow over either of us after that.

CLARE: Would she know?

DOVER: Oh yes, sure, yes, yes because I express myself very vividly and so does she when required.

CLARE: So there's some of him in you?

DOVER: Oh yes, for sure.

CLARE: But it's your mother you would prefer to be like?

DOVER: Yes.

CLARE: You said, I think, that the three most important influences in your life were this chest deformity, and that certainly influenced you in terms of the way you thought about yourself, you also indeed included in that I think circumcision?

DOVER: I can't remember now whether I took against circumcision after or before I realised my chest deformity. They both belonged to the same time, around about the age of 12 and, as my two closest friends at school were uncircumcised and one of those two boys was the one who exclaimed in horror at my chest, so it's all terribly mixed up and I cannot now remember which came first. But I'm inclined to think I wouldn't have worried about circumcision if it hadn't have been for the deformity because they seemed to go together.

CLARE: Did it worry you to the extent that you would worry about your sexuality?

DOVER: Oh no, no.

CLARE: No. It was more your attractiveness?

DOVER: Well, the circumcision I think was in a way sort of independent. I wasn't worried about whether it was attractive or unattractive to girls because in my generation in England half the boys were circumcised. So there's nothing unusual about it. It was really a sort of self-condemnation, a feeling of inferiority above all *vis-à-vis* those two friends.

CLARE: And when you met the Turkish prostitute, did you actually have a discussion about the deformity?

DOVER: Well we couldn't because she spoke no English at all and my Arabic was pretty elementary and I've no Turkish.

CLARE: So how was it communicated to you that this wasn't so bad after all?

DOVER: Gesture and facial expression.

CLARE: And that did go a long way towards helping you?

DOVER: Oh yes, yes, it's very curious. Because this was a very traditional thing to do of course for young officers going out to the Middle East; 2,000 miles from home at 21 and you discard your virginity as soon as possible. And this was a very clean, up-market officers' brothel and this particular girl was very sort of unpretentious, kindly looking, fairly pretty ordinary looking really, not particularly made up or anything like that, and I thought of her afterwards as just a very nice person who I would have liked to get to know in more leisurely circumstances. It's the only time I've ever been with a prostitute actually.

CLARE: And you remember her to this day?

DOVER: Oh yes, for sure.

CLARE: The second influence in your life we've touched on, the bad relations between your parents and that's left a legacy in terms of the way you see the unpleasant expression of emotions and the importance of reasonableness. The third influence is interesting in the sense that I think you and I would probably agree that it's hard to explain it. As a child, as a baby, you were more interested in paint than pictures.

DOVER: Well, that is what my mother told me and I don't find that impossible to believe because I can't remember ever not reading and I do remember you see that first day at school at the age of five, being confronted with a children's reading book and shrinking back and saying, 'That's a baby's book' and that incident has stuck in my mind.

CLARE: Was it a bookish house?

DOVER: Oh yes, yes, both my parents had, had a fair number of books.

CLARE: Yes, and of course, you were an only child. You'd a lot of time on your hands.

DOVER: Yes, well particularly because so few of my parents' friends had children.

CLARE: Really?

DOVER: We didn't know many close neighbours who had children. I didn't grow up in an ambience of other children until I went to school at the age of five, and then it was different.

CLARE: But you didn't have any troubles with other children?

DOVER: Well no, I didn't actually. My friends and I we used to sort of come home together after school and then, if there was time, go back to a friend's house and then walk back to mine and so on, and go out together on the common at weekends because at Thornton Heath at that time there was a lot of open common land. Mitcham Common, Streatham Common and so on, much of which has now gone, but it was quite easy then for boys to find somewhere to play.

CLARE: Would you describe yourself during that period of late adolescence as hyper-stoical?

DOVER: Perhaps like that. I don't know. I felt after I'd left school that there'd been an awful lot of good friendship on offer that I hadn't really taken up. There were one or two people I knew very well, people in my own subject particularly. Not many outside it. And I felt really I must have been a pretty cold fish.

CLARE: Really?

DOVER: And fairly friendless. But then later on, when I met people who had been at school with me, they didn't react like that. I can't in fact have been as stand-offish and solitary as I felt in my memory I was. I think perhaps I was maybe both misapprehending what sort of person I was socially at that time and almost misremembering and it was these encounters with other boys, with people who taught me and so on, who were very come forwardish and friendly and so on, that made me feel, well, maybe I wasn't as bad as I thought.

CLARE: Is it possible do you think that while you were very intent on suppressing feeling, or keeping it under control, that actually in your late teens it wasn't all that easy? It would come out from time to time.

DOVER: I suppose so, yes.

CLARE: The ideal would have been stoic.

DOVER: Yes, yes. I don't actually recall occasions on which it came out but plainly that doesn't mean there weren't any.

CLARE: You said, and this is always a, a difficult one in this kind of interview, you said that some experiences are so painful you weren't willing to write them in your autobiography because it would mean reliving them. Now, that intrigued me. If you had just said some experiences are so painful I don't want to write about them, but it was because you added in an explanation that rather intrigued me – because it would mean reliving them. Because it suggests to me that you actually know what they are, you know what these experiences are.

DOVER: Oh yes.

CLARE: They're not buried, in other words. You don't have to excavate them. But if you wrote about them then the full detail would emerge, whereas at the moment, what, you've just got an image of them?

DOVER: I wouldn't be worried about communicating them to others, I'm worried more at my own revulsion against them. I'm not going to go into details about them but they are imaginary experiences in which I'm being sort of forced, so to speak, against my will, into committing great cruelty. But that's really all I can say.

CLARE: Yes. Again it echoes, a great, a seeming conflict in you between your sense of order and rationality and this business of uncontrolled emotion.

DOVER: Oh yes, yes.

CLARE: That recurs.

DOVER: Yes, yes I accept that.

CLARE: So of course that is in a sense why the Aston affair involving this troublesome, difficult academic in Corpus Christi, that's why it rather interests me, not so much because of all the hype that occurred around the time that you wrote your autobiography, but because in a curious kind of way it represents again an example of this conflict in Kenneth Dover between reason and order but also, of course, other feelings that you're honest enough to admit you had.

DOVER: Yes, I could I suppose give a misleading impression over the feelings, because if I had simply got fed up with Trevor Aston, as of course I did after eight years of trying to do my best with him, if I'd merely got fed up with him, I knew I'd only got a year to go. I knew I was retiring in the summer of 1986, and I could have put up with that all right. It was this sort of passion, which some people would say was a misguided passion, to get the situation straight for the college and when I referred to thinking about how to kill him, I did choose the word 'kill' against the advice of one or two people. One, a fellow of Corpus who otherwise was a hundred per cent behind me, and also my daughter, who thought the words were ill chosen. I did nevertheless go ahead with using the word 'kill' because I do think it's awfully important that people should realise what they're doing when they're doing something and if, in fact, you're contemplating not saving a man from death when you've reason to think he's taken an overdose, that is killing him. And I think that should be recognised and one should use brutal words to describe things. But of course, I wasn't feeling 'My God, I must get rid of this bastard.' I was thinking, 'Now is there any way in which the situation can be improved for the college. Is there any way in which I could bring about a situation in which this man is dead.' And there was only the one I could think of and then I discovered by asking a lawyer, it's illegal anyway, so that was that.

CLARE: As I read it, I was, I suppose, a little puzzled that that was the only alternative. Being a psychiatrist I can ask you whether it ever crossed your mind that really this man was clearly amongst other things not well, he was ill?

DOVER: Oh yes, indeed.

CLARE: He was not in control of himself. It wasn't clear to me from reading your book, the extent to which the psychiatrists regarded him as ill and therefore warranting really something more than just an occasional intervention when he was acutely unwell, or was bad with occasional bits of illness. And the crucial decision it seems to me that you made was that there was no other alternative. That this man either wrecked Corpus Christi or he died. But people reading this would feel, 'Well, he was a manic depressive, he was an alcoholic, he was ill.'

DOVER: Yes, had been for 20 plus years.

CLARE: That's right, although he'd only been in a hospital once or twice, as I understand it, or a few times in acute emergencies but never for very long.

DOVER: No, he wouldn't go, you see. I have said something about this in the book actually, that one of the difficulties was talking with Trevor. And it's the thing that eventually made me feel 'Well, I give up', his complacency.

CLARE: How do you mean?

DOVER: Well, it didn't ever seem to worry him in the least that he was making a lot of trouble for other people. One of the occasions in that last summer, when he talked about his own illness – incidentally, of course, as long as it was advantageous for him to proclaim that he was absolutely well and rational, he would do so. When that didn't succeed then he would try to evoke pity.

CLARE: By saying he was ill?

DOVER: By saying he was ill. And the way he talked about how he'd never been able to find a psychiatrist whose principles he agreed with and so on. That may not sound in itself a particularly awful thing to say but I was there and I remember the complacent expression on his face and the complacent tone of voice which made me think, 'Well, I can't do any more.'

CLARE: And at the same time, as I understand it, and both his widows I think have emphasised this, he was actually a college man. In his own way he too had done a great deal for Corpus Christi.

DOVER: Yes, certainly, he did a great deal for the college.

CLARE: Indeed it was his life in a way. He didn't seem to have had much outside the college?

DOVER: Well, I think that was exaggerated by him and by his friends because although one of his early achievements, from the 1950s onwards, was the creation of a very good college library, I know from his confidential file that he was applying for other jobs at that time. It isn't as if he was content to be in the college all the time. And also he was very ready to condemn the fellows as a whole, or the majority opinion among fellows, in the event of any disagreement. It isn't as if he thought, 'Well, this corporate body is my life, I will respect it,' because he didn't respect it. He certainly didn't respect majority decisions on the part of the governing body so that I think the extent to which his life was the college has been a little bit exaggerated.

CLARE: Did he ever remind you of your father?

DOVER: Yes he did. Of course, I think any unreasonable person was pretty well bound to remind me of my father on occasion, yes, no doubt about that.

CLARE: And, it wasn't clear, you actually said that you put a dagger in his hand?

DOVER: Yes.

CLARE: Some of what you did seemed to me to be eminently reasonable, indeed quite humane and kind. You wrote, what seems even from the bits you revealed, a kind letter in that you said, 'I would like so much to have the good Trevor and ...'

DOVER: Well, the psychiatrist seemed to think it was just the right letter.

CLARE: And that you 'don't want to talk to the bad Trevor'. So there was that, but there seems to have been this meeting that you had with him and you seem to feel that by what you didn't say you put a dagger in his hand. Can you just tell me a bit about that?

DOVER: Yes, what I meant by that was that he said something which was absolutely untrue, namely that until then he had always enjoyed very good relations with all the fellows and now I was being used by his enemies. That was so untrue. Ever since 1982 he provoked me and perhaps this is where I ought to have been more hyper-rational. So he provoked me into saying, 'Well, good lord, when your fellowship was renewed in 1982 it was a hell of a job to get it through.' I felt I suppose after I'd said it, this must have been an awful wound for him and in fact that's when he said, 'You're trying to push me out of the college' and I couldn't deny that, because I was, of course, trying to push him out of the college. And then he said, 'Well, that's more than I can take on board' and that's the last time I saw him really.

CLARE: Well, did you think at that moment that that was a very significant exchange?

DOVER: Well, I certainly thought it was very wounding to him.

CLARE: You did.

DOVER: Now, I don't remember thinking, 'This will be too much, he'll kill himself.' Because at that stage, having discarded this idea of doing something illegal, and incidentally, of course, if he actually had rung me up at night and said 'I've taken an overdose' of course I would have tried to save him. I couldn't help it really. One can't just leave people to die like that.

CLARE: Would you have helped him?

DOVER: Oh, I'm sure I would, yes, when it came to the point. That didn't prevent me from contemplating what a marvellous relief it would be if I could avoid doing that. But then you see, after that stage had passed, what I was interested in then was making him resign his fellowship because I had that advice from another fellow who was very close to him who had experience himself of rehabilitation from alcoholism, who said, 'An alcoholic will never get anywhere until he really hits rock bottom and you have to pick them up out of the gutter.' And that in fact encouraged me to feel, 'Well, suppose we do try and push him into resigning?' The striking thing to me is at the end of the day, of course, when he did in fact kill himself, the letter he left by his bedside said nothing at all about bad relations with the college or with me, it was entirely a very, very affectionate letter to his wife, against whom in fact he had been inveighing the previous day because she was divorcing him. And there was a sort of long, rambling letter about the nurses in the Warneford Psychiatric Hospital and how unreasonable they were, but nothing about me, nothing about the college. So I don't in the end think that my desire to push him into resignation was a major cause of his suicide. And, of course, although I in fact corrected him over what he said, that it was only just recently that the fellows in the college had turned against him, it was he himself who had told me two years earlier that he was aware of that and maybe he'd dredged that up out of his memory and realised that this had been going on quite a while.

CLARE: You felt a sense of relief. It was that as much as anything else that caused critics to tear their hair because you said, 'I got up from a long, sound sleep, and looked out of the window across the fellows' yard. I can't say for sure the sun was shining but I certainly felt it was. I said to myself, slowly, Day One of Year One of the Post-Astonian Era.' Fine, but did you ever feel guilt as well?

DOVER: No.

CLARE: Never.

DOVER: Never. I don't really go in for guilt. I don't feel guilty.

CLARE: You're not Irish!

DOVER: Shame certainly. I'm often ashamed of things that I've done and feel that I should have done them better or should have done them differently but I don't have feelings that I would call guilt. I don't know if I'm defining guilt very narrowly but I associate guilt with the feeling that one ought to be punished. That feeling that it's right that one should be punished. And I don't in fact have that feeling. This may be a deficiency in some way.

CLARE: What if I said that guilt is about feeling that you've done wrong?

DOVER: Well frankly, no, I didn't feel and still don't feel that I did wrong.

CLARE: I don't know if you wrote this but I saw somewhere something about you'd never actually experienced grief at anybody's death?

DOVER: Ah.

CLARE: Is that right?

DOVER: Yes. I'm sorry in a way that really from carelessness I let that statement stand in 1994 because it wasn't true after 1984. It was ten years out of date when I wrote it and I can't quite explain why I did this unless I was sort of looking at the state of affairs I've described through eyes which were already out of date.

CLARE: What changed it then in 1984?

DOVER: The death of a very good friend. The sudden death of a very good friend in Dundee, a man called Leach Adams who was the professor of education and I realised how saddened I was by his death. Since then there have been other people whom I've very greatly missed and grieved.

CLARE: But would it have been true prior to 1984?

DOVER: It was true before 1984 yes.

CLARE: Your parents, when would they have died?

DOVER: My mother died in 1973, my father in 1978.

CLARE: So you didn't grieve either of them?

DOVER: No, I didn't grieve over my mother because she wanted to die, she told me so. And I felt, well, relief but a different kind of relief of course from Trevor Aston. And then I couldn't grieve over my father really because he got, not exactly worse, but duller, you know. He was 86 by that time and in some ways more and more inclined just to create an unpleasant atmosphere, so I couldn't be sorry about him.

CLARE: There was relief again?

DOVER: Well, yes, it was relief really and other people, friends, relations. I ought, I suppose, to have grieved over the death of my Uncle Kenneth whom I had so much admired when I was a boy but as a question of fact, I was not in fact stricken by grief although I am sure if I'd been asked, when I was a boy, if I would be grieved by his death, I would have said, 'Good heavens yes!'

CLARE: And your explanation for that paradox?

DOVER: I don't know. I really don't know. I don't think of death in itself as suffering. I react very strongly to other people's grief or pain. I'm certainly stricken by that. But death, for some reason or other, not. I think of that as an end of suffering, an end of grief.

CLARE: And loss?

DOVER: Well, yes, one, one is sorry for people who experience loss but that is again a form of suffering. To take a particular example over the last two years, one of my oldest friends in life lost his wife a couple of years ago and both of them were people of whom my wife and I were very fond as we are very fond of him. And I realised that what grieved me there was my friend's own grief and loss. I couldn't feel sorry for the wife who had died because she was dead, if you see what I mean. But I could certainly feel grieved over the living.

CLARE: Do you find other people's responses to your feelings puzzling? For example, when your mother died, I would assume that people would come up to you and they'd express their condolence to you for you. But in truth, if they but knew, there was no point, was there?

DOVER: Yes, that is true but I think some of them at any rate knew how, well to use the cliché 'quality of life', how awful her quality of life was because she was finding it very difficult to swallow food for example and it was difficult to tell what she said. She died of atheroma but it seemed to affect her lungs and her intake of food and so on and she was very weak and the last time I saw her when I said, as one does, 'How are you?' she sort of smiled wryly and said, 'I want to die.' And that was so obviously true, I couldn't put on an act and say, 'Oh no, no mother, you mustn't say that' and so on. All I could say was, 'Yes, I understand.'

CLARE: No. She'd taught you anyway that you must never say that. But I do empathise because my mother did the same. My mother made it very plain that she wanted to die and it does, I agree, at least it did to me, make quite a difference to the way I responded to it. I don't know if a lot of other people understand that though. There's still a difficulty with the notion of matter of factly accepting someone is going to die and dies. But what adds a little piquancy in your case is that you have expressed a sense of, if not indifference, then certainly a lack of any sense of the sanctity of life. You've got a prosaic attitude to life.

DOVER: That is true, that is true yes, yes.

CLARE: Where does that come from do you think?

DOVER: I honestly don't know. People have suggested of course it comes from my excessive immersion in Ancient Greek civilisation because the Athenian democracy used capital punishment lavishly, one might say, for all kinds of things. But I think possibly this absence of horror at the very idea of ending somebody's life, that absence has always been there, if you forgive the paradox, and I can't remember at any time thinking to myself, 'My God yes, the Greeks had the right idea after all.' You see, I've always felt like that and I find there are quite a number of other people who do too, who've told me so, but they don't necessarily go around proclaiming it themselves.

CLARE: I wonder whether it's tied up with this notion of empathy, that some people are excessively squeamish perhaps, or sensitive, it really depends on your viewpoint, because they can very easily, if you like, live out Christ's injunction. They find it very easy to imagine what it is like to be the sinner or about to be executed, they identify with the individual to the extent that their judgement about what should be done to that individual is affected. So they wouldn't necessarily say, 'Yes, well the Athenians had a point, capital punishment for, say, fraud or whatever' because, as I said, either the empathy extends to 'I could commit fraud myself' or the empathy extends to 'God it must be awful to sit in the electric chair waiting for the volts.' Whereas what I don't sense with you is that element of empathy. The emotions are there, the rationality is there, but I don't sense any great sense that you can or wish to enter into the dilemma of the other.

DOVER: No, I think there are quite a lot of types of people if you like, with which I don't empathise. I suppose contemplating different ways of behaving – at one end of the scale there's the heroic, the saintly, the quixotic and so on, of which I would say I couldn't live up to that. At the other end of the scale, monstrous ways of behaving of which I'd say I couldn't possibly do that. And most of us are somewhere in the middle between those extremes. I can't in fact at all easily put myself in the place of the monsters.

CLARE: Right.

DOVER: So there isn't any empathy there.

CLARE: What about the not so monstrous?

DOVER: Well, yes for sure, as you get up towards the middle of the scale, you get nearer and nearer home, so to speak.

CLARE: But let me press it again. There is in this dilemma, a conflict between an individual's rights and needs and the community's, rather illustrated by Trevor Aston and Corpus Christi. In this conflict you would tend to come down on the side of the community?

DOVER: I do tend to and this is a matter of feeling, and I can't really justify it rationally in such a way that I could persuade somebody else to agree with me. It seems to me the sort of area where the individual makes fundamental choices or inclines basically one way or the other and one can't really argue about it, or at least not very easily. And this is where the moral choice is, in the strict sense of the word I suppose, arbitrary.

CLARE: So, you could conceive of a situation where a community, like Corpus Christi say, could for the sake of the community eliminate the individual?

DOVER: Well, it wouldn't need to, of course, because it could simply deprive them of membership of the community.

CLARE: Why didn't it do that in the case of Aston? Why couldn't they have got the two-thirds together and taken his fellowship away?

DOVER: There are an awful lot of people, I think, who didn't know enough about it. You see there are professorial fellows and so on who were not familiar enough with the situation. One or two people who actually liked him. I don't think there were many. I can only think of two who actually liked him and felt they were indebted to him. You'd have to be absolutely sure that you'd get the two-thirds majority if anybody proposed depriving him of his fellowship because if you didn't get that majority, things would be much worse afterwards. And, of course, even if you did get it and he appealed to the Visitor who was the bishop of Winchester ex officio and the Visitor upheld his appeal, that would be a hell of a situation after that. This was really the dilemma I think.

CLARE: But it is an interesting suggestion that you make, that we are drawn to the individual or the community when we're trying to make those balances by temperament. I'm struck by, say, Swift or Orwell or Dickens, even with their dislike of the community, Swift hating mankind but liking Tom and Dick and Harry and Orwell always being very sceptical of smelly 'isms' and groupings and so on. But then there are other people who are wary of individualism. I wonder what is it about you that you say, 'Yes, I'm drawn to the community.' What is it about the individual that you feel warrants certain circumspectness?

DOVER: I honestly don't know. I probably feel that if we all as individuals take against the community of which we are members, then nothing will ever get done. A tremendous lot, after all, does depend on individuals co-operating, on one individual saying, 'Well, I don't really like that but for the sake of harmony, I won't object' and so on and so on. Each of us drops the particular things one might have held out for to concentrate on the things which are common to oneself and to other people, and things then move. And this is true, I think, of a body taking any kind of collective decision. And I think collective decisions are rather important.

CLARE: Yes, but at the same time your reputation rests on so much individual action. You are working away at Greek texts, going and visiting that country and writing.

DOVER: Yes, I think in academic work, of course, it's the individual who has the good ideas. Even in the sciences a lot of actual discovery is the work of individuals, however large the team that works together on working out what it all means.

CLARE: And some of them are maddening individuals, I understand your endorsement of the community, although I wonder why you're not so worried about the dangers that community can lead to. Some of the academic communities you and I know have their own strange aberrations. They can become closed in, they can become very indifferent to individuals and let them decline and rot until crisis point. I wondered again, does it go back to your father? Is it the notion of individuals running riot or is there a chaos you associate with it?

DOVER: It could be that, yes. You mentioned Orwell's hostility to 'isms' and so on. Well, I'm pretty hostile to 'isms' too. I don't like words ending in 'ism', or 'istic' and labels of that kind.

CLARE: You're not a believer in any of them?

DOVER: Very often they're false substitutes really. But, of course, Orwell might have been a little bit deceiving himself in thinking that he was hostile to communal action, communal decisions because I should have thought he was, in a way, a natural communitarian.

CLARE: True, but of course, I'm not suggesting for a moment that you are in practice hostile to individuals, because I think you're a very individualistic man yourself.

DOVER: Could be, yes.

CLARE: But I'm struck by the fact that when you talk or write, if you're allocating a value, it tends to be a greater one to the community than to the individual?

DOVER: Yes, yes.

CLARE: So there was a striking irony in the fact that it was Mrs Thatcher's honorary doctorate from Oxford that came up at the time when you were a crucial president of Corpus Christi because of course she very strongly took the opposite view in that famous statement in which she said, 'There's no such thing as society.'

DOVER: Well, I can see what she meant in the sense that people sometimes use the noun 'society' as the subject of a verb in a very misleading way, when, instead of saying 'society', one could say 'other people'. In that sense I think she recognised there were some silly statements going around about society, but of course, she went right over the top, as she commonly did.

CLARE: Did you ever meet her?

DOVER: No, not to speak to. I've set eyes on her once from close quarters.

CLARE: When all that thing blew up, did that lead to a lot of personal inconvenience for you?

DOVER: There was a certain amount. There was a certain amount, yes. I had the honour to be attacked in a *Times* leader by name and it's always an honour to be attacked by the Murdoch press. There was a pretty hostile article in the *Telegraph* by Max Beloff and I got a sort of what you might call anti-fanmail, of about 30 letters, all of which I answered. And that was it really, that was it.

CLARE: But as you say, you're not a believer in 'isms'. In fact, you're not a religious man in the sense of believing.

DOVER: I'm not religious, no.

CLARE: But from time to time there are these interesting experiences that you describe quite openly. You leave them for others to make sense of. There was what you describe, and I was very taken by this, as a religious experience in reverse, when I think the heavens opened and a voice declared, 'You have no need of God.'

DOVER: Yes, yes, the A. J. P. Taylor experience, yes.

CLARE: When did that happen to you?

DOVER: Oh, that was in 1961 when I was 41 at the time, when my wife was in Stratheden Hospital and I was driving to see her every day and it arose out of a suggestion from a Baptist friend of ours that one put one's sorrows upon God and that's when it happened. I was driving along towards the hospital.

CLARE: Tell me what happened?

DOVER: Well, I can only describe it as a sort of mystical experience in reverse. I say mystical because I felt at the time that all of a sudden I understood something which I had not previously understood but I couldn't possibly put into words what it was that I understood. And it was really just a process of my thinking, you see. Is our Baptist friend right? Should I really take religion more seriously? Should I put my troubles upon God and so on, you see? And then, no, from the sky, so to speak. And I remember describing it to somebody afterwards as being rather like going through the sound barrier only not so noisy, and I felt as if I'd gone through religion, not that I'd pushed it aside, but somehow I'd gone through it, I'd come out on the other side. And the words that came into my mind were, under a clear sky on a calm sea. And, well, that's how it was. Some years later, quite a while, it must have been 12, 15 years later, when Alistair Hardy at Oxford was collecting experiences of the supernatural and so on, I wrote, well not to him but to whoever was organising it at that time, telling them about this religious experience in reverse, and whoever it was, I've forgotten now, wrote back and said, 'Well, this is not unknown. We have had other people who've told us the same sort of thing.' And then years later, of course, I wrote about A. J. P. Taylor's experience when he was a boy.

CLARE: And was it also accompanied by a sense of serenity?

DOVER: Yes it was, really, yes.

CLARE: Sweetness even?

DOVER: Oh no, I wouldn't say that, no. It was more a sort of matter of factness, in a way. I felt I can cope with this situation with my wife being depressed. What I need to do is find out much more scientifically about depression and that salvation lies in knowledge, scientific knowledge, technical knowledge and so on. And that's really how it turned out, you see. But after all, my wife has essentially a scientific turn of mind so that we were very much on the same wavelength really over how to cope with depression.

CLARE: A biological model of depression as a disorder, treatable with anti-depressants or indeed, in the case of your wife, a course of ECT. That, I understand from what you've written about her, has helped her.

DOVER: Oh yes, oh yes indeed.

CLARE: As an academic I know you would have met many other academics around the time of your wife's depression, and if the decision concerning a course of electro-shock therapy came up, I would have anticipated if others knew about it, I don't know whether they did or not, there would have been a lot of antipathy to it, or opposition?

DOVER: Well not actually among adult academics. Students took against it.

CLARE: Now in the case of your wife, they wouldn't have known about it would they?

DOVER: They wouldn't actually have known so far as I remember, though I would not have objected to telling a student about it. But I didn't know actually that there was feeling against ECT because the only experience I'd had of it before was by my tutor at Balliol, Russell Maggs you see, who had this awful cyclic depression where the mood switch was turned in a matter of seconds for a few months, then turned back again. He had ECT and after each lot of treatment, he did bounce up, he was a great deal better. So that that's all I knew about ECT.

CLARE: When was your wife severely depressed?

DOVER: Oh, my wife really started from that bad flu which we both had in the winter of 1958–59, when she got these sort of periods of lethargy, sometimes accompanied by a slight fever and so on, every month and nobody could find anything wrong. She started to get depressed and in the spring of 1961, when she went into hospital, she started getting better.

CLARE: Yes, the reason I ask you is that would have just been before the big anti-psychiatry movement and the rise of Laing?

DOVER: Before Laing and Cooper. But of course one of the awful things is that to this day, ECT in fiction is painful, not in reality. One of the friends who read my book in typescript said that I didn't show enough compassion for my wife going through this terrible experience and he admitted that his knowledge of ECT was entirely derived from *One Flew over the Cuckoo's Nest*.

CLARE: And was given with no anaesthetic and no muscle relaxant and the patient conscious.

DOVER: And people don't know, and, you see, I couldn't be sort of shedding tears over my wife's experience because what she had was such an immense sort of injection of hope and optimism that it wasn't the occasion for being upset.

CLARE: And she has done reasonably well since?

DOVER: Oh yes, I forget what medication she was on but in 1963 she had a relapse, not as bad as in 1961. She went to a day hospital then and actually she had by then learnt to drive, she was able to drive herself to the day hospital and back and then there she was put on Pertofran, an anti-depressant, and that did fine really for nine years. Then it seemed to lose its potency a bit and she was put on to another drug, the name of which I've quite forgotten now and that lasted about nine years, then she was put on to something else and at the present time she's on Paroxetine, which seems to work fine.

CLARE: Have you ever yourself suffered from something similar?

DOVER: Oh yes, indeed. In 1962 I had a spell of feeling pretty depressed. It stopped.

CLARE: How long did it last?

DOVER: Well, I think it was just that I felt pretty miserable for several weeks but it didn't actually stop me working. Work in a way was a refuge from it, you know. Then in 1963, while my wife was going to the day hospital, I had arranged to go to Greece for a couple of weeks because there were various things to do with something I was writing and needed to fix up there. And my mother-in-law was staying with us at the time, so they said, 'You go' so I went. And one day in Greece I quite suddenly got the most awful sort of misery descending on me for about 24 hours and then the odd thing was, after 24 hours, I was in the train going towards the port where I was going to go on a trip to Italy, and within about 30 seconds the misery just lifted like clouds lifting suddenly, and didn't come back. I've never known the explanation of that but I have from time to time had spells of weakness and tiredness which seemed to be associated with stress rather than with overwork. I do seem also to be rather liable to post-viral depression if I get flu.

CLARE: Have you ever contemplated suicide?

DOVER: Yes, I have actually and on each occasion it was to escape from a situation that I couldn't see any other way of escaping from. And really I think, in all cases, ludicrous really, no reason to choose that particular route of escape.

CLARE: Can you remember the situations?

DOVER: Well, one occasion I remember was actually during the war, on the retreat back to Alamein which was of course a colossal defeat, a rout. And I had a troop of light anti-aircraft guns with part of the Second Rifle Brigade and I had to switch over and report to somebody or other so I left my guns where they were and I went to see the bloke and when I came back I couldn't find the guns. The whole area, of course, was moving and units in the desert on the move cover an enormous area because you have to keep at least a hundred yards between one vehicle and its neighbour because of air attacks. After about an hour of toing and froing and looking for my own guns, I felt suicidal about that. I thought, 'I just can't face the humiliation of being here, not knowing where the unit I command is.' But of course, I suppose the circumstances were slightly exceptional because one had the unhappiness of defeat and also of course a great shortage of water, which doesn't help.

CLARE: Again, I'm struck that when you said earlier, shame rather than guilt, shame would be something very powerful in your make-up?

DOVER: Oh yes, yes.

CLARE: Shame you could see driving you to do something, guilt not so?

DOVER: Shame would I think, and guilt would not.

CLARE: Yes. You said, 'One falls in love with someone who is or comes near to being the right recipe for oneself' and I wondered in what way your wife hit the right recipe. What is the right recipe for Kenneth Dover?

DOVER: Well, this is very, very curious really to define. I think a high degree of complementarity in a way, but seasoned so to speak with an awful lot of things that we do enjoy doing together.

CLARE: And the complementarity, tell me what you think complements you?

DOVER: Well, her education was essentially scientific and she's inclined to be reductionist. And we got married, of course, before I'd taken my finals at Oxford. And I used to try and explain philosophical questions to her and she was inclined to think that philosophical propositions are either armchair and ignorant science or they are quite meaningless rigmarole, which made me feel very insecure for a while but it had a very good effect in fact because I took a fresh look at all the philosophy I was doing from that point of view. In fact it stood me in very good stead by the time I'd worked through the whole mass of stuff. That kind of thing I mean in complementarity. But then, you see, we both have a passion for wild country and at the present time we both have a passion for gardening, a fair degree of passion for birds and things like that. I am very, very much more musical than she is. But in many ways she's a great deal more practical than I am. So it's what I mean by the right recipe, the right sort of ratio of complementarity and supplementarity.

CLARE: Presumably as you wrote about the important influences in your life and from the deformity all the way through to the way in which you've managed your academic life, your personal life, you have looked at it carefully. Do you think that you're unusual?

DOVER: Goodness knows. I have to accept the statements of others that I am unusual in revealing so much about myself but whether I'm unusual in having these things to reveal, I cannot know. If other people don't, one doesn't know, you see. This is one of the curious things about autobiography.

CLARE: You're very candid about the importance of sexuality to you and the impact of ageing.

DOVER: Yes, yes indeed and so far as I know, I don't know of any autobiographical work which is candid on that particular subject.

CLARE: And did you have to think long and hard about whether you would be?

DOVER: No, no it comes naturally.

CLARE: And that's really the question I thought I wanted to ask most of all – why do you think that is, why does it come naturally?

DOVER: I honestly don't know. I think it has something perhaps to do with the war. Because I spent the greater part of the war in the company of young, working-class, lower middle-class men from Lancashire. Now, among them, I don't suppose this will be recorded on the broadcast, if A showed B a photograph of A's girlfriend it was perfectly natural for B to say, 'Has thou fucked her?' And in many ways the way I talk about sex I think was determined by that part of my life and it's something of course that academics of the younger generation perhaps have not had. Indeed, many of my generation have not, because so many of them went into code breaking, Japanese, intelligence work and so on and it just so happened that I joined the artillery section of the OTC at Oxford on the outbreak of war and people who came up a year later, they mostly ended up at Bletchley.

CLARE: That's interesting. I hadn't thought of that, I had wondered how much it was a reflection of your mother's original exhortation – not her exhortation, her . . .

DOVER: Habit.

CLARE: Her habit and her injunction not to say things like 'You mustn't think that' or 'You mustn't say that'. The opposite way round, not that you must say them but that it's reasonable to say them if that's what you're thinking. When you were thinking about Aston, you feel, 'Well, if I was thinking that I should say I was thinking that.'

DOVER: Oh yes, well I certainly thought that if I was thinking that I should say so because there's no point in writing an autobiography if one conceals things.

CLARE: And when it came to sexuality, because you describe very interestingly as you age, your anxieties about waning potency and your delight when it returns and you describe this in terms of your relationship with your wife, how did she feel? Because it is unusual for someone such as yourself to write very candidly about your anxieties about sexuality and then indeed, how the performance returns and it involves your wife. I wondered how she felt about that?

DOVER: She had absolutely no objection whatever to anything that I've said in the book about her, or about sex. People have asked her this question and I'm not sure she even understands why they're asking.

CLARE: What seems to me to make you unusual is that you say things people don't say and you say things that you think that people think but don't say. And I'm still struck by that. I wondered whether, before this autobiography ever appeared, whether that had got you into trouble in other situations?

DOVER: I don't think so, as far as I can recall, at least not what I would regard as real trouble. Of course, in what I've written for the general public, I have said one or two things that rather to my surprise people who I would have thought would have known better, have taken objection to. For example, in that very general book about the Greeks that I did for the public in connection with the BBC 1 programme, I was talking about how the Greeks seem to portray in art humans and gods and goddesses absolutely on the same level, whereas in other cultures, of course, you very often get grotesque gods and goddesses and so on. And I said if you see a statue of a girl with 16 tits and a crocodile's head, you know she's not the girl next door. And one or two people thought that was letting the side down, so to speak, to talk in those terms. Now the curious thing was that once the phrase had started to form in my mind, it followed the rhythm of, what is it, 'Sixteen men on a dead man's chest, yo, ho, ho, and a bottle of rum,' you see! And rhythms of words do enter into some of the things I write.

CLARE: Do you have any regrets?

DOVER: Never, never. You mean for anything I've written? No, except saying I've never been grieved by anybody's death because I should have stopped and realised that was no longer true.

CLARE: And at the very beginning of your book you raise the question of what is the purpose of life. What would you say is the purpose of yours?

DOVER: I'd give the same answer – to be useful.

CLARE: And do you think you have been?

DOVER: I'm told so, yes.

CLARE: Sir Kenneth Dover, thank you very much indeed.

Stephen Fry

You have to be very careful interviewing someone like Stephen Fry. He is very clever, very witty, very sharp and very articulate. He is a consummate actor and a shrewd communicator. There is virtually nothing that can be said about him that he has not said himself. That, as he helpfully points out, does not necessarily mean it's true! I knew I had to be careful not to be taken in by what could have been his latest act – the reflective, introspective, slightly agonising and deeply questioning multi-talented star anxious to be helpful, to muse thoughtfully on the patterns and pressures in his full and colourful life, and provide plausible and meaningful responses to questions. I don't know whether I succeeded.

He is one of a number of subjects who has participated in *In the Psychiatrist's Chair* who has seen a psychiatrist professionally in the past. In his case it was during his troubled teens when he was arrested for shoplifting. Unlike, for example, Martin Bell and Tony Benn, Fry's adolescence was a turbulent and rebellious one. He was expelled from a number of schools, was described by fellow pupils as too clever for his own good and something of a loner, and had considerable difficulty coping with his abilities and his own and other people's expectations. He was physically awkward, gangly, clumsy, hopeless at sports, and coming to terms with his homosexuality. He knew he was a disappointment to his father. Fry senior, serious and hard-working, a scientist, mathematician, electronics engineer, inventor and musician, regarded Stephen as something of a superficial, clever show-off whereas Stephen found his father to be a 'very, very brilliant man'. While Stephen, unlike his older and more stable brother, Roger, shared his father's competitive temperament, he could not, dare not, compete with him but deliberately turned his back on his father's life of mathematics and music. He didn't just fail these subjects, he did, in his own words, 'spectacularly badly'.

The psychiatrist he saw at the time apparently was tempted to attribute Stephen's stealing to some kind of nesting response to a constant moving around of the family. In fact, the Frys were immobile in Norfolk. With the benefit of hindsight, it would seem more likely that it had much more to do with Stephen's anguished relationship with his father about which he talks with energy and understanding in this interview. He admired his father and clearly craved his attention, his approval and his admiration. He continued to do so well into his adult life and successful period as a writer, actor and television performer – there is a revealing little cameo in which Stephen parades a series of increasingly flashy and expensive cars before his parents, provoking little or no response from his father while his loving mother gushes approvingly. But it is the father's approval he wants. He has found it hard to get. As recently as 1994 his father was quoted as saying of his son, 'He spends a lot of energy doing things that aren't worthy of him.'

He was, like most adolescents, preoccupied about his identity – who was he, what was he about? In so far as he had answers he apparently was not very satisfied. He was like his father but he had no wish to emulate him. A meteoric professional career as a multi-talented performer has not taken him much closer to the answer. But it has intensified his search. He finds now, to his surprise and some irritation, that people take his public mask or persona at face value. He feels he is seen as cool, urbane, detached and in command. In fact, he has a terrible fear of losing control, of failure. This division within himself came to a head when, in 1995, he found he could not go on stage playing the role of the spy, George Blake, in Simon Gray's play, *Cell Mates*. He walked out and fled to Belgium.

Initially and since, he blamed his punishing workload. But, in a letter to Simon Gray, he blamed himself for the show's poor reviews: 'I simply could not live with the shame, humiliation and embarrassment of having failed so completely. I only know my confidence is so blown away that I can never tread on a stage again.' He subsequently returned to London to be treated in hospital for depression. He still finds it hard to hit the right note when talking of his feelings. Reveal the full extent of his unhappiness and he risks being told he should stop complaining: he is a whingeing luvvy and has so much talent, wealth, so many opportunities, achievements and friendships, for which he should be grateful. Cover it all up and be the urbane, suave, witty man in control, and he ends up living a lie.

During the interview, Fry manifests considerable difficulty in acknowledging that some of his troubles in adult life may derive, to some extent at least, from the clash between his father's value system and expectations and his own. He knows they are connected and indeed provides much supportive evidence. But he is uneasy that any such linkage might constitute blame. It is as if unravelling the connections constitutes an act of disloyalty. 'I have,' he says at one point, 'a natural resistance to blaming anything in the past for anything bad in the present.' It is a common and understandable anxiety. Many people prefer to blame genetics or personality, constitution or biology – and sometimes they are right to do so. Yet it is not easy to listen to Stephen Fry ruminating on his unhappiness with life and success without recalling his father's world view in which there is a direct and stated correlation between the effort one puts into something and the reward one receives at the end. Science is serious work. Research is serious work. Performing as Jeeves or General Melchett on television, or even George Blake on stage, is not serious work. The fact that it is ludicrously rewarded in material terms is perhaps to compensate for the fact that in the great scheme of things it is trivial. Stephen's father despises things that come easy while Stephen, by virtue of his uncanny memory and quick mind, finds that a great many things come only too easy indeed. 'I think,' Stephen remarks about his father, 'he always knew that I never really had to sit and think and I think that upset him. It upset him because he didn't like the idea of a world in which you could succeed and apparently be praised without ever having made any real effort.' He claims that while he resented his father's attitude as he was growing up, after university he understood and accepted it. Yet there is considerable evidence that, while he certainly opposed his father's view, he incorporated much of it within himself despite himself. The *Cell Mates* crisis was hardly just a crisis of identity, a question of 'Who the hell am I?' and 'What am I doing here?' or indeed only a matter of loneliness, although clearly that was a significant factor, but a question of 'What is the point and value of my doing this in the first place?'

The irony is, of course, that life is getting harder for Stephen Fry and his father's adage that nothing really worthwhile comes without effort is coming true. At the time of the *Cell Mates* débâcle, the theatre critic, Jack Tinker in a perceptive *Daily Mail* article, observed that acting does not become easier the longer and and the harder people work at it, it becomes more difficult. 'The bold confidence and blissful ignorance of charmed youthful promise is no longer available to carry you through the reckless process of testing your talents nightly against an audience of strangers and reading the judgements of critics in the first-night reviews afterwards,' wrote Tinker. 'The more you learn about the craft the more you know what can go wrong.' As I write, Stephen Fry is once more being subjected to criticism, comment and analysis in terms of success and failure. His talents as a movie star are being thoroughly scrutinised. This time it is in relation to something that I suspect even his father would regard as hard and demanding work – playing Oscar Wilde in the film *Wilde*.

In previous interviews Stephen Fry had made a number of characteristically witty and entertaining observations concerning the messiness and the destructiveness of sex. He had renounced sexual intercourse, revelled in the joys of celibacy, and expressed a vigorous distaste for the basic realities of physical relationships. In a pugnacious interview with Lynn Barber he declared uncompromisingly, 'I have many good friends whom I love dearly and couldn't bear to be without; I just don't want to rub the wet slimy bits of my body all over them.' When I interviewed him, this had all changed. His previous Swiftian repulsion, it became clear, was in no small way a consequence of the fact that at the time he just did not have anyone to call his own – no relationship, no lover, no significant other. But when I met him that had changed. Stephen Fry now had a lover and all that had been said before was quite simply redundant – a useful reminder that what people say in interviews is often true but only for that time and place. Change those and a lot else can change as well!

CLARE: The term 'a man of many parts' could have been coined to describe Stephen Fry, comedian, actor, lyricist, reformed juvenile delinquent, bestselling novelist, noted wit, celibate homosexual, master fundraiser for charities, friend of the rich and famous and what used to be called 'man about town'. He was born in 1957 in London, he grew up in Norfolk, was expelled from three schools for various misdemeanours, spent three months behind bars for using stolen credit cards, yet managed to win a scholarship to read English at Queens' College, Cambridge, where he shone not only academically but also in the *Footlights*. He made his name as a comedy actor in such television hits as *Blackadder*, *A Bit of Fry and Laurie* and *Jeeves and Wooster*. He co-wrote the musical *Me and My Girl*, which is said to have made him a millionaire at the age of 27. Since then, he has written a number of bestselling novels, fled to Belgium from the leading role of a West End play and has starred as Oscar Wilde in the film, *Wilde*.

Stephen Fry, when you were 14, or thereabouts, you were sent to a psychiatrist for the treatment of what would be called kleptomania and of the experience you later said, 'They, psychiatrists, don't recognise the diagnosis of a bad lot, which I was.' Are you still a 'bad lot'?

FRY: Well, somewhere inside myself I feel I may be. I think, it's very hard to tell. I'm not a kleptomaniac any more. The point is that if one is truly a kleptomaniac it wouldn't matter how much property you had or how secure you were financially, you would still steal things. But I stole things as a teenager because I wanted them and it was really that simple. And I remember the psychiatrist being slightly confused because my father wasn't a diplomat or in the armed services and he obviously had a very tidy and quite understandable theory about kleptomaniac adolescents who had parents who moved around and therefore didn't have a stable nest and were stealing in order to create some sort of permanency about them; you know, collect property because they felt, you know, a lack of confidence in their background. But I had the most stable background you can imagine, so I didn't fit into that pattern. And I wouldn't say that I was a bad lot. I don't think there is such a thing. It was a sort of flip remark really. I don't think it helps, necessarily, with things like that to explain it. My father was very good, I remember. When someone said to him during my turbulent adolescence that maybe I'd got in with a bad lot, a bad set of people, he said, 'No, I think Stephen is the kind of person that other people get in with.' You know, that I was the bad influence other people get in with. You know it used to be said about the Krays or whatever, that as twins they got in with some people who were a bad influence on them, which makes one puzzle about who this kind of primal evil person is at the centre?

CLARE: But presumably it was your parents who felt that you should see a psychiatrist?

FRY: Yes, I think they . . .

CLARE: So they were worried about it. It didn't seem to have an obvious explanation to them. You say you did it because you wanted the things you stole but, is it, was it, as simple as that?

FRY: Looking back I think it was very difficult to explain. I had a brother who had more or less the same upbringing as me. He was, he is and was, as honest as the day is long. And there was no real explanation as to why I should want to do it other than the usual sort of clichés about a cry for help or attention or something. I mean, one can say that I was advanced beyond my emotional development or something, and I think actually that is something that the psychiatrist said, that I suffered from, what he called 'developmental delay'. I was academically quite bright in as much as in those days you were encouraged to do O Levels at a time when you could pass them, so I did them when I was 14 just because I could. But, you know, inside I was probably an eight or nine year old and I think that was part of the problem, that I was mixing with people who were 16 and just that much more advanced than me and I somehow knew that I wasn't quite, quite grown up yet, but I could do exams and things like that and I had a retentive memory. And also I was in love, I suppose, when I was 14, and that's a very disturbing thing to be.

CLARE: In love with?

FRY: Well, in the usual tedious kind of clichéd public school way, with a very beautiful boy, and it's very, very upsetting, it's very disturbing. You know, you can read *Romeo and Juliet*, you can read various novels and autobiographies, as I did, that show you that you are not alone and that it is a common thing and that this sort of infatuation is, you know, very normal, particularly in that sort of hothouse society but it still knocks you over.

CLARE: What hothouse society?

FRY: That of a public school, that of an all male public school. And, you know, it wasn't a sexual thing, it was a really kind of devastating, overwhelming event in one's life that made one think that the rest of existence was rather meaningless. And I think this is quite common with adolescence, you know. You have a sort of solipsistic belief that no one else can really see the beauty of nature, or the wonder of beauty, or really appreciate it in the way that you can and that you are alone and isolated. That's certainly how I felt and I knew there was no way that this could have expression. That it wasn't the same as the love one saw on television or in movies or in the usual books. That it was a sort of, you know, something other. And I was very proud of it, I didn't want to lose it. It's that sort of pain that you have when you're adolescent that you know is pain but is a pain that you don't want to lose.

CLARE: As you discovered that this was your sexuality, this was your orientation. I don't get a feel from reading about all of that just how that came across to you and to your family. You make it sound as if in fact it all, it all worked out pretty well.

FRY: I think it's not exactly a paradox, but I think it's a strange truth about British culture, or certainly the kind of Britain I grew up in, that sex is, is something rather splendid and easy to be proud of but that love is something rather shameful. I found it much easier to talk about homosexuality or to say that I was gay and, and for people to imagine that that was a sort of sexual expression and, and I think that's what homophobic people can't take. You know one's very used to those strange right-wing Tories who say, 'Do you know what these people actually do, do you know what buggery really is?' and you know deep down that that doesn't actually worry them because a lot of heterosexuals use buggery as a form of sexual expression. What they really can't cope with is the idea of people the same sex loving each other. That, to them is far more shocking, and I think it is to oneself. It is to me, it is to most people. I think love is shocking to heterosexual people, let alone to homosexual people. And that's the thing that is hardest to cope with, I think people hide behind the fear of the physical act of homosexuality, and what they really can't cope with is the emotional side of it. And certainly that's what my problem was and as far as my parents were concerned they both were aware of it at least as early as I was. But it's a common problem with some parents that they may be worried but they don't want to hear it, they don't want it stated as a fact. But my parents were fine about that and if there was any private pain for them about it, they certainly never let me feel guilty about it or bad about it.

CLARE: When would they have known?

FRY: I've never really asked them about that but there was a time when I was at Cambridge when I, as it were, came out to them, in the phrase, and, you know, they both were absolutely fine about it. There was no difficulty at all.

CLARE: You have described them quite differently, your father and your mother. There's much more talked about in relation to your father, his fierceness, your relationship with him, whether in fact you could or couldn't or wanted or didn't want to compete and all of that, and doubtless we'll talk about that in a moment. But your mother is much less distinct in the kind of picture I have of her, other than that she seems to be splendid. But you know, obviously I'm going to be more sceptical than that. I wondered what was she like?

FRY: I think consistent, which is the one thing that one values in that she has always been immensely supportive of me and even in the darkest moments of imprisonment or expulsion I knew that she believed in me, which she always did, from when I was very small. She believed that I could do something in the world and that I had qualities that she valued.

CLARE: What were they?

FRY: I think she enjoyed the fact that I had a sort of social side to me, what my father rightly I think, when I was a teenager, regarded as a kind of cheapness in me, as it were, a sort of easy charm or whatever one wants to call it, a skill at pastiche, an ability, you know, to get on with all sorts and conditions of people and to talk to them in their own terms.

CLARE: She liked that?

FRY: Show-off basically, and my mother, I think, valued that because my father, it's one of his greatest qualities, but it's a problem, it's a problem sometimes as it is with anyone with that quality, he has a kind of integrity and a kind of lack of interest in the shallower side of human affairs. It's not that he disapproves I don't think, actively, of some of the things I've done in terms of sitcoms or whatever, it's just that his own standards and his own sort of intellectuality, as it were, are not particularly interested in that kind of thing. I think my mother always liked that side of me. It may be something to do with being Jewish, a sort of social thing, a sort of, if you like, warmth that she has.

CLARE: She is good at it herself?

FRY: Tremendous, yeah, she's, I don't know what the word would be, eudemonist or something is the word. She's someone who sees the best in everybody and has a sort of active quality when she meets people which makes them feel good because she so sublimates her own ego to their conversation, as it were. And so everybody always says, 'Gosh, I love your mother, she's so wonderful, she's so warm' and she is.

CLARE: You have an older brother by 18 months, and then there's yourself and then you've a younger sister. Did both the Fry boys go to boarding school?

FRY: Yes.

CLARE: Do you know why that was, apart from the usual explanation that that's what a lot of people did? Do you know why in your case it was?

FRY: Well, both my parents did.

CLARE: Did they?

FRY: And all the people around us that we knew did. It's not that we lived in an immensely remote sort of socially county sort of world, it's just that all the boys of my age that I knew went off to boarding school. The only thing that was slightly odd about it was that it was 200 miles from home, that's to say we lived in Norfolk and the prep school was in Gloucestershire, so it was quite a long way away. And I was seven which was I suppose a pretty young age to be sent away. It looks it now but I have to say, with I think my hand on my heart and more or less honesty, I don't, I can't honestly feel any sense of rejection. I think it's fair to say, that I would have felt rejected if I hadn't been sent away because all the boys I knew were and I would have wondered what was peculiar about me that I wasn't going off to boarding school. And I knew my father had been to boarding school. He'd been a chorister at St Paul's Cathedral and had been evacuated to Truro during the war, so he'd been, you know, a boarder at prep school age and then at public school age. And my mother, similarly, had been hidden away in some ways in a boarding school, her father and mother being Austro-Hungarian Jews during the Second World War. They were, as it were, tucked away during the early part of the war under a very English name, just in case the Germans invaded, because their parents knew perfectly well what would happen. So it was just what happened in our family, as it were.

CLARE: And was there anything particular about this boarding school, that it was chosen, all 200 miles away from home?

FRY: It's friendliness actually. It was the fact that it was run by a splendid old chap who had three daughters who were all absolutely devoted to the school and to horses and to a very sort of country world in Gloucestershire and everybody rode the ponies and learnt the tack vocabulary and it was a very warm place. I think that's what appealed to my parents about it. They actually went to a scholastic agency, and said what they were after was somewhere with a very family sort of atmosphere. And we kind of knew that, my brother and I, and so I don't think there was any sense, like all seven year olds who might be sent away or feel sent away, it wasn't, you know, an act of absolute joy to go to school, there were moments of homesickness, but I don't ever feel now, or I can never remember a feeling since that time, of rejection. I think it really did seem most natural. And of course, people who criticise that sort of education forget that everybody you're at the school with is in the same boat so it seems the most natural thing. It's not as if you're the only boarder in a school of 99 day boys and so you're somehow isolated. In fact, there were plenty more isolated boys who had parents in Africa or Malaya or somewhere who actually sometimes had to stay at the school during the Easter holidays, the shorter holidays, and they seemed to cope all right. It's very hard to say. I have a natural resistance to blaming anything in the past for anything bad in the present.

CLARE: But isn't that the problem that as you try to make sense, as any of us, as I try to make sense of my own life, there's a sense that if I see an association between something that happened to me early on and now, it looks like blame?

FRY: Yes.

CLARE: But aren't you then left with the alternative model? I'm very struck by the fact that essentially, if you don't see links between any of this, you in adolescence clearly at odds with all manner of things – expelled from a number of schools, described by others as something of a loner, having difficulties, in some sense coping with your high intelligence and other aspects of yourself, you fall back in the end on, 'Well, it's a rum bit, there's my brother, 18 months older, he came from the same environment as me, he's one and I'm the other.' You're left with no explanation at all, other than I suppose genetics, and even that's not a particularly helpful one.

FRY: But you, one only seeks an explanation, I think, if you have a sense that your life or your identity is worthless. That's a feeling a lot of people may have.

CLARE: Really! Do you think that's true?

FRY: Well, you know if . . .

CLARE: I know people who look at their lives and, and sketch in the influences, but I don't think they think their lives are worthless.

FRY: That may be overstating it but I . . .

CLARE: And there are times you clearly think yours is?

FRY: Yes, of course, one goes through that. There may be moments in one's past, you talk to people, one has friends who have an abused childhood or a sense of rejection or they've done various things, you know that they feel there have been wrong turns in their life. If they're satisfied with the way they are, they don't go on about it. I mean, there is that, you know, wonderful phrase about the lady protesting too much. Methinks, people who say, you know, 'This happened to me and it's fine, I've coped with it, it's OK, but you know, I think it made me this, it made me that, it made me the other,' obviously they haven't dealt with it. I can look back generally speaking with a kind of wry amusement at my past and know that there was real pain there, just as when I broke my arm I know there was real pain but one doesn't feel it any more. I certainly know some people, and I've been in that position myself, who will dwell on things exterior to themselves now, either because they're the past or because it's their birth sign or because it's something the *I Ching* has told them.

CLARE: So when did you make the transition from being someone who wasn't making sense of it all to someone who has made sense of it all?

FRY: I wouldn't claim for a minute that I've made sense of it all. It's just that I've believed, like W.H. Auden, that if one were to expel one's devils one runs the risk of expelling one's angels as well. That the very things that caused me pain as a teenager and made me feel different and alone and separate, are things that also created qualities in me that I like, or at least qualities with which I can fulfil myself. For instance, my main emotion as a teenager was a sense of physical self-disgust, which I think is extremely understandable in someone who looks like me but that's a sort of cheap remark. But, it was very strong. It was extremely strong. It was partly because of a lack of physical co-ordination so I could never excel in the games field and the school I was at set quite a high store by athletic prowess on the rugby field, the cricket pitch and so on. I wasn't good at seeing the ball and moving gracefully. I was growing very fast and I was a bit of a bean pole and I was all arms and legs and very clumsy and unco-ordinated. I also felt unattractive and so on and it was a genuine problem and I wanted to be a brain with no body at all. I wanted just to be all essence, all mind. I kind of knew it was nonsense but rather earlier than most people do. I read the literature of the aesthete against the athlete, you know. I read that Kipling poem about the flannelled fool at the wicket and muddied oaf at the goal. I kind of felt it was a war, that there was an England which was physical, dull, prosaic, had no life of the mind.

CLARE: Philistine?

FRY: Philistine, bourgeoisified, and there was a life of light and ideas and freedom which was represented by all kinds of different writers and people. Ironically, some of them were at the same school as me, people like Sir Norman Douglas and Ronald Firbank as well as E. M. Forster. The central text I suppose is 'Only connect'. And I felt that it was a war and that they were having their day and making hay while the sun shone, but I knew that the one power a human being can have was over language and the mind and intelligence and so on. I thought that I would get my revenge in a very cheap sort of way. Of course, the irony is I now love sport with a complete passion, and if I could go back I would want to be perhaps something else because I, I think there is a great glory in the brief summer of sporting prowess and all the rest of it.

CLARE: But you still are inclined to talk quite disparagingly of the physical.

FRY: I think less than I was perhaps a few years ago.

CLARE: Why is that?

FRY: Well, I think there are a number of reasons. Deep down one knows intellectually as it were that the answer is a balance, a sort of dualism.

CLARE: But deep down you knew that two years ago, or three years ago. What's changed you? That's quite a change.

FRY: Oh dear, how do we express this? Something has happened to me which goes against your introduction which is to say the word that had been attached to me for so many years, celibacy, is no longer appropriate. And I always said at the time when people interviewed me about this celibacy business that it wasn't a religious or spiritual or psychological decision that I was going to be celibate, it was just something that as each day passed was an observation about myself.

CLARE: There was a reference to Swift which interested me, a reference expressing physical repugnance and you articulated that very powerfully. Now maybe you were persuading yourself, but it seems to me legitimate for me to push you a little on this because it wasn't just you saying, as I've heard people say, 'This tedious business sex, it gets you into all sorts of trouble so I'm really giving it up for a while.' You were saying something I thought more interesting and in some ways more profound, which was there is something quite repellent about physical sexuality.

FRY: Yes, I'd played precisely with those Swiftian ideas and it all started with an article that I was commissioned to do for the *Tatler* years and years ago, when Jonathan Meades was a features editor and he called me up and said, 'We're doing a Christmas special about things that people don't do. Like, for example, the fact that he never drives and Brian Sewell was doing something about the fact that he never watches television or goes on holiday or whatever it was. He asked, 'Is there anything that you don't do?' And this was about 1985 or something, and I said, 'Well there's sex, does that count?' And he said, 'Yes.' So I wrote this article in which I made a sort of Swiftian reference to the repugnant insistence of God on placing the elements of the sexual quest contiguous with the elements of faecal expulsion and excretion and so on. I said how cruel and unpleasant it was and talked about the damp tufted areas and how unpleasant they were. But in the article what I was saying actually was that the fact is I'm not very good at it and that's what it was all about really. And I spent many years having to cope with people who imagine that I look down on them because they lived a sexual life and they thought that I was superior for not doing so, which I never thought. It was in me simply fear. It is one of the problems of the gay world that because of the availability of casual sex in heathland, clubs and bars and so on, and the sort of slight kind of body fascism, that I've always had this absolute horror of going into gay places where you see these cold eyes who just look up and down and then turn away. And most people find it shallow when someone has attracted them just because of their physical appearance. I find it depressing and shallow when people are attracted to me just because of my voice or the way I talk or my personality. And I was simply afraid of rejection. I just hated the idea of people turning away from me. That's why I never went to gay clubs and couldn't bear the idea of pursuing a relationship. And I kind of knew this and I think that was part of the crisis a couple of years ago in *Cell Mates*. It was a sort of realisation somewhere that I was unhappy and I couldn't work it out. It made me very cross with myself because I thought I had no right to be unhappy as a lot of people do feel if they have no worldly explanation, as it were. People who don't know where the next mortgage payment is coming from and who are about to be evicted, or whose marriage is in tatters, can find easy explanations as to why they're unhappy and you know, they may well be right, but if you apparently have a successful, in inverted commas, career and enough money floating around, one tends to buy the worldly idea that therefore you have no right to be unhappy. I didn't want to conform to what always struck me as that lazy cliché of the Pagliacci, the tears behind the clown and all that sort of thing, because I just felt, as I always did, that the human world is bigger than anything, that one's will can overcome things, and I still think that's true.

CLARE: Do you?

FRY: But of course. There's that strange paradox that you have to have the will to use your will. For some reason a moment came, and there are all kinds of explanations why, when I suddenly realised I was unhappy and it took me a long time to work out why.

CLARE: And why?

FRY: Because I was lonely. Because I was not, as the Americans like to say, in a relationship, and I had thought that work, friends, public success and doing what I'd always imagined would be wonderful things to do, like writing books and appearing on television and meeting heroes and so on, would be as fulfilling a life as one could have.

CLARE: So were some of your declarations about relationships, was some of that what the analysts would call denial?

FRY: Absolutely, it was denial, which as we all know is a river in Egypt, and it was as bad a case of denial as you can get. But the odd thing is I kind of knew it. I kind of knew, really, that I was missing a sexual life or a life of complete dependence upon the happiness and connection with another person, the strange sort of banal details in a relationship – being able to say 'we'. I suddenly would see some of my friends and hear them say 'Oh yes, we saw that, didn't we?' And I thought, 'I can't use a first person plural, I can't say "we did this, we did that", it's always "I did this".'

CLARE: You remind me of an image of something you wrote. I never get the words right so forgive me, but it was something about that you really did not feel particularly drawn to the notion of waking up next morning with somebody, in your inimitable way, you then described all those tedious things that you feel you have to say to somebody who no longer is there for any particular purpose. And you were pretty powerful in your dismissal of that kind of ongoing relationship.

FRY: Yeah, indeed, and, and that's the problem. One gets swept away by one's own rhetoric and certainly other people do. I mean one's friends very often who are in relationships, straight or gay. I suddenly realise that they often felt that they had to apologise to me, or they thought I might disapprove of them and in fact, of course, you know, the boot was very much on the other foot. I used to envy them.

CLARE: Is there some truth in the notion that you're weary of relationships – because you describe yourself sometimes as very selfish? Indeed there's virtually nothing that one can say about you that you haven't said about yourself!

FRY: Yes, it doesn't mean it's true on the other hand.

CLARE: I told somebody I was seeing you and they said, 'Well, he'll be very difficult because he is so many things to so many people.'

FRY: Yeah, I mean that has always been part of the problem with me, this desire to please, this chameleon sort of quality. It's a kind of egotism and there's no way of expressing it without either sounding falsely humble or superior or whatever – a sort of self-consciousness is the problem really. I've always had this desire to please, this kind of eagerness to be liked, stroked, admired. And I've naturally found that the easiest way to be liked is to like other people and to enjoy their company and to listen to them and to let them be themselves and to subsume myself to their level so I can have evenings with poker-playing, snooker-playing friends, after watching a soccer match on Sky then it turns into some snooker and then some poker and I would talk about nothing but sport and manly things. I can have other evenings with, you know, painters, and other evenings with musicians or whatever, and I will live on their level and so on.

CLARE: So, turning it round a bit, why isn't it enough? There'll be people who will say, 'Stephen Fry gave him what he was looking for, he's always going on about relationships and he did it. He came and he gave him, because that's what Clare goes on about all the time, families and relationships and children and God knows what.' So let me turn it round just for a moment and say, 'Well, what you've just described sounds quite attractive. It's kind of *Peter's Friends* really – all these people, the Sky Sport and snooker and some very attractive people and they're all very fond of you and you're a stimulating, entertaining, intelligent man, then why make it complicated, why make it messy?

FRY: Absolutely, there's no reason to. Except a moment came when I was knocked all of a doo-dah by the realisation that I was, well, I'm over dramatising it, I was profoundly unhappy and part of the unhappiness was the realisation that, or at least the thought that, I had no right to be this unhappy, that I had what you've just described, every reason to be pleased with my lifestyle, in inverted commas, that I had a nice flat in central London and a nice house in the country and friends and I could buy a car if I wanted to and go on holiday wherever I pleased and so on and it ought to be enough.

CLARE: But of course around the time of *Cell Mates* you had something that reminded you that you didn't have everything, in the sense that clearly you didn't have the appreciation of the critics about a performance in full view of the public. A lot of people were saying, or people you seem to feel very sensitive to, were saying unpleasant things about Stephen Fry.

FRY: Yeah, and it's certainly true to say that I find it hard to cope with criticism. I mean, I actually don't mind criticism, it's not the criticism of something I've done, but, I do find it very hard to deal with people whom I've never met describing my character.

CLARE: Now do you know why that is because I could say to you, what does it matter if they're people you've never met?

FRY: Absolutely, and I've done that. I've had friends, you know, anybody in our business has had to cope with friends in tears because they've read their character being destroyed and they've come round and you've given them solace and said, 'Listen it's of no importance.'

CLARE: Did you worry that someone might read it whose opinion mattered to you? Do you know what I mean?

FRY: I know exactly what you mean. I don't think so. Naturally one of the things one dislikes about sort of any kind of character assassination or particularly virulent criticism is not the effect it has on oneself but the idea of one's mother reading it or one's parents' friends or people who slightly know you. But it's very hard to say what it is and of course the reason . . .

CLARE: Your father reading it?

FRY: No, I really don't think that was it. I know he'd be supportive, I know he would, you know, he has the ability to judge the true from the untrue.

CLARE: I read the reviews recently – they're not terribly savage. Therefore that made me then think because I know this of myself, that one thing that really does upset me is to read criticism even if it's written by people I despise, and sometimes they say something close to the truth.

FRY: Mm, yeah.

CLARE: The criticism that one critic said – 'that he never stops being Stephen Fry' – I thought that maybe you did not like that, that's because of how you feel about being Stephen Fry, and then another critic said of your performance that it was 'another of his studies of lofty, smiling, superiority . . . the all-time façade, so damnably English on the one hand and so completely inexpressible on the other. That suave, clubbable, heartless voice.'

FRY: I think you're buying the public perception that I left the play on account of the reviews. The reviews were part of it but it simply was a very bizarre day and the reviews contributed to it in that I suddenly became aware that there was some terrible problem inside me. That I was completely miserable and that I couldn't cope with life and that I wanted to drop out of it and I don't think there was any phrase or any particular review . . .

CLARE: Was it somehow the last straw?

FRY: It was somehow a last straw.

133

CLARE: What was it that drew you to the character? *Cell Mates* was a play by Simon Gray and it was about George Blake who was a spy who was sprung from Pentonville.

FRY: Wormwood Scrubs.

CLARE: Wormwood Scrubs. And you played Blake. What about that part? It's a curious part, particularly played by a man who has many, many façades, as you have. In some, some ways you might be ideal to play it because you're in one sense, a very enigmatic man. You could be a spy for all I know!

FRY: Yes.

CLARE: What about the part itself, did it stir you up or aggravate the stirring up?

FRY: It's a very interesting question and I don't know the answer. Part of the reason for doing the play was that I had a relationship with Simon Gray in as much as I'd done, a couple, three things with him before and he was an amiable companion and I like the idea of working with him and with Rik Mayall again. Also there was something very appealing about playing a character as blank and as unreadable as Blake, who was actually Dutch but had become English. And I think people often sense in me a sort of, a falsity of Englishness. I don't know where it comes from. A sort of over-English Englishness. Which is something that I . . .

CLARE: Is it related to the half-Jewishness?

FRY: It may well be and I often find it a peculiar snobbish thing about the British which is that they will say of me 'Oh, I'm so English', whereas they wouldn't say that about the average cab driver, who actually is just as English or, you know, a Huddersfield bank clerk, who's just as English. But because my voice seems to come with, you know, instead of fleshy fibres in my larynx, it seems to be tweed, people think that's more English. But actually I don't think it is. I think there's a sort of over-English quality about it you might say, and some people perceive that and find it uncomfortable or irritating or false.

CLARE: So there was an element, there was an echo in this character of a certain sense of Stephen Fry being not what he seemed.

FRY: Exactly, and one of the sort of things I kept, as it were, shrieking to myself during this crisis of leaving was that I didn't know who I was. You know, that I didn't believe that people who wrote about me, as you know, in a phrase like 'He is always himself', I thought, 'Well, I don't know who I am so how do they know who I am. What do they mean by saying he's always himself?' It's a thing actors often have to face is that some people's character or perception of their persona seems to shine through each performance they do, however different they are. And I can remember seeing a review that said that, you know, 'He's always the same – Jeeves, General Melchett – always the same.' And I remember thinking, 'Well, I don't know how Jeeves and General Melchett could be more different.' You know, one is shouting, bellowing, mad, stamping about, absurd, moustache bristling and the other one is completely placid, cold, unemotional, quiet, respectful. But because people see it, I'm not blaming them because they see in it some quality that they think is me, they say, 'Oh, it's Stephen being Stephen again.' But because at this point I didn't know what I was, as it were, I found it particularly upsetting to think that there were lots of people out there who thought they did know what I was, who thought they knew what I thought, who second-guessed my opinions about things, my views on this that or the other, the way I was. People who'd never met me imagined that they knew who I was and that they were able to say things like, 'He is always himself', and I felt that I didn't know who I was. It was all, as it were, coming apart. I'd had this 15 years or whatever of amiable, successful, all the rest of it, very enjoyable, highly energetic work in which I'd done lots and lots of different things, and somehow, although I didn't regret any of it in its broader sense, I was glad I'd done this job, glad I'd done that, what I realised was that if I carried on doing that, you know, another novel the following year and another play that year, perhaps a bit of film, another television series, if I went on doing all that I would not go to my grave a fulfilled and satisfied human being. I was in some way in that sense on a wrong path because this was not what was going to give me happiness and I'd always thought it was. I'd always thought, you know, yes, if I do this, and then I've done this, a novel, it's a success or a play or a television series that's watched by a lot of people, that is what I'm about, that will give me happiness. And although there is pleasure to be got from doing a job well or satisfactorily, or in a way that pleases other people, it's a heck of a lesson to learn that it doesn't give you joy. And one had, of course, precedents. Everybody knows about the very public self-analysis of the most successful comedian of our age really, John Cleese, or certainly one of the most successful. And so one knew as it were, intellectually, and through history, that being funny and successful was not necessarily a path to happiness. But I'd always imagined that I wasn't like that and I didn't want to be like that. I didn't want to be, you know, self-examining, I didn't want to take myself apart in front of others. I didn't want to burden others as it were. I thought it was sort of bad manners.

CLARE: What about self-examining or taking yourself apart in front of one other?

FRY: That's right, I mean that's what I realised I was missing and that's the point. I realised I was lonely, not because I missed having sex or I missed a relationship in terms of just someone to talk to, but I sort of missed someone to worry about, someone who would worry about me in a way other than parents and friends do. Someone whose happiness was contingent upon mine and vice versa.

CLARE: But going back to something we said earlier, wouldn't knowing who you are, or knowing more in so far as any of us know who we are, wouldn't that to an extent depend on you making the kind of connections, devoid of blame now, the kind of connections between Stephen Fry when he was three and five, and seven and ten and 16 and 21, his relationships with the people in his immediate environment, his school, his mother, his father, his brother, his sister. That's what I meant really about looking for connections. You instantly saw it as a kind of passing the parcel of blame, which I accept many psychiatrists make it sound like, so I'm not defensive here, you're absolutely right, but I was thinking how do you find out who you are. You said, 'I realised really I didn't know who I was when they said there is Stephen Fry being himself again.' It's a wonderful missing the point really and yet hitting a different one. But surely to make sense of who you are does involve making sense of your Jewishness and your non-Jewishness, your mother and your father?

FRY: Yes, I think there is an element of truth in that and I think it's not a forlorn or necessarily an Oprah Winfrey quest. But, on the other hand, the irony of it is, is that I've always known those things. I knew when I was an adolescent. I came across a diary entry I wrote when I was 15 which was addressed to myself aged 25, that said I know when I'm 25 I will read this and be embarrassed by it and think that I was a hysterical teenager and think, 'Oh my God, can I really have written this?' But I'm telling myself in the future that what I'm writing now is real and what I'm feeling now is real and that when I'm 25 if I disown my 14- or 15-year-old self, I will be betraying myself, you know.

CLARE: It was your feelings then.

FRY: But my feelings had always been, I'd been lucky enough, painful as they were, to have them endorsed in a way that some people aren't lucky enough to have them endorsed by art, by literature, by music, by painting. And if art is said to have a function, which I don't think it should have, a function as such, it is one of the extraordinary things that art does. I knew I was not alone in that sense. I knew that there was nothing uniquely guilty or shameful about myself, my identity, either sexually or emotionally, that set me apart from others. I knew that actually.

CLARE: At a rational level you knew?

FRY: Yes, at a rational level. It doesn't mean that one forgives oneself for it or one comes to terms with it in an absolutely sane level way, because nobody ever does, but on the other hand I feel that there are all kinds of things in my past that may explain this, that or the other, but I don't think they're unique. They're unique literally because no one else has lived exactly my life, but they are absolutely typical and symptomatical, if one wants to use a slightly medical term, of other people's lives and experiences. They may have coped and dealt with it in different ways, some more satisfactorily, some less satisfactorily. And I think the point is to deal with things now.

CLARE: But the answer to the question, 'Who am I?' . . . Let me give you an example. You wouldn't have the faintest idea who you were if I took your memory away or if somebody took your memory away.

FRY: I would have a clue because I would have like all animals a sense that I knew I was a human being, just as all cats know that other cats are cats or know other dogs are dogs.

CLARE: That's true.

FRY: And the point is one sees one's identity so much in other people, not in oneself. I agree I can overstate this but I remember reading something somebody sent me, it was a newspaper clipping and it was about someone who, at the age of 82 or whatever he was, learnt his fourth language. He's now learnt his seventh musical instrument and he continues to dance, to garden, he sails every day, and it was just a description of this extraordinary life in an 82 year old – it was James Cagney. And at the bottom it said, 'He puts down the richness of his life to a complete lack of absorption in self.' Now, that is not to say that I have decided to be unabsorbed in self. I'm doing this programme which some might regard as the most egotistical or egoistic programme that a human being can decide to do in this country, so, you know, I can't claim that I'm not absorbed in myself or keen to put across an image or to talk to myself in a loud way, or whatever, but I do think it is a sickness of our culture that people are absorbed in themselves. This is not because self-absorption is a bad thing. I believe I'm Socratic in that sense, I think 'Know thyself' is as good as a creed as one can have, but I don't think one knows oneself by looking at oneself. I think one knows oneself by looking at others and connecting with other people and seeing that one's experiences do not isolate one, but conjoin one in the John Donne sense to the continent of man.

CLARE: But so much of what you say I have no problems with. The one thing that I do have a problem with is why it is such an either/or. It could be said of you, Stephen, that you were very self-absorbed. You talked about yourself a great deal. Admittedly, it didn't necessarily reveal a great deal but you talked a great deal. People were interested in you and, I don't think you really necessarily pushed them away. You didn't. You had the same attitude as many of us have, a sort of love-hate relationship with this exposure business. Many people who wrote about you at the time would now be saying, 'How can Stephen Fry describe himself as not interested in himself?' And the answer to that paradox you're saying is that there are certain aspects of yourself that you are interested in but making connections, only connect in this sense, is something you're a little wary of doing because it seems you feel it would be utter self-absorption to do it.

FRY: It's also as an explanation I think that's the fallacy. That's the point. One is not explained, it's like a cheap Hollywood movie where some of the characters are explained by a flash that they witnessed their mother being murdered when they were three.

CLARE: Like the end of *Psycho*, yes, yes.

FRY: At least in *Psycho* it's a joke, you know, it's kind of comic.

CLARE: But, for example, if we were to say that your relationship with your father, shall we say, was a different relationship to that which your brother had with your father, and it was different because, while of course there are similarities between you and your brother, there are differences too. First of all, he is 18 months older and he's the older brother and that, we know, has subtle influences. The older brother's relationship with your father, doubtless we could talk about but he's not here and therefore that's not particularly helpful. But when you said to me, 'Well, you know, we all were exposed to the same man and the same woman,' you were indeed but there are immediately subtle differences. The second point is, you were a very bright boy. I don't know how bright your brother was, no doubt very bright but not as bright as you. You were very bright. Thirdly, for reasons that doubtless you could tell me, you certainly developed a self-consciousness, a physical self-consciousness, and you coped with it by being verbally skilled, you learned very quickly to use words, I suspect to keep people away, to control them, to bring them to you, to entertain. You did all of that and your father, you touched him on a particular raw nerve and that was, he has a profound sense of the seriousness of life, of its moral worth and its integrity, and he might see this, the danger of this is, this boy, you, will become a popular star, but won't amount to something serious. And you've written all of that. Now, that doesn't reduce you. It doesn't blame your father. It makes a certain kind of sense which I've no doubt, given your intelligence, you've long made these connections or maybe you haven't, I don't know. But anyway, they're not connections that necessarily demean you or blame him, or explain too much, but they go to help give you a sense of where some of the drive in you comes from. I'm very conscious that on the one hand you're very good at denigrating things you do well. It is a tiny bit English, this sort of self-denigration.

FRY: Yeah, yeah. No, that's absolutely true. I suppose all I'm bleary about is the idea that, that it's an explanation of what one is.

CLARE: But let me interrupt you there. Is it not in a sense far simpler and more profound than that? Is there not again a certain fastidiousness about feelings?

FRY: Yes, absolutely right. I think there is.

CLARE: And you can intellectualise almost anything?

FRY: Yeah, but also it's a problem of being in this culture now where, you know, feelings seem to be presented as an antithesis of logic and reason and to me part of the real beauty of humanity and the world is reason and is thought. It is one of the most beautiful things we have and one of the most moving and most profound. Yet we live in a culture in which people generally think that if something is well expressed it's less likely to be true than if it's badly expressed. That a fumbling for words is an index of sincerity and truth and a mastery linguistically of expression of feelings, however complex, must mean a callous disengagement from them, as this sentence might be regarded as an example of precisely that. That I'm describing something that means a great deal to me emotionally but doing it in language that is not that chaotic. And people distrust that, and perhaps rightly and perhaps I distrust it myself. I think it's very important and it sounds almost like a right-wing point in that I'm profoundly moral not because I think evil should be punished and that blame should be apportioned. But I think that the universe is meaningless if we don't reward those who have overcome difficulty through some quality in themselves, whether it be called human will, which sounds rather Nietzschean and unpleasant. If we constantly say, 'He is like this because of that,' this may not be a whole explanation but goes some way towards explaining why he has trouble doing this and trouble doing that. All that is very good and very believable but

I do think there is so much to be admired in those who have dealt with these problems in terms of not giving other people grief about them, and the way I've been honest or frank in the past has always been at a slight remove and has been partly to do with the fact that, out of pride, that I would rather tell the press, say, that I was gay than have them find it out, as if it was a guilty secret because I'm damned if I'm going to be made to look ashamed or found out about something. I never really found that the press are actually interested in things that one truly feels, they're interested in the persona and so one kind of goes along with it, as it were. Like the celibacy thing, they want to hear you reiterate the sort of jokes about how disgusting the human body is and they find that quite amusing, and that's sort of fine and, you know, I don't feel the need to burden people, as it were. This is turning into Jimmy Savile now! I don't feel the need to burden people with the particular history of my own emotional development because partly, I get it out of my system in my books. I think if someone wanted to see what I felt about that, they could read *The Liar*, say, where the hero is accused of living by pastiche and pretence and having an intelligence which actually renders his own emotional life meaningless and makes him callous. And his articulacy far from being charming, becomes irritating, and all the rest of it. And this is self-critique, if you like, and self-explanation, and you might look at the parents in that book and say they were pretty similar, and in that sense, I did not work through it because I don't think, you know, that's the point, I don't regard these things as a burden to be worked through, but in as much as they have meant something to me and they've been a path down which I've felt I've had to go of self-examination, I've had the great good fortune to be able to do it in the guise of fiction or even occasionally in three-minute sketches.

CLARE: But the problem with a relationship is that another person does want to know, doesn't just want to share and see things and be described as a 'we' and provide company, but the problem about loving relationships, if it's a problem, is that the lover usually wants to understand, to know, the object of their love, to possess and know. And there is about you a sense in which there's an unease about that, I feel, about this self-knowledge business. It becomes a distraction. It's a sort of weakness.

FRY: Yes, I think that's absolutely right and I think it's particularly a weakness because . . .

CLARE: You think it is a weakness?

FRY: Oh absolutely.

CLARE: But then won't you face a problem in a relationship that somebody will be intrigued to know what it is that makes you tick?

FRY: I think that's the beauty of an intimate relationship that that can happen. But it's almost an insult to that intimate relationship if it were to happen in precisely the same way, in this conversation with you and me talking, as it did with my lover, because that would be most extraordinarily insulting, because that's one of the joys of that relationship. But one of the problems I have, I suppose, is that people don't believe me when I tell them about some emotional state I'm in because I'm aware that I give off this aura of self-containment, self-control, of being 'sorted'.

CLARE: Of being sorted, yes.

FRY: Yes. And some of my friends are aware that I am not but also, will say, you know, that 'Oh, it's easy for you.' And I will say to them, 'Two years ago I was sitting in a garage with a duvet against the garage door and my fingers over the ignition keys, absolutely determined to end my life.' And they'd go, 'Yeah, yeah, yeah, but actually, my problem is if my bank manager, blah de blah de blah.' And you'll think now why don't they want to know that about me. Why is it when I try and say to them, 'Look, you know, don't look on me as some source of security and massive control and self-knowledge. Believe me, I have been in as bad a pit of despair as anyone else I know. I mean, almost as bad.' I haven't actually topped myself. I'm not going to overstate it but, the fact is that is not what a lot of people want me to be, oddly enough. To be able to put everything in brackets and inverted commas, to be able to comment on it rather than seem to live it, although people may use that as a criticism of me, it is also what they want of me and if I don't fulfil it . . .

CLARE: But I don't want it of you and yet ...

FRY: No, I realise that.

CLARE: But you're giving it to me.

FRY: I am giving it to you because, unfortunately, the very act of describing it sounds like disengagement, that I'm talking about someone else. Now short of weeping on the programme, saying ...

CLARE: Yes, but it doesn't, honestly, it doesn't.

FRY: Well, I hope it doesn't.

CLARE: No, no.

FRY: But you know this is the problem I tried to wrestle with in *The Liar*, which is you know, what is one's identity. It's an Oscar Wilde point too about masks, and the image I used to use was ...

CLARE: Strip away the reality and there's the mask.

FRY: And the image I used to use was that of a signature. That, you know, when you're a teenager it's quite common isn't it, to reinvent one's signature, or to say I'm going to use a Greek E from now on or I'm not going to do a hook on the end of a Y, I'll do a straight line or whatever. So, for a few days, you have this new signature, which you've invented and then it becomes your signature and it is your signature and no one else's. It is the way you write your name and in that sense, it's the truth about you but you've invented it. Similarly, when you're a teenager, you decide you're going to walk with books in this particular way in front of you, like, you know rock your shoulders up and down and you're going to hug the wall and you're going to throw your head back. All those adolescent things of reinvention, they become you. And it's very hard, or it has been for me ...

CLARE: And you were particularly analytical about that, and observant and you were very good at changing it, I presume, and altering it?

FRY: Yeah, but eventually it becomes one's manner.

CLARE: But I understand that. Are you saying though that the other side of that is that when you feel you are being authentic, is there a little voice at the back of your head saying, are you being authentic?

FRY: Absolutely.

CLARE: Is this really you, Stephen?

FRY: Yeah, funnily enough, I also have this thing about not somehow being able to get drunk. I enjoy a drink and I'll have long evenings with people, but I'm always in control and I'm often told by people, 'You know, I'd love to see you drunk one day, Stephen, I'd really like to see you drunk.' And I always have this, I call it a little voice in my head, that at some point if I'm working the next day will say, 'Time to go Stephen,' and I will trot off home.

CLARE: There was something about your driving licence or some stag party of Kenneth Branagh's wedding or something, a stag night, you got drunk?

FRY: Oh, yeah, I mean I've been over the limit but what I mean is I haven't reacted in the way other people do when they're drunk. I don't get loud, you know, I never lose the thread of a conversation.

CLARE: And you never lose the little voice?

FRY: Yeah.

CLARE: And, of course, that's in there in the sex thing too, isn't it, of course, because that is the one maddening area that your film persona, Oscar Wilde, of course, came to grief over, not just his sexual but his whole erotic, his human relationship. It is the area where you have to, in one sense, lose control.

FRY: Yeah, that's right. And, and of course, I love that. That's what I've always loved about sex, it's why I find it a fascinating part of human experience, because I think far from dragging us down to the same level, as it were, it actually, it keeps us rising above. I always loved that remark of Kinsey's, whether it's true or not, when someone said to him, 'You know, Dr Kinsey, according to your report 96 per cent of American males masturbate regularly, what do you think this says about American males?' And Kinsey said, 'It tells us that 4 per cent of American males are liars.' I've always thought that, you know, British life could be so improved by having captions on *Today in Parliament*, or the Westminster live transmissions from the House of Commons in which every time a Member of Parliament got up to speak, to make a speech, this caption would say when they last masturbated and what they used in order to masturbate and what they thought of when they masturbated. For the first two weeks everyone would snigger and say, 'Oh, how awful,' but eventually we'd just get very bored by it, and instead of being embarrassed by it or thinking that we're unique for having this strange fantasy world, this strange libidinous drive, we would actually feel that it was actually OK and that there was no guilt attached to it and that it wasn't a bad thing.

CLARE: But what is one to make of Stephen Fry, who can very persuasively describe sex, quite repulsively, by saying, 'I have many good friends whom I love dearly and couldn't bear to be without. I just don't want to rub the wet slimy bits of my body all over them.' You were very convincing. Clearly, you convinced a lot of other people that this man, Fry, is the nearest thing to a twentieth-century Jonathan Swift. Yet now you're saying, 'No, not really, that's not me. I'm as sexual as the next man or woman.'

FRY: I think I've always said that, I've said it both consciously in interview and I've said it in . . .

CLARE: It didn't come across.

FRY: I mean when people said, 'Are you celibate?' I said, 'Well, I have been.' That doesn't mean that tomorrow I won't be struck by the thunderbolt, as they say in Italy, you know. I've always believed that that was possible.

CLARE: You are verbally so skilled that you can really convince yourself of almost anything though, can't you. I mean you're intelligent enough.

FRY: What one can't do is convince others of it, though. You see, I can't convince you that I've said that every time.

CLARE: Well you're getting there, you're getting there.

FRY: Yeah, and when I do that in interviews, they don't print it, it's not what they want to hear. I don't want to overstate this into a kind of paranoia, but there are definitely things that journalists want to say about me and they don't want to hear the opposite, so they didn't want to hear it when I said, you know, this is not an achieved or considered state, this celibacy, tomorrow I may well be thunderstruck and fall in love and the whole thing will change, and that rather spoils their image of me.

CLARE: When you talk about who you are, there is the half-Jewish, half-English side. There's an example that doesn't necessarily involve blame, it doesn't involve blame at all, when one looks at one's own antecedents and starts to see the extent to which the Jewishness of your mother's side is part of you. That's what I meant about making sense of the past.

FRY: Absolutely.

CLARE: What about now, do you feel clearer about who you are?

FRY: I'm more interested in things like the Jewish side of myself. I used not to be uninterested but it didn't really take up much of my time. I remember making a remark when I was at university, to someone saying, 'Gosh, you know, I sometimes think if I wasn't Jewish and queer I would be the most appalling right-wing person.' It's very easy to be liberal, to understand bigotry if you happened to be born with two quite crucial separate characteristics, one of which is almost a symbol of man's bigotry in our century, which is to be born Jewish, and the other one which is pretty big too. I sort of questioned my liberality and sympathy for other minorities and other people because it was easy for me to be liberal because I had every reason to be, because I myself could so easily be a victim of illiberality. Whereas someone who was absolutely white, heterosexual, English, Christian, when they were liberal it was more achieved, you might think. Auden wrote about that too. But being Jewish is such an odd thing to be because it's neither necessarily religious nor racial. My family has never been religiously Jewish, or at least none of the family that I've known have ever been, so I've never had Sabbath candles lit or celebrated Hanukkah and the only times I've ever been to Passover have been with friends in London in the last few years, with whom I'm not related. They just sort of invited me. So it's not that sort of Jewish background, it's never had a cultural identity. My mother went to a girls' public school. She did flowers and vegetables for Harvest Festival in the local church. She never denied her Jewishness. She was always very proud of it but I was brought up in the Church of England.

CLARE: What is your father's faith or religious background?

FRY: The family was originally Quaker though it stopped being Quaker in the sort of late nineteenth-century thing, and so he was brought up also in the Church of England and as I said earlier, he was a chorister at St Paul's Cathedral when he was young, he was very musical.

CLARE: And a scientist and a mathematician. A rigorous man.

FRY: Yes.

CLARE: What did he want of you?

FRY: There's a cheap answer – I could say you'll have to ask him but I, the feeling I got was ...

CLARE: Have you ever asked him?

FRY: Yes, it is something we talked about. We're on very good terms these days and I think part of it was that he recognised in me someone who was rather similar to himself in some ways and so there was always a rather grating antagonism between us because he was a man of pride and I was a person of pride. And looking back one could see that the very subjects I most deliberately ignored and failed were maths, physics, music, when I was at school. I just made no effort at them whatsoever. Indeed, I wasn't going to be seen to have tried and failed. I did spectacularly badly at them.

CLARE: That's common enough. You weren't going to compete on his terms.

FRY: That's right.

CLARE: You say you were like him – do you mean, in terms of personality?

FRY: I think so.

CLARE: Would that have been different from your older brother?

FRY: Yes.

CLARE: So you would have been more like him?

FRY: I think so, I think yes. I think that's right.

CLARE: Is he quite competitive?

FRY: I think he's only been so with me. Part of the thing that frustrated me is that he has no sense of competition socially in the world at all. He's never shown the least interest in, you know, business or projecting himself or becoming as it were one of the great and good and being on committees for this that and the other, which he could easily be. He's a very, very brilliant man and certainly awesomely so when you're growing up because it reveals itself not just in the mind but also in practical things. He could make anything, you know, and solve problems and express things in numbers mathematically and so on and with logic and reason. One of the things we most disagree about these days, of course, is that he finds my scepticism rather hard to cope with, which is sort of ironic really, that I was always the art-side person and he was always the maths-side person and he's much more, as it were, open minded about things like ghosts or ESP or things than I am. I find it absolutely intolerable if people dribble on about ESP and telepathy and so on and he doesn't, I don't think he believes it but it doesn't annoy him as much as it annoys me.

CLARE: But he was more competitive with you?

FRY: Yeah, I think so. I think he saw that I could be like him as it were and maybe part of it is that he actually felt that he should have been more worldly and that he should have been more involved in competition and proving himself and you know, shouldn't have dropped out of the, you know, the human race, as it were, the rat race is what I meant I suppose. Looking back on it, I used to turn up in the early days of being on television and almost every time I visited him I was in a different car, you know, a Jaguar, then a BMW, then an Aston Martin and Austin Healey and all this kind of thing. And looking back on it, it was the most naked and embarrassing act of crude self-assertion you could imagine. 'Look at me, I've got this car this time.' It's amazing my father had patience enough even vaguely to nod at it.

CLARE: But you wanted him to?

FRY: Of course, yeah, I wanted him to and of course he didn't. He was not so cheap as to pretend it didn't exist and just turn his back on it . . .

CLARE: Would your mother go 'Gosh!'

FRY: Yes, she was sweet, absolutely, 'Oh gosh, lovely isn't it?' and all that sort of thing, but she was also worried that it might upset my father, not because he was jealous but because he would be worried that I actually set store by such stupid things as bits of metal one hurled around country lanes, you know, he was extremely decent about it. I know a lot of parents would have been a lot more problematic.

CLARE: But did you have a sense of what he would have wanted of you?

FRY: I think he wanted perhaps to see evidence of work like most physicists. There's a very high doctrine of work because work is essentially just another word for energy or heat, which is the only thing that makes the universe move.

CLARE: Work?

FRY: I think he equates work, not in the sort of protestant work ethic way but more with thought, thought and work.

CLARE: But so do you of course.

FRY: Yeah, and I think he'd always been aware that things had come very easily to me. That I've never had to revise for examinations, that I'd never had to learn things. I'd just been able to reproduce, to give people what they wanted in exams, to know exactly what the examiners were after and to give it to them, to deliver. And that it never was an honest wrestling with ideas. It was never trying to answer the question, it was trying to give the answer that I knew would give a pass.

CLARE: A worry I had with you today!

FRY: Yeah, exactly, and in the world you might say this is one of the both successful and terrible things about exams, that exams prepare people for the world because in this world you are rewarded if you are sly and facetious, facile, and very often you are not rewarded if you do honestly wrestle with ideas, and try to solve problems with thought and integrity. Very often people aren't interested in employing people like that. They want people who will, you know, click their fingers and make smart short-cuts. I think he always knew that I never really had to sit and think and I think that upset him. It upset him because he didn't like the idea of a world in which you could succeed and apparently be praised without ever having made any real effort. And also he didn't feel that he could rightly be proud of a son who just didn't fulfil himself, didn't realise himself, wasn't all that he could be. I was sort of aware of that and earlier on of course resented it deeply but, after university, I kind of understood it, you know, and I continue to understand it.

CLARE: The paradox is, of course, that those very qualities and abilities have taken you a long way.

FRY: Yeah.

CLARE: So you're left with this strange tension which is that that which isn't necessarily serious or work in the physicist's sense, has none the less given you and a lot of other people enormous amounts of satisfaction and, in your case, considerable rewards.

FRY: Yes, but, that was, that's the problem, that was the crisis.

CLARE: That is the problem?

FRY: Well it was.

CLARE: How was it resolved?

FRY: It was not something that gave me happiness. It was resolved by me realising that this simply was not enough, that it was a rainbow being chased and I can perfectly understand why people might say I should have such problems. I've always thought, for example, if there is one clear advantage, probably the only real advantage in having gone to Cambridge, is that I've never had to deal with the problem of not having gone to Cambridge, which a lot of people regard as a problem and feel that somehow if only they had, their life would have been better and easier. But, by having gone there, it's not a problem I have to deal with. Similarly, by having made a bit of money and a name for myself, I never have to deal with the problem of not having made a name for myself or becoming famous or whatever it is. But, it also means that because I have been there, I know that that is not an automatic route to fulfilment and happiness but that's very hard to express because it's very easy for people who are struggling in that direction to see me coming back from this golden city, footsore saying, 'Don't bother to go there, it's not worth it.' But they could say, 'So it's all right for you, you've been there, you've had all the pleasure of being there, don't tell me not to go there, I know if I go there I will be fulfilled and happy.' And I can fully understand why it sounds very easy to say that it isn't a satisfying way to be, because I have to admit that I have had a great deal of pleasure and happiness from my career in films but I know that it is not what will fulfil me or realise myself or whatever phrase one wants to use.

CLARE: I see what you're saying. It's a difficulty even running through this interview that you feel that you've been very fortunate, very talented, you've been given a lot of gifts, you've been to Cambridge, you've a very fine, agile mind, you've made a lot of money, you've got a public persona, so in a sense, if you say anything negative about these things, if you say that it can lead to difficulties, it has made problems for you, it's not all that it's necessarily cracked up to be, you're sounding like a whining luvvy.

FRY: Exactly, and I can quite understand why whining luvvies are immensely irritating to a large number of people. It's also a class problem.

CLARE: We'll come back to that, but the other problem is that if you don't do it, if you don't do it, then some of the people I see who are in dire straits, see people like you and say what is it about people like them that their lives are so perfect?

FRY: Absolutely, and indeed that's one of the things one realises when you have a public wobble, from the mail you get, it is that people are rather pleased, they're thrilled. It's not because they want to see you skid and fall, it makes them more fond of you. They'd rather see a fallibility and so on. And they also feel that it's rather encouraging to know that success doesn't give one total security.

CLARE: You mentioned class.

FRY: Well, only in as much as I think it is not something one can whinge about because it's, it's absurd to do so but to give you an example, I remember being in a bar with a friend who was also at Cambridge and we were having quite a serious conversation and a rather drunken woman came up and chatted to us and we sort of answered, and then she went away, then we carried on talking. She came up again and the other person said, 'Actually would you mind, we're having rather a private conversation?' and she said, 'Oh well, sod you, I thought you were supposed to be nice,' and off she went. And it really upset the other person. He said, 'Well, I mean, how nicer could we have been? You know, we listened to her, she was very drunk, very unpleasant,' and I said, 'Yes,' and the odd thing is, isn't it, is that if we had been, say, I don't know, Jimmy Nail and Robby Coltrane, and as soon as she'd come up first time we'd said, 'Why don't you bugger off?' she would have gone. You know, 'It's really great, Jimmy Nail's just told me to bugger off.' Part of the baggage you have to handle with a Cambridge or a public school education, is that you are expected to be a great deal nicer to people, a great deal politer to people, a great deal more dissemblingly cheerful and all the rest of it than someone else. I used Jimmy Nail perhaps unfairly but you know, then someone like Jimmy Nail, who everyone recognises, he's fought his way up from working-class routes, and he can say, 'Why don't you bugger off?' and people won't think any the less of him. Whereas people who are supposed to be smart and tidy and neat and grateful to the good fortune of their public school education and all the rest of it, have a sort of duty to be absurdly apologetic all the time, essentially. And as I say, it doesn't fit well to apologise for it because one realises that there are a lot of advantages in coming from a comfortable prosperous family, getting a classical education, going to what's perceived to be an excellent university and making good friends, and having the time to develop one's personality when young and in a way that other people don't. And so to complain about it is absurd because these are wonderful things that one wishes everybody could experience. On the other hand, I think there is no doubt that because we are a snobbish nation, the British, not usually in the sense that we look down on people of lower class, but we rather weirdly look up at people that we can perceive to be of, as it were, higher class. So that, for instance, you know, I can say 'fuck' on television and won't get any complaints, whereas if someone like Ben Elton says 'flip', it will get 300 people jamming the phone lines saying, I don't need to be addressed by this yapping Jack Russell of a vulgar man. Whereas I say 'fuck' in a nice tweedy accent and people go, 'Oh bless him, you know, he's a toff our Stephen,' you know what I mean? And it's sort of one of the things one plays with, you know, professionally, it's part of one's comedy to investigate that strange quality of the British. I get the impression that I sort of have to be something for other people, both people I know and people I don't know, that they are pleased to think of me in certain ways and they like the fact that I widen the gap more than others might. That I will suddenly leap from silly verbal games to rather direct emotional language in some speech about a charity thing, or whatever, and they will like that and think that's a good quality. But thus far and no further is the impression I get. Now, it, it's my own problem, it's not other people's problem, and I accept that.

CLARE: You've reminded me of something that you said of yourself. You said there was a time when you felt that you were the only person alive, that if you came around a corner everybody then hopped into their act and behaved, but you were the only really live person. It is not an uncommon adolescent vision. Everyone else is a kind of extra, that was the sentence I was looking for, I scribbled it down. How much, again risking you putting me down on this one, how much is this related to being a very bright little boy. Sir Peter Hall was another very bright little boy, enormously hard-working man, haunted I felt, certainly he told me he was, by never feeling he ever did anything that was really worthwhile. And again, he was the centre of a fair amount of expectation and attention because he was a bright little boy.

FRY: It's a very interesting point. I don't know how much it's to do with that. I think it's partly to do with that and partly to do with the fact that I've always felt I wasn't quite bright enough. If you are going to be very bright, I would like to have been just a bit brighter.

CLARE: This of a man who, I understood, memorised the *Guinness Book of Records*. Perhaps that is memory rather than intelligence?

FRY: It's just a sponge inside me and it soaks things up.

CLARE: It carries you through.

FRY: God it does, and that's the point. One can never separate in oneself how much is simply memory and ability to reproduce, a sort of mimetic gift, and how much is genuine intelligence. It's as if I have this perhaps fantastic idea that there is this thing that is intelligence, which is an ability to solve problems, academic problems, intellectual problems, not necessarily life problems, whereas the great chess player, mathematical prodigy, genius novelist or artist is as incapable of solving their life problems, their relationships as anyone else, often more so. So it's not as if I think that is an answer, but I just feel that if brightness is an explanation of me, it's not quite good enough because I'm not that bright. I know brighter people and it's brightness rather than real intellectual power, than real discipline. I am in many ways extremely lazy. I've relied on this memory and there are scholars, there are real thinkers, there are people who research and absolutely work at ideas and I know that I don't. I know that I don't read as much as I should because I'm so capable of picking up so much so quickly that I can carry on a conversation as if I've read lots of things that I actually haven't and that I've read things years ago and still remember and haven't re-read. Whenever I do re-read something that I've read that's important to me, I find that although I've remembered enough about it before, when I've re-read it now it means something different to me. That's not to say I don't read or that I'm entirely kind of shiftless and dishonest about things, but because I give this impression of intelligence it does make me wonder. How much of this intelligence is worth anything and how much is it simply like anything that is advantageous, like a skill at cricket or something that is charming and delightful for many people but has no real meaning in the sense that it is just a sort of games-playing ability with words and so on?

CLARE: Or like being tall?

FRY: Or like being tall or anything else, and it has no moral value.

CLARE: And what is that like?

FRY: Being tall?

CLARE: Have you always been tall, in the sense of being a tall boy?

FRY: Yes, I wasn't that tall until I was about 13 I think and then I started to shoot up very spectacularly. It's like what we were saying earlier about class and background and so on. Everybody can understand why short people put their chins up and it's considered rather impolite to mock them for it. No one is going to feel sorry for someone because they're tall, unless they're so extraordinarily tall that it's just embarrassing and they always think it's some kind of advantage. But like a lot of tall people, I keep one arm folded across the front of my body to kind of create a horizontal that breaks up the vertical and I stoop and I bend one knee and I cock my head and I never use my height as it were. If I actually were to use my height by stretching it would look extremely alarming I suspect and so I have that rather sort of stoopy . . .

CLARE: Diffident?

FRY: Apologetic physical attitude because one is aware that it's very off putting, particularly to people who regard themselves as short. Although one of the strange things is I've always regarded shortness as a very attractive quality.

CLARE: Would you prefer not to be as tall?

FRY: Oh absolutely, God, I hate it. I absolutely hated being tall, loathed it. The people I always admired at school were those kind of scrum-half types, those nippy, dodgy, balanced, active sort of children and youths and adults too. I think there's something kind of so splendid about slightness, neatness, agility. It's just a matter of the other man's grass being greener I suppose.

CLARE: And was there a stage at which you were really preoccupied about your tallness?

FRY: Yeah, I mean, if the wish fairy came along I would certainly have liked to have lost a couple of inches.

CLARE: But did it mean that when you looked at, say, a mirror image of yourself, you didn't like it?

FRY: No, no, not at all, never. I think like most people a mirror image one can sort of cope with because that's what you see every day, but one of the problems actors have is, and indeed increasingly ordinary human beings, is that, because of VCRs and things, they see real images of themselves. It used to be, as you probably know, that portrait painters would often paint people through a mirror because that's how they were used to seeing themselves and they couldn't cope with seeing themselves as others did. It's only in the last 100 years that human beings have been able to see non-mirror images of themselves on a regular basis on television and in photographs.

CLARE: In many of the things you say about yourself there is a certain kind of fear of failure which you share with a great many, a fear of losing control, or not so much losing control but certain anxieties in relation to that. There's a sense of not getting things right. We're back to relationships, of course, because you have to play them to an extent by instinct and each one is different to the other. There are in one sense no roles, or at a certain stage there are no roles and that's where I sense you get quite wary in a way?

FRY: The point is that eight months ago I entered a relationship and I think that has changed me to some extent, and my friends say it's changed me in ways that I'm slightly amazed because I don't think I have.

CLARE: Like what?

FRY: Well, they just say they've never seen me more relaxed and more cheerful or, you know, things like that, or more tactile. I've never been particularly tactile and I'm surprised they think I am now but they've actually said, 'You've started to put your hand on people's elbow when you want their attention and you never ever used to do that,' and I said, 'Did I really never do that?'

CLARE: You're not physical?

FRY: And they would say, 'Yes,' and similarly, 'One didn't put one's hand on your elbow because you didn't exactly flinch or blanch but because you were not the kind of person one would do that with whereas now you are,' and I honestly hadn't noticed this and they'd say this to me. And I'm very pleased that they should notice that I seem to be more relaxed and cheerful and I do feel I've embarked on this adventure and I'm enjoying it enormously. And part of what I'm enjoying is a kind of new-found, not exactly physical confidence, but much less of a physical lack of confidence than I used to have.

CLARE: And is there a sense in which you feel less of an enormous urge to do so many things?

FRY: Absolutely, to the extent that I'm slightly worried I'm actually never going to get anything done because I so relish now the idea of not working and of doing things that I would before have regarded as a waste of time. Like, you know, watching television for a whole evening or going for a drive along the coast or things that I just wouldn't have done really. The odd weekend, staying with people, if that's what they want to do, of course I'll do that, but usually I'll try and devise a game or, you know, something to structure the occasion, be the sort of larky, spare bachelor, who assumes he's been invited to these occasions in order to be pert and witty and make up limericks about people or whatever it is that one is supposed to do if you're the sad old uncle who's invited. But now I'm not part of that any more. I rather enjoy it, so much enjoy, in fact, pottering and mucking about and not working that maybe I'm going overboard in the other direction and I'll become a lazy old cuss.

CLARE: When you described to me earlier the garage and the duvet and the ignition, when you were really on the edge, when you were in that state, was your view of death different to what it would be now?

FRY: Yes, I assume, and again this is relying on the experience of past human beings, which is sort of cheating but it's also, it seems to me, the point of past human beings and what they write and think, I assume that death becomes more interesting to one as one gets older. I've never been in the least bit interested by death but I'm fully prepared for the possibility that in five years, maybe two years, maybe six months, I will become more interested in it in the way that human beings do as they age, and indeed obviously come closer to it.

CLARE: Even though on a couple of occasions you're flirted with death?

FRY: No, what I was interested in was life, and stopping it. Death as a positive thing was not what I was thinking about. The only thing that stopped me from ending my life was the fact that the death would have such a huge effect on people I cared about and I just couldn't, you know. That's the one thing that stopped me and in that sense the desire to please other people is a very healthy one because the only thing, I think, how can one know, but the thing I think that stopped me was the idea of how it would affect my parents and my friends. And I just felt that that was something that I couldn't do to them. But it wasn't death, you know, that I was wanting to embrace, it was just that I wanted to stop this pain, I just wanted to stop being alive, which was a miserable, seemed to me a miserable thing. But death, as a thing that I know a lot of people do think about and get more interested in as they approach it, has never really figured in my thoughts or worries. Like everybody I would quite like it if it comes for it not to be long, drawn out and painful but that's a worry about life being painful, it's not a worry about absence of life. I happen, like the Ancient Greeks, to believe that anybody who thinks they can tell you what happens to you after you're dead is either a liar or a fool because it is simply perfectly clear from all experience that nobody knows. Nobody has come back and told us and so it's a great mystery and a great adventure in that Peter Pan sort of way but it is not something I think about. I don't think it's particularly healthy or unhealthy to be very interested or very uninterested in death. I think it's just something that happens to you rather like I used not to be particularly interested in being Jewish but now I do find it more interesting, and I find it more interesting when I think of other people who are Jewish and think about the Jewish effect on our culture in the nineteenth century and, you know, famous Jews through the ages, or whatever. Fifteen years ago I was much less interested and that's not a conscious effort of will, it's just something that happens, it's like, you know, when you're 14 and hairs grow, or, or when you're four, language blossoms, or whatever. You know, whether it's pre-programmed or just part of what happens in a human being, certain things become more interesting to you at certain phases. In your early twenties, particularly in our field of comedy, there is no doubt that teenagers, late teenagers, have a really high, they would call it bullshit antennae, but it is a real high embarrassment of emotional language. We find it very easy to find things embarrassing, and a very good index of that I think is when you're 17, 18, 19, everything that's written in Pseud's Corner in *Private Eye* is pseudish and ridiculous. Suddenly you enter your thirties and you start reading things in Pseud's Corner that you don't think in the least bit ridiculous and you wonder why it's reproduced there and you think, 'Oh my God,' and you start getting angry with *Private Eye*. And then you start worrying about yourself, have I become pretentious, I don't actually think there's anything wrong with that, why is that considered pretentious, you know, and one observes in oneself again, at the risk of sounding very disengaged from myself, we observe in ourselves these sort of changes and they're there to be embraced, to be welcomed, the fact that one doesn't know what one is going to think and feel in five years' time. It is a very exciting thing about getting older. One continues to be surprised by what one always knew was going to happen, like the hairs were going to lose their pigmentation and skin was going to sag, we always knew that was part of the life, you know, from the age we were sentient, we could see and we were told that was what happened when you age, but none the less when it happens we still go 'Ah!' as if it's the most shocking thing. But the excitement is that one does get interested in other things and I suppose one day I will be very interested in death and start boring people with my ideas about death.

CLARE: Stephen Fry, thank you very much indeed.

Uri Geller

Interviewing Uri Geller was a very strange experience. For one thing I did not know what to believe. The interview is riddled with fantastic stories, colourful accounts, dramatic descriptions concerning events and influences in his life which make his notorious ability to bend spoons recede into the comparative insignificance of a party trick. Just consider some of his assertions. At six months, he remembers, *remembers*, a British soldier in Palestine shooting two bullets through the window and glass falling on to his pram. Aged ten, he claims to have rescued an Israeli pilot from a plane which crashed near his kibbutz. Aged 11 in Cyprus, he says he saw people killed in front of his eyes, people blown apart. He becomes an Israeli spy cycling around Nicosia with top secret material from Syria, Egypt and the Lebanon. He leads a UN convoy of tanks to the Turkish quarter in Nicosia to salvage a piano belonging to his stepfather. And all of this over and above his famous and notorious claim to be able to harness his strange ability to bend spoons, start and stop clocks, and read other people's minds. During the interview I suspend belief and disbelief. I let Uri Geller talk.

He is a charming, articulate, persuasive and exceedingly plausible man. Like the character Shaun in the breezy novel of the same name which he published in 1990, he is a very handsome, lithe, youthful man with effrontery, nerve, the Jewish word is best – *chutzpah*. He is a self-confessed entertainer and showman and he has a compulsive need to perform. Uninvited in the interview, he none the less offers and proceeds to bend a key in the BBC's basement studio. I decline to offer one of my own – for some reason Geller is able to bend a key but claims to be quite unable to unbend it and I want to drive home – so I suggest the car key of my producer, Michael Ember. True enough, after some gentle stroking by Geller, the key proceeds slowly to bend and continues to do so for some minutes after the stroking has ceased. I make it plain that I am impressed but that since I cannot fathom the simplest magic by the local town conjuror I am not a credible scientific assessor. I stay, as Uri Geller puts it, 'in the neutral zone'.

In this interview, Geller refers me to a paper which appeared in one of the world's most distinguished scientific journals, *Nature*, giving an account of a series of scientific assessments of his spoon bending carried out at the Stanford Research Institute between 1972 and 1974. The published paper was, however, accompanied by an editorial highly critical of the research methods employed. Geller's most persistent and bitter critic, the American magician, James Randi, who maintains he has duplicated Geller's performances, insists that the Stanford studies prove nothing.

Throughout the interview, I neither endorse nor dispute what Geller claims – a position similar, I understand, to that adopted by David Berglas, one of Britain's most accomplished magicians. He should stick to bending spoons and mending watches, sniff his doubters, and indeed he has done financially very well out of such activities. He owns a mansion near Reading, a Cadillac covered all over with assorted, suitably distorted cutlery belonging to the rich and famous, and has been the subject of a Ken Russell film. However, I am more interested to see what kind of picture Geller presents of himself. He does indeed exhibit many of the characteristics of the charlatan, the magic man – there are the mesmeric eyes, the seductive charm and physical attractiveness, the blatant egocentricity, the bombastic claims, the control freakiness. In this conversation, he refrains from elaborating on his more bizarre theories concerning dead extraterrestrials and universes in inner space preferring instead to list the three explanations he has for his 'power' (none of which involve conjuring). But I am aware of the proliferation of Geller paraphernalia which amounts to a complex and highly successful industry – a Uri Geller board game, a Uri Geller mineral prospecting company, a Uri Geller film, and a Uri Geller Mind Kit consisting of a tape, a small book, the *Mind Power Book* with a supportive quote from none other than Sir David

Frost, and a rock crystal, all designed to help us tap into our own potentially awesome mental powers.

In discussions I have had with people who heard my interview with Uri Geller, the commonest question asked is: 'Is he a con man?' The process of the con, of being conned is where one is put in a position of helplessness by someone else, a con man who makes the rules, knows the game and exercises total control over not merely the end result of the interaction, of the 'trick', but of the processes involved. The con man adopts an omnipotent position and maintains this illusion by a repeated enactment of behaviours which ensure that others are 'fooled', 'screwed', 'taken for a ride', are kept in a position of helpless dependence. Geller, quite apart from his spoon-bending, appears a man preoccupied by power and keeping helplessness at bay. He gives a history of addictive bingeing and vomiting which tapped his need to feel in control even when manifestly he was not. He experienced panic attacks – which are frightening precisely because they challenge a person's preoccupation with control. Many people negotiate fear and panic with only moderate difficulty – they are rarely too bothered by issues of control and hence do not react excessively at each and any suggestion that they might not be in as much control of themselves and their environment as they would wish. Those preoccupied or obsessed with control react to experiences of anxiety and panic badly. Bodily sensations appearing out of the blue – the palpitations, stomach churnings, sweating palms, dry mouth – threaten and accelerate unease into panic attacks precisely because they appear without being bidden and cannot be dispelled. It is as if biology decides to remind overweening psychology of a few basic physical realities. We cannot be in total control of our destinies. But Geller is obsessed with control, with physical fitness and with age, or rather with slowing down the ageing process and his beliefs in this area do suggest more than a touch of crankiness: 'You can,' he assures me, 'actually talk to your cells and you can actually instruct the ageing cycle to slow down.' It is not difficult to imagine a concoction of such ideas and beliefs solidifying into some kind of quasi-religious movement.

There are hints too that he is quite controlling in other areas of his personal and social life. But it is difficult to make any coherent sense of the life picture he paints. Perhaps his desire to be so intensely dominant does owe something to the disrupted and fragmented early years in Palestine and Cyprus, the separation from his father and his mother's remarriage. It is difficult to get any feel for close, intimate and loving family relationships. Geller appears to inhabit a world of drama and fantasy. The impression I come away with is that the histrionic and exaggerated quality of his early childhood and adolescent experiences persist into his adult life. He clearly is fascinated by the limelight, manifests a high degree of self-dramatisation and theatricality, and has a style of speech which is remarkably impressionistic if a little lacking in precise detail.

In general he does no great harm. He does not promise people healing, as many faith healers and so-called alternative therapists do, nor does he does arrange for bereaved and bereft individuals to be linked up with their dead relatives. He did once assert that a Swedish woman tried to sue him for an unwanted pregnancy caused, she insisted, because her intra-uterine device bent while she was watching him perform on television. Apart from that unlikely complication, Geller's trickery, if trickery it is, does not seem to be particularly sinister. He feels compelled to claim important political and diplomatic powers in adult life which sit side by side with the extraordinary statements he makes concerning his childhood. Mark Biedlinkmayier, acting executive director of the Arms Control and Disarmament Agency in Geneva, insists that Uri Geller was never invited to sit in on the arms limitation talks between the US and the Soviet Union in Geneva in 1987 to beam 'positive thoughts' at chief Soviet negotiator, Yuli Vorontzov. Geller insists that he was there and there is a photograph to prove it. The Department of the Environment has maintained a benignly sceptical view of Geller's claim that he stopped Big Ben in 1989, pointing out that the clock had a history of intermittent malfunctions and the claims of interference tend to come after rather than before the event. Geller remains convinced and can be extraordinarily convincing. The only certainty is that doubters and believers will continue to argue and the spoons to bend.

CLARE: At the height of his fame in the early 1970s Uri Geller was a truly controversial figure worldwide. Hailed by some as a psychic superstar courted by celebrities, politicians and heads of states, and denounced by others as an outright fraud, his ability to bend spoons, start and stop watches and apparently read people's minds, was the subject of some 15 books, innumerable articles and lengthy tests by scientists and magicians, with inconclusive results. The Geller phenomenon was best summed up by Ken Russell during the filming of *The Mindbenders*, which is based on the Uri Geller story. 'Only God knows,' says Russell, 'and He's not telling.' What is certain is that Uri Geller was born on the 20th December, 1946, in Tel Aviv, the only son of a Hungarian father, who later became a sergeant-major in the Israeli army, and an Austrian mother, who is said to be a distant relative of Sigmund Freud. Following his parents' divorce when he was nine, he lived for six years in Cyprus, where he learnt to speak English, joined the Israeli army at the age of 18, trained as a paratrooper and was wounded in the Six Day War.

Having achieved his childhood ambition to become rich and famous, he dropped out of the limelight, moved to England in 1985 and now lives in a picturesque village by the Thames in reputedly luxurious splendour where he cultivates his various business interests.

Uri Geller, most people, it seems to me, don't quite know what to make of you, but, what about you. Are you a puzzle to yourself?

GELLER: Oh, I think that my abilities, my powers puzzle me, not myself.

CLARE: You don't puzzle yourself?

GELLER: No, I think I know where I come from, I know where I'm going to, I don't know if I'll get there but it's the abilities I have. Many a time I describe myself as a little ant crawling between the jigsaw puzzle, you know, that game, and I'm sort of struggling in the lines, not being able to see the overall picture. If only something could just elevate me above this jigsaw puzzle, then I'd see the picture.

CLARE: And the picture, what would be the picture?

GELLER: Oh, I think it will be something to do with infinity, with untapped powers that come from the universe, from the cosmos, something to do with the creator, something very big that I will have difficulty in understanding myself.

CLARE: You said once, or wrote once, 'A lot of what has happened to me is due to my childhood.' What do you remember of your childhood? What's your first memory for example?

GELLER: OK. Strangely enough it is quite fascinating that I do remember, and this was when I was about, believe it or not, six months old. My mother put me in a pram under a window and she was playing cards with my father and friends in the main living room. Now, we lived in a very sort of shabby apartment near the railroad tracks, and on the other side of this, the tracks, there was a British post, because the British occupied Palestine at that time, and a British soldier shot two bullets into our window. And Anthony, I remember the glass shattering and sort of falling on to my face. I remember it in almost slow motion. So that's my first recollection.

CLARE: And did your parents talk to you about that afterwards? Was it a very frightening experience?

GELLER: It wasn't frightening. Nothing happened to me. I wasn't even scratched. Now, as years went by and when I was about four or five years old, I remember that I took a penknife and I actually got the bullet which had embedded itself in the other side of the room near the ceiling and I carved it out. And I used to play with that, pretend that it was a spaceship. I went down to the little garden we had and I pretended that the trees were a vast forest and I was some kind of an astronaut and this was my little spaceship, so we never really talked about that happening. My mother, you know, tells me that it was miraculous and that it was amazing that nothing happened to me.

CLARE: You were an only child?

GELLER: Yes.

CLARE: Do you know why, why your parents didn't have any other children?

GELLER: It's really a rather sad story now that you bring it up. My mother, believe it or not, was pregnant eight times. My father didn't want children. And I came, almost as consequence, of a fight with my father. My mother said, 'I want a child.'

CLARE: What happened to the other eight pregnancies?

GELLER: She had abortions.

CLARE: Goodness.

GELLER: Can you believe that? I learnt of that later on. So it's amazing that sometimes I feel that, who knows, maybe there are some guiding forces above me that, that were supposed to be my brothers or sisters.

CLARE: What was your father like? He sounds a controlling man. Was he?

GELLER: He was a controlling man because he was a military man. He was in the Hungarian army, then he joined the British army and became a sergeant. He fought Rommel in Tobruk in Northern Africa. Then he went to the Haganah, which was an underground movement trying to liberate Israel, and then he joined the Israeli army. So you see – military, very Germanic thinking. I remember that when I got out of bed if my shoe was half an inch misplaced he would immediately tell me to correct that. He was an extremely good looking man, he was very, very handsome. And I'll never forget this. When I was about six years old, he once took me to a coffee shop on the main street in Tel Aviv, and in it tens and tens of people were having coffee and cakes, and he entered the coffee shop and I was right behind him and Anthony, for 15 or 20 seconds there was silence. All the clattering of coffee cups and cutlery went dead silent, and everyone looked up. That was my father. He had such a presence and the military uniform made him look, you know, like a movie star. And that was very unfortunate for my mother because women were chasing him day and night.

CLARE: And what was he like with you? You gave an example about the shoes. What other examples have you of the way he would regard you or how he related to you?

GELLER: He was a good man, a loving person. For instance, one night he woke me up in the middle of the morning, it was like three or four o'clock in the morning. I was maybe six or seven, and he said, 'Uri, go to the balcony, I've got you something.' And I went to the balcony and I found a little puppy that he found in the street. He loved animals. No, he was a good father but there were the women and then there was the thinking, military thinking that was hard for me to understand when I was very young.

CLARE: Things like discipline?

GELLER: Yes, it was discipline, and I wanted to be like any other child, you know.

CLARE: What did he want for you? Was he ambitious?

GELLER: When both my parents discovered my powers, you know, when I started showing them that I could actually bend spoons and make watches move and clocks go to different hours, my father wanted to take me to a psychiatrist, strangely enough. My mother was saying, 'Just let it be, leave him, it's a talent, it's something he was born with.'

CLARE: But your father thought it was creepy or ill or something?

GELLER: It was bizarre. He thought it was, I was, it was freakish. Because we were poor they wanted me to be a doctor or a lawyer or something like that and they wanted me to be successful.

CLARE: And your mother, what was she like?

GELLER: Very hard-working, she was a seamstress and a waitress and she couldn't take the women. I remember also times when women would whistle up to my father from downstairs and my mother was working at the sewing machine and she was making money and he was spending it on all these women. So she had to divorce him and it was very hard. I was then around nine, ten years old, and I saw her struggle. Then from being a seamstress she became a waitress and I remember her pulling down tens and tens of times a day cappuccino machines, you know, working very, very hard. So I got a picture of what I'd got to get out of this. I'd got to make a lot of money to sort of give back my mother what she gave me.

CLARE: What happened to you when they split? Did you go with one or other of them?

GELLER: Yes, when they divorced they sent me to a kibbutz for one year, which was quite a strange experience for me because I was very, very homesick. I wanted to be with my dog.

CLARE: What age were you?

GELLER: Nine, ten.

CLARE: Why did they do that?

GELLER: Because there was a quarrel going on, there was a divorce going on.

CLARE: Was there a battle over you?

GELLER: Yes. My mother of course wanted to keep me, my father wanted to visit me more often and so on. But it was for them to sort out this battle so they sent me to the kibbutz. But it was a great experience for me that one year, being away from home. It's strange because I was more homesick for my dog than for my parents. It's very interesting, and I used to go out at night and look at the moon in the kibbutz. The kibbutz was in the south of Israel, and what relaxed me is knowing that that same moon, my mother could also see.

CLARE: Would you have been closer to your mother?

GELLER: Yes, yes, definitely.

CLARE: Do you remember the break up? Would you have been very upset or were you more detached over that period of time? What kind of ten year old, nine year old, eight year old were you?

GELLER: I was quite an intelligent ten year old because I knew it was better for them both and sort of went along my mother's wishes.

CLARE: You wouldn't have wanted them to stay together?

GELLER: No, because it was too late. If this had happened five years before that I would have thought, 'Yeah, I want them to be together.' But too many things went, you know, down the river.

CLARE: Was it distressing? Was there violence?

GELLER: No, there was no violence. None at all, but there was sadness and unhappiness, for my mother mainly. And you know, my mother was an old- and still is, an old-fashioned sort of Jewish mother, she would never dream about finding another man or sleeping with someone else. You know, the old values. So it was a very, very unusual childhood because of my powers, because of my parents divorcing, because of the one year in the kibbutz, it did a lot of things to me. There was an airforce base near the kibbutz, for instance, and one morning I told a teacher that I felt that something terrible is going to happen. And that day an Israeli jet crashed in the cornfields, and I ran there, I was the first to pull out the pilot from the cockpit and later on the same pilot, months after that, came and gave me a little gift from the airforce base. So, just being by a smoking jet and pulling out a pilot from the cockpit, bleeding and the parachute was half open. You know, that does something to a ten year old.

CLARE: And who else was there?

GELLER: Where?

CLARE: When that happened?

GELLER: Oh, the whole class ran to the fields because we actually heard the crash. And immediately we heard sirens from the airforce base, but we got there faster because the, the fields were really close to the school.

CLARE: What sort of little boy were you? Were you a loner?

GELLER: No, I had friends. Actually not long ago I met someone here in London, and he reminded me how we used to play together. No, I had friends and I had in a way a very normal childhood. It was a very Tel Aviv kind of surrounding.

CLARE: Would you have liked to have stayed on in the kibbutz?

GELLER: No, I hated it.

CLARE: Did you? Why?

GELLER: Because I had no privacy, everything was shared. Homesickness was the main thing.

CLARE: What do you make of the notion of the kibbutz as a method of helping people to develop independence, self-reliance, and yet at the same time to be collaborative and not to be too self-obsessed? The criticism of the modern nuclear family is of two little children being the centre of parental attention – in a kibbutz you were sharing with many of your contemporaries.

GELLER: You're asking me what I think today or what I thought then?

CLARE: What you thought then?

GELLER: I just didn't like it. There were scenes that were outrageous. My mother came once to visit me and she came with this man from Cyprus, a Hungarian Jew, who wanted very much to marry my mother, which they did actually. And my mother was wearing lipstick, and I was tortured for weeks after that because my mother was wearing lipstick.

CLARE: By the other kids?

GELLER: Oh yeah, by the kibbutzniks, who were born there. And there was another outsider, they used to call us outsiders, and he used to instruct his mother not to put nail polish on and not to wear make-up because they would make fun out of us after that. It was a no no in the kibbutz, there was no such thing as make-up, for goodness sake, that's a taboo. Everything changes. Today it's a whole different story. But then it was terrible, and so I was very, very much scared when my mother used to come and visit me.

CLARE: What do you think was the legacy of that? When you say, 'A lot of what has happened to me is due to my childhood,' what would you attribute to that experience? What's left of that whole kibbutz experience in the adult Uri Geller?

GELLER: I have to think about that. I think what it gave me is protecting my privacy. That's it. I remember since I left Israel I always looked to a house that would be very secluded and it would be on many acres and there'd be a big gate that no one could come and interfere with my life.

CLARE: Really? To an extent that perhaps mightn't have occurred had you not had that experience?

GELLER: Yes.

CLARE: Did any of your father's meticulousness, perfectionism, discipline, order, any of that rub off on you? As a little boy, did you keep things in a highly organised way?

GELLER: That's interesting, a very good question too because reflecting on my son, on Daniel, he's exactly like my father. I can't believe it. When I walk into Daniel's room and I move something on his cabinet, half an inch, he corrects it and he is very, very proper. When he takes off his clothes, everything is folded away. I mean it's unbelievable. So it's so interesting. Maybe my father's genes are in him. But I am exactly the opposite. My poor Hannah has to pick up my socks, and shirts and all that. I'm very, very clean, I've learnt that. I look at people's fingernails and that's what I've learnt from my father. If I see a little dirt that's a no no for me. So I'm very clean.

CLARE: Tell me, when you say it's a no no for me, what would you do?

GELLER: Oh well, you know, I'll give you an example. For instance, if I was some kind of an executive and I had to hire people to work for me or for the company, and they would enter the room, the first thing I would look at would be their hands, their nails – are they clean, are they black, dirt around the collar of the shirt? That's my first observation on people.

CLARE: So you're quite preoccupied by that?

GELLER: I'm not preoccupied by that. I just think hygiene is very, very important.

CLARE: Right, what else?

GELLER: I learnt that from my father.

CLARE: What else?

GELLER: I guess that's where it stops really because, I don't know what to call myself but when I go home and I take off my clothes, I don't fold them, I just hang them, here one, there one.

CLARE: What about punctuality?

GELLER: Yes, I try not to be late to meetings if I have to but then I've changed. I think I'm one of the very rare people that change their Type A driving character to that of a very relaxed person.

CLARE: Say more about that. You mean you were once . . .

GELLER: About 15, 20 years ago, I was very, very strict in things. I would shout at people, my secretaries, for instance. I used to surround myself with a lot of people who worked for me, and if things weren't done on time and things like that I would be very, very upset and very angry.

CLARE: Would you have been there driving, putting a lot into your day, chasing deadlines?

GELLER: Yes, yes.

CLARE: A Type A personality.

GELLER: Type A, that's what I said.

CLARE: Why did you change?

GELLER: Because I realised, Anthony, that life is too short and that, that's not what life is about.

CLARE: And why did you realise that? What provoked that change, because I'm interested in this.

GELLER: I think what I'm saying is that because people out there are struggling to make ends meet, it's the financial security that relaxes you, that puts peace of mind around you. I guess that's what it was. Suddenly from being very, very poor, and struggling, I became very, very wealthy. That metamorphosis changed over night. Suddenly it catapults you into a totally different dimension where you suddenly discover that you have more time, you can do what you want and not have to listen to other people, and that can lead you into a very relaxed life. And then I saw that my priorities were my children, my wife, nature, just enjoying life, the rustic way. And that totally erased all the punctualities and the order in my life.

CLARE: When you left the kibbutz you went back to your mother. Had she remarried then?

GELLER: Yes, she married the Hungarian Jew who lived in Cyprus, in Nicosia.

CLARE: And what was he like? That must have been quite a blow.

GELLER: He was a very, very nice man. Unfortunately, he didn't live long. He died one year after my mother married him. It was an incredible time for me because, you must realise, Cyprus at that time was going through a war, the Greeks were killing the British soldiers, the Turks were killing the Greeks, we were weeks upon weeks in curfews. He had a little pension, a hotel, a little 11-room motel. I've seen things that an 11 year old just doesn't see. I've seen people getting killed in front of my eyes, I've seen British soldiers shot from behind the back, I've seen little children on their backs fall on the ground. I've seen body parts, I've seen people blown apart, I've seen blood ooze from morgues that were next to our school. It was an incredible experience.

CLARE: How long were you in Cyprus?

GELLER: About six years.

CLARE: The reason I ask about your stepfather was that I understood from reading one or two of your books that you actually didn't like him, that you disliked him.

GELLER: I disliked him for one reason. I'll tell you why, I disliked him because they put me into a boarding school and the boarding school was like the kibbutz but it was even worse. My stepfather took me to a Catholic school out of all the schools in Nicosia. And I remember my first vision – we were driving towards Terra Santa College which was this Catholic school with fathers and nuns and the grass was cut out to look as a huge cross, that was the entrance to the school. So suddenly I'm being driven to this huge enormous place and all the teachers were wearing brown, you know, Vatican monks' clothes. So that was a terrifying moment in my life.

CLARE: And how long were you in the boarding school?

GELLER: About two years.

CLARE: Why did he pick a Catholic boarding school?

GELLER: Because it was the best school in Nicosia. But I must tell you of an incident that again melted this fear away. One day, Father Camillo, who was the head of the school, calls me into his office and he locks the door, and of course they all knew that I was the only Jew there and he said, 'Come close to me.' And so I come close to him, I didn't know what he was about to do to me and suddenly he starts unbuttoning his collar. And then he pulls out a bunch of little trinkets on a gold chain, and there was a cross there and then came Mary and a St Christopher's medal. And suddenly he pulls out a little Star of David from behind all the crosses and he says, 'Look, I'm wearing it.' And that was it for me. Again, totally, all the barrier that had built up between Jews, Judaism and Christianity disappeared, evaporated, and I knew that this is it, there were really no religions, there was only one God and that was a God I always believed in.

CLARE: Even though I assume in the school you would have been exposed to some baiting as the only Jew in a Catholic school?

GELLER: No, I was just accepted as all the other kids.

CLARE: Some people would expect of this childhood – the separations and the kibbutz and then a Catholic boarding school as a Jew, a stepfather and so on – that it would have left a variety of marks on your character or would have moulded you in certain kinds of ways. For example, that it would have made you emotionally wary, careful of people?

GELLER: Well, it didn't do anything to me. Now I look back at my childhood and the early twenties as little sort of clusters of lessons that I had to go through.

CLARE: But what about your feelings at the time? All these sort of things happen to you caused by these adults – your parents warring, then you go to a kibbutz, then you're taken out of the kibbutz, then your mother marries again, then you're off to a Catholic boarding school, then you're out of a Catholic boarding school. Given what I've no doubt we'll talk about subsequently, namely this issue of power and control and prediction, I am struck that the childhood of Uri Geller was a childhood where you had little power and certainly not much control. That's what I'm struck by – the, the sense in which, as you describe it, you're a bit like a cork bobbing about on an ocean that's been stirred up by other people.

GELLER: Well, I have to disagree with that because what I derived out of it, what I sort of was exposed to is things that happened around me without my control, but, as a person, as me, as Uri Geller, as a little human being, I had to swim in this turmoil and I had to make rules for myself, so I actually got energy from this. I learnt from it. I became a little grown up in a boy's body. That's what it gave me and it taught me a lot, I must tell you. So I was very much in control. Actually I was in such control that, at the age of 14, I led a convoy of tanks to the Turkish quarter in Nicosia to salvage a piano that belonged to my stepfather that was rented in a hotel. And I told the UN soldiers what to do and, and I was only 13 or 14, so I became a little person.

CLARE: So, as ever, the psychiatrist can be right either way! What you're saying is that I'm right in that it was a very unpredictable world but it taught you to exercise control.

GELLER: Exactly.

CLARE: Would you say that you were an adult in a little boy's body – it was that kind of childhood, was it?

GELLER: I would say.

CLARE: Leaving aside for a moment the powers you describe in terms of your effect on inanimate objects, I'll come back to that; what about your power on people? The example you give, which sounds rather extraordinary, of leading this convoy of tanks, did you become aware early on that you actually had an effect on other people?

GELLER: Leaving my powers aside?

CLARE: Yes, yes – that you as a person had an impact on others?

GELLER: I had an impact on others but it came naturally, it came automatically because of the circumstances.

CLARE: You mean you didn't have to work on it?

GELLER: No, you must understand I'm not telling you a lot of things because this interview is not that long. Our hotel turned out later on to become an Israeli spy safe house and I met Israelis who went to spy in Arabic countries and they would do all the dealings in the hotel and I was actually asked to be a courier boy for top secret material that would come in from Syria and Egypt and Lebanon to our hotel. And I would bicycle it to the head, the ambassador or the consul at that time in Nicosia. So I was going through all these phases and yes, I had to have responsibility very, very much so. And that responsibility gave me, in a way, credibility and respectability in the eyes of the people who were around me, so it was an automatic thing.

CLARE: An image that stuck in my mind from early on in this interview is that description of you as a little boy going with your father into a café and his presence, which I think people would call charisma, certainly his presence had this effect on people. Reading about you now, as distinct from the spoon bending and the mind reading and the influence of other people, just leave that for a second – there is something of this charisma, there's something of that about you, or certainly about the way you would like to be.

GELLER: Oh, of course. Come on, I mean Anthony, you know very well that when you have a good looking person, you know, that has also charisma, and that person is given a gift of being able to entertain other people, they are more successful in life than not good looking people, I'm not saying that out there there are no successful not good looking people, but I was lucky to have been born in a way handsome. And again, you listeners out there, I'm not boasting or anything like that, but I had that sort of thing from my father and that helped me terribly in my career, you know. Because there I was, a young 20 year old, I was a model, you know I modelled clothes and all that.

CLARE: Yes, how long did you do that for?

GELLER: For about two years and that also came by coincidence. One of my girlfriends dragged me to this photographer and a male model didn't show up and the photographer looked at me and said, 'Hey, you're pretty good looking, come on, why don't you do it instead of him?' So, suddenly, I found myself in double-page spreads in the Israeli newspapers, not as Uri Geller but as a model. So, of course, it helps to have good looks. Everyone will tell you that.

CLARE: And how early were you aware that you had an impact on other people?

GELLER: When I suddenly found myself in newspapers as a model. But I think I already had an impact on people when I was demonstrating my powers in school, but that was another impact.

CLARE: Did you do that at school?

GELLER: Oh yeah, I used to tell children to bring in their keys and I didn't like school and I used to manage to move the clock an hour ahead. Now, Anthony, although this is radio I know, and I'm sure you're not expecting this to happen, but I do want to demonstrate to you what I do, and it's fascinating. I know these keys here are not mine, you know, I don't know whose this key is but I'd like to show you ...

CLARE: I think they're my producer's so do what you will with them!

GELLER: These are your producer's?

CLARE: Yes.

GELLER: I want you to hold these two and I want you to observe very carefully what I do. If I begin to stroke the key very gently, you can describe what I'm doing.

CLARE: He has got the key, one of the keys of my producer, the key of Michael Ember's car I fear and he's ...

GELLER: And I'm saying 'Bend'.

CLARE: And he's rubbing very gently this brass key.

GELLER: Look, it's beginning, it's beginning ...

CLARE: And he's ...

GELLER: See, it's beginning to bend upwards.

CLARE: Yes, I have to confess ...

GELLER: And this is not an illusion.

CLARE: I have to confess that, yes it's certainly bent enough to ensure that my producer will have to take the underground home.

GELLER: Look, I just want to show this and it is not sleight of hand, it's not chemicals.

CLARE: Now, you did that at school?

GELLER: Oh yes.

CLARE: And what did they make of you?

GELLER: Oh, the kids loved it because it was entertaining. Some, the teachers thought that it was magic, that I had some kind of chemical.

CLARE: The endless argument that goes on to this day.

GELLER: And then they saw it happening so many times that they knew it was real and they accepted it, like all the other scientists that tested me. And you know, this is a thick key, there's no way to bend this physically even.

CLARE: And what is your explanation? Do you know how it's done? If it's not magic how is it done?

GELLER: I have no explanation to what bends the key. I have theories. I want to believe that my mind is doing it, that there is either a frequency that goes into the key when I stroke it or the spoon.

CLARE: But you have to stroke it?

GELLER: No, no, in laboratories I was not allowed to touch the spoon. They were put in glass tubes and bell jars and they bent also. And look at your producer's key, it continues to bend. You see, I'm not touching it any more, you know, but still, you have to admit that it continues bending.

CLARE: Well yes, now, I fear he'll be travelling in the underground for some considerable time because it is bent considerably.

GELLER: And I'm not trying, yet for two or three minutes it continues. Now I'll tell you, given you asked me what I think it is. Unfortunately, the scientists who tested me, they validated the power, because I've done it under controlled conditions, but they cannot capture this energy on any tool, on any computer. They've put magnetometers, they've put electrometers. There is nothing that registers the power, the energy that goes into the metal and bends it.

CLARE: And is there any suggestion that your brain is more powerfully active at some period during the bending?

GELLER: Some EEG results come looking strange but there is nothing really conclusive on what this power is. Mind you, I don't know how much you studied about me, but many years ago there was already a paper published in *Nature*, 16 pages long.

CLARE: Oh yes, I know about it. Why is it that, as I understand it, now you tell me if I'm wrong, there is only one Uri Geller?

GELLER: I don't know. You know, this is something that has been bugging me for years. Actually, I'll tell you what I've done to discover another Uri Geller. I've just created a Web site on the Internet and I've placed a spoon on my Web site and that spoon is being filmed 24 hours a day and the real live image of this spoon is being televised on to my Web site, and I'm offering people a million dollars to try to bend the spoon. And I do believe someone will do it. A child, a teenager.

CLARE: But let's stay with you for a moment about this power. You've just bent this key, all right. Now, you're very well known, and certainly in the 1970s you were exceptionally well known. And your phenomenon, this key bending, was well known and it was demonstrated on television round the world. So if people haven't come forward with this ability then I'm puzzled and I think to myself that if this is a mental power, you know, telepathy, an ability to predict, the ability to read minds, the ability to influence inanimate materials, why shouldn't it be found in many other people? And you're well known so it's not as if people don't know about this.

GELLER: All right, the answer is simple. I'll tell you what the answer is. When I appear on television, I can trigger this power in people, mainly in teenagers. And they can do it for a few minutes. I mean my last programme with David Frost, 13 million viewers, and out of 13 million viewers, 2.6 million people called up the station. Actually, the British Telecom in Scotland blew up because it stopped functioning for five minutes because of the massive response. Now, those people weren't lying. They were reporting something that happened to them. The question is, why doesn't it last in people? Why am I triggering it only for two or three minutes or maybe for a day? I don't know. There are certain things that I can't explain.

CLARE: Of course the other problem is that you're dealing here with a novice. I don't understand how magicians do the simplest things. I hasten to add that lest people start ringing up here and say, 'What's all this about blowing up power stations, what on earth is he on about? This man is an absolutely brilliant magician.' Let me come back to something else, though, about you and that is the extent to which this power has changed you. Now, your life has been much altered in material terms, I accept that. What about the effect of all this on you as a person? Has there been a down side for you?

GELLER: Oh yes, you know when you come from a poor family and suddenly you earn vast amounts of money and fame – overnight I became world known. It was just incredible how in one day I was headlines all over the world. What it does to you? It puts stress, definite stress on you. And I'll tell you what happened to me. You know some rock bands who make it suddenly, they go into drugs, some go into alcohol. What happened to me was very strange, for a man. I suddenly got bulimia. I know what triggered it. A producer looked at me and said, 'I want to make a movie based on your life story but I want you to lose weight.' And because I wanted to keep everything, all my materialistic possessions, this was about 18 years ago, I even wanted to keep food. It was that deep, that psychological. I wouldn't even let food go. So what I did is I binged, and very secretly excused myself away from the table and I started vomiting. I thought I was inventing it. I didn't know there was a thing like bulimia.

CLARE: What age were you about then?

GELLER: This was about 18 years ago.

CLARE: At the height of your fame?

GELLER: Yes, and I didn't even want to give food up, can you believe that. And I was killing myself, slowly, because I was getting weaker and weaker. I went to very laborious ways to hide the bulimia, like stuffing towels under the doors of the bathrooms and drowning the noise of vomiting with showers and toilets flushing. It was unbelievable what I went through to hide it.

CLARE: And did you lose weight during this bulimic phase?

GELLER: Oh yeah, I went drastically down to almost 58 kilos, 60 kilos. And then, one day, in Manhattan in New York, I couldn't get out of my car I was so weak. I had to lift my hand and pull myself out of my car, clutching the roof and as I was struggling towards my apartment doorway, I said to myself, 'I'm going to say now, one, two, three, and I'm going to say stop, and I will stop this vicious cycle.' And I did it. I said, 'One, two, three, stop.' And I summoned my willpower and it never came back to me again. I stopped this addiction, it was an addiction.

CLARE: How long had it gone on for?

GELLER: For a year.

CLARE: Did anybody know of it?

GELLER: No.

CLARE: Were you married at that stage?

GELLER: Yes, I was with Hannah. Hannah thought that I was losing weight because I was over-exercising. I knew how to hide it away. It was fascinating too because that's when I realised that willpower is so strong and we all have willpower. It's dormant in most of us.

CLARE: You didn't take alcohol?

GELLER: No.

CLARE: And you weren't a drug taker?

GELLER: And I don't drink, I don't smoke.

CLARE: You're not someone who loses control in that sense?

GELLER: No.

CLARE: But this was an addiction that allowed you, in a sense, to retain control?

GELLER: Yes. And it was just my thing, it was just . . .

CLARE: A secret?

GELLER: A secret, my thing. I didn't share it with anyone.

CLARE: Did you get depressed about it?

GELLER: Not depressed but I got concerned because it was an addiction.

CLARE: Well did you get frightened, for instance, that it was out of control?

GELLER: Concerned, not frightened.

CLARE: Not frightened?

GELLER: Concerned, and I said to myself, 'Am I the only person in the world that has it?' Because I thought I had invented a great way of losing calories. Eat, eat, eat, vomit, vomit, vomit.

CLARE: I read that at some stage you developed panic attacks, you got panicky. Was it around this time?

GELLER: It was around this time. That is strange. It was attached to bulimia in a way. It's a very interesting phenomena.

CLARE: Do you remember where you got them?

GELLER: Where?

CLARE: Yes.

GELLER: Where I used to be alone. Once I went running in Spain, somewhere in Barcelona, and I'll never forget it. I found myself alone out somewhere in the wilderness in the outskirts of the city, and I thought, 'I'm going to die.' It was just a panic attack. You feel your heart race 200 beats per minute and you think you're going to drop dead and there was no one to help you. There was no one around. So then you even get more scared and then you run faster and it is as if you see civilisation on the horizon there, you know, you're getting closer and closer to it and you feel more secure and more secure.

CLARE: Did it get to the stage where you wouldn't go into certain situations?

GELLER: No.

CLARE: No. You never got panicky about getting panicky?

GELLER: No, I think the anxiety and panic attacks were because I was losing so much weight. I was so thin that I almost damaged, started to damage my nerves.

CLARE: You're involved in things like fitness, jogging, exercise, nutritious diet, you take care of yourself.

GELLER: Because of that. That triggered my sort of entering into a healthy way of living.

CLARE: I wondered what you feel about the one thing that none of us seems to have any control over and that's getting old?

GELLER: Well, look, I believe that you cannot stop the ageing process, no way. You can't stop getting old. But I'm trying for myself and for my family to try to slow the ageing process. And you can do that, definitely, that works.

CLARE: How do you do it?

GELLER: Oh, by eating the right foods, by taking the right vitamins, by lowering stress, by exercising. Your mind is very powerful. I've found ways – I call it mirrorising. I do it maybe once every week. I just look and I say to myself, in my mind actually, you know, I wrote about it in my Mindpower Kit, about how to slow the ageing process. Because we are built out of so many billions and billions of cells, those little cells are little worlds in themselves. You can actually talk to your cells and you can actually instruct the ageing cycle to slow down. You can't stop it but you can slow it down. And it's something that I look at as very natural.

CLARE: How do you know you can slow it down?

GELLER: Because I look at myself. I look at my inner self. I feel great. I'm going to be 50 in December. I'm fitter today than when I was in the paratroopers when I was 18. Mentally I'm fitter. I'm happy. I don't think I look my age. My body's my barometer for that.

CLARE: You can, of course, spend so much of your time ensuring that you live longer, that it interferes with the process of living at all. You know, you're paying so much attention to your diet and your exercise and your sleep and your waking, your emotional temperature and so on.

GELLER: Well, if people say that then they're wrong because I enjoy what I'm doing. It's strange because in 1972, Anthony, when I was boarding that El Al flight out of Israel, into the world, as I was walking up the stairs of the plane, I said to myself that I'm going to look at my life as one big vacation. No matter the ups and downs and the struggles that I'll have to go through, I will look at it as some kind of a gift from God and mould it as something happy, a big happiness, a vacation. And I've never stopped thinking that way.

CLARE: Do you find yourself given to talking to yourself? I don't mean in any psychotic sense, I mean in the sense of reflecting with yourself about life, having a conversation with yourself about how you're doing, how you're experiencing, what's happening to you, where you're going.

GELLER: No, my conversations are with God, and that's a form of prayer. I do reflect about my life when I pray to God, which I do every day. That's, that's, that's the only time I find myself talking to, to something.

CLARE: Now that example of going up the steps of the El Al plane, you were reflecting with yourself. God wasn't entering into it at that time?

GELLER: No, but I was giving myself some kind of a role in life, it was just something that I did then. But remember, since 1972 I've changed a lot. So it's hard for me to look back at what happened to me, you know, 27 years ago and bring it into today's life. But I do believe in the power of prayer. I don't go to synagogues but I do, every morning, I put up my hand on my head, you know like the Jewish custom, you have to wear a *yarmucka*, but I put my hand. And I just thank God for everything he has given us and I look at my life as one day. For me a day is a life, and then next day is another life and so on and so on and so on until the day I'll die.

CLARE: Do you think of yourself as Jewish?

GELLER: Yes, yes, but I don't believe in religions. I think there are no religions. I think there is one God and that's it. And that the religions, Christianity, Judaism, Islam and Hindu, all are just customs that we formed as the centuries went by.

CLARE: And in terms of one of the great religious questions, and that is the question as to which there is another life, what's your belief about that?

GELLER: There's no doubt in my mind that afterlife does exist. There is no way you can destroy energy in your body. That is the soul, the spirit, I am sure.

CLARE: How about you as a person?

GELLER: I believe in life after death.

CLARE: Will you survive afterwards?

GELLER: Everyone will. Everyone will. My soul will go somewhere. Don't ask me where because that's another whole thing, philosophy and so on. But I do believe that some people can reincarnate if they want to come back.

CLARE: Oh you mean it's a matter of choice?

GELLER: That I don't know, I don't really know. But some people do come back, they reincarnate. Some people stay haunting a place and they are a form of ghosts. Some people do go to Paradise, some people do go to Hell. I believe in that, I believe in the old way of thinking.

CLARE: Your father is dead isn't he?

GELLER: Yes.

CLARE: He is still contactable or available or accessible?

GELLER: Of course, of course.

CLARE: Not just in terms of a memory now?

GELLER: I get signs from my wife's mother, trivial signs to you or to your listeners, but for instance, almost every time my wife's mother's birthday comes along, a little bird flies into our conservatory. Why didn't that bird fly in a day before or a day after? Or on someone's anniversary, you know, the day they died, the alarm system in my house will go on, you know. Things like that give me the sense that they are saying, 'Hey, we're around, we're looking, we can see you, we can hear you.'

CLARE: Did you ever think that this power of bending keys emanated from somewhere else?

GELLER: Yes. I have three theories, Anthony, and I'll tell them very quickly. The most believable one is that it's coming from our minds, and we all have it, I have it a little stronger, I don't know why. The next theory is that maybe I'm tapping into some outside force in the universe. I'm just tapping into it and it allows me to do this. And the third one, which is the most unbelievable one, is that it is extraterrestrial. This is the most strange one, that there is a UFO out there, somewhere and it is maybe a little extraterrestrial child that ran away from its parents and it's playing little tricks with me. That's the third theory.

CLARE: Do you know, you've reminded me, there was something I wanted to ask you. I read, you wrote a novel.

GELLER: Yes, *Shaun*.

CLARE: Called *Shaun*, which is a very interesting novel. It's about a young extraterrestrial who comes to earth with this preternatural ability. I think he can crush grenades.

GELLER: Yes, and turn them into oranges.

CLARE: That's right. You published it in 1990 and it rather intrigued me. There's a rather cynical publisher in it called Codewaller.

GELLER: Yes, Codewaller, from America.

CLARE: Yeah. At one point he says of the ET, of Shaun, who incidentally gets I think rather fed up with the world and the way it treats him and he goes back. He says of him, just let me quote this, he says of Shaun, 'He's going for the big lie and he's sticking with it. What else can he do. Still, it's a temptation. He could cop out, couldn't he? No, not really, he couldn't. He said he's from up there and so if he admits now that he isn't, that he's just like you and me, then he's through, isn't he?' And, actually, on the same page, I'd written, 'People want to believe in magic, but the ultimate magic is that magic is not magic.' I wouldn't know how you do this, or how you do any of this.

Only you know in a sense. And, the paradox is that if you're like Shaun, or if you are Shaun and you're some kind of force, fine. If you're the Codewaller Shaun, if you're . . .

GELLER: The magician?

CLARE: That's right, then there's no way you would ever say to anyone like me, that's what I am, because the whole thing rests on this mystery.

GELLER: Look . . .

CLARE: You are as fascinating because you can do this, as you are fascinating because we don't know how you do this.

GELLER: Anthony, I'll tell you something. You are a brilliant interviewer because you're very clever to stay in the neutral zone. You know, many, many broadcasters shout, 'Wow! The key's bending, you're great, it's the power of the mind.' But you're careful and I take my hat off to you on that because, you know, it's an important programme, you're credible, it's prestigious and you have to stay in the middle, not believing either this or that. But I must tell you that what you've seen here today is real. The key continued bending on the table and whoever's key it is will attest that it was straight before. Yes, I love the mystery around it.

CLARE: Yeah, you do, that's honest.

GELLER: But believe me.

CLARE: You do like the mystery around it?

GELLER: Even if this were not real, I could probably now come up with this big, bestselling book entitled, *How I Fooled the Whole World*, but I can't do it because I didn't. It is real and to the conversation, the mind is mysterious and it works in very odd and bizarre ways sometimes. And I like the controversy around me – up to a point, by the way. I will not take people libelling me and defaming me. That I will not take because I sue people for that.

CLARE: Yes and you've been in some intense controversy.

GELLER: But the mystery is something that we are indulging in. It's the powers out there. Is there life after death? Is there religion? Can the mind bend metal? And that's the essence of life. Do you understand?

CLARE: I do.

GELLER: Let it be mystery. So the controversy actually propelled me to stardom in a way, you can say that. And I love it when people are still mystified and I like it to be that way, although if people do their homework and read all the scientific books that were published about me, it will sort of explain that Uri Geller, what he does is real but there is still no explanation to it. And I will be very disappointed when there will be an explanation, very.

CLARE: Will you?

GELLER: Yeah, I'd like to go on into another life and let the explanation come then. Do you understand me? When finally science will be able to build some kind of device that will be able to capture the energy that moves from my mind into the key and makes it continue bending. That's when I'm finished, because that's when the mystery will be wiped out.

CLARE: Well, let me ask you something else, much more cynical and corrupting. I think to myself, that if I had these abilities I might well use them to, I don't know, put a couple of thousand pounds on a horse running in the three o'clock at Wincanton or I would build a fortune. Now of course you have built a fortune. I remember the 1970s very well, Uri, and I remember the extraordinary publicity and the fact that your name was everywhere and so a bit of me says, 'He made a fortune, a fortune accumulated through this enormous influence resulting from the fact that he became a world name.' Have you put to personal effect powers which seem to me to include an ability to forecast the winner of the 3.30? You have talked about being able to influence soccer players for Reading to score goals against Manchester United. What about the ability to say what's going to win the Ascot Gold Cup?

GELLER: Yes. There are many things that I can't talk about. I would say 98 per cent of the things I do privately I cannot talk about. I've made a rule in my life. But I have used my powers to find oil for big major mining companies. I've found gold for mining companies. I've found diamonds for big corporations. And I dowsed very successfully with my powers so I became multimillionaire from that.

CLARE: Are you plagued, by people like me writing in and saying, 'Uri, can you help find diamonds in such and such a place?'

GELLER: All the time. People come up to me with the lottery, to predict the lottery and all that, sure. I mean even coming in here into the building, there were two people downstairs asking me to choose them the six numbers.

CLARE: Did you?

GELLER: Strangely enough I'm mystified. Why am I allowed to find oil, but I'm not allowed to gamble? Because I tried and something terrible happened to me. That's a mystery to me.

CLARE: What happened to you?

GELLER: I once went into a casino in London and I won at that time what was a lot of money, £17,000 sterling, and the next day I was being driven in a limousine somewhere and I heard some terribly loud noise in my head, it was like shouting at me, and I got so scared that I grabbed the driver. I actually smashed the glass partition between us, because it was this big limousine, and I started shaking the driver and he stopped the car. And the door opened, like an invisible hand opening it, and I was thrown out of the car and I felt a massive weight on my chest and body. And I threw out the money on the M4, £17,000, they were all in bundles in rubber bands, and I never gambled after that happening. So the mystery to me is why am I allowed to fly in an airplane and open maps and point to big mining companies where to drill, but I cannot try to do the lottery and I'm not going to go into a casino. I don't know.

CLARE: But that story suggests that your power is under some kind of external influence?

GELLER: It could be.

CLARE: No, no, no. There's no 'It could be' about it. You've just described an example which on your own testimony means it is.

GELLER: Who knows?

CLARE: When you say 'I'm not allowed,' and as you said it you actually pointed upwards, 'I'm not allowed to gamble,' you said, that suggested to me that there's some kind of external power that regulates this gift.

GELLER: But, Anthony, I told you my three theories.

CLARE: You did.

GELLER: One of them is right, which one, I don't know.

CLARE: Yes, but let me just take you back through it again. You're in a taxi. You've been gambling the night before. You've got £17,000 in rolled notes in your pocket. You're driving along in a chauffeur-driven car and you have this experience.

GELLER: Yes, so what are you asking me is whether it's an external power, governing me or is it coming from my mind? Maybe it was me, maybe it was my inner conflict telling myself never to do it, and it translated it in such a way that it scared me and it was me shouting at myself, and it was me building an energy force around me, being able psychokinetically to open the door of the car and some force grabbing hold of me, throwing me out of the car. I will never know those things. I can't say I will never know because I never know what will happen to me tomorrow, but it's a feeling I have that either this power is totally coming from my mind, or it's totally coming from an outside force.

CLARE: Do you have a feeling one way or another about people's beliefs in you? For example, do you want people to believe that this is mind power? You wrote somewhere, 'I'm an entertainer for goodness sake, I'm a showman, I never wished anyone ill, I never stole anyone's money.' Now, I wondered the extent to which actually you quite like the controversy. That it would be awful not only if science could show how this is done but if everybody believed it to be what you believe it to be?

GELLER: Yes, I would like people to believe in what I do, when I show them what I do. I'm not going to force anyone. I can't force anyone to go out and buy my books or buy the videos or come to my lectures. It's up to you people out there to decide whether you want to see Uri Geller or not. I can't force anyone.

CLARE: Tell me something, why don't you now live on your laurels?

GELLER: And not do anything?

CLARE: Yes, move from a Type A, driving, driven kind of life to just living your life as a vacation, as you put it?

GELLER: Because, Anthony, I enjoy doing what I'm doing. I wouldn't be sitting here otherwise. Why am I here today? Because I've got a Mind-Power Kit out which I'm promoting and I love to promote it because I want a lot of people to buy it. Besides, a big piece is going to Save the Children, which is a good charity and it's a good cause. So, I'm doing what a singer would be doing, you know, promoting his record, or his CD, or a movie actor promoting his movie.

CLARE: Is this a power that's inherited. Did either of your parents have it, will your children have it?

GELLER: I don't know. My parents, I don't think they had it. Daniel, my son, can do telepathy with me quite incredibly, I mean, it astounds me, but he can't bend spoons or keys.

CLARE: He can't? By telepathy, you mean he can read what you're thinking?

GELLER: Yeah, telepathy is something that, if you don't mind, I'll demonstrate to you. Take this marker, I will turn away and close my eyes, believe me, I will not look. I want you to draw here something very simple, and then cover it with your hand. I'm not looking, go ahead. Tell me when it's finished. Draw it big, simple.

CLARE: Very simple.

GELLER: Yes. Anything that you want but something you can visualise in your mind. Did you finish your drawing?

CLARE: Yes.

GELLER: You have to cover it so I don't see it. Your people in there [the recording studio] didn't see it either, I hope. Can I look now? You didn't see it. Now. But you did draw something, you didn't leave it blank?

CLARE: No, no, no, I drew something.

GELLER: Now, I'll demonstrate to you now telepathy. I close my eyes and I visualise, like a TV screen in my mind and into the screen I have to get your drawing. And many a time my hand draws it millimetrically, the same size. Keep drawing it, Anthony, keep drawing it over and over, I'm getting something. Keep drawing it over and over in your mind. Yes. I'm getting something but it's not a drawing. What I'm getting Anthony is, usually when I tell people to draw something they either draw a house or a tree or a flower, but I'm getting more like a shape, a geometrical shape and that's basically it. And I'll show you what I'm getting, something like a diamond shape. [Geller shows Clare a drawing of what he thinks Clare has drawn.]

CLARE: That's exactly what it is.

GELLER: I did it, exactly. Look. Wait now, wait a minute. Now comes the mystery. I'm going to show you something that is quite mind blowing. If I measure my line from here to here and now we'll measure your line from here to here. It's the same size. You take a ruler later on and you will see that it's millimetrically identical.

CLARE: I believe you!

GELLER: Millimetrically the same size, so sometimes I wonder. OK, telepathy, I read your mind, I can see the image in my mind. But how does my brain hold my hand, control my hand, with a pen, and make it the same size? I'm astonished myself at this.

CLARE: You are? You're constantly surprised?

GELLER: Yes I am. To be very honest with you I am.

CLARE: I suppose one could say, 'Well, given this ability, what do you want to use it to do?'

GELLER: Well, I have a fantasy in my mind at this stage of my life. I've been studied at big American universities and laboratories, one of them was a place where they build atomic bombs. And the Americans asked me to do many things throughout my life when I worked for them, and just lately the chairman of the American Foreign Relations Committee, Senator Claiborne Pell, and actually Vice-president Al Gore, they invited me to the Nuclear Arms Reduction Treaty and my task was to bombard the Russians to sign the nuclear arms, the nuclear treaty, a guy called Yuli Vorontzov and I was there in the room sending my vibes and saying, 'Sign, sign, sign.' So you ask me what is left; my dream is I hope that soon, somehow, three or four billion people, billion, will be able, will be united together, through the media, through a television show like, like the end of the Olympics, where there are four billion people, and instead of bending a key, or instead of saying, one, two, three, work, to a watch, I would like to see four billion people saying, one, two, three, disarm, because right now, Anthony, while we're sitting here in a London studio, there is a nuclear weapon aimed at England.

CLARE: The example you picked, without wanting to introduce too critical a note, that is itself much argued about. You claim that you actually influenced the chief Soviet negotiator by doing what you did. But I understand that the acting executive director of the Arms Control, representing the United States, says you were never there!

GELLER: Oh, nonsense, that's not true. Of course I was there. This is a perfect example of how misinformation and how the press can twist things. Now, I don't know where you got that information but the only way I can prove it to you is I actually have a picture with Vice-president Al Gore standing right next to me, and with Yuli Vorontzov standing right next to me, and with Senator Claiborne Pell standing next to me, and that picture is real and it's from the American Nuclear Arms Reduction Treaty in Geneva. So you see, there you go, misinformation.

CLARE: Well actually ...

GELLER: Of course it happened.

CLARE: To be honest, the question of whether you were there or not was less relevant to me. Much more significant to me, because I'm much more of a sceptic than I think you realise, is that even if the power exists, sadly, it being like penicillin, if it works it will be abused. So there's Uri Geller sitting with three million people willing the Soviet negotiator to think certain things, but sadly if we have such powers, I've no doubt that there'll be an Adolf Hitler sitting somewhere willing people to think quite different things. I'm no great enthusiast for mind power than for any other power because power can be misused. Which takes me to a question I really wanted to ask you and that is, why is power so important to you?

GELLER: There are two meanings to power here. There is the power that bends keys, energy, and there is another power, you're talking about the power that Adolf Hitler had on people. Well, I don't care about that kind of power.

CLARE: Well, mind power is a power, mind power can influence. Hitler is a very good example. Hitler, through a variety of extraordinary skills, was able to move a nation of some 50 million people.

GELLER: Negatively.

CLARE: Yes, indeed. Which makes many of us rather fearful of power. Why are you not fearful of power? Why do you immediately think in terms of this power as something benign and useful?

GELLER: Because I myself cannot do anything negative with it.

CLARE: You can't?

GELLER: I can't, I can't. Now, if you're telling me that you know for a fact there is someone in Russia, some psychic that can destroy people with the power of the mind, you know, that would scare me. I don't believe you can do it.

CLARE: You don't worry about this kind of power?

GELLER: No, I've been too much in intelligence forces and secret meetings and I'm well read about this area. There is no one out there that can mind control people. You can't really do it. You can do little things like the telepathy. Yes, you can influence people. I can do a drawing here and put it in your mind. You can do those things, but you cannot abuse the power. That's why I leave an opening to the door; the door is open to the possibility that something is above us, something protecting us.

CLARE: Are you an optimist?

GELLER: Very much so, I'm a dreamer.

CLARE: Do you dream much?

GELLER: I'm a dreamer. I believe that things will happen. I'm optimistic. I think good things are going to happen.

CLARE: What do you worry about?

GELLER: The little things or big things? The big thing is that there will be a malfunction in a computer, artificial intelligence will take over a computer and the red button will be pressed and missiles will go up.

CLARE: What about personally? Do you have worries, personal worries? Do you worry about death?

GELLER: No.

CLARE: Your death?

GELLER: No, I think of it sometimes, but I don't worry about it. Little things that worry me are safety.

CLARE: Do you worry about disease?

GELLER: No.

CLARE: You've never been seriously ill?

GELLER: No, thank God. I will worry about it if it hits me. I was wounded in the war.

CLARE: Did you ever get to the stage where you felt you couldn't go on?

GELLER: No, no, never. Luckily, I'm really blessed. I have a great family, you know, my kids, my wife, my friends.

CLARE: What does your wife make of this power?

GELLER: She's just a very simple woman. Excluding the times where the cutlery bends in her kitchen – she's grown up with me together, you know. I've known her since 1968 and we've gone through a lot of things together, phenomenon things, you know, strange things. And she just is my wife, you know.

CLARE: And the future?

GELLER: For me?

CLARE: Yes.

GELLER: Remember I told you I live every day as a little life, I don't really want to know the future. I just hope and pray that God will give us health, all of us, because that's the most important thing. And I've learnt that very, very important lesson in my life that it's great to have money, but it won't bring you health, it won't bring you happiness and love. So if I can stay with those three things, with health, happiness and love, I am the richest man in the world.

CLARE: Uri Geller, thank you very much indeed.

Kay Redfield Jamison

The subject of this interview is a very remarkable woman indeed. She is a professor of psychiatry at one of the most prestigious medical schools in the world, Johns Hopkins in Baltimore – an impressive achievement for a non-medically trained, female clinical psychologist. She has written a stunning book on the relationship between manic-depressive illness and the artistic temperament, entitled *Touched with Fire*. Drawing on recent advances in genetics, neurochemistry, psychopharmacology and psychology, she re-examined the constellation of afflicted artistic giants and concluded that the suspected association between mood disorder and creativity is indeed a reliable one. In some families, most notably those of Tennyson and Byron, she was able meticulously to trace the genetic transmission of the disorder back more than 150 years. She has also written, in collaboration with Frederick K. Goodwin of the US National Institute of Mental Health, one of the most substantial and lucid texts on manic depression currently available. Indeed, when teaching young doctors about manic depression I myself have been fond of quoting a passage from it in which a manic-depressive patient pays a moving tribute to the skill, compassion and genuine understanding of the treating psychiatrist. The passage ends: 'You taught me that the road from suicide to life is cold and colder and colder still, but – with steely effort, the grace of God and an inevitable break in the weather – that I could make it.' I sensed the passage was authentic. What I did not know was that the patient was Kay Jamison herself, that the world authority on manic-depressive illness, who had written on the subject with such impressive scientific detachment, had herself on a score and more occasions soared into the destructive dizzy heights of manic madness and plunged into the abyss of melancholic despair.

Early in the interview we consider the implications and misgivings of people with a history of mental ill-health going public and discussing their experiences. Clinicians ordinarily are no more willing than others to admit to having been ill. There is understandable concern too – the impact of untreated manic depression on a doctor's professional competence is inevitably disastrous. Kay Jamison has herself observed many medical students, psychology graduates and medical doctors denied permission to continue their work because of their own medical histories. But, as she argues powerfully in the course of this interview, manic depression is eminently treatable.

Born to a quixotic, temperamental and intense air force officer with a history of depression himself, and a kind, generous and talented mother, Kay Jamison suffered her first episode of manic depression at the age of 17. It was the beginning of a roller-coaster ride through college, a research career and academic preferment. At virtually every stage there are sudden, shocking confrontations with the full implications of her illness and its impact on her life. She does not duck its reality. She uses frank, uncompromising words to describe it – 'crazy', 'insane', 'ravingly mad'. 'I think to try and bleach the English language of expressive words,' she argues, 'is ultimately more stigmatising because it says you're so frail, you're so vulnerable that you can't handle normal language.' People who have this illness, she adds, 'really should be able to use whatever they want to describe themselves.' The term 'madness' bluntly describes what she herself has suffered. During one manic spree in London, for example, she spent several hundred pounds on books having titles or covers which somehow caught her fancy, books on the natural history of the mole, 20 sundry Penguin books because she thought it would be nice if the penguins could form a colony. At UCLA she took a massive overdose of medication prescribed to help her cope with her suicidal depression and was rushed to the very emergency room where, not long before, she had helped manage a distraught, incoherent manic patient.

Kay Jamison provides a remarkable insider's picture of what it is like to be manic and depressed. There is a particular kind of pain, elation, loneliness and terror involved in the illness. When she is on a high, she feels marvellous. Ideas and feelings fizz and flash like shooting stars. Sensuality expands, a sense of ease, intensity, omnipotence, of quite extraordinary well-being takes over. But the foot cannot be removed from the accelerator. The mood becomes uncontrolled and uncontrollable. Behaviour becomes frenetic, aimless, bizarre, destructive. Sleep disintegrates as do personal relationships – 'Volatility of moods is something that does split people apart.' Then there is the decline into despair, desolation, suicidal destruction.

Both from the perspective of her professional knowledge of the state of research into manic depression and of her own life history, Kay Jamison is in no doubt about the essential nature of the illness. In her remarkable autobiography, *An Unquiet Mind*, she has written, 'It is an illness that is biological in its origins, yet one that feels psychological in the experience of it; an illness that is unique in conferring advantage and pleasure, yet one that brings in its wake almost unendurable suffering and, not infrequently, suicide.' She acknowledges the extraordinary insights, the sensual enhancement, the sheer excitement of the manic experience but she is no longer bewitched. True she inherited the Laingian era's inconsistent attitude to drugs – accepting LSD while abhorring antidepressants – but this interview reflects the sober 1990s not the exotic 1960s. She describes her dislike of drugs and her resentment, like that of so many of her fellow sufferers, at having to take them. But she argues convincingly about the need to take major tranquillisers to control her highs, antidepressants to avert her suicidal impulses and lithium to anchor her to a normal mood level. Without medication, she tells me quite matter-of-factly, 'I would be dead or insane so medication is central in keeping me alive.'

The war that Kay Jamison has waged against herself is not an uncommon one. The major clinical problem in treating manic-depressive illness is not that there are no effective medications but that patients, like Kay Jamison in the early stages of her condition, refuse to take them. Many sufferers, because of stigma, ignorance, poor medical advice, fear of personal or professional reprisals, do not seek treatment at all. In the wake of early episodes of manic depression, sufferers frequently deny that they suffer from an illness. It can also be difficult to give up the high flights of mind and mood in mania. Jamison admits to missing the intoxicating highs and at times finds a normal stable mood boring. She was, however, fortunate in her psychiatrist and in this interview pays him a glowing series of compliments. He never gave up on her. He kept her alive with his psychotherapeutic skills and his use of medication. He always kept the basic choice in perspective. The issue was not whether lithium had or did not cause side-effects. Few medical treatments that are any use are free of side-effects and, all things considered, lithium causes fewer than most. It was not whether medication was consistent with some idealised notion of the illness. Medication works and, as Kay Jamison is well placed to remind us, the research is there to show it. The choice in her case was, as it is in virtually every case of manic depression, between sanity and madness, between life and death.

One of the most bitter and most contentious disputes in psychiatry is that between physical treatments and psychological treatments, between drugs and psychotherapy. For Kay Jamison there is no conflict. Despite her view of manic depression as, in essence, a biological disorder, both treatment approaches are essential. No pill can help her deal with the problem of not wanting to take pills. Likewise no amount of analysis can on its own prevent her manias and depressions, her highs and lows. She needs both. It is, as she admits, an off-putting reality, owing her life to pills and to the strange, profound and ultimately rewarding relationship involved in psychotherapy.

She does not provide a particularly romantic notion of madness but rather the plain, unvarnished truth. She has had to learn how to live her life suspecting her feelings, keeping a wary eye on her enthusiasms. She has a number of favourable factors in her life to help her – a supportive, informed husband, a sympathetic group of colleagues and parents, family and friends who have sustained her through bad times and good. And the closing stages of the interview are optimistic. To those who have had illnesses and have recovered she reminds them of the words of another sufferer, the Hollywood director, Joshua Logan, who was told by his psychiatrist that if you walk into a room and act normally people will treat you as normal. That is valuable and reassuring advice for all of us!

CLARE: Kay Redfield Jamison was born in 1946 the daughter of an American career air force officer. She trained at the University of California in Los Angeles, St Andrews University in Scotland, at the Maudsley and St George's Hospitals in London and she was senior research fellow at Merton College in Oxford. She is currently a professor of psychiatry at the Johns Hopkins Medical school in Baltimore.

Kay Jamison is the author of more than 80 scientific publications, mainly about mood disorders, suicide, psychotherapy and lithium.

CLARE: Kay Jamison, you must have had considerable misgivings about revealing as a professional practitioner in the behavioural sciences that you suffered from the very illness about which you had written and become an international expert?

JAMISON: Many, many, many reservations, over many years, yes, ranging from the personal to the professional, reservations about professional repercussions and licensing and hospital privileges and how people would see my work, would see me. I think from a personal view just how one would be perceived differently by people.

CLARE: We'll talk about the professional perceptions in a moment. A consistent statement by people who experience psychiatric illness and who have been hospitalised and treated as you have, a consistent statement they make about 'coming out' about illness is they fear that subsequently all that they say and they do will be seen through a sort of veil of illness.

JAMISON: Yes, I think that's true. I think that when it came right down to it that was my major concern. That all of a sudden, if you were a bit irritable and cantankerous, that all of a sudden it would become that you were getting a bit manic. Or if you were a bit enthusiastic. I'm sort of naturally enthusiastic and a little over the top anyway, that all of a sudden that would be seen as illness, as pathology rather than who one is.

CLARE: And does that happen?

JAMISON: We don't know actually, that's the ungluing thing. I have experienced less of that than I thought I would from a work sense, but of course you don't know what people are really thinking. You don't know what people all of a sudden are seeing you as because they don't say. People aren't going to come out and say, 'Well, I think you look manic.' They might say it to somebody else but they're not going to say it directly to you. I haven't felt as self-conscious about it as I thought I would so in some respects I don't think it's as bad as I thought it would be.

CLARE: And when you came to write it, when you started to put together the story, what I wasn't clear about was the extent to which you sought to find in the origins and the early years of your life, anything that would meaningfully contribute to your understanding of why you suffered from this illness, in other words, the classic public view of how psychiatrists and psychologists work. Did Kay Jamison plough her own background to discover the antecedents of this strange illness?

JAMISON: I think the antecedents are so clear in my family. I have manic-depressive illness everywhere I look.

CLARE: Really?

JAMISON: Yes. I think of it as clearly a genetic illness. My grandmother, my great uncle.

CLARE: That's your father's mother?

JAMISON: My father's mother. My father's uncle was in a state hospital virtually all of his adult life. Probably half of my cousins on my father's side.

CLARE: And when would you have known that?

JAMISON: Well, I didn't know that until I was diagnosed as manic depressive the first time. I don't think I really knew it in any intellectual sense. I think you have a sense obviously of a certain moodiness and temperament floating around the ethers but I didn't go round labelling it as manic depressive. But certainly, when I wrote the book, I knew all that and I understood that and really believed it. What I think I was much more aware of doing was trying to find out the things that sustain you actually in childhood, how you survive. I was very interested in going back and seeing the things that kept all this together. You know the strengths as well as perhaps the vulnerabilities. So, I think at least in writing it I was much more struck by the fact that I was interested in those things.

CLARE: When you say what kept us all together, that suggests that there was some kind of impulsion to split you all apart?

JAMISON: Well, I think, yes. Volatility of moods is something that does split people apart. It does draw them together as well. I think crisis and awfulness can draw you together. I had the great fortune of having two wonderful parents in terms of basic values, very kind people, decent people, good people, smart people, curious people, very supportive. But all that doesn't protect you from the ravages of severe psychosis and mental illness. They're such terrible, catastrophic things to happen in a family so that you get protection from it and sustenance from it but it doesn't keep you from it.

CLARE: How many were in your family?

JAMISON: I had an older brother and an older sister, yes.

CLARE: Three of you and your parents. And it's your father's side that carries the illness. Your mother's side would have been free of it?

JAMISON: Yes, absolutely as normal as one can imagine really.

CLARE: And did that mean that in the Jamison family, that in addition to your father and yourself, was there anybody else that you would see as affected by this volatility of mood?

JAMISON: Yes, certainly my sister. Many of my cousins have been hospitalised for mania. As I say, my grandmother and her brother, yes, and then who knows who else?

CLARE: What was your father like? He was an air force officer and you moved around quite a lot.

JAMISON: Yes, he was an air force officer. He was a pilot and a meteorologist. He was a scientist really in terms of what he did most of his time, he was a scientist. He was intense, is intense, mercurial, very romantic, very imaginative and so I think that life was always full of great descriptions and great magical moments. When that was withdrawn during depression, it was, it was very devastating but when it was there it was fabulous, you know. So it was sort of very tidal really.

CLARE: Would you remember the periods of depression when you were growing up?

JAMISON: Yes, again, I don't think you grow up thinking, 'My father's depressed.' I mean it's a very strange way of looking at the world. I think what I was aware of was that he got quiet, he withdrew, he got irritable, angry, a great enthusiast by temperament, he wouldn't be enthusiastic any more. If you get used to

someone's enthusiasms and warmth and that leaves, I ⸻
much worse than if that isn't there to begin with becaus⸻
take it more personally and you try and reconstitute it. You⸻
and recreate it and you try and do everything you can to mak⸻
that person enthusiastic again. I think that's one of the things
that's very compelling about moods actually, that because they
are so contagious, you feel responsible for other people's moods
in the same way you, as you are very affected by them.

CLARE: You used the word, and you're careful with words, you
used the word 'contagious'.

JAMISON: Yes, very definitely, yes. Because if you're in a room with
somebody who's profoundly depressed, that mood is contagious
unless you're cold as clay. You're affected by that person's mood
because we are interactive and if the interaction ceases and
there's no energy going out and no eye contact and no warmth
and no gesticulation, there's nothing, that's contagious. That's
part of what moods do in life, they let you know how someone
else is, they let you know how the situation is.

CLARE: What you're just describing is what people ask about when
they say to a psychologist or a psychiatrist, how do you stay
sane in the context of the misery, the pain, the depression that
you meet? Now not too many admit to what you've just said. In
my experience not too many say, 'You're right, it is contagious.'
They usually hide behind reference to professional training, and
separation of feelings and so on.

JAMISON: Well, I think it's both actually. If I'm in a room with
somebody who is depressed now, I think your professional
training does go on because you have been around it so much
and it's so obvious and it's almost stereotypical. There is a
distance there. There is a professionalism and there's just a
distance. If you're with a friend, though, who's very depressed
and you don't have your professional armour on, then that's a
very different sort of situation. I think it's still very hard for
people, however much professional training, to avoid being
impressed and affected by mania, or hypomania. It's a more
invasive mood, in a way, because by definition it's a mood that
reaches out and grabs you.

CLARE: Most people have some kind of handle to understand

depression by reference to those little depressions we all get when life is a bit unfair to us, or we feel it to be so, bat squeaks of the real thing. They're not the real thing in that profound, severe depression is really an extraordinary thing, both to see and to experience. But none the less, there's a sense that depression shades into everyday sadness and debility. But mania, and I think you write this in your book, you really have profound doubts that anyone who has not suffered it can really understand it. I wanted you to say something about that.

JAMISON: Yes, I think it's true. I think that perhaps exaltation and great excitement, enthusiasm is a second or third cousin of the beginnings of mania. Perhaps when you get very, very frenetic, over-committed and are rushing against time schedules and you've got 700 things to do and time to do only 300, you might get some notion of that, of the irritability and the overload and whatever of mania. Or religious ecstasy. I think people who describe religious ecstasy clearly have much of the same language that one would have in describing exultant states. And a mania only for a while is exultant, of course, and then it just sort of splutters into horrible chaos and, and fragmentation and so forth.

CLARE: Could you describe for me a typical experience you would have of how it would start and then how it would develop?

JAMISON: Well, I think mania, like depression, is a matter of severity. Typically, if I'm describing myself, I would start getting enthusiastic. Colours would seem much more intense to me. I would listen to music and music would be not just music but music that was vivid and meaningful with a capital M, not just wonderful music but a sudden extraordinary sensation, bodily sensation, physical sensation, much more so. I would start having a lot of ideas, getting out notepads to write them down, being enthusiastic about just having a lot of plans and being convinced that my ideas are really quite a contribution. Of course, often they're not. Usually they're not any contribution to anything except chaos, but at the moment you're convinced that you have some sort of profound insight into what's going on. You start buying things. You see something and you may know in your mind of minds that you don't have the money to back it up or that you can't really afford it in any sort of realistic sense, but it doesn't matter because your mood just totally dominates it. You just know that you have to have it. You just know. For example, when I got severely manic the first time, I was quite delusional after a certain point ...

CLARE: How do you mean?

JAMISON: Well, I thought there was going to be a major crisis of rattlesnakes in the San Fernando Valley. I was teaching at UCLA at the time and there is actually a snake problem. Let's not minimise the snake problem in Los Angeles but it's not something that people stay awake at night worrying about usually. But I was awake at night anyway because I was manic, and thinking of all the problems that there were in the world and how I might solve them. And the snakes were one of them. So I went to a store and I bought all the snake bite kits because I wanted all of my friends to be prepared. Well, this is just vintage mania. It's a combination of just being crazy as a hoot owl and doing something about it and being convinced that what you're doing is really going to make a difference. Of course, it didn't make any difference. All it did was look absurd and, and when I was depressed, look particularly absurd. But it's that kind of thing. And then, at some point you hallucinate. Not everyone who gets manic does that, of course, but in my case I had very severe mania and I did.

CLARE: What age would you have been around this time?

JAMISON: Well, the first very severe mania I got I was about 27, I think. I had gotten many, many, many mild manias before that from, when I was about 16. But again it's very hard to separate from your temperament. My temperament was one that was high energy, high voltage, loved life, loved a lot of things, had a lot of friends and was out, out and about in the world. So it sort of gradually creeps up on you that you were doing things ... You see it in other people really. You see the fact that you're wearing out other people. You see that other people are getting exhausted being around you and they make it very clear they're getting exhausted being around you.

CLARE: They find you tiresome. But most of them wouldn't know what on earth this was, or didn't then anyway?

JAMISON: Oh heavens no. That's part of the difficulty I think for people who have manic-depressive illness. They don't know that it's an illness. It doesn't seem like an illness until you go absolutely psychotic when it's very clear to you that something is seriously wrong or when you're severely depressed. It doesn't seem like an illness. It seems like a part of your personality or your temperament.

CLARE: And is it the fact that you can't control it, that makes you see it as an illness? Is it the fact that this is a mood state over which you've no control?

JAMISON: No, because I think often you can be very depressed and feel like you can't control it and still not see that as an illness. I think when your mind goes and you start seeing things that you are aware that are not there and when you . . .

CLARE: Like what with you?

JAMISON: Well, the first time I got really manic I had both very wonderful hallucinations and very awful hallucinations.

CLARE: Visual?

JAMISON: Visual hallucinations were the terrible hallucinations. I saw blood splattering and a woman and it was just terrifying. The marvellous one was when I went through Saturn. I went on a trip around the planets but I sort of focused in on Saturn and there is no way to describe how unbelievable it all was. You know, it's still with me in some sense. These are very intense experiences like I think a lot of drug experiences are perhaps but internal.

CLARE: And did you ever have auditory hallucinations? Did you hear voices?

JAMISON: No, I didn't. I suppose I heard sounds when I was going around Saturn but I didn't think about it.

CLARE: Is there a moment in your head, your reason at the back of your head, saying, 'This is madness'?

JAMISON: There was for me a very clear moment and funnily enough it was not when I was hallucinating or delusional. It was before that. The obvious psychiatric jargon is 'racing thought'. It's one of those many phrases that is just so reductionist that it doesn't begin to convey the terror involved. But racing thoughts is when your brain, your mind, your thinking is just going so fast. I would start a sentence in my head and again, you're not aware of how close a friend you are with yourself intellectually until your mind goes. You have all these conversations with yourself and you just take it all for granted. You take it for granted that that person you're talking to in your head, yourself, is going to be there in some sane sort of version for the rest of your life. And so I would start a sentence in my head and I couldn't remember it after I was about half way through because I would have had four or five more thoughts. Your brain splinters. When you talk about losing your mind, I think that's as much losing your mind as being psychotic in a funny sort of way.

CLARE: This racing of thoughts – it is going on in the sentences that you're not even speaking, that you are mulling over with yourself?

JAMISON: Exactly because what comes out manifest to other people is rapid speech, compulsive speech, very, very fast, chaotic speech. What goes on in your head is what's frightening. What happens to you with other people is less so.

CLARE: But of course, in these milder states, some of the things you've described are quite advantageous. You're sparky, enthusiastic, conversationally uninhibited, open to new ideas, you fire with enthusiasm. Certain kinds of activities, business, or salesmanship activities that demand staying up late at night, in the media world or the pop business or whatever, this kind of personality in the mild stages is perhaps something of an advantage?

JAMISON: No question about it.

CLARE: Was it to you in the early stages?

JAMISON: Oh it was to me absolutely.

CLARE: You were a student when some of these experiences started to occur.

JAMISON: A student. When I first went wildly manic, I had just joined the faculty as an assistant professor at UCLA, at the University of California.

CLARE: In the medical faculty?

JAMISON: In the medical faculty. Basically you get promoted in the universities on the basis of publications and I could write a paper in a day without any problem, it would just flow. I would have all sorts of ideas, most of which were not useful in the least. But some of which were and later on you sort of prune them out. It was very advantageous and I think that's one of the reasons why mania is not only seductive but genuinely addictive. It is an intense experience and up to a point, for a certain window of time, it is highly productive in some people. You really can get a lot done. And you engage in life and that transmits itself to other people. If you have high energy other people feel it and are attracted to it. Now, after a certain point that energy gets to be very discombobulating and very uncomfortable for other people to be around because it gets very irritable and angry. But, on the way up, it's great.

CLARE: And you would have been first hospitalised when?

JAMISON: I wasn't ever hospitalised because all of my friends, most of my friends were physicians and my concerns and their concerns about my losing privileges, clinical privileges were realistic and so for a long time . . .

CLARE: Realistic in the sense that?

JAMISON: That I probably would have lost my licence to practise and I would have jeopardised my job if I'd been in the hospital, I think there is no question about that. And so they kept watch over me. I had a lot of very good friends and at some point I was under a literally 24-hour watch and they were great. Looking back on it I'm horrified that I imposed upon my friends in that way but they volunteered and they felt very strongly that if I went into hospital I would possibly lose my job. When I look back, one of the worst things about it is that I wasn't hospitalised, I should have been hospitalised, there's no question about it. I needed to be in a hospital.

CLARE: Because?

JAMISON: Because I was certainly dangerous to myself at many points but I also was in no condition to look after myself.

CLARE: Dangerous to yourself while manic?

JAMISON: Well, on my way down from mania, yes, yes, in terms of suicide. But also I just was psychotic. I think people should be in hospitals when they're very sick. It's a tremendous burden, in addition to having an illness, to feel that you can't get the right kind of treatment for that illness. I mean it's bad enough being psychotic without feeling that you can't really get the kind of treatment that you need for it.

CLARE: And would that still be the situation now in the United States, that if you had been hospitalised, you would have lost your privileges to practise?

JAMISON: Not always. Actually one of the things that has been very interesting to me since I have written the book is that I've gotten hundreds of letters from lawyers and teachers and doctors, particularly doctors, who have lost their privileges or been put on severe restrictions, who've been kicked out of medical school, thrown out of residency programmes and so forth. And, you know, perhaps some of that's justified if people certainly aren't taking treatment, but a lot of it is stigma and not just a stigma, it's very real the jeopardy of losing your job.

CLARE: Well, can I ask you, did you take the precaution of ensuring that you had some mentor protecting you before you wrote the book, before you published the book? You know, somebody who would stand by you?

JAMISON: Well, I have always told the people that I practise with that I had manic-depressive illness because I always wanted to be removed from clinical work if my judgement seemed to be going. Now, actually, nobody's had to do that because I actually removed myself, but I don't think you can trust yourself to make that decision. So I've always told the doctors that I've worked with that I have the illness. The chairman of my department at UCLA knew it and I have been very fortunate in the chairmen of both my departments of psychiatry. I think they're unusual men. They were both wonderful. My chairman at UCLA said, 'Learn from it, write from it, teach from it. Just keep taking your lithium and I will back you entirely.' And he did. When I went to my chairman at Johns Hopkins, Paul McHugh, I said, 'Look Paul, I really want to write this book and I'm concerned because I love Hopkins and I don't want to put Hopkins in a difficult situation.' And he said, 'You know, Kay, Professor Halstead, the first professor of surgery at Johns Hopkins, everyone knew that he had a major morphine habit and everybody knew he had a major cocaine habit and the faculty had felt they had two obligations. One was to protect Professor Halstead's patients, and the second was to protect Professor Halstead, so that he could teach and write and do research.' And he said, 'If Hopkins can't do that for you, we have no business being in business.' He said, 'I will do whatever it takes to back you and support you,' and he has done and, and, the department of medicine and department of psychiatry at Hopkins have been very wonderful. But that's unusual and I know it's unusual. I would have written the book anyway.

CLARE: Would you?

JAMISON: Yes, I think I would have but he made it much, much easier for me because I went out knowing that Johns Hopkins and actually a lot of my colleagues at other universities, at Harvard and Yale and so forth, also supported my doing it.

CLARE: What about the stigma? Bound up with this obviously are reasonable professional concerns about your safety as a psychologist, working in medical school, your safety with patients and your safety with yourself, concern about litigation, all of these things, these are reasonable concerns. There are also, of course, washing around in this mix a lot of other concerns. Let's take one you must also wrestle with and that is this notion of psychiatric illness as a kind of weakness, as a flaw.

JAMISON: Yes, yes, I think that everyone who's had severe psychiatric illness has to struggle with that. I think what I've come up against at the most is in the case of suicide. Manic-depressive illness is a very lethal disease and it kills 20 per cent of people who have it through suicide. I nearly died, I was in a coma for days.

CLARE: What did you do?

JAMISON: I took an overdose of lithium and a lot of medications to keep me from throwing up my lithium.

CLARE: When did that happen?

JAMISON: That was when I was about 30.

CLARE: And you meant it?

JAMISON: Oh, no question about it. I was saved totally and in a completely unpredictable manner. But the reaction of people to suicide attempts tends to be to see them as evidence of weakness and neuroticism. And, you know, I don't mind being classed as psychotic but I don't like the idea of being thought of as weak or snivelling or neurotic. We all have our sense of discrimination.

CLARE: But, putting it in non-jargon terms, you prefer to be thought of as mad than weak?

JAMISON: Right. It's all meaningless at the end of the day but there is an assumption, you know, that you just sort of didn't have the guts to survive. My sense is that there's a reason why people kill themselves who have this kind of illness. The pain is simply unbearable. You also think you are unbearable to other people. I couldn't stand what I thought I was doing to other people, I simply couldn't bear it. I thought I was taxing the resources of everyone I knew. I thought everyone would be better off without me. There's a study, a classic study, asking terminal cancer patients, some of whom had had very severe clinical depressions and some of whom had not, asking them what the difference in levels of pain was. And the people that had had the clinical depression said, the terminal cancer pain was so much easier. I think there's no way of, of describing the amount of anguish in severe depression. But people can't understand that who haven't been there. There is a tendency to think of people being weak. I was reading an article recently in a, a New York paper that had, had been written about me and my book and I was interested that one of my colleagues, who I've been at many, many, many meetings with, had said, 'Dr Jamison should just have kept this to herself. She's a scientist, she's a researcher, she shouldn't be talking about her personal feelings in public.' Now that's been a very unusual reaction, fortunately. People mostly have been very supportive. But I read that and my blood went cold. It was my worst fear. I was brought up in a WASP sort of family where you're expected to keep your feelings to yourself and it's been a very real struggle to do this. I hope to help people out of it and open up the debate and discussion about severe mental illness, particularly in the professions. And to see a colleague that you go to meetings with all the time say this, it just was awful. It's like a sense of betrayal and you think, well, who else is really thinking that out there?

CLARE: I was interested there when you said you were brought up in a WASPish family and feelings were to be controlled and so on. Were you conscious when growing up of the tension that your father must have experienced therefore. What kind of conflict do you recall?

JAMISON: He wouldn't go to a doctor. If you saw a psychiatrist at that time in the American air force, and certainly if you were a pilot, a fighter pilot, you would immediately lose your flight privileges. He wouldn't see anybody. He didn't believe in psychiatrists. I mean, none of us believed in psychiatrists. There was a general feeling, I think, in the military in general that psychiatrists were weak and ineffectual and anybody who saw a psychiatrist was weak and ineffectual. That was clear. That was out in the open. It was overt.

CLARE: So he suffered his depressions untreated and those manic enthusiasms untreated. Other people suffered.

JAMISON: Yes, and eventually he got fired.

CLARE: Oh really?

JAMISON: He became a scientist at the Rand Corporation and he was fired for basically being completely off the wall.

CLARE: What age were you then?

JAMISON: Perhaps 20, I don't know. Yes, probably 20.

CLARE: You've written strongly concerning the genetic factor in manic-depressive illness and your own family bears you out. But sturdy environmentalists will say to you, is it possible that in the interactions of your moods in relation to your father's moods and his moods in relation to his mother's moods, that there's, there's an environmental element as well perhaps? That, emotion becomes something very difficult to get right. You're growing up in the context of someone who has extraordinarily mercurial moods. You described it yourself, like when you're in the presence of someone else's depression, your mood is affected, I suppose in one of two ways, you can either get depressed yourself or you can adopt a slightly manic response. And I wondered what about that contaminating this fairly simple genetic model of transmission? In your case, in your family case, do you recall your moods affected by your father's moods?

JAMISON: Oh, I certainly recall my moods being affected by my father's moods. I think there is a difference between your moods being affected and your thinking getting very very fast and hallucinating and delusional, being delusional and being suicidal. And then there is the fact that only one or two of you in a family get it and others don't. But I don't think that most people who study the genetics of manic-depressive illness think it's a simple genetic model for starters. But that it is a genetic illness is unquestionable. You can take identical twins, raise them apart so there's no common environmental influence, and they have a concurrence rate of up to 80–90–100 per cent. There's studies going on now, I'm sure within a year, we will have at least one of the genes for manic-depressive illnesses. It's down very close to one portion of chromosome 18. But I think there are very few things that are genetic that aren't also tremendously influenced by the environment. At the most reductionist level, take light. We know that light has a tremendous impact on mood disorders. We know that in the case of manic-depressive illnesses, the single, easiest way to get somebody who has manic depression to be manic is to deprive them of a night's sleep. The sleep cycles are enormously important. I know that the easiest way if I wanted to get manic would be just to stay up all night. This has been shown in experiment after experiment after experiment. That's an environmental factor. When you get stressed, the first thing that goes is sleep. In postpartum illnesses a lot of the changes are due to sleep deprivation. So that's a subject that's related to a psychological variable and psychological experiences. But it has a tremendous impact. But certainly there's no question that you learn moods to some extent being around people who are very moody. But I think psychosis is something else again. I think the severity is something else again. And I look at my brother, for example, who clearly isn't affected in that sense and he's much more my mother's son in that sense. And you know, he was around the same things that I was all the time and he's perfectly normal, never had a depressed day in his life as best I can make out.

CLARE: What have your family made of your book because in turn, of course, it casts light on your father. I don't know whether he was already confronting his cyclothymic moods, his mood-swinging tendency before you wrote the book. But the book clearly involves him. It raises the issue that when you write about yourself, you write about people around you?

JAMISON: Right. I think, it's an issue with writing about a genetic illness. There's no question of writing about your family. Both are very separate things. Funnily enough my mother and brother were quite opposed to my doing it because they thought I had been through enough already, enough pain, and that I was just going to expose myself to a lot of public criticism and hospital and professional repercussions. That I wouldn't know the implications, for example, that people wouldn't come out and sue me, you know, patients and so forth. I would never know what the professional repercussions would be. And that I had been through enough, and enough was enough already and I didn't have to sort of do this. I sent a manuscript to my father because I wanted him to see it and my father wrote and called and said, 'I think it's wonderful. I think you're very gutsy to do this and I admire you for doing it and I love you for doing it.' So, actually my father in an odd sort of way was much more understanding of why I did it. I think my brother and mother were very, very understanding. There was a concern for me and I think that it wasn't a concern in any way for the family being exposed. I don't think they felt that way and it's not that kind of book. I love my family. But my father I think understood intuitively the reasons why I did it and didn't do anything but say go for it.

CLARE: And the reasons why you did it were what?

JAMISON: A lot of different reasons I think. One was at a very, very specific level. I see people in professions who have manic-depressive illness who are very successful who don't talk about it, who are at the highest levels of government and the law and entertainment and so forth in the United States, and they don't talk about it because of the stigma. And I understand that totally, I don't think they should. I don't think people have any obligation to be open about it. But what happens is that people have no idea that people can be very successful with a very severe illness. So what happens is that people read in the newspapers about somebody who's gone psychotic and taken 20 people out with a machine gun and that's their notion of severe mental illness. It's not the people who are working in the White House. It's not that thing. And I thought I was at least in a position to understand manic-depressive illness from having written about it and having seen it in many people, and then, of course, having been through it myself and with my family. Also, because I think people don't understand how attractive mania can be, early on, and the major clinical problem in treating manic-depressive illness is not that we don't have good drugs, obviously we have, we have lithium, we have two anti-convulsants that work very well. There are a lot of drugs in the pipeline, the major clinical problem is that people won't take their medicine.

CLARE: And you wouldn't?

JAMISON: And I wouldn't.

CLARE: And you wouldn't because?

JAMISON: I wouldn't because of side-effects. I had very bad side-effects because I was given a very high dose which was very common when I was given lithium. It was the very early stages of lithium treatment, 20 years ago, and in that day and age people were taking high, very high, levels and I was very sensitive to lithium.

CLARE: Let me just get this in sequence. You clearly had a psychotic episode when you were 27. What age were you when you said, not just to yourself, that this is an illness, that you better get something done about it, that you must have some kind of treatment for it?

JAMISON: It was when I was 27 that I got treatment because I was clearly mad.

CLARE: You had to be treated?

JAMISON: I had to be treated. It was a psychiatric illness.

CLARE: But that was done to you so to speak.

JAMISON: It was done to me but I also knew that I was very sick. I knew that I was completely out of control and that something awful was going to happen, had to happen to me.

CLARE: So you were given heavy tranquillisers and ...

JAMISON: Yes, I was given heavy medicine.

CLARE: Slowed up?

JAMISON: Right, and then I was on lithium and I took lithium for about six months.

CLARE: Lithium being the salt that stabilises mood. Now, you had one advantage over the average manic depressive, and that is, you knew about all these treatments and you knew about lithium?

JAMISON: And I knew that it worked. And I knew that it worked in me. It was very clear that it worked for me.

CLARE: You knew that it worked. You also knew it had side-effects. In those days they were using higher dosages as you say. But, none the less, people had to stay on it. So the side-effects were one reason that you weren't terribly keen on it. But my understanding is that that's not the only reason?

JAMISON: No, that wasn't the only reason. In fact, I think the first time the side-effects probably were not the reason, the main reason anyway, they certainly were important.

CLARE: The main reason was?

JAMISON: Well, two. One was I really thought I was an exception, which I think is what happens to a lot of people. I thought that willpower would see me through. I knew that was irrational but it didn't make any difference. You don't live by your rationality, or I didn't anyway.

CLARE: That you could control it?

JAMISON: That I could control it, that I would be OK. Sure I'd had a crisis, sure I had gone stark ravingly mad. I'd gotten treated for it. I thought it wouldn't come back because I thought I would be the exception. Now, I knew the natural course of this disease, I studied it. But I thought I would be an exception. I really thought I just could get by without medication and I think that's true for an awful lot of people with manic-depressive illness. The level of denial is phenomenal. But that's true for a lot of people on a lot of chronic medications. I also missed the highs. I missed those periods when everything was so easy. It's very much I'm sure like being a cocaine addict only cocaine doesn't last nearly as long and it's not as intense. Mania is just an indescribably, incredibly productive state for the time that it lasts and I wanted to recapture that. Because what happened after I got manic the first time was, as night to day, I became severely depressed and I didn't get anything done and I was just inert and basically a cabbage. And being a cabbage is unattractive, you know. And I thought well, you know, gee, if I just stop because I blamed the depression on the drug. I thought, gee, the reason I'm feeling this way is because of the medication and while I knew it wasn't true I really believed it.

CLARE: None the less, the evidence suggests that lithium does reduce the amplitude of the swings, that it stabilises mood.

JAMISON: There's no question of it, sure.

CLARE: And with lithium you can lose the highs.

JAMISON: Yes, well, sure enough I did.

CLARE: As there is a terrible, physical pain with depression, is there not a great physical sensuality with mania?

JAMISON: Oh yes, there is. It's just indescribable. For a while.

CLARE: For a while?

JAMISON: Oh yes, absolutely. It's very seductive. You're very seductive. You love life and it's a vivacious state.

CLARE: You sexually act out?

JAMISON: Yes, I didn't so much because I was involved with somebody. But that's very common certainly and it's very understandable. Everything is excessive, everything that you could enjoy in life is excessive. So to give that up, saying goodbye to that, I was not ready at that time in my life to do it.

CLARE: Does that mean that a stabilised manic depressive tends to feel that life in comparison is just a little bit grey?

JAMISON: I don't feel particularly grey because I actually keep my lithium very low. I don't see my psychiatrist very often because he lives in Los Angeles. But my level is quite low and I know I take a certain risk and I'm prepared to take that risk at this point in my life. But no way would I ever go off lithium again.

CLARE: You take it every day?

JAMISON: Absolutely. So I don't feel grey. I think a lot of people opt for what I do, which is to sort of cycle around a wee bit so as not to feel medicated. When I was on a higher dose of lithium I felt very medicated, and I felt very grey, and I felt like my passions were gone, my enthusiasms were evaporated, my thinking for sure was slowed up, so there was not much good to be said for it except that I was sane – which is a lot.

CLARE: You've written about the relationship between creativity and manic depression. Is there some truth in the suggestion that had lithium been around in earlier times half the creativity of Western civilisation might well have gone down the tubes?

JAMISON: I think we don't know. One of the things that as a scientist bothers me is how little that's been studied actually. It's a terribly important thing and it's not studied nearly enough.

CLARE: Well, what about your own creativity?

JAMISON: My own creativity I feel at this point is the same as it's ever been. I don't have those great rushes of ideas, they come in wavelets instead of waves. And I'm much more productive so there's a sort of productivity trade off there because if you're sick a lot of the time you are not very productive. Actually, the two studies that have actually looked at artists and writers and have asked them about lithium, the artists have said that they feel as creative or more creative on lithium because you just spend so much of your life being sick otherwise, you know.

CLARE: You trained as a psychologist and you work in a department of psychiatry. You are a clinical psychologist, so you work with patients that I, as a psychiatrist, work with, patients suffering from manic depressions, and schizophrenia, and people with personality difficulties and anxiety states and obsessive compulsive disorder and so on. The difference, really the only difference between us, is that you're not medically trained.

JAMISON: Yes, that's right.

CLARE: And you don't prescribe medication.

JAMISON: I don't prescribe drugs, I have a degree in psychopharmacology but I don't prescribe drugs.

CLARE: In which case you know a good deal more about drugs, I suspect, than many medically trained psychiatrists. The reason I ask this question is, when you were training as a psychologist, you would have been reading about the great psychoses – illnesses such as schizophrenia, manic-depressive illness – and you would have read these textbook descriptions of mania, for example, or indeed, depression, or indeed mild mood changes, cyclothymic mood and so on. Now you know the way as a medical student you read about subarachnoid haemorrhage and you've got a headache in the back of your head and you think, my God, I'm having a haemorrhage, did you ever, when reading about mania, say, 'This is me. This is what happens to me!'

JAMISON: No, I think when I was an undergraduate, not a graduate, when I was an undergraduate I did read about depression and I did start to go to student health psychiatry and I ended up not going, because I just couldn't do it. I just had been so brought up not to see psychiatrists. I did sort of recognise myself in that but that was a fleeting moment of insight. No, I didn't. I look back and I'm horrified at my lack of insight. I mean, it's exactly the opposite of medical student syndrome. It's exactly the opposite. I just blithely went on my way thinking I was who I was and I think a lot of people do that. It just seems so much part of your temperament. My temperament had always been that way and reading about it didn't make it any less so.

CLARE: But of course it is part of your temperament and, and this raises a somewhat painful philosophical dilemma. We're talking here about Kay Jamison who is a mercurial person. That is what people would say. Sometimes when you meet Kay she's bubbly and she's full of ideas and she's enthusiastic and she's zesty and she's going to the theatre and she's writing interesting things about Byron and Shelley and Keats. And then another time you meet her and she's subdued, hasn't very much to say, she may even dress differently, more colourfully the first time, more soberly the second, she keeps her opinions to herself, she doesn't have much to say.

JAMISON: Or you wouldn't meet her because she . . .

CLARE: Or you wouldn't meet her. But in one sense you're saying, as you were reading these texts, that's the way I am, that's me. You reconcile the two elements by declaring they are both you really, that's the essence of who you are. Now, how shaken does that get when you realise that these manifestations of mood, which so affect your life and your relationship with other people, your family, your lover and so on, that they're actually just epiphenomena really of some genetic twist or quirk?

JAMISON: The genetic part doesn't bother me in the least because I think we are all made up of genes. The only metaphor that I think makes any sense to me is that fire is very useful most of the time and that every now and then there's just a huge conflagration and it's totally destructive. It doesn't mean you want to get rid of the fire. I think of a temperament like that. Basically your thyroid works most of the time just fine and then every now and then you have a thyroid crisis if you've got thyroid disease. I see that I have a temperament that goes a particular way and has certain risks attached to it. It's a temperament that is my own and I don't want to change it. I have no interest in changing it really. I'm sure perhaps some people I know wouldn't mind changing it but I don't. It's who I am, you know. But I think that I'm aware that it can go completely awry and I know that it has the capacity to kill me at some point. That it is a temperament that ultimately can kill but it also gives me a lot. So I just think it's enormously complicated. It doesn't bother me in that sense. I sort of enjoy it.

CLARE: Are you glad you've had it?

JAMISON: I'm glad certainly, I'm certainly glad I had the intensity of it and the complexity of it because it's all I know. It's the only experience I know so it's the only language system I know in a sense. I do respond very well to lithium. Yes, I think I'm glad I've had the disease. I think it's forced me to look at a lot of things that I would not otherwise have looked at.

CLARE: Like what?

JAMISON: It's made me much, much, much more aware of my shortcomings. I think that until I went flamingly mad, I thought I was somewhat invulnerable. I think things had come very easily to me. Despite the fact that there had been some turmoil in my family, I actually thought things had gone my way in life very, very well and I really had no reason to complain. It was so inconsistent with my notion of myself that I couldn't handle everything. It really, it sent me back to the drawing board in terms of myself and I think that was a good thing. I think it was a very good thing actually. I think that I'm always aware of that capacity for terror and that capacity for dreadfulness and awareness of death.

CLARE: Has it made you more sympathetic? It is said, often, by patients, they need, they want a wounded healer. They want someone who has been touched by fire. That can be a disadvantage to healers who don't appear at any rate to have been touched by too much fire, but in your case, is it an advantage?

JAMISON: I think sometimes it's an advantage. I think it's probably more of an advantage in teaching actually. I've come up against this a lot since my book came out because a lot of people have called up wanting consultations and so forth with this notion that somehow ...

CLARE: Yes, that you'll know what it's like.

JAMISON: Right, and I'm not sure that's such a good recommendation for anything really. I think that what you want is a doctor who really knows about an illness, who is compassionate, sympathetic, intelligent, witty. I mean, any number of things. I don't think you have to go to somebody who's had Hodgkin's disease to have somebody treat you well for that disease and understand the suffering that you go through. Sure, maybe I can recognise mania, my diagnostic skills may be a little up there because I might be a little bit more finely tuned but I don't think having the disease is any great recommendation for anything really. It may give you certain things, but I know too many empathetic doctors who are terrific with mood disorders, you know, and people who have mood disorders who are terrible with patients. In teaching, I have focused on aspects of the illness different perhaps to those that typically would be focused upon. That might be some edge. I hope so. I hope that it has affected my teaching.

CLARE: How do you feel about the current swing, that some people indeed will see your book as a manifestation of, the current swing most noticeable in American psychiatry but true, I think, across the world, the swing away from psychoanalysis and to some extent psychotherapeutically oriented psychiatry to a very biological psychiatry, in which a disease like manic-depressive illness, a condition like manic-depressive illness, will be seen as genetic and biological and for which there are now effective physical treatments, lithium, anti-convulsants, other psychiatric drugs, a number of major tranquillisers? In so far as your modern psychiatrist needs therapeutic skills, they're the therapeutic skills of being (a) able to tell you what the condition is (b) to persuade you to take the medication and (c) to be around when you don't or when that medication needs to be monitored. And that is the model of the late twentieth-century psychiatrist in the management of manic depression.

JAMISON: Yes, well, I think it's very frightening. Though, you know, I believe that the evidence is overwhelming. I think you have to be a flat earther not to believe that manic depression is genetic and biologically based, it is psychologically expressed and it is psychologically manifested. What you feel is a change in your moods. What you feel is a change in your thinking and in your energy. What you have is a devastating disease that is not totally taken care of by pills. Pills are probably the most important thing but certainly not the only thing, and actually one of the things I think that's good at the moment is that there are actually a lot of studies now showing that the combined use of psychotherapy and medication is more effective than medication alone.

CLARE: Well, take you. What made the difference? What made the difference when you look back and you had this catastrophic psychotic episode when you were 27? From there on your treatment starts to take shape and there's relapses and remissions, I understand, that are a very characteristic pattern to your illness and your coming to an acceptance and an acknowledgement that things are going to have to change in certain ways. How would you identify the elements that made your treatment, as I assume it was, good treatment?

JAMISON: Well, clearly without medication I would be dead or insane so medication is central in keeping me alive.

CLARE: You'd put it that strongly?

JAMISON: Unquestionably. It is unquestionably true. But having a doctor who had the sense not to equivocate on my diagnosis, not to equivocate on the fact that I needed medication, who didn't buy in to all of my discussions of why I didn't need to be on medication, who was compassionate, deeply compassionate, humanistic, who knew my love for the arts and my concerns about losing the edge, and who never for a second doubted that I ultimately would be able to get out there and compete again. And I asked him not long ago exactly that, 'Did you ever really doubt?' and he said, 'Well, I assumed that if you stayed alive long enough, you would get out there and compete again.' He never gave up on me. He was just an unbelievably intelligent man. I think he was just a superb doctor and I think that that kept me alive as well. I can't divide the two things. I can say that without medication I would be dead, but I could also say that without superb psychotherapy I would be dead because much of my illness was really of a psychological nature. I didn't want to take the medication. That is not a medical problem, that's a psychological problem, and that's a psychotherapeutic problem.

CLARE: But listeners will also think in terms of psychotherapy as exploring your family dynamics, examining your relationship with your husband or your marital circumstances, your attitude to your career, the meaning of this illness and of course there's the speculation as to what the disease means?

JAMISON: Yes, tremendously important. I think having to sort out what impact your illness has on your life, on your relationships, on your work, the ravages of life as well, no it's not just psychotherapy around a drug or around a disease. It's psychotherapy, I think, in the best sense of psychotherapy, that in the case when you have severe disorder of moods, where your moods and perceptions are changed, I think you need extra-intelligent psychotherapy.

CLARE: But it's not psychoanalysis in the sense of exploring particular conflicts, oedipal conflicts and transference relationships between you and the therapist?

JAMISON: No, no, although a lot of people who are on lithium do go into psychoanalysis and seem to profit from it. I wasn't interested in doing that. It would not have been indicated at the time. As Freud was the first to say, you know, you don't do that kind of psychoanalytic work on somebody who's severely depressed or psychotic. You really have to do that when somebody is well.

CLARE: You mention that psychotherapy in your instance helped clarify, if you like, issues around yourself and your illness. That is a fascinating topic because you and I know that in the history of medicine is this battle between the notion of illness as a sort of rarefied thing out there, that afflicts you and you wrestle with it and you eliminate it and you get rid of it. I suppose the most classic being, say, pneumonia caused by the pneumococus, between that notion and the idea of illness as a kind of adaptation to life that we all go through to a greater or lesser extent. This latter model suggests that illness and self are enmeshed to a far greater extent than the first model and with something like manic depression, the second model sounds closer, that the illness and you cohabit almost in the same self.

JAMISON: Yes, well, you certainly cohabit with the potential for disease. Unless you're completely on another planet or denying, you're aware all of the time of your potential for getting ill again. And because it is wrapped into your temperament, the mild, very mild part of it is wrapped into your temperament, it is you to a certain extent. Now there are some people who just get manic and it has nothing to do with them. I mean it really has nothing to do very much with who they are and how they go through life day to day. It is genuinely like having a Martian land inside.

CLARE: Or having TB or something.

JAMISON: Right, something like that. It comes in, you get an infection and you get rid of it. For other people who, I think, are more cyclothymic by temperament, it's more.

CLARE: Well, then the question arises about the distinctions at each end of the spectrum. Let's for a minute take mania and happiness or ecstasy, because you referred to that when we were talking about how does one get an insight into what mania is like. Now you yourself, how do you tell when what you're experiencing is intense, wondrous happiness and when it is a manic episode?

JAMISON: Well, it's difficult. It is kind of a horrible thing that you have to mistrust your enthusiasms to some extent. In some respects, I suppose, other people in your life take on that task to a certain extent. My husband, for example, who is a psychiatrist, is a little bit more sceptical about my enthusiasms than I am. I start to think, 'Oh God, this is marvellous,' you know, I feel terrific and you get this kind of cosmic hue and you start staying up later at night and so forth. As soon as I start staying up late at night, he gets very worried and insists that I take something to sleep and for good reason. I've told him that many, many times, you know, that that's fine. I need somebody who does that because otherwise the tendency is to stay up and stay up and then get manic. But it's sometimes very difficult because I cycle, my mood cycles, swings a lot now but it's generally into these mild, mild, very, very mild manic states. I enjoy them. I feel like

I get a lot done. It's just that at some point you have to sort of cast a cold, beady eye on it, you know, because although it's fun but then the first moment depression sets in or you get too agitated or irritable, and then it ceases to be fun and you learn over time it isn't worth it.

CLARE: But really mood, it's like blood pressure. It edges into pathology.

JAMISON: Right. Now some people obviously just switch over night and they become wildly manic but in most people . . .

CLARE: You haven't had that?

JAMISON: No, no, most people sort of start to get ill slowly.

CLARE: And what about the opposite end of the spectrum, and how often as a psychiatrist I get asked this question, the difference between grief and depression. You lost a lover of some years standing, you had a strong relationship and he died very tragically. This was before you were married. And you describe that in *An Unquiet Mind*, the grief. But how does one distinguish between that profound melancholia of loss and severe depression?

JAMISON: Well, you know, it was strange but they actually seemed almost completely unrelated to me. Very different. When he died it was like my future going, his leaving, and unbelievable sadness and so forth. I didn't lose hope, I didn't think that I didn't want to live. It never occurred to me, suicide. It didn't occur to me for a second. I didn't lose hope. I think that hopelessness is such a part of depression and I didn't lose my capacity to feel. I think a lot of depression, clinical depression, is you don't feel anything but pain. It's not sadness, you know.

CLARE: Though some bereaved people describe a kind of numb-ness, don't they, a loss of feeling?

JAMISON: There's a loss of feeling but it's a different kind of thing, it's like being in shock. It's very protective. For the first several days after he died I sort of went on automatic pilot and you are protected by that. It's something that does numb you out but that is being numb, that is not being depressed. It's not that everything is grey, flat, you want to die. It's being numb and sad simultaneously. It's very different. It is just almost unrelated in a funny sort of way.

CLARE: When you were talking about your enthusiasms, there is always a little eye keeping a watch so that you're not going to go over the line. Is there something equivalent when you get sad? Because there is a deliciousness about a certain kind of melancholia and one indulges it a little, the sweetness of nostalgia and so on. Is that quite the same?

JAMISON: No, that seems to be an issue quite different to me. That kind of mild melancholia is a certain intensification of sensation actually because you may be more aware, as you say, with a nostalgia, aware, you may get morbid. When I get concerned is when things start to seem very flat and I don't see any point, just everything turns grey and there just seems no point in anything. I don't feel that way when I'm sad.

CLARE: Is duration a factor? Every now and again I may feel like that, I do feel like that, but, I wonder whether duration is important. To feel it for a day, or to feel it for a couple of days even, that 'Oh God, there doesn't seem any way out of this, that or the other' is, in a sense, different from it persisting over a period of time. You know the old GP adage, 'Let's see how it is over a week,' and often indeed it clears.

JAMISON: Right, and I think that, you know, for good reason, the diagnostic criteria require at least two weeks. And it's usually longer than that. Actually, untreated bipolar depression is usually 9–12 months long, so you're not talking about being depressed for a day or two, you're talking about very extended, very severe and very disruptive sleep patterns, very disrupted energy, a total loss of energy and so forth. So it's both severity and duration.

CLARE: What about the emotional turmoil of falling in love, of being in love? I was particularly struck reading your account of your experiences, you had three relationships in your life, your first marriage, the relationship with David who died, and now your current marriage. And you write very powerfully about the emotion of love as much as the emotion of mania. I am immediately struck that there's quite an overlap sometimes. It's a single-minded focus, falling in love. It's a bit different from virtually all other enthusiasms. So it would seem sometimes to me from reading people who write powerfully about being in love. When you had accepted that you have this condition, did it make you then distrust your feelings of love, of involvement with people?

JAMISON: No, I think I've been very lucky in that respect. I think I could if I had not been lucky, I can see how I would but I've actually been fortunate in falling for men who were very nice. Both David and my husband, and my first husband actually, are all remarkably stable men.

CLARE: Your first husband, I can't remember what happened?

JAMISON: Yes, he was a painter and we got divorced.

CLARE: It didn't work out?

JAMISON: It didn't work out, no. I wanted children and he didn't and there was a series of things. But we're very, very good friends. They all are, were, very steady people and they somehow understood me or were able to leave me alone. You know you can get into relationships where people exacerbate the illness and make it worse, and make you more agitated and put demands upon you that are impossible. I've been fortunate in a sense that I have had people who've been pretty, pretty understanding.

CLARE: Yes, how important is that? Your present husband is a psychiatrist but he's a psychiatrist of a somewhat different school?

JAMISON: He studies brains. Yes, but he's not detached. I think, fortunately in many ways, he's not a terribly introspective person. He's not that kind of psychiatrist and I'm not sure that would be great in our relationship. It might be. It would probably be very different.

CLARE: You mean if he were introspective?

JAMISON: Yes, if he were introspective, oh yes certainly, if he were volatile. I have been involved with people who were more volatile and it's a different kind of experience.

CLARE: Is it explosive?

JAMISON: It's explosive and more intense, you know perhaps more good and bad in a way. But my husband is quite wonderful because he absolutely loves me and has this sense to sort of leave me alone, but sort of hang around on the fringe for sort of security. It doesn't happen very much that I get sick very much any more or disturbed, but he's very understanding about that.

CLARE: How often would it happen?

JAMISON: Now, it's actually much more inclined just to kind of go up for a while and I may be a bit irritable. The one thing that we do is we buy a lot of video tapes because if I get at all depressed, which isn't very often at all, but when I do, I don't feel like going out to the movies, I don't feel like doing anything and just pop video tapes. So there are certain things, you know, kind of practical things.

CLARE: But is his lack of introspection a protection? Does it mean that he finds it easier to curb your enthusiasms because he doesn't necessarily share them?

JAMISON: Yes, and he doesn't get caught up in them. I think he doesn't. If he were perhaps more wired like me, he would be more inclined to get into the fray. I find it impossible to be with somebody and get deeply involved with that person. I think he loves me very deeply but he leaves it at a comfort level for him which is good for him, it's good for me.

CLARE: As we've talked, we've used words that are politically very incorrect. You've used words like 'crazy', 'insane', 'ravingly mad'. You have preferred 'manic depression' to the more technical 'bipolar affective disorder', though you're a world expert in both since it's the same condition. I have to confess that I'm split on this because, on the one hand, I worry about the way in which the language of psychiatry is used to smear and stigmatise, on the other hand, there's something very robust about these terms. They're honest. What you're describing is close to the truth and the newer words are scientifically detaching, dehumanising in a way. You've used these words and I wondered whether you feel (a) you do it deliberately and (b) what do you think is going to be made of that by your colleagues?

JAMISON: If I use the word 'crazy', I mean something by it. If somebody uses the word 'crazy' to be insulting or demeaning, then I get just as angry as anybody else. But I think to try and bleach the English language of expressive words is ultimately more stigmatising because it says you're so frail, you're so vulnerable that you can't handle normal language. These words do describe things. I think 'madness' is a great word. Again, if people use it to stigmatise, then they're going to stigmatise anyway. I don't agree with my colleagues that you just tidy up the language and you solve problems of stigma. I think that's ridiculous. I think it's so absurd that I can't even begin to believe that people think that way because it's not that simple. If it were that simple it would have been solved a long time ago. I think that people who have this illness really should be able to use whatever they want to describe themselves. And some people definitely feel more comfortable saying they have 'bipolar illness' or 'bipolar disorder'. A lot of people feel like I do, that they feel more comfortable saying 'manic depressive'. I mean, to me 'manic depressive' is descriptive, it's what it is. If you have bipolar disorder, you still have mania and you still have depression. You don't get rid of the problem by calling it something else. One of the reasons why Fred Goodwin and I, when we wrote our textbook on manic-depressive illness, used the term 'manic-depressive illness' is because, scientifically, it's incorrect really to say 'bipolar'. It assumes a distinction from regular depression that we don't know is true and it's very often a mixed states. You very often have mania mixed in with depression. So it's an historic term.

CLARE: Yes, that's something I think people don't quite realise. When you say mania mixed up with depression, you mean simultaneously the same kind of experiences. You've had that? What is that like?

JAMISON: Well, probably the most common form of quote, mixed states is to have a very morbid mood, very morbid thinking and a very high energy level. So you have this almost electrical sensation, very agitated, impulsive state, physical state.

CLARE: But depressed?

JAMISON: But depressed. And that's when most people kill themselves. It's a very lethal state and a not uncommon state. So when people say 'bipolar', they assume that depression's over here on one side, neat and tidy, and mania's over here on this side. But, clinically, it doesn't make sense to describe a lot of manic-depressive illness that way.

CLARE: You talk about the genetic research and you say they're close to identifying at least one of the genes because there may be many involved. The implications of all of that of course are that, in another age, someone like you won't exist? We'll breed you out or you'll treat us out or whatever it is. How do you feel about that? This is a paradox. You are what you are, illness and all. You are a very good example, I suppose, of this very interesting question of the evolutionary value of an illness. In fact, it could be said that Laing picked the wrong illness when he picked schizophrenia and thought it was an illness that said something about the sane, that it had its own voyage to reality. Manic depression is closer to that. In it's milder versions it gives considerable insight into the human condition and most, certainly many of the great artists, as you have skilfully identified in another book you wrote, *Touched with Fire*, many of the great artists have been touched by this illness and their art is enmeshed with it, and perhaps many of us would argue, enriched by it. So there are moral questions, or philosophical questions, raised by genetic interference with an illness like manic depression that I think over-arch or certainly are of a different order from the moral questions raised from, say, genetic interference in schizophrenia, which seems to be an utterly fragmenting and disintegrative disease, for many people, not for all, but for many people. So, coming back to you and putting it very personally, a gene available, perhaps when you were in your mother's womb or perhaps even before, but certainly then, would mean that Kay Jamison as we know her, we would not now know her?

JAMISON: It's very frightening to me. I spend a lot of my time actually on this issue. I think on the one hand that genetic research has the capacity to give us better treatments, less problematic treatments, more accurate diagnosis, earlier diagnosis, so people don't have to die, don't have to suffer. So I think those things are extraordinarily important and I actually spend a lot of time raising money for genetic research for these reasons. However, I spend more time trying to deal with the ethical issues and, in fact, later this year we're having a large meeting at Coldspring Harbor Laboratory on the evolutionary biology of manic-depressive illness and why it survives in the gene pool. Because my concern is, OK, once you do find a gene, of course you do have a genetic test almost immediately, and if you have this genetic test, would people abort? It turns out this just hasn't been studied. I supervised a medical student at Johns Hopkins on this and asked about 50 manic depressives and their spouses, 'Would you use this test and would you abort a foetus if it did have the manic-depression gene?' Actually, it turned out that most of them said that they would not abort. I don't think we know. If you could prevent this gene from occurring at all in the entire gene pool, would you get rid of it? Well, I think that's a horrifying thought. I think actually most geneticists think that's a horrifying thought. Manic-depressive illness is frequently used as an example of an illness that confers advantage to society while not necessarily conveying an advantage to the individual. So the decisions you would make as a clinician or as an individual patient or as a family member, might be very different from the decisions that you would make as a member of society. As a member of society the thought that people would start tampering with the gene pool is just terrifying to me. But if it were a nephew or a niece of mine, I would want to be able to have that information available for them. I would want them to have that information available to know in terms of their own treatment, not to prevent them being born but for clinical reasons, you know, so that they could get better earlier treatment, if they needed it.

CLARE: Did you not have children because of manic-depressive illness?

JAMISON: No. I did not have children because the man I wanted to have children with died. And my husband, my current husband, has three children already. But, it's a consideration. It was not a consideration for me, I would have had children.

CLARE: You would?

JAMISON: Absolutely.

CLARE: Knowing as you do that . . .

JAMISON: That it's genetic, yes.

CLARE: That you not only know that it's genetic, you can give a rough estimate of in, say, four children, how many of them might well have an illness very similar to yours or even more severe. But you still would?

JAMISON: I would have children because I have a treatable illness. I think if my illness were not treatable I would be concerned about how well I could raise a child. But it's a treatable illness. In 15 or 20 years when a child would be born, it's going to be much more treatable, it's not going to be less treatable. So it's not like Huntington's disease where you take a test and you've got a 50 per cent chance of having the disease, whether you would pass it on or not. I think that's very different.

CLARE: Do you think that your upbringing was less traumatic because it was your father who had the cyclothymic mood swings and not your mother?

JAMISON: It's an interesting question. Probably, yes, I think probably. Yes, probably. It's hard for me to say because actually my father was very involved in our upbringing. It was a very nice thing about my father. He was a very involved parent. The stability came from my mother. Oh yes, my mother was a terrific mother. She was always there, always available, very supportive.

CLARE: Is she still alive?

JAMISON: Yes.

CLARE: What is she like, temperamentally what is she like?

JAMISON: Temperamentally she's very stable.

CLARE: Is she to your father what your husband is to you?

JAMISON: Yes, I think so. Characterwise you know, she is very strong and very loving, very unmoody. I've never seen her really depressed. I've never seen her wildly enthusiastic. I'm glad I had both. I'm glad I had my father the way he was and my mother.

CLARE: It sounds as if it's a good recipe.

JAMISON: Yes.

CLARE: The worst thing to do is for a manic-depressive person to marry another manic-depressive person.

JAMISON: But it happens all the time of course.

CLARE: Indeed. Is not having children a major regret?

JAMISON: Yes, without question. I always thought, growing up, I would have a house full of children. I regret it almost every day, yes. Yes, I wish I had children. I do fortunately have great nieces and nephews but that's not the same.

CLARE: Do you regret having manic depression?

JAMISON: I regret having manic depression in the sense that it's taken a lot of years of my life and it's cost an enormous amount of pain. Given that it's treatable for me, I would choose to have it, but I think that that's just because my form of it happens to be very treatable. As soon as I get depressed, I would never say that, you know.

CLARE: As soon as you get depressed?

JAMISON: I would not say this if I were depressed. I would not say this if I were manic. I say this with the luxury of having been relatively stable for many years now and seeing the benefits in my life. But the disadvantages of manic-depressive illness are so overwhelming and so ghastly in terms of your notion of yourself and losing your mind and losing all the years. You lose a lot of your life to this disease.

CLARE: When you said that you have to keep a monitor on your moods, you have to keep a check, you were talking about you personally keeping a check. But, of course, it means that anyone who knows you really well, and loves you or is involved with you, also keeps a check, keeps a wary eye out. Your mother, your husband, your colleagues.

JAMISON: Friends, yes.

CLARE: Sometimes people jib at that. They get irritated. They feel it suggests that once a manic depressive, always a manic depressive.

JAMISON: In a way. Though, you know, that's true up to a point. But when you're well, people who know you treat you as though you're well. I don't know on the fringes but people just sort of assume you're fine when you're fine. And I remember a great line that Joshua Logan, the film director, wrote in his autobiography about his manic-depressive illness, and he said he was talking to a psychiatrist and he'd gone up and down the eastern seaboard naked, he was just really, really out of it, and he said to his psychiatrist, 'How can I ever go back to Hollywood, how can I ever convince anybody that I'm sane again?' And his psychiatrist said, 'Because if you walk into a room, and you act normally, people will treat you as though you're normal.' And I remember reading that and for some reason, in the mist of all the chaos, that really sustained me. And the fact of the matter is if you're *compos mentis* and sane and normal, people forget about your illness, people who know you. People who don't know you may be seeing, may be reading all sorts of things into you. But my friends don't sit around, I don't feel people are kind of fluttering around me hovering and so forth. I think people know me better than that and don't do that. Occasionally my mother worries, which I think is very natural. I think it would be pretty abnormal if she didn't. And occasionally my husband. I think, well, why don't you just give it a rest, but that's very unusual actually.

CLARE: Has this illness, like other illnesses do for other people, has this illness sharpened your sense of mortality?

JAMISON: Unquestionably, unquestionably. And for everyone I know. I have a lot of friends and colleagues who have manic-depressive illness and we talk about the big D a lot.

CLARE: The big D being . . .

JAMISON: Death.

CLARE: Not depression?

JAMISON: Death, death, yes, yes. I think that if you're severely depressed you think about death and dying so much and then when you get well, you're very aware of wanting to pack in as much as possible. I always feel a little bit like a squirrel, you know, storing up nuts for the bad times. And I think you do that in relationships. One of the things I tell my patients is you've really got to take care of your friendships when you're well. Be aware that it's very depleting when you're ill. It may be that people ought to be terrific, nice and so forth, but it's not in human nature just to give endlessly. You wouldn't want to do that to somebody else and so forth. I think you really have to nurture that and I think the sense of death and the awareness of it from depression does make you much more inclined to try and live life pretty intensively, yes definitely.

CLARE: And is that because you're anxious about your mortality, you are anxious that you might get into a state where your life would end? You quoted a suicide rate of 20 per cent. That is a statistic with direct relevance to you. Are you saying that you're never that confident that this illness is beaten? You never can tell when it might grab you by the neck?

JAMISON: No, I think that's true. I think that's realistic, to be concerned about remission. I think I have every good reason to be optimistic that my illness is in control, but I also know the illness well enough to know that it can come back. That's just life and I know that I have the kind of violent depression and violent manias that make me much more likely to commit suicide than somebody else. If I just take a cold-blooded clinical look at the kind of disease I have, I am an extremely high risk for suicide if I'm not responding well to drugs. Now I also have the kind of illness that's very responsive to drugs but I know that that can happen again, sure. In the same way my husband had stage 4B Hodgkin's disease about 20 years ago, he nearly died, he had cancer everywhere. When he gets sick now, I first think does he have a recurrence of Hodgkin's? And then he gets well and I don't think about it any more for a while. I think you have to be completely dead not to think about these things. Manic depression is a recurring illness.

CLARE: Kay Jamison, thank you very much indeed.

JAMISON: Thank you.

Nigel Kennedy

'If you wish for reputation and fame in the world and success during your lifetime,' Oscar Wilde once remarked, 'you are right to take every opportunity of advertising yourself. You remember the Latin saying, Fame springs from one's own house.' He could have been speaking of Nigel Kennedy, widely regarded as Britain's finest post-war violinist and simultaneously described as madcap, nutty, scruffy and a boozy yob. In the early years of his public career, Kennedy cultivated an extravagantly laddish, wilful, disorganised persona, a sort of classical punk/grunge yob. There were hints of abuse of alcohol and even more of drugs. A spiky haircut, baggy trousers, luminous socks and Doc Martens, together with a slang-filled vocabulary and mangled vowels, combined to suggest an overgrown schoolboy with the personal habits and social manners of a drop-out on acid. In spite of or, if Wilde is right, because of, such much-publicised extravagances married to his virtuoso musical ability, Kennedy during this period enjoyed quite extraordinary fame and fortune and effortlessly bridged the previously awesome chasm between the Albert Hall and *Top of the Pops*, between Jimi Hendrix and Fritz Kreisler.

It was not, however, until I interviewed Nigel Kennedy that I fully realised what a repetitive family cycle of talent and abandonment his own life story contains. Nigel's father was an alcoholic who walked out on his wife just before Nigel was born and whose own talent sadly burned out. That much I did know. I did not know that his father had himself suffered precisely the same fate at the hands of *his* father, Nigel's grandfather, an exceedingly talented cellist, who played with such artists as Heifetz and Kreisler. I was

234

interested in the effect on the young and growing Nigel Kennedy of this absent father. Nigel is himself fairly scathing about him and quite reluctant to forgive him for the emotional pain and the financial and other difficulties his abandonment caused. His father's behaviour was blamed on alcoholism but Kennedy remains unsympathetic despite the fact that his father was left in the hands not of his mother, as was the case with Nigel, but in the care of somebody who was not family at all. The very self-reliance that Kennedy has had to develop and sustain as a consequence of the paternal separation fuels his continued rejection. He does not mince his words: '. . . I had never much sympathy with my dad for being a wonderful talent who was destroyed by alcohol because at some point in his life he had the choice – is he going to drink a lot or get on with his job?'

Kennedy has got on with the job. The violin and the music – they became the reason he survived, the reason anyone seemed to take note of him, to care for him, to educate him, from the earliest of years. There is much anger in Kennedy still concerning not merely his father's abandonment but his mother's decision to send him off to the Menuhin school while she made a new life, a new family for herself. Note during this interview the way in which Kennedy, obliquely for the most part, but on one or two occasions explicitly, refers to his loss of family. Of his mother remarrying and going off to the Midlands, he remarks, 'my whole family circumstance was obliterated and I didn't really have a chance to get into the new family because I was at Yehudi's school.' He felt like a cork floating on an ocean of other people's destinies and seems to feel that that is where his steely determination, his absolutely incorrigible insistence on doing things his way, comes from. For much of the time in the Menuhin school he appears to have coped with the traumatic separation, the unfamiliarity, the loneliness, by withdrawal into his own inner world. The image he conjures up at that time is 'a bit of hibernation' while to Yehudi Menuhin, as he relates in his autobiography *Unfinished Business*, he seemed 'almost becalmed'. Menuhin, incidentally, confirms that an important influence on Kennedy, musically and psychologically, was the late, great jazz violinist Stephane Grappelli, who took him under his wing and quickly gave the adolescent a sense of confidence in his ability not merely to interpret the great classics but to improvise and experiment. There seems little doubt that Menuhin and Grappelli made an important contribution as surrogate fathers of Nigel Kennedy through late childhood and early adolescence and mitigated, to an extent at least, the absence of his own father during this time.

The psychological problems of child musical prodigies are well recognised. The British pianist Terence Judd was found dead at Beachy Head aged 22. He had spent over half his life as a public performer. The Greek pianist prodigy Dimitri Sgouros was burned out and finished as a performer before he even reached his twenties. Another pianist, the Australian David Helfgott, broke down with manic depression, driven by a relentlessly ambitious father – his breakdown and subsequent recovery portrayed in the Oscar-winning film, *Shine*. Nigel Kennedy, sometime before I interviewed him, had expressed quite bitter and critical views of the demands placed on young musicians, declaring that there is 'something monstrous or abnormal about prodigies playing at the ages of ten or 12'. In addition to the very real stresses of public performance and parental expectation, there is the difficulty for child prodigies in distinguishing between how much they are loved by their parents for their own sake, that is to say as children in their own right, and how much because they possess a rare talent which is avidly prized and diligently cultivated by the parents. In the worst cases, over-ambitious parents invade and take over their children's lives, live out their own fantasies of fame and success. In Kennedy's case, this conflict was exacerbated by the fact that, while his mother was concerned enough by his musical talent to ensure that he got the very best scholastic opportunities available – at the Yehudi Menuhin school – she did not appear sufficiently concerned about his feelings, his psychological development, but went off and established a new relationship for herself and a new family from which the young Nigel clearly felt excluded. Where he blames his father for wasting a musical talent, he blames his mother for putting that talent before himself as a person. Perhaps his mother saw in the Menuhin school and in Menuhin himself the opportunity to ensure that her seven-year-old prodigy could be enabled to do what her husband, Nigel's father, was unable to do, namely to develop as a mature adult and as a talented artist. But for Nigel there just appeared to be an irreconcilable dilemma – confronted by the sense of himself as a child and as a prodigy, he asks himself, 'Which one of me is the real thing?'

That question holds the key, in my view, to understanding Nigel Kennedy and the rollercoaster life he has led since his productive and talented years at the Menuhin school. There has been a conflict between the Nigel who wants to be accepted for what he is, no matter how outrageous, provocative and difficult, and the Nigel who does not want to be like his father, a disappointment, a waster of prodigious talent and a failure to his son. And without a resolution or an acceptance of the dilemma it was unlikely that Kennedy could continue as a musician. Success, such as he had with the 1990 album of Vivaldi's *Four Seasons*, only exacerbated his sense of being owned by his talent rather than the other way around. He had to find himself not merely as a performer with an interpretative style and an emotional approach to the music distinct from Menuhin but also as a man, free-spirited, multi-talented and with many interests, who happened also to be the finest young violinist in the country. And so he stopped playing in public for a while. An operation to remove cysts on his neck, which had developed as a consequence of his repeated playing, gave him, as it were, an alibi to take time out, but the real value of this break is that it enabled him to take stock of just who he was and where was he going. It is interesting to note how he spent this period of reflection – maintaining and developing his other interests, particularly football (the attractions of Aston Villa being described in those familiar family terms), and putting his musical talent into some kind of balanced perspective. And it does appear to have helped him come to terms with some aspects of his past, in particular the difficult choice his mother made all those years ago.

Now he himself is a family man, a father to another young Kennedy, his son Sark. He has a new responsibility over and above that he owes to his girlfriend, Eve, Sark's mother, and to his music. I ask him whether the cycle of paternal abandonment is going to be broken. He is crucially aware of the importance of family life to him but honest enough to admit that in any conflict between the demands of his music and those of his family he is not absolutely sure for which side of the divide he would opt.

CLARE: 'The wild boy of the classical world' as he is often referred to, Nigel Kennedy was born into a family of musicians. His mother, like his grandmother, was a pianist; his father, who walked out on his family just before Nigel was born in 1956, was a principal cellist. At the age of seven he was sent away by his mother to the Yehudi Menuhin School, and at 16, continued his education at the renowned Juilliard School of Performing Arts in New York.

Following his debut as a solo concert violinist with the Philharmonic Orchestra in the Festival Hall in 1977, he enjoyed quick success and popular acclaim. He has performed all over the world both as a classical and jazz violinist, secured a place in the *Guinness Book of Records* with his recording of Vivaldi's *Four Seasons*, which has become the biggest-selling classical album of all times and was voted Show Business Personality of the Year in 1991.

While his innate talent is never in question, he began to attract derisive comments from much of the classical establishment. His trademark punk hairstyle, sartorially challenged way of dressing, suggestions of heavy drinking and laddish antics as an Aston Villa supporter, all went against the grain and earned him such nicknames as the Liberace of the 'nineties or the Clown Prince of Cringe. Then, still in his thirties, he announced that he was going to abandon the world of classical music for ever and disappeared from public view for five years, during which time he was laid up for some months following two operations to remove cysts from his neck where the violin digs deep into his skin. He began his comeback in early 1997 with a highly praised concert in the Festival Hall, in the words of *The Times*, 'the wild boy of classical music has found an astonishing new maturity.'

Nigel Kennedy, people seem to detect in you a change, a transformation, do you feel in some way a changed person?

KENNEDY: Well, not particularly at this time any more than other times. I think it's one's job as a human being, particularly myself in my trade, where you're making music and analysing in hopefully as objective way as possible what you're doing, it's your job to analyse yourself, so maybe that carries over into my other aspects of life, outside music as well. But I think change is a healthy thing and, if there's one constant thing in my artistic life or in my so-called, rest of my life, I think change should be the constant really.

CLARE: Are you interested in yourself?

KENNEDY: It's difficult to say. Sometimes I'm really not interested in myself at all because I spend so much time dissecting and being very self-critical of myself in my work that when I've finished working, it's almost like I want to forget about myself and maybe either go off on my own somewhere and find total solitude, or else be surrounded by a lot of people who take me out of myself. Because it's such an inward-looking, almost destructively critical job, playing music, you know you have to take yourself to pieces and almost build up afresh every time you approach a great masterpiece by someone like Beethoven or Bach. It's no good if you say, 'Oh well, I've played this Bach work last year so I will start from there.' The only way that you can really communicate properly the music that you're going to play is if you start afresh from square one each time you approach that work, and that requires unlearning lots of bad habits, being very self-critical in order to then get to that area of freedom where you can really communicate the music truthfully instead of just by habit.

CLARE: Now when you talk there you say, 'unlearn bad habits' and I'm thinking, 'bad habits of playing, of technique, of musician-ship'? or 'bad personal habits'? Are you talking about both?

KENNEDY: Well, there's a bit of each there. Obviously, I'd be going for the musicianship habitual-playing type of thing because habitual playing is no good to anybody. If you've got an audience listening, they want to hear something as if it's new and if it's fresh, and if there's been real interrogative thought put into it, and so the habitual things in the violin technique, definitely, the bad habits can grow quite quickly and they take longer to get rid of. You know, unlearning things is quite a lot more difficult than learning things. But then it goes to the rest of my life. You know, if I've got an important project coming up, I'll give up things like drinking, treat it a bit like a boxing match, how the fighters prepare to focus their mentality, they prepare by cordoning themselves off from any activities which might be derogatory to them doing a good job.

CLARE: So you're quite focused?

KENNEDY: I like to be very focused when I'm doing my work and obviously I pay for that in other areas of my life a little bit.

CLARE: I'll come back to that in a moment. Are you unapproachable when you're focused? Take that comeback night in 1997 – in those days and weeks before it, were you a different sort of person? Were you less approachable, more turned in upon yourself? Or are you still the same friendly, cheerful Nige?

KENNEDY: Well, I think at home, things are a lot more difficult than after I've finished a gig. You know then everything's relaxed and everything's cool, but when I'm preparing for something I have to find my own space where I can work. Maybe because I'm picking on myself as a musician I might start picking on other people as well. So quite often what happens is that a few days before an important gig I'll go off and leave the rest of the family in order that I don't start picking on them and I can just get on with picking on myself.

CLARE: And would you physically go away somewhere?

KENNEDY: Yeah, yeah. I'd come down to London or something and just work on my own. If I've got any negative repercussion from working on my music, it's not other people who are being hit by it.

CLARE: And would that be for some days you'd do that?

KENNEDY: Yeah, a couple, two or three days.

CLARE: What are you like in your own company?

KENNEDY: I'm very happy in my own company because playing classical music requires a lot of practice, which you do on your own. So I'm used to having that time every day on my own and I tend to get a little bit disturbed if I don't have that space any more. And becoming possibly more successful in my musical career aspects, you tend to find you're getting less, less time to yourself and it's something that I really covet quite a lot, and so I feel very happy being on my own for a certain amount of time. Obviously I enjoy people's company as well but there's times when people need time on their own, I think.

CLARE: And, you're a man with many interests. I wondered how does that live with the life of a professional soloist? The question I put to you I'd put to say a top class businessman or a sportsman or a single-minded politician, and that is, how much of your work is so absorbing that it becomes harder and harder to protect the other aspects of your life?

KENNEDY: It does tend to be overwhelming the work that I put in. Sometimes it could, without me knowing it, lead to neglect of other aspects of my life.

CLARE: And other people?

KENNEDY: Well, and even people sometimes. I suddenly realise I haven't called up a friend for six months or something and then I feel so bad about it I can hardly pick up the telephone to call them up. It tends to be this kind of chicken and egg thing, you know, got to pick up the phone sometime and call them, but feel really bad about not having done that. Even in my close circle, people have to learn to be a little bit independent themselves and have some interests of their own as well, because for so much time each day that I'm pursuing my own interest in a very isolated way. So my little kid swinging on the curtains and like pulling all my CDs out of the shelves while I'm trying to play the violin! Music has to come from total silence otherwise it doesn't mean anything because music is a contrast between sound and silence and colours of sound. So you need to be starting from a blank canvas to be able to do that. If you've got noise, it's a bit like asking a painter to paint on an already started canvas by somebody else. So that way it makes it difficult for me to actually pay attention to other people as much as possibly people in another job might. Although on the other hand I have the advantage of when I am at home, being at home for long periods of time. You know, I'm not governed by the nine to five thing of – got to be out of the house in someone else's office doing the work.

CLARE: Are you good at saying no?

KENNEDY: To whom?

CLARE: To people who want you to do more and more. People are always asking things of you – help with various things, concerts, appearances, interviews like this and so on?

KENNEDY: Well, I think I've become very good with the interviews like saying no to the ones I don't want to do and I've got an instinct as to which ones would actually interest me that I can actually contribute something hopefully useful to it. Concerts, maybe. I think every musician has this problem. Coming from a background where every college has got 1,000 people leaving each year, all looking for work – and I've played in front of empty concert halls in the early stages of my career – so maybe concerts are something I find a little bit more difficult to turn down, because there's that slight insecurity from the very beginning of my career that, you know, I'm really lucky to have people coming to my concerts. For so many musicians are finding it difficult to get concerts and stuff, so I find it difficult to turn down concerts, particularly with people that I'd really like to work with. There's always new things around the corner and I always end up trying to do too much.

CLARE: Do you ever have a feeling that this is a heavy responsibility, this talent?

KENNEDY: Sometimes I think about the areas of my life that have been sacrificed for the talent which I'm trying to give the best chance of fulfilling its potential, because I know I've got some talent in there. I think lots of people I've met have had equal talent to myself but maybe wouldn't have had the obstinacy or courage, or whatever you want to call it, to pursue the fulfilling of their potential and so it does mean that you have to give something to gain something.

CLARE: Do you feel you have been pretty single minded?

KENNEDY: Yeah, I'm very much one of those type of people who focuses on something and says, 'Well, that's what I want to do.' People who've worked with me have learnt that either to their regret or otherwise – that once I make up my mind I want to do something, then I'm pretty much going to do that before I do anything else.

CLARE: Really! And this would be what you'd sacrifice everything else for?

KENNEDY: Yeah, if you get a vision of what you want to do. Maybe being born into playing classical music has been particularly lucky for me and jazz music equally lucky. There is a standard already there to live up to and to learn someone else's way of thinking who's on a par of Beethoven or Bach, for instance, is just such an amazing thing and to have a vision of something and to actually be able to go and do that and have it come off and work, that is something that is so fulfilling that it's very difficult to say no to afterwards. I think it's a very privileged position to be in, to actually be able to think, well, this is what I'd like to do and I know that if I put in the amount of work that is necessary, I can probably do it, you know, with a little element of luck as well.

CLARE: And what would you have sacrificed?

KENNEDY: Probably being able to play for a football team every week! The normal things, like going to the pub every night and having one pint too many. Maybe you know, going out for lunch and all of those things that people do, being able to forget about your job at six o'clock every evening, for instance, that's one of the main ones. I can't really do that. Because I like writing music as well, quite often I find myself waking up at three in the morning and having to go to the piano to check out the idea and put it on to a tape somewhere.

CLARE: And what would your partner say about this?

KENNEDY: 'Man, I think it's a bit weird!'

CLARE: She wouldn't just throw something at you?

KENNEDY: No, no. She knows that if she throws something at me it will only make more inspiration for another melody!

CLARE: There's this sense of the suffering artist. Now I have to say I've never seen you like that. There are many images of you and we'll come back to some of them but not the suffering Nigel. But that may be because we've missed it. Is there a sense in which sometimes you find this more than a sacrifice, but something that eats at you a bit?

KENNEDY: Well, when I'm writing it certainly affects my health sometimes because I just write so late into the night that I forget what time it is. I end up forgetting what time it is and getting not enough sleep. It's bad for your health sitting in a room crouched over a bit of paper, or over a computer or something, trying to get something finished and things are never finished when you're writing. You can always improve it so there is that trap of neglecting yourself and ... what was the question again, sorry man?

CLARE: Whether you ever suffer, really suffer, almost wish that it would all just go away?

KENNEDY: Well, yeah, but I've tried going on holiday and stuff and sitting on beaches and it doesn't really work for me. I can't really do that.

CLARE: Can you go on holiday and wander around museums and sit in café sidewalks?

KENNEDY: I need something cultural to like kind of latch on to like a vampire, you know. One of the best holidays I've done I suppose was going to watch England play in the World Cup in Italy, World Cup Italia, that was great because there was something that I loved there and it was something I could follow and it was an involvement.

CLARE: And you put the violin completely out of your mind?

KENNEDY: I still practised for an hour or two every morning. You know I get a kind of withdrawal thing, like, if I don't play.

CLARE: Do you? What's it like?

KENNEDY: It's kind of feeling dissatisfied, you know, however good things are around you. You can be with the sun beating down on you but, there's a tactile thing that you miss. It's even a physical thing as well as an emotional and mental satisfaction. It's just the tactile thing of vibration of the instrument and being in touch with some thoughts which are just so grounded. Because if you're playing other people's music, like the composers I've mentioned before, you know, Bartók, Bach, Beethoven, Brahms, it's such grounded music, it really gives me a good grounding for approaching the rest of the day if I've done something like that.

CLARE: But it would physically affect you, you would feel physically unwell?

KENNEDY: Physically I feel just a little bit uneasy not having done it, which is probably because it is an habitual thing that I'm used to doing it.

CLARE: So you'd play every day?

KENNEDY: Yeah, I like to play every day. Maybe I'd have one day off a week, you know, because that's more healthy for the violin and myself but if I'm three or four days off then I start to get a bit itchy about it.

CLARE: In the book that you wrote, you said, 'They say that your background, your schooling, all that stuff, moulds how you turn out in later life, well, I fought like hell all the way through mine not to turn out as other people thought I should and I'm proud of that achievement.' What was it that other people thought you should turn out as?

KENNEDY: Well, everyone's got preconceptions about everybody and how they should be and probably it was more of a general battle on behalf of myself as an individual.

CLARE: Well, what did your mother want you to turn out as?

KENNEDY: She wanted me to turn out as something which would be a totally fulfilling thing to be doing but she never put pressure on me by estimating my talent as being so good that I should be the next Menuhin or the next Heifetz but, inwardly I think, perhaps that is what she would have liked me to have become. But that doesn't take into account the changing of generations and the fact that people actually do have access to more different kinds of music. I think class, hopefully, is a thing of the past now. I mean people still like to live the roles of it but I'm not favouring any political vision of a classless society, which is a rather clichéd phrase, but I think, you know, people relating to each other, and not being stuck in one background, is a freedom of the intellect and a freedom of the potential of each individual involved. And so as far as music is concerned, you can't say, 'Well, I want my kid to be the next Milstein or Menuhin,' because they were born in the early 1900s, late 1800s and were from a different background.

CLARE: People of their time. What has she made of you?

KENNEDY: She's happy now because she hears me play and luckily it seems to give her some joy, you know.

CLARE: Did she worry that you would turn out like your father?

KENNEDY: She's never actually voiced that sentiment, that she was worried about that, but I think she was quite keen that maybe I would have a chance to satisfy myself through my music and not blow it in a way that maybe one or two generations of my family have done before.

CLARE: Was that the picture you'd got? That would be the story, the family story told was of talent wasted?

KENNEDY: Really, yes. I think it's not a totally unique scenario to my family, because I think there's been a British attitude towards the arts and sport which has been that they should be strictly amateur and we shouldn't be seen to be trying. But unless you try you can never know really what you can do. But, on the other hand, if you do try, there's always a danger that you find out that you can't do as much as you thought your potential will allow you to do. So there's always that kind of what you would call fear amongst the English culture of trying their hardest because they might find that their best isn't as good as what they could hypothetically make it, by saying, 'Well, if I had worked, I could have done this and that.' Which is the typical scenario with British musicians that I've noticed. So many are so talented and then they go to the Royal Academy of Music, drink the subsidised beer at like, 50p a pint, and then say, 'Well, if I had practised I could have done this and that.' Whereas to get in there and practise ...

CLARE: You could be Nigel Kennedy?

KENNEDY: Yeah, well you know, and so she was worried I think my mum, about that scenario developing.

CLARE: Your father left before you were born. I know you've been asked about it many times, but what I'm particularly interested in, because this often happens, is that an image of the absent father is created and all sorts of things go to form that image, and some of them are perhaps true and some aren't. What's interesting is the effect of it, and I wondered, what was the image that you did have of him? Did you know, for example, that he had been a musician?

KENNEDY: Well, yes, I definitely knew about him and that he'd been the first cello under Thomas Beecham, who was one of the greatest conductors. People would come up to me when I started playing with orchestras and it was quite disconcerting that they'd know my dad much better than I did, because I'd only met him on maybe two or three isolated occasions.

CLARE: So he had been a talented man?

KENNEDY: He had been talented and quite an individual and people just estimated his talent as being very high and they said what a waste.

CLARE: And the second question is: had you any idea what was the cause of the waste? It must have intrigued you people saying to you, 'Oh, I knew your dad,' and so on, and of course they'd be communicating a number of things to you – he was very talented and there was a waste; but did you ever get any sense of what had gone wrong?

KENNEDY: Well, it's been blamed on alcoholism and I've got to admit it may be not a very pleasant trait of my personality but I don't really have much sympathy for people who become addicted to drugs of any type or alcohol, because I really believe in playing a hand in your own destiny. I really believe in that and so if you let something take control of your life, you've made that choice and, you know, you've got to do something about it. And so I never had much sympathy with my dad for being a wonderful talent who was destroyed by alcohol because at some point in his life he had the choice – is he going to drink a lot or get on with his job? I think the whole of modern-day society seems to be basing itself on less self-determination for each individual person and more on reliance on computers, on everything else apart from the individual's own will to get from A to B. And I'm very much subscribing to the opposite philosophy – that as an individual if you're lucky enough, I know there are some adverse circumstances which people get born into which then negate the odds shockingly, but if you're lucky enough in the way that I was to have been born into a piano-teaching family, not a lot of money but great access to something that I really loved, if you're lucky enough in that area, then there's no excuses, you know. You can't make excuses for things, you've got to get up there and do your best.

CLARE: So my next question would, in a sense, be a kind of excuse! Did you know anything about your father's life that would explain, not necessarily justify or even excuse, but would make meaningful why a man with talent destroyed it?

KENNEDY: Well, yeah, because my dad's life was very similar to the beginnings of my life. He was, well to put it in a cruel way, abandoned by my grandad who was busy touring and was a cellist himself. He was actually a very good cellist, if I may be kind of orientated towards how great my family was for a second. He played in the same quartet as Heifetz and Fritz Kreisler and things like that, so he was an excellent player.

CLARE: And a Kennedy.

KENNEDY: And a Kennedy as well. He left Ireland. He was taken off by my great-grandad as part of a vaudeville troupe which went to Australia and I've got pictures of the wagon with 'The Kennedy Troupe' written on the side and apparently my grandad got up and played bagpipes and stuff like that at first. But he learnt the cello, good talent at it, and played really well but then decided to leave my dad in the hands of someone else not related to the family at all. So, in that respect, my dad had it worse than myself – maybe a slightly turbulent, unrooted beginning to his life. So maybe that's a good excuse. But you find so many orphans and people who have done so well with their life, you know, people who've come from much worse circumstances than any of my family have, and they've done so well for themselves and for the people around them that you can't really use these things as excuses I don't think.

CLARE: When you met him, did you talk much? You met him twice I think you said.

KENNEDY: Yeah, we didn't really have a lot of chance to talk because he was too busy telling me how to play, which at my age, at that point I was 17 or 18, I was a bit bolshie and not wanting to be told by anybody how to play. And so I said, 'Well look, if you want to tell me how to play, get the cello out and show me.' But, unfortunately, the alcoholic excess had taken too much toll because I would have loved it if he had got the cello out and we could have communicated in that way. That would have meant something a whole lot to me actually really. But he wasn't able to do that.

CLARE: What I'm getting at and do resist it by all means, what I'm getting at is ...

KENNEDY: You're getting in there, you're burrowing in!

CLARE: I wondered whether in your determination not to be certain things that people expected, that that, in its own way, that that has been a powerful influence? Let's take the issue of alcohol. You've certainly flirted with it, you've drunk a bit in your time, but would you always have had at the back of your mind that warning, that notion that this was something you weren't going to let master you. Were you even conscious of it as a problem, as a possible problem?

KENNEDY: Well, being the performing musician that I've been for the most part since the age of 18, or less maybe – although when I was younger than that I wouldn't have thought of getting near alcohol and would have got a severe reprimand from the Yehudi Menuhin school staff for doing it. I remember trying to ferment our own beer in that establishment and we were so impatient that we couldn't wait for it to be ready and so we drank it and puked our guts out. But from the age when I could have been involved in alcohol, I've always had important projects which I've put first you know.

CLARE: The problem with people like me is that we'll argue that childhood, and childhood experiences, have an influence whatever you say. In that I'll say your very attempts, your very insistence on not being in a box, of dressing and speaking the way you want to, of living the kind of life you want to, is itself influenced by your early childhood; the things you were not going to do were reactions to the things that other people wanted you to do. It's very hard to be uninfluenced by these things. An example of this is, I suppose, your father's career and life experience, that there are certainly clearly things that you've decided about yourself, in relation to that. His drinking, for example, has that influenced your attitude to drinking?

KENNEDY: Well, you are the psychologist and I'm not but, you know, first of all I think if people were too influenced by their surroundings and by their family background, we would all still be in the cave, and so there's got to be some . . .

CLARE: There's more to it than that!

KENNEDY: Yeah, there's some aspect of humankind which has always battled against the acceptance of the surroundings and been responsible for us moving on a bit. Hopefully, we call this progress which some people might argue about. But the aspect of me being influenced by my dad's predicament?

CLARE: Yes.

KENNEDY: It depends when one's attitudes are formed. I've always heard that people's attitudes are more formed from maybe seven to 14, or earlier ages than when I was really aware of my dad's predicament. Maybe some of the things which might have formed my attitudes were being sent to a boarding school at the age of seven and also quite a small boarding school with only 34 students in there, and my family, my mum remarrying and going up to the Midlands. So my whole family circumstance was obliterated and I didn't really have a chance to get into the new family because I was at Yehudi's school and almost like my destiny had been chosen and I didn't want my destiny to be chosen. And so maybe that's got something to do with it, with the way that I go about my life. I strongly believe, which is probably some belief I had to form at Yehudi's school to give myself some hope of light at the end of the tunnel in a situation which I wasn't particularly enjoying in the first few years.

CLARE: What was it like?

KENNEDY: It's an old Victorian house, understaffed really with people who would understand the make-up of a child, over-staffed with people who know how to make children progress in musical domains. Really the situation that I was confronted by was maybe emotionally not having the back-up that I needed, but having wonderful music to be in touch with. Not that I've analysed it myself much, but I'm sure that's where my mentality and philosophy towards my own life started.

CLARE: You would have had to be pretty self-reliant emotionally?

KENNEDY: Well, it does teach you that. I think a lot of people who have been to boarding school, even of a broader kind, would say this. Being at a school like that, with only four or five people of your own age range there, you had to make sure that you were self-reliant and able to get on and enjoy your life.

CLARE: So there would have been only four or five other seven year olds?

KENNEDY: Yeah, I would think there was only two or three, in fact, and then there was about three eight year olds as well.

CLARE: And was it physically spartan? Would it have been fairly basic?

KENNEDY: Well, I think things were quite basic but on the other hand, it hadn't exactly been luxurious at home anyway so. Piano teaching doesn't exactly bring in Rolls-Royces and Daimlers and things, so it was pretty basic in both places. But obviously being from a single parent family the motherly care which I'd become accustomed to was suddenly lacking.

CLARE: Of going there for the first time, is that a vivid memory?

KENNEDY: Yes, I remember meeting my room-mate, a guy called Michael Stanley, who I think conducts musicals nowadays, we haven't been in touch for God knows, 20 years, but he was my room-mate at the time. I remember meeting him and that was quite cheering, but it was kind of a dark day and I remember it as being a bit of a dark day really, because it was a bit of a shock suddenly finding yourself away from the umbilical cord.

CLARE: Had you been prepared for it? Did you know it was coming?

KENNEDY: Well, I knew that something was going to happen. Yehudi's parents and Yehudi himself had clubbed together to make the scholarship to facilitate my being at the school because my parents didn't have the financial background to be able to do that kind of thing. And that scholarship only got confirmed about one or two weeks before the term time started. Yehudi, particularly at that time, had loads of touring to do and other things to think about, so my parents, my mum was left wondering what on earth was going to happen to me because there was only two weeks left until the school term begun, and then she finally got the confirmation that the scholarship had been brought into reality.

CLARE: Were you her only child at the time?

KENNEDY: At the time, yes.

CLARE: How did she cope with you going? Do you remember that?

KENNEDY: I think it was a hard decision for her to make. She put a good face on it on the day but, talking in retrospect, she says it was one of the hardest decisions she ever had to make. You know it's a kind of, of balancing between doing something for my talent, which I'm supposed to have had, or doing something for me as a person. And, you know, I think in the end it's worked out both ways, that she helped my talent and I as a person am happy doing a job which I love doing.

CLARE: And if I reversed your roles, if you were her and she was you, would you do it?

KENNEDY: No, I wouldn't do that, not to a kid that young I don't think. I think so many things in the world are transient at the moment, you know. No one can rely on having a job for the whole of their life like they used to. Marriage isn't a concept which holds people together for life any more. People are having to travel to get jobs. Nothing is kind of solid any more. So I think maybe it's even more important now, if you can, everyone's human and makes mistakes, but if you can give a child a solid background at least until they're a teenager. That's got to be a good thing, I would have thought.

CLARE: So if Sark, who at the moment is seven months old, but in seven years he looks as if he's the talent you have, and an opportunity came up like that, you wouldn't take it?

KENNEDY: No, I mean if it was visiting the FA school of excellence like every now and then, that would be fine!

CLARE: Every now and again. And so you say, that's something that shaped you. I've already suggested ways in which things might shape you but what would you name as the characteristics of Nigel Kennedy that you think, 'That's where they started to be seeded, that's where they really took hold of me'? What are you thinking of?

KENNEDY: Well, I think I went dormant for a few years.

CLARE: You did yes! One of the reports described you as follows: 'He is something of a dormouse and much of the time seems to be hibernating'!

KENNEDY: Yeah, I mean there was a bit of hibernation while I kind of evaluated these circumstances of having a family which I couldn't get into really because I wasn't there.

CLARE: How long were the terms?

KENNEDY: They were three months each, three terms of three months each and then a pretty decent summer holiday which was the one where I could really get involved and see what the new family was all about.

CLARE: But I interrupted you, you said that initially you kind of were wary and took a look, like a dormouse?

KENNEDY: Yeah, but then I started finding out that areas of spontaneity were things which brought a lot of joy into my life in the music and outside it so I think I turned into a little bit of a comedian at that point because I found it was the one way of getting interaction between myself and other people around.

And also, in the music, I found that maybe not always adhering to what the teachers were saying once I started playing in front of audiences but giving reign to my own feelings within a structure, hopefully, of some kind of preparation beforehand, that the spontaneity would actually bring something more to the music.

CLARE: How early were you performing before audiences?

KENNEDY: I'd say by about 11 or 12.

CLARE: In the school?

KENNEDY: Yeah, well in the school we'd perform in front of each other and the parents, you know, pretty frequently, but then by the age of 12 we were going out, I was going out with other kids from the school and playing to real audiences.

CLARE: When did you get a sense that you had some personality? Did you get any sense that you were unusual amongst these pretty unusual kids, that you had something else?

KENNEDY: No, because I think each one was an unusual person, you know there were only 34 kids there and they'd each been chosen because of some particular talent that they had but I did find, by the time that I was about 12 or 13, that I could get things sorted on the violin with about half the amount of work that most of the other people were doing. So it suddenly became easier for me, which sometimes can be a bad thing because it means you don't devote enough time to it but I'd always only do about an hour and a half of work and then skive off and, you know, benefit from daydreaming and stuff.

CLARE: And do other things?

KENNEDY: Yeah, exactly. I think also one sign to me that I could use music as a flexible medium rather than a preconceived one was when Stephane Grappelli came to the school and quite a lot of the kids got interested in improvising but it seemed like I was the only one who could really do it. And that gave me some kind of feeling which was an obvious one, you know, I was getting involved in jazz and going off every weekend and playing with Stephane when the rest of them were just continuing to play the prescribed medicines.

CLARE: OK, they were all unusual in different ways, but I'm trying to get a sense of whether you realised you were unusual, because you are unusual. You're extraordinarily talented but you're also unusual, you're a character, you're a personality. I wondered whether you had a sense, even an intuitive sense, that you had something that you could put across that deepened people's appreciation and attracted them to you?

KENNEDY: Well, in my musical work, I had this feeling that I could go in there, on to the stage and in a way command the situation a little bit rather than be a passive recipient of the bad luck which might happen to a performer on stage. I noticed with some of the other kids, they'd get nervous and shaking bows started to invade the mood of the music and uneasiness would ruin the mood and I had a feeling that from about this age, 12, 13, that I could actually go there and communicate something I wanted to without being too uptight about it. The sense of enjoyment that I got out of the music was something I was able to communicate. It's a matter of being able to let go, I think, and also being able to leave behind the preconceived doctrine that one might have been taught. In classical music, things are quite often over-taught, as in maybe some other subjects, but definitely classical music. And in the same way that we're taught to believe what we read in every newspaper, we believe things that we read, and it's the same with musicians. People believe what they read, the notes, whereas a lot of the music has to come from your own feelings and from maybe other things, you know, other stratospheric influences.

CLARE: In a sense that calls for a certain degree of dissent, to be slightly subversive or rebellious. Was there that too?. There are a number of reports that you very helpfully provide in that book of yours and they suggest that you're changing, perhaps not changing, you're coming out of yourself. There's an image that is used about you, which I thought was interesting, that is a reference to a volcano, volcanic regions, but it's a quiet volcano, it stays dormant for a while. Did it explode from time to time?

KENNEDY: When I was at Yehudi's school I think I was pretty well within the framework of expected behaviour. There was one instance where I fell out of a girl's closet late at night when the matron was checking on the room and then I had to be housed in the headmaster's quarters so that things wouldn't go that badly awry again. But overall, I wasn't the most troublesome person at the school by a long way. Probably New York was the area, when I went there ...

CLARE: To the Juilliard?

KENNEDY: Yeah, to the Juilliard school.

CLARE: You were 16 then?

KENNEDY: Yeah. The Juilliard school was maybe neither here nor there within my formative progress as a musician, but the city itself, with all the cultural elements that it has and people having a good time, that was where I was really able to let loose and have a good time and also develop as a musician.

CLARE: So what were they getting at when they talked about being volcanic? What were they tapping? The dormouse I can understand, hibernating and so on, but there's a sense that people felt there was a passion inside you. There was some kind of anger even, or rage?

KENNEDY: There might have been some, you know, I can't really fathom it exactly because it's something which obviously someone perceptive said at the time when I didn't know what was going on in my own heart or mind. I think they saw that I could devote myself to music and do a great job within that, but for the first few years I wasn't expressing myself as a person very well because I felt a little bit amputated from the things which I'd been accustomed to having in my life.

CLARE: Yes, it's a good description, 'amputated'. And amputated suggests that there was no real way of reconnecting them?

KENNEDY: There wasn't really, you know. A new family involving my mother was starting 150 miles away with me having no access to it. There was nothing I could do about that really. I couldn't find some false circumstance of being able to become a growing part of that family.

CLARE: But did it make you angry? You refer to a new family starting up hundreds of miles away and you've in a sense been amputated from the source of that family, your mother.

KENNEDY: Yeah.

CLARE: What feelings are there?

KENNEDY: Mainly unhappiness, I think, it was really unhappiness. It didn't get transferred into anger until a little bit later on.

CLARE: In your teens?

KENNEDY: Yeah, maybe in my teens and early twenties.

CLARE: And was it a directed anger? Would you and your mother, for example, have fought and would she have been the target of the anger even if you hadn't been aware of why or was it just spread all over the place?

KENNEDY: It was mainly directed back at my mum. If she would criticise me. In the past, when she criticised me early on, I'd just take that criticism and think, 'Oh dear!' But when she criticised me later, I'd come back with some of the things which were on my mind, you know, which is probably the same case as many other teenagers. That's how it expressed itself.

CLARE: And would it have been some of the resentments about the school?

KENNEDY: Definitely. The choice about putting my music before me as a person. You know, there's always been that kind of 'Man with Two Heads' kind of scenario going in my mind, you know. Which one of me is the real thing, when in fact I've realised that both of them are the same real thing, but at one point I felt that maybe she'd chosen my career above me as a person.

CLARE: And what would she have said to you when you said that?

KENNEDY: Well, she said she couldn't forgive herself, like, if she hadn't have given me a chance to excel in an area which I could have been good at and I'm surely happy, which is right, I'm happy making this music and having access to such amazing musicians to work with and such fulfilment. But on the way up towards that point, there was a lot of thinking in my mind, 'Well, has it been worth the sacrifice?' you know. But now I'm very happy with the way things have gone.

CLARE: But there were times when you weren't sure?

KENNEDY: Yeah, there were times when I was thinking, well, particularly, actually at the height of my fame, you know, it happened yet again that I wasn't able to give myself time as a real person.

CLARE: When the Vivaldi made Number One in the charts, at the height of that, what was happening?

KENNEDY: Then it all started seeming to happen again, that I was being taken away from any semblance of real life and the music, or my career aspects of the music, were taking over and at the expense of me as a person. And so it seemed like a repeat of a scenario which had happened when I was a kid and that made me react quite, what would you say, quite forthrightly against it. You know, that's why I probably stopped playing in public for a little while, just to make sure that I could get a grip on things and nourish myself as a person and not just be this kind of commodity which was fulfilling the use of a career for a record company, or for a manager, or other people.

CLARE: So, there's always that sensitivity in you, that you've got to be very careful to protect you, the person.

KENNEDY: I think that's happened, yeah, from these two examples. I'm quite keen now to find that I can look after my own life as well as just career aspects of my professional life.

CLARE: Would you consciously have said, 'I'm taking time out?'

KENNEDY: It happened that I had to have this operation on my neck.

CLARE: Because of the cysts?

KENNEDY: Yeah, because of the cysts which grew there.

CLARE: That was directly related to the violin, was it?

KENNEDY: Well, no one's really ascertained if it was absolutely directly related. It was a totally harmless thing but it was starting to hurt me because it was so big and it needed removing. What I'd been told before the operation was that it would only result in me being away from the violin for seven or eight days before I could recommence my world tour, which involved concerts in Germany, Japan, America. It actually turned out that I couldn't play again for about six or seven months and so that gave me a window. So at the same time as feeling very deprived about not being able to play the violin, it gave me the chance to evaluate my life and say, 'Are things going in the direction that I wanted?' and I was able to say, 'No, they're not,' and decide to alter the structure of it a bit.

CLARE: What did you do?

KENNEDY: Well, I decided that I wanted to make music which is based on the admiration I've got of the colleagues I'm working with, have a lifestyle which wasn't going to be influenced by, you know, front-page pictures or all the more frivolous aspects of the media, hang out with people who weren't necessarily ambitious, success-orientated people but just be with people who've got some maybe more grounded values than that.

CLARE: You sorted out your personal life too?

KENNEDY: I feel very happy about the way life is at the moment.

CLARE: When did you meet your present partner?

KENNEDY: I met Eve just prior to the second operation I had to have on the neck because in the first one I didn't really receive enough after-care of a sufficient nature to make sure that things didn't get worse. And so I met her through friends of mine in Malvern and it was a very natural thing.

CLARE: She's not a musician?

KENNEDY: She's not a musician.

CLARE: So in that sense she's grounded in other . . .

KENNEDY: Yes, she's got artistic leanings. She's very good in visual arts and she actually designed an album cover for me actually after we'd started living together and she's got great gifts in that area.

CLARE: Were you influenced by what other people said about you? I don't mean tabloids necessarily, but are there any people whose views, even if they are painful and you initially argue with them, you listen to, you think they have an effect on you, or are you very much your own person?

KENNEDY: I'm pretty much my own person, I think. Every now and then, sporadically, I pick up a bit of information about myself which I learn from some kind of inner instinct type of thing, but it's not necessarily one person. There's one guy called David Heath, who's a composer friend of mine over a long time, who musically, if he said something I'd believe it about me.

CLARE: Given that you're a self-reliant person, we'll take that for granted, does that mean that you're not affected by what other people say about you or their comments or their advice?

KENNEDY: Well, I'm a bit of a ploughing type of guy in that once I get going it takes a lot to stop me. I've got some fixed idea in my head but there are some, one or two people, who are very close to me that, whose opinion I would trust and maybe take heed of. And then there's other scattered areas of advice. I remember doing, for instance, a concerto appearance with Yehudi, my mentor, for a very long time, playing the Elgar Concerto, and I thought I'd really done my greatest and I'd played it in his spirit and got very close to maybe the spirit which was evident on the record that Yehudi made with Elgar himself, or later with Adrian Boult, the other great recording that Yehudi made. I was almost moved to tears by the performance I'd done, in fact I was moved to tears by it, I have to admit although for a grown man that's totally shocking in the macho British society we are, but I was moved to tears by it. But one of the reviewers, this is one of the very few times I've actually been influenced by a music reviewer, but this guy next day in the papers said, 'Well, you know, is this what we really need, to hear someone playing just like Menuhin did. Wouldn't it have been nicer to hear an original interpretation of the Elgar?' And that struck home. There was something true in there which struck home. That it's my job representing music to people, not to do it through coloured spectacles of somebody else, but to actually relate to that music truthfully myself and honestly give an interpretation that I care about, not what Yehudi would necessarily endorse. Obviously, I owe everything to him as far as being a professional musician, but at some stage, if people are coming to hear me play and if I'm playing with musicians myself, I've got to give something which is from my heart to the musicians I'm playing with and to the audience. And so that was a moment of truth. There's another couple of friends that I've got who I've had for a very long time who are honest enough not to come up to me and portray things in a sweet way so that I'll like it, and those people I can take something off, but overall I'm pretty pig-headed and get on with my own thing, really.

CLARE: I interviewed Yehudi and, apart from the fact that you were both prodigies, I know it's a word neither of you probably like very much, I cannot really think of a man less like you, or you less like him. You're very different. What was your relationship, what is your relationship with Yehudi like?

KENNEDY: Well, given that I was lacking a father figure for the first few years of my life, Yehudi became almost like that to me and certainly musically was a father figure for quite a long time. I

admired his catholic taste, you know, and I think some of the
things have rubbed off on me. The fact that when I was at his
school he was playing with people like Ravi Shankar and
Stephane Grappelli, maybe has lent that quality to my musical
life. So that I'm ready to go and play possibly with people who
would be seen as more diverse than that now but at that time
that was hugely diverse for a classical musician to be doing that.
So now maybe I'd be challenging the boundaries in the same
way. He was a very passive person and I'm someone who
doesn't channel my anger physically. I'll find ways, maybe
intellectually or instinctively, to communicate what I want to,
but it's not like I'm going to go and hit someone or do things
like that. And Menuhin was never like that, even musically. He
never portrayed anger in his playing, which is something
actually I think I do. I think, having listened to someone like
Isaac Stern, for instance, who really can, I think, all emotions are
important in music. Beethoven is someone who's got huge
anguish in his music.

CLARE: Passionate.

KENNEDY: Yeah, sometimes it needs anger in there too. You can't
play certain music without the anguish. There are the transcendental aspects which are wonderful, but also there's an anger in
there sometimes and so . . .

CLARE: And how would he have coped with that, with the anger
being expressed by you?

KENNEDY: Yehudi?

CLARE: Yes.

KENNEDY: I think he would have seen that as a foreign concept. He
likes the rhapsodic approach and he's very much a man of
another world, and you know, I think he expresses himself in a
very angelic, transcendental way.

CLARE: Lyrical, pastoral.

KENNEDY: Yes, that's where his heart is and he's got a pulse there
which is always living in the music which is like a human pulse.

CLARE: Was he fatherly in other ways?

KENNEDY: He's always been too busy travelling around the world
really, but he's been a fantastic inspiration to so many young
players, and I was one of those people. But it's very difficult for
him to be fatherly too; he's got his own kids after all.

CLARE: Was there a rebellion in this relationship?

KENNEDY: Well, there was a situation where I thought for my own musical well-being and for the honesty of the task that I had at hand, that I had to unlearn every Menuhin mannerism that I'd learnt in order to be able to portray the music in my own way. So possibly if one's talking about a father–son relationship . . .

CLARE: Because you had learned them, had you?

KENNEDY: I had, you know, and I was doing things which he might have done.

CLARE: Like what?

KENNEDY: Certain ways of sliding between notes and diminuendos at the end of every phrase to make it gentle and things. I had to unlearn these and really get my own thing sorted out. So it wasn't really rebellion. I've never really seen myself as being a rebel, like sometimes people have written in newspapers and stuff about me being a rebel. I've never seen it, I've only seen myself as establishing that I want to do something in my own way, which I thought in a democratic society, and particularly in an artistic society, might have been something easy to accept, because art is certainly, to a certain extent, an expression of freedom and an expression of individuality.

CLARE: But you yourself have hinted, none the less, at a fire inside you. You wrote somewhere that 'a mixture of circumstances and musical potential fused to create a time of much unhappiness and isolation for me, of anger and sacrifice.' So this isn't something you've picked up recently. This is something you've been aware of for some time – the conflict and the passion within you.

KENNEDY: I think, you know, you've got to be passionate to enjoy life to the full. You've got to at least take heed and pay a certain amount of due to emotions that you might have. And being an artist is something which makes it easier because you're put in touch with your own feelings and it's not a criminal thing to entertain those feelings that you have. Whereas in some other walks of life, maybe that's not a cool thing to do as far as peer pressure and that.

CLARE: Music is a very direct way, it's the most direct way, into the emotions. Can I ask you, is there an after-effect? Do you find that when you've, for example, expressed anger, appropriately, in a piece that calls for it, are you different at the end of the piece? Do you feel different?

KENNEDY: Sometimes. It's so difficult to say. Sometimes I just feel a little bit like that, I feel a certain amount of freedom after having expressed something. It is almost like when you've had a dream, you know, whether it's a pleasant dream or an unpleasant dream, you wake up and you feel cleansed and kind of relaxed because you've got it out of your system. That's how I feel after I've done a performance of a certain work of music which might have portrayed, as you're saying, anger.

CLARE: Do you feel purged?

KENNEDY: Yeah, yeah, you definitely feel cleaned out, yeah, which is a good feeling.

CLARE: And how long would it last?

KENNEDY: If it's been a really good one, it can last for possibly a week, but all too often you're on to the next town and doing another concert which you are paying attention to equally as much as the previous one.

CLARE: Are you a risk taker?

KENNEDY: I'm a risk taker on the background of having really good preparation before hand, you know. All of my preparation is a bit like the guy trudging up the hill with the hang-glider on his back, in order to get that moment of freedom when he can just fly and go free. That's what my work is all about, I think. On the basis of a lot of preparation, that preparation is totally so that I can take more risks in a performance and be more open to the moment, respond to the musicians instead of prescribing to a preconceived method of performance. Method goes out of the window when I'm playing actually for real in a concert and risk taking is what I really want to do. In the rest of my life, I think it's equally the same, you know. I have periods of like, conservation, building up, and then I always end up taking risks in the end.

CLARE: There is that tension. You said something very interesting about the fact so much of your life was planned in a way not by you – the decision to go to the school, the school itself, the structure of your life and so on, right up to 16 – it was pretty well planned not by you but by your environment. There is then in you a sensitivity to plans. You accept that the work that you have calls for discipline, preparation, application. You accept that. You accept the rules of music clearly are the fundamental elements. But there's a tension there. There's a sense that too many rules are constrictive and too many rules can be implemented by other people, so you're always having to re-seize control of your life from time to time.

KENNEDY: Yeah, and I'm really one of the worst people that I know for taking plans, being told what to do by other people and having my life planned out. I react so badly to that, it's unbelievable.

CLARE: Really? So working with you one would need to be a shrewd manager. A programme planner with Nigel Kennedy would be somebody who would absorb you into the process of the planning?

KENNEDY: Yeah, exactly, I need that, you know, I really believe that we're in a music industry today but industry is already only a real small fraction of what the word should be to describe music. It's called industry because of some kind of professional thing and that's already derogatory to the art form, I think. And at the moment there's this formal laden thing that we all have to try and work with where people see what they call the music product; it's all about shipping bits of plastics around the place and somewhere in that, hopefully, there's room for a musician with some fresh creative impetus. But, overall, people prefer it if the musician is exactly like the last one so they can do the same marketing formula on them.

CLARE: And package and programme.

KENNEDY: Yeah, exactly so.

CLARE: There's a very good example in your book about this. You gave a couple of encores in an American concert and this threw them all into chaos because the package didn't include that.

KENNEDY: Exactly, exactly yeah.

CLARE: But what about in your personal life, say, with Eve? Would she have to be sensitive to this? Would something quite innocuous that she would have planned or set up, would that something lead to an unexpected explosion from Nigel? Do you see what I mean? Is this something that you're aware of, not just in your professional musical life but in your personal life?

KENNEDY: Well, maybe I'm lucky in this aspect because she, I think, has an instinctive sensitivity to that type of thing. And there are also other areas of my life in which I totally don't mind this type of thing happening.

CLARE: Really?

KENNEDY: Yeah. So, for instance, she's just an absolutely amazingly instinctive, wonderful mother to our child. It's natural for the mother in the earlier years to be more responsible for the child and when I see her, it's such a beautiful picture seeing her and our little monster and it's just such a natural thing. Some people are just wonderful mothers, and she's a real madonna with that kid.

CLARE: What about you? How has it affected you having a kid? You're breaking, I hope, the family tradition, the grandfather leaving your father, your father leaving you, now, you're here and you've got a seven-month-old son, the Kennedy line continues.

KENNEDY: Yeah, and I'm the last one of my particular Kennedys as well, so it's kind of a laugh, you know, that people do build up these lines around the male. It's one of those little areas we still got our hands on.

CLARE: Don't we just? But what has it made you think about that?

KENNEDY: It's made me think about it and I just hope that I'm going to be able to do something on a long term better than what had been with my dad and grandad. But it's brought out things in me. I'd never been interested particularly in little lumps of protoplasm before and obviously with your own, suddenly this whole new world, you live your kid's world, don't you, and it gives you a whole new perspective on things, and enjoyment of things which you'd otherwise take for granted.

CLARE: Are you a person who thinks much about the future, about your own mortality or ...

KENNEDY: Not really no, I haven't got to that stage yet. I know having reached 40 one's meant to be thinking about these things but somehow one's playing. A lot of my world obviously revolves around the music and when you're playing works by composers which have been dead over 150 years somehow mortality doesn't come into it any more, you're in touch with immortality a lot of the time.

CLARE: When you were out of action, so to speak, I'm not terribly clear whether you stopped playing for all of those years, four years was it, before the concert in early 1997 when you burst back on the scene, was it about four years?

KENNEDY: It was about four or five years.

CLARE: Were you playing?

KENNEDY: I was playing every day, I was playing Bach every day and working, apart from the recovery period from my neck operation. I was writing music. It wasn't actually as if I was doing nothing. I was just doing things which weren't particularly designed to take headlines. I was getting on with creative things. I was learning other instruments, how to play other instruments.

CLARE: Was it a big decision to decide to have a comeback concert?

KENNEDY: It was a little bit of a hard decision but I had to do it, in a way, because, you know, it's a chicken and the egg thing which you can fall into where you never make any movement at all. I'm interested in playing jazz. I'm interested in playing classical. I'm interested in getting in rock-orientated areas. I'm interested in collaborating with other people to write music and interested in many areas of music. For a long time I'd wanted to be doing something, but I was surrounded by people, professionally, who were waiting for the big album, and then, before the album came out we couldn't do anything, but then the album couldn't come out until we did something, and so it was this which was coming between the chicken and the egg. And suddenly I woke up and thought, well, I've got to do something myself to make this happen, so I just changed the whole lot of people I was working with to people who were more acclimatised with the fact that, primarily, I'm a live, performing musician who might be supplemented by recordings, rather than waiting for this big record which then my life can revolve around. I'm not that type of musician. I'm happy playing in a pub. I'm happy playing in a concert hall, in a club, whatever, and I want to be doing that, you know. If I'm playing four times a week, I'm a happy person, you know. So that's the way my career's going to go and it took a while to realise that's what I should be doing.

CLARE: What is the appeal of football?

KENNEDY: Football, I think, is this collective thing which the appeal is gradually being whittled down, if I may be permitted to say this.

CLARE: The appeal to you is being whittled down?

KENNEDY: I think the appeal to me and a lot of other people, who got into football for the same reason as myself, which is the collective feel of the crowd and what a fantastic atmosphere it is.

CLARE: Yes.

KENNEDY: It is now being taken over so that, you know, the football match isn't on a Saturday, it's whenever the television wants it to be. The crowd don't matter, the scaptegoatism after Hillsborough, where the police wouldn't admit their mistake until long afterwards, meant that we're not allowed to stand. The innocent people who've done nothing wrong in football, we're all being made to sit in situations with less atmosphere.

CLARE: It's lost its character for you?

KENNEDY: Yes, lost its character, and the people who've actually supported football from the beginning, the crowd, have been put last, and that really, for me, takes a little bit of the magic out of it. Everyone can, like, wax on lyrically about how great these all-seater stadiums are and how modern they are, but there's some atmosphere of the game which has now definitely gone. Before the game starts, they play that 'We Will, We Will Rock You' song instead of letting the crowd give voice to their own feelings. You know, everything's been taken over.

CLARE: Packaged?

KENNEDY: Yeah, and I don't like that at all. Premier league, to me, I'm becoming a little bit alienated from it and what I really want to go to football for is to get away from the corporate thing and to get into what people want to do.

CLARE: But you're vice-president of Aston Villa.

KENNEDY: Well, I have been that for four years. But I've served my stint and they're wonderful to me. They still give me all the free tickets that I wouldn't get otherwise.

CLARE: What do they say when you say that to them about losing the atmosphere?

KENNEDY: Well, I've never actually broached it because it's only been a dawning realisation lately. And I do know that clubs, if they've got too old fashioned a vantage point on it, they go under, you know. So I mean, in a way, it's a no win situation. Doug Ellis, chairman of Villa, he lives football and he's someone who's ensured the future of Aston Villa for many, many years to come, and so we owe him this. But no chairman can stand on his own and say, 'Hey, we want to like stay how football was before,' because otherwise they'll just go under.

CLARE: And, you describe your involvement in football as belonging?

KENNEDY: Yeah, there's a fantastic group consciousness.

CLARE: That was important to you.

KENNEDY: Yeah, that is something important to me.

CLARE: To belong to a club?

KENNEDY: Well, for one thing there's a nice family atmosphere about Aston Villa which is fantastic, but also the group of people, 30–40,000 people, all who want the same thing. It helps me put my life on a back burner for a bit and forget about myself and get involved in something else.

CLARE: How important to you is the notion of family?

KENNEDY: Family, well, that's an interesting one. It's something I've done without obviously so maybe the importance of it will not be really recognised as far as I'm concerned until I've managed to get somewhere with my kid and my girlfriend.

CLARE: Because you now have a family.

KENNEDY: Yeah, and then the values will unfold before me I think.

CLARE: You went through a time mulling over whether a relationship, a long-standing relationship was possible.

KENNEDY: Well yeah, there's lots of people I know who wonder about this concept, the religious concept.

CLARE: You wondered about it in relation to yourself, did you?

KENNEDY: Yeah, I've wondered about it, obviously. I think every relationship is as good as it is at the time, but sometimes relationships take a lot of work to get through to the next good spell and sometimes, you know, today maybe people have more freedom to say, 'Well, this isn't going well, we're off.'

CLARE: For instance, the decision to have Sark, you've now got a responsibility over and above you and your art and Eve?

KENNEDY: Yeah, there's something else going on there which is a far longer-term kind of responsibility.

CLARE: How do you feel about that because you've prided yourself on your self-reliance and you have been in one sense a free man?

KENNEDY: Yeah.

CLARE: It could be said, well, now things are different.

KENNEDY: Well, it was a freedom of choice to be able to get into this scenario in the first place, and I think there's a freedom of seeing the world through the kid's eyes. To be able to help someone is an act of freedom and to like someone, for someone to be able to rely on me, that's also a freedom. You can get into another trap where no one can rely on you.

CLARE: That's true, that's true. Let me put it slightly differently. You once said, I can't remember where I got this from, you said, 'I suppose I've devoted myself unconditionally to the violin and the music. I can get through it. I know the violin is going to be there so any relationship which has finished, I've still got the music. A lot of my emotional needs are met by the violin.' Now, while you were certainly your own person and had no one really depending on you, that's a statement that you could live with. Once you get involved in a relationship, perhaps great creative artists shouldn't, but once they do, the question is then about the potential conflict. What if it came to a sacrifice of your career versus your child?

KENNEDY: Well, actually, I remember having a conversation with someone else about it, with the same predicament, except there were three ingredients: there was the child, plus girlfriend, obviously.

CLARE: Eve?

KENNEDY: Yeah, and then there was my violin, and then there was my season ticket to Aston Villa.

CLARE: All right, I'll leave them in there.

KENNEDY: And I remember having a very hard predicament to think which one should go first. With the kind of TV-orientated business ruining the schedule of football, I can't say to my music manager, 'Well, I can't play the violin on Saturday, I can't do a gig on Saturday, I can't do it on Sunday, I can't do it on Monday and also I can't do it on Friday, in the awful scenario that we might have got relegated to Division One. But, you know, there is no day left in the week where you can be absolutely sure there's not a football game on, so maybe that's a slightly easier one – music wins. So then I'm left with the violin and my kid and Eve and it still is an unconditional commitment to my music that I've made. And I think in some ways, you know, every child and person in a relationship has to accept some things about the partner, and the things that people have to accept about me is that I will be touring for the rest of my life, it's something that keeps me ticking.

CLARE: That music comes first?

KENNEDY: It really is there and it's part of me as a person now, it's not something I can just divorce myself from.

CLARE: And in that sense, Eve, or anyone who gets close to you, would need to know that. There's a little bit of Nigel Kennedy . . .

KENNEDY: Always in the music which maybe no one else can get. And if I didn't have that I think life at home would be a less pleasant proposition probably because I'd be some miserable, down-on-the-world type of guy. Because, you know, people who are deprived of what really they love doing are turned into cynical people, I think, in the end.

CLARE: And your mother must have had that too, she must have intuitively decided that the music would have to come first?

KENNEDY: Maybe she planted it there, I'm not sure which way round it happened. There's obviously a natural affinity I've got with music which makes it worth the dedication, so if I didn't have that it would be an easy thing to give up.

CLARE: To people who have no musical talent, try just and help me about what it is like when you are playing Elgar or Bruch or Brahms or Beethoven. Is there anything, physically and psycho-logically, that is like that sensation, that experience? Is there anything you can say to someone who doesn't have that experience that, well, it's like this or that, it's like sex or it's like a really good meal, or it's like some other physical sensation?

KENNEDY: Well, there are some of those elements, I think, some of the areas which music takes you are so aesthetically out there that possibly people a couple of months ago, if they saw the comet, for instance, seeing something like that or seeing an amazing sunset somewhere, something of an intense kind of spiritual beauty, possibly almost like a religious experience if people are into religion, they might understand it from that vantage point.

CLARE: What used to be called ecstasy but unfortunately that word has got attached to something else, but the sense of being outside yourself?

KENNEDY: Exactly, it definitely takes you outside yourself and puts you into an area of communication which is so deep that language becomes a superficial thing.

CLARE: Do you ever sometimes in that moment, feel that you will just completely lose yourself?

KENNEDY: Well, I have felt danger. I've actually had out-of-body experiences once or twice. Like on particularly good nights and I've been away from my body at the back of the hall wondering, 'Well, my body's going through that thing and I'm hearing the music from the same vantage point as the audience and being carried away by Beethoven,' and I've never had the courage to go out of the hall because I've felt I'm this spirit, which can go straight through the wall out into the stratosphere as far as I want, but I've never dared leave because I've thought well maybe I won't get back into my own body, you know.

CLARE: And does it last long?

KENNEDY: No, I think it's only lasted for about five, ten minutes at a time. That seems like eternity at the time that it's happening. But I mean, even on a more superficial area, you are getting into someone's thought patterns, like Beethoven's, who's been dead for a while and so it takes you out of yourself just doing that, assimilating someone else's thought patterns and emotional patterns to the extent that they feel like they're your own. It's a very much out-of-yourself experience.

CLARE: Do you have an ambition? Is there something you want to do?

KENNEDY: It's difficult to say. There might be particular musicians that I want to play with. Obviously seeing my kid grow up into a happy person, that would be a major ambition, probably the most focused one that I've got at the moment because musically I'm having a very creative, very fulfilling time. And so if things just carry on in that way, you know, I obviously want to be able to change musical direction every now and then and, like, go off and work with someone, to work with someone like Herbie Hancock would be amazing, to work with. Like discovering the pleasure I got working with Klaus Tenstedt, if I meet someone else like him.

CLARE: Are you a worrier?

KENNEDY: A worrier?

CLARE: Yes.

KENNEDY: Yes, I do get nervous about gigs that I've got to do if they're particularly important ones, like the London gig we were talking about. That's the time when I have to separate myself from the family and go down for a couple of days and work somewhere else so that I don't make life a misery for everybody else as well. So I do worry about things like that. But those worries are seeming to be dispelled quite a lot at the moment because I'm getting so much satisfaction out of playing and having made my so-called return, although I've been playing music every day, coming back in front of people and playing and knowing that I've still got that communicational thing happening with people who listen to the concerts, the worries are subsiding a little bit and I'm just enjoying it. But I think overall I'm a worrier because I pay attention to detail in the musical preparation that I do. So I'm always like picking away at something.

CLARE: You're quite a perfectionist?

KENNEDY: Yeah, I'm kind of down on myself a lot at the time.

CLARE: Would you regard yourself as a happy person?

KENNEDY: I'm happy, yes, I think I'm a happy person, yes, definitely, in many different type of circumstances. Happiness is a very subjective thing. My life might make a load of people really miserable, but I'm really happy in it.

CLARE: Nigel Kennedy, thank you very much indeed.

Carla Lane

The reason I was keen to interview the writer Carla Lane was not because she is the creator of a staggering list of television dramas but because she exemplifies a particularly interesting group of people who make no bones about the fact that they prefer animals to human beings. I had read a spiky piece by her in the *Independent* in the summer of 1994 in which she unblinkingly equated the murderous destruction of babies in Rwanda with the the killing of animals for food. 'Don't let syrupy tales of humane slaughterhouses blind you,' she exhorted her readers. 'They are the most shameful dark corners of our society and, unlike Rwanda, have been and will be with us for ever, to the tune of 130 million animals a week in this country alone.' She insists, when challenged, that she does not compare human beings to animals because likening people to animals would be flattering to people. 'My idea of animals is that they're the only pure things we have left in this world.'

Her move from London to Broadhurst Manor in 1992 was a forced one – she had rescued so many New Forest ponies that she needed somewhere to look after them. She has lived there since, surrounded by over 1,500 cats, dogs, birds, ducks and geese, squirrels, peacocks, rabbits, herons, badgers, foals, donkeys and deer. Though she writes brilliantly, amusingly and affectionately about people, has been married and divorced, has two sons and five grandchildren, she is quite unabashed in insisting that animals are preferable to human beings any time. In this interview, for example, she spends much time talking about loss – loss of animals as well as humans.

Consideration of the death of her father and her mother is quickly followed by reference to the deaths of dogs and cats. 'My father died so young, my mother so quickly. Dogs, cats, you know. You go through losing so many well-loved persons that I think we're all equal in that way.'

What is it about human beings that so repels Carla Lane? She insists that it is their cruelty and describes it with detail and disgust. But as she talks of her own experiences with people, the people in her life, it soon becomes clear that there is more to it than that. For a start, she finds the actual demand of relating to another person in an intimate way threatening. 'If I love them,' she declares of her lovers and friends, 'I'll make them happy in the loving but it's the living with them, I found that difficult, I really did.' She speaks of 'being devoured' in a relationship, of her dissatisfaction with having to share her space with someone 'who's going to keep making demands on me'.

Her experiences – with her own parents, with her children, with the husband she subsequently divorced – are all sketched in terms of demand, restriction, control, sacrifice. The contrast with her relationship to animals is stark. Again and again the word 'purity' is the one with which she chooses to describe them. She rebukes me for suggesting there is a simplicity about animals, rightly observing that in many ways their abilities and skills are highly complex. But the simplicity to which I was referring concerned the nature of the relationship human beings can have with them. You can lavish intense affection on an animal, you can care for it, protect it. But, as Carla Lane points out with a degree of relief, you can at any stage let it go free. The relationship involves no true element of dependence, and it is the dependence that is part and parcel of any truly intimate personal relationship between human beings that really deters her. Purity is the state human beings were in in the Garden of Eden, before free will and choice. To say, as Carla Lane so often says, that animals are the only pure forms of life left on the planet is not really saying very much. Animals do not, as she acknowledges, have evil thoughts but they don't have good thoughts either, or indeed any thoughts if it comes to that, or at least not in the sense that we traditionally think of thoughts. Thoughts, pure and evil, are what humans have. It might be more accurate to say that it is the very fact that animals are thought-less that makes them so appealing. They don't think, they are.

But all of this only goes to raise the question as to why the impurity of human beings should so distress and disturb her to the point that she prefers dumb animals to them? It is tempting to wonder about the effect on the adolescent Carla of the death in very distressing circumstances of her father. She explicitly describes her active dislike of death, her fear of dying, the dreadful last days of her father during which time she lost over a stone in weight. She refers on a number of occasions to her anger – anger about life, about people, about dying – and to her panics which occur in settings in which, once again, the fear and threat of being controlled, restrained, contained, recur. At one stage in her life she was a nurse – a person whose role it was to sustain, care for, show compassion, be there. It proved too much – perhaps the human demands became too entrapping – and now she is playing a very similar role but for dumb animals who, whatever else they will do, will not express in coherent and enmeshing words their needs and their demands. Carla Lane eloquently and powerfully expresses their needs and their demands for them. She is in complete control of these relationships. She, it is, who can decide when and whether to loosen the binds, ease the dependence, hers on them, theirs on her, and free them.

For a woman whose professional currency is words, the silence of the animals may well reinforce this sense she has of them as less demanding and purer souls. 'Most people who have animals,' she argues, 'do say they're better than humans.' Many people might agree. The problem, however, is that some of the people who agree take things further and decide that when the issue becomes the so-called 'liberation' of animals, then the very superiority of these animals justifies any method, including violence if necessary, to be taken to free them. In this interview, Carla Lane denounces violence but she does readily admit to a sympathic understanding of why the protesters at Shoreham, for example, gave vent to their violent impulses in their protest against the live export of animals from British ports.

The interview ends with a paean to human eccentricity. Carla Lane engagingly agrees with those many commentators who have decided that, not to put too fine a point on it, she is psychiatrically disturbed when it comes to animals. But it is not her love of animals, interestingly enough, which makes her think of herself as cranky, eccentric, 'mad'. No, it is the fact that she likes being on her own, not in the social sense for she has a squad of helpers looking after her every need, but in the psychological sense. She doesn't need people. She is, quite simply, 'selfish'. And therein lies another important clue concerning her preference for animals over humans. Get involved with a human being and your tendency to self-obsession and self-preoccupation is challenged. It does not mean it is overthrown. Many people come to grief in personal relationships precisely because they can never, or hardly ever, put the other person first. But with animals you never really have to put them first. You interpret what they want and give it to them. They can't complain. Carla Lane's foxes don't eat her chickens because she feeds them fit to burst – with what I quite forgot to ask her. She doesn't ask her foxes if they would prefer to behave as foxes normally behave. She decides how they should behave and indeed that they should wish to behave as she wishes them to behave – as showing a respect and tolerance of their fellow creature, the chicken. In so far as animal lovers have needs to meet, they are simple and basic needs – the provision of food and safety. They are not psychological needs.

The purity of animals, of which Carla Lane speaks so passionately, is surely a projection of the human wish for a simple, uncomplicated purity in human relations in which the other's needs can be made identical with what one wishes them to be. It is a wonderfully romantic vision akin to her pastoral view of Rome.

CLARE: Carla Lane is the highly successful and prolific author of such hit television comedy series as *The Liver Birds*, *Butterflies*, *Mistress*, *I Woke Up One Morning*, *Solo*, *Bread*, *Leaving* and more recently, *Searching*. The Queen is said to be among her many fans of her writings, for which she was awarded an OBE in 1987. She is also famous for being a fervent animal rights campaigner and for turning her Elizabethan manor house in Sussex into an animal sanctuary, with something like 1,500 creatures great and small, from cats, dogs, ponies, sheep, to a frog with a broken leg.

Carla Lane was born in Liverpool, the elder daughter of a chief engineer in the merchant navy. She says she was a real dunce at school, the 35th in a class of 36, yet she won a poetry competition in the *Liverpool Echo* at the age of 10. She left school at 16, married at 17 a draughtsman, Arthur Hollins, who was to become a naval architect and the father of their two sons, Carl and Nigel. The marriage lasted 27 years and ended in divorce in 1976. She has been single ever since and has no intention of remarrying. About the man in her life she said in a newspaper interview, and I quote, 'In my affection he is marginally ahead of birds, level with cats and way behind the dogs.'

Carla Lane, reading about you made me wonder what the people who know you made of your decision to come and talk to a psychiatrist?

LANE: I think that's best explained by one of my sanctuary workers who ran me to the station. He said, 'Where are you going now?' I said, 'I'm going on that programme *In the Psychiatrist's Chair*.' He said, 'Oh my God, make sure they don't keep you in!'

CLARE: You are aware clearly that people think of you as a highly unusual woman. Eccentric, I suppose they'd say?

LANE: Yes, I am aware that they think that but at least I'd be pleased if I thought they thought I was eccentric. I think, because of the tabloids mainly, a lot of them just think of me as this silly blonde who pats little animals and the seriousness behind me is often lost.

CLARE: How do you see yourself? Let me put the question differently. You are clearly interested in humanity. You write about it. You've called them more tragic comedies than anything else. You write about the darker side of life in a highly interesting and amusing way. You analyse and examine human behaviour. You are clearly interested in humanity but you don't much like it I sense, and I wonder when you look at yourself, do you like what you see?

LANE: Not entirely. There are lots of traits I have which I could well do without.

CLARE: Like what?

LANE: Well, I am quite dogmatic and I'm afraid I'm a little

judgemental and I do hate that. I make very quick decisions about people. And I know very quickly whether I want to spend time with someone and I think I'm a little hasty in those judgements.

CLARE: You say that as if you can think of actual examples of when you were wrong?

LANE: Yes. Sometimes I think, oh well, you know, I'm not very keen on that person and they turn out to be really quite warm and nice – not too often to worry me but I know I'm a bit judgemental. I think probably I do have a problem. I'm angry all the time.

CLARE: Do you know why?

LANE: Yes, I'm angry because of my own species. I'm angry with them. I'm constantly aware somehow and I don't know why. It's as though it's fed into me from some source that I don't know about. I'm angry about what they're doing to the planet, their attitude toward things that are trying to survive on our planet, cruelty. I'm angered by all those things.

CLARE: How long have you been angry? Have you always been angry?

LANE: I know when I was very small I used to rescue the earwigs out of the dogs' water dish. I would have probably been about four. I didn't like earwigs but I couldn't bear to see them drowning. And I remember even at four I used to wonder why other people didn't feel the same, and it disappointed me even then that other children and other people didn't mind them drowning. Do you know what I mean? So I feel that the anger started probably a long time ago.

CLARE: You have a sister?

LANE: I have a sister, yes.

CLARE: And she's younger than you?

LANE: Yes. She's nine years younger than I.

CLARE: Oh, quite a bit younger. So you were for a long time an only child.

LANE: Well, I have a brother and he's younger by only 15 months.

CLARE: Would he have been different to you in that regard? He wasn't going round worrying about earwigs then?

LANE: Not then. He's very like me now, more sort of in the last five or ten years. He's become a little the same. But now I think I just inherited something, probably from my grandfather who fought all his life for animals and I just feel maybe I've inherited chips of him.

CLARE: He was your father's father or your mother's father?

LANE: My father's father, yes.

CLARE: And what do you know of him?

LANE: Well, it's sad what I know of him, because he was a very aristocratic kind of man, he wore a velvet coat to smoke and he had works of art around him and he was very noble really. And he had a private income and because of this he was able to do what he wished. And he joined the RSPCA in the days of uniform and silver braid and pride and he worked diligently through his life. He travelled with the animals across to France. He fought for them and finally got separate holds for them and his name is mentioned in the Minute Book. I feel as though he's actually intruded into my life so strongly that I seem to be carrying on where he left off. But as a child I didn't appreciate him at all.

CLARE: You knew him?

LANE: Oh yes.

CLARE: What was he like?

LANE: He was a stern man and he used to put terror into my heart because he didn't really have a way with children. But now I just wish I could talk to him because I know I would appreciate him.

CLARE: And what was your father like, his son, your father?

LANE: My father? He was just a lovely, lovely man, my father. He died when he was 50.

CLARE: Of what?

LANE: He died of a coronary. He was artistic, although he was an engineer. He wrote poetry now and then but we didn't know until after he'd died. He was just a very nice man. I don't know how else to describe him. He was gentle and nice. He brought us up in a way that was clear and there were no frightening moments, no hitting, no bullying.

CLARE: Was he angry or was he at peace?

LANE: I think he was peaceful until he had the coronary and then he had a year of knowing that he wasn't going to live and he was angry then but because of that. Not the things that I am angry about.

CLARE: How did it express itself, his anger? What did he do?

LANE: He became a tiny bit bitter and spoke in terms of, you know, why should it happen to him when he had so many plans. I think he resented the fact that people he knew and perhaps felt were not as kind as himself were healthy and robust. I imagine it would happen to us all. He resented the fact that he was the one that wasn't going to live very long.

CLARE: Do you remember his death?

LANE: Oh yes, I was with him.

CLARE: Were you?

LANE: Yes. We'd been out for the day, the whole family, and I knew when we were driving back in the car there was something wrong. He kept looking at his hands, turning them over and looking at them and it was a strange thing for my father to be doing. And he had another attack and he made me promise not to call the ambulance, he was frightened of going to the hospital. And I waited for as long as I felt necessary and then, in order for him not to hear me, I went out to a phone box. My mother was there. I called an ambulance and he died just before they came. The sad thing was, although I don't think it affects me, but I'll tell it to you, his last words to me were, 'I'll never forgive you.' I really don't believe it affects me at all because I don't believe my father meant that. At the time it was upsetting for a few months but I hardly ever think of it now. It was the ambulance he wasn't forgiving me for. I went through a stage where I thought I hastened his death because he knew I'd gone out to call one. But I had to do it. He needed help.

CLARE: What sort of relationship had you with him?

LANE: Oh, a lovely one. You know, I have been really lucky with my upbringing. My parents loved each other and it showed. We had a happy house. We had not a lot of money but enough to go places and do things. We had a little country cottage which we went to and I think, you know, I had an ideal childhood.

CLARE: What was your mother like?

LANE: Brilliant, beautiful, bright, she was extraordinary my mother. She never resented anything. She never tried to stop us doing things. She had a wonderful giggle. She always used to giggle behind her hand. She had a lovely broad smile and she was my favourite person, always.

CLARE: When did she die?

LANE: She died last year, very suddenly. I suddenly felt I had to go and see her. I didn't need to because I saw her regularly but I'll never forget the sense of 'I must go and see my mother'. It was my birthday. I didn't normally go and spend my birthday with her. I'd been with her two days when she took ill, and she was dead within 48 hours. I couldn't really wrestle with that for a long time but now, you know, when grief goes, I think of her and smile and think of the many, many wonderful things she said. May I tell you one? She used to say to me, 'You know you get your animal-loving stuff from me, don't you?' And I used to say, 'Look Mummy, don't give me that. You know my father was the one.' 'No, no,' she said, 'you get it from me.' I must tell you first, she was very vain.

CLARE: Very vain?

LANE: Very vain, beautifully vain. She had her make-up on at seven in the morning. I said, 'You're walking along the road and there is a little pigeon stuck in the mud on the other side of the road. You're walking down there and you see it. What would you do? Would you go and pick it up, take it home?' And she thought for a while and she said, 'Well, it depends what shoes I had on!' Oh she was lovely, she was great, my mum.

CLARE: You said that you'd only discovered your father wrote poetry after he died.

LANE: Yes. We found some in his bureau. It was really nice poetry too. I think he was a little shy of it. He was a big man, you know, not the kind of man you'd think would write poetry. I think probably he was a bit embarrassed. He wrote a very nice little poem to my mother, and he wrote quite a funny one to me when I had my first baby. But that was an open thing because it was funny, he wasn't worried by it, you know. He was quite a nice painter, my father, like his father, he was an artist too as well as the RSPCA. It sort of runs through the family but not to me, I can't paint. I thought I could and I went to art school and I couldn't even draw a bottle so I gave up. I don't have that talent at all.

CLARE: And the growing up? You say it was a happy time.

LANE: Yes, it just was. It was lovely largely I think because of the obvious passion, if you like, my mother and father had for each other. They were a very handsome couple and I used to be very proud when they came, when my father was home from sea, and they used to come and stand outside the school. I wanted everybody to know, you know. She was small and dark, he was tall and dark and he had a lot of gold braid on. And I was always very proud of them and I can't fault my parents. They never did anything that makes me as an adult, think, 'Fancy doing that, you know, you're responsible for this and that.' I can't think of a single thing.

CLARE: No.

LANE: It was a nice household.

CLARE: So when you do think of them, what would you think you've inherited from either, or indeed both of them?

LANE: Well, I've inherited my mother's spirit. This business of you must keep going, you mustn't think about age, you must always present yourself in a bright light. She gave very much of that to me. My father probably the poetry bit, the secret writing which became a non-secret but for a long time it was a secret. The artistic bit, if you like to call it that, I think came from him. But because it was so long ago that he died, my mother is much fresher in my mind because she was my friend right up to last year. I used to take her to Paris with me, or America, or wherever I had to go, and if I had to choose company it was always her.

CLARE: What did she make of your career?

LANE: She never quite got the hang of it, to be truthful. She used to watch the programmes and I don't think she ever realised or thought how they came about. You know, she used to ask me what I was writing and I'd tell her and she never asked for detail. She boasted a lot about me, that was the only embarrassing thing she did. When she was in hospital, not the time she died, but she became ill a few years before and, you know, how in hospital they ask you if you want your hair doing, and she said, 'Yes.' She went to have her hair done and when it was done, she waved her hand about casually apparently and said, 'Put it on my daughter's account!' Oh dear!

CLARE: When your marriage broke up, was that a painful time for her? Did she get close to your husband?

LANE: She did like my husband, but she did something terribly cliché and terribly northern. The first word she said was, 'What am I going to say to the neighbours?' And I more or less expected that because my mother did worry about what people thought. I did once but I'd overcome that by then. But she was worried about what she would explain to people. It doesn't matter now but we're going back a little while. She was more concerned about what people would think, you know. But I just gave her a bit of cheek and we got over it.

CLARE: What sort of adolescence did you have? Given that background, were you a reasonably, reasonably secure person?

LANE: No, I wasn't secure, in spite of the family, because I went through a very ugly stage. I'm not sure that I ever got over it but I did. I remember feeling quite ugly between probably 12 and 15. My teeth seemed to stick out and I had wiry hair, which was right for today but not for then. I developed quite early. I seemed to be the only one in the class that was doing that and I really wasn't very secure at all. I just felt that nobody would really want to bother with me. But it didn't last too long. It was quite painful and I remember I used to dress up, you know, and try and make myself look pretty but I never seemed to achieve it. I had a few years of that but I think most girls go through that.

CLARE: Did it stay with you? Is it something that you still worry about?

LANE: No I stopped worrying about those things and I straightened out a bit when I got to be 17. And nothing like that has ever really occurred to me since.

CLARE: Did you enjoy school?

LANE: Oh no, I hated school.

CLARE: Why?

LANE: Oh, I couldn't bear it. Well, I would describe myself as thick. I really do believe I was thick at school.

CLARE: Why were you thick at school?

LANE: Well, I just couldn't cope. I couldn't cope with school and I certainly couldn't cope with maths and stuff like that. I used to look out of the window, and I always remember we used to have milk in little bottles in those days and they used to stack the crates up outside the school, and I used to watch the leaves swirling around, and I was so interested in these things that I didn't hear half the things the teacher was saying. And I used to count the bricks in the lavatory wall because that was opposite and there was a nest in a tree and I used to watch that. I was always a dreamer, you know. I could never take anything in and actually I'm a bit like that now. I can't take facts in too easily. I've got a fax machine, right. I hate it. I've got a computer because my sons bought one and I put a velvet cloth over it and put flowers on top. I couldn't cope with it. No way can I go near a computer. I can't bear technology. I have old telephones. I write longhand. I don't have a word processor. I am sure that there's something wrong in my head about these things but I never could take in anything that was factual. It has to be a vividly painted picture for me to be interested. And the saddest thing of all was, I never did read. I never read books and the moment I started to read a book, I wanted to put it down and start to write a book and I really think I've missed out there. The only books I ever read, and I've read them over and over again, are the life stories of da Vinci, Van Gogh, Rubens. I loved all that, the Renaissance. I have such an affinity with it, not in an intellectual way. I feel as though somewhere, this is going to sound awfully silly, but I feel as though somewhere I came from there. When I go to Rome I feel as though I came from Rome.

CLARE: What is it about Rome?

LANE: I just feel at home there.

CLARE: Well, analyse it a bit more. What makes you feel at home?

LANE: I don't know, I feel, it all sounds silly. I feel as though I can see my own ghost, if you like, running through those streets. I feel as though I've been there, been brought up there. Everything about Rome seems right for me, I love it.

CLARE: When you say everything, so what are the things about Rome that you think of?

LANE: It's the back streets of Rome, not the very upper-class Rome. It's the back streets. It's something about peasants, or gypsies, or people who were very colourful and danced and wore long black skirts and lots of beads and earrings. Those people, I identify with them and I don't know why.

CLARE: It's not great open spaces and nobody around?

LANE: No. It's lovely urns on tops of pillars and not the clichéd beautiful things that we all know. It's the little streets and the sudden coming upon a courtyard and . . .

CLARE: Little squares . . .

LANE: Little stone fountains which are not very embellished, just a piece of stone with water coming out of a pipe. It thrills me. I feel elated and I never can trace why. It's only there that it happens. I can feel elated about many things, you know, a bit of sun or even rain. I'm very easily transported to elation.

CLARE: Does that mean you're easily transported to depression as well?

LANE: I never have depression but I have melancholia. I think the difference is that depression is something you can't lift. No, I never get depressed.

CLARE: And melancholia, on the other hand?

LANE: Melancholia? I feel a phone call, a bright voice, something going right, you can move out of it. That's only my own theory. I've had a slight depression lately because of this, going back to animals, the live transportation of animals. I've been down there in Shoreham bellowing and trying to stop it with the rest and I did get a bit depressed at the sight of what I saw. But I've only to have somebody ring and say, 'Oh, I heard today, you know, that the government might do something,' or some little ray of hope and it goes. So I don't call it depression for that reason.

CLARE: When you have this feeling in Rome, you know, and you're in those little back streets and the little squares and so on, what about the people that live there? Do you have any feeling for them?

LANE: Yes, I love them, you know, the old ladies in black, the people who carry dried flowers in baskets. It's all wonderful. I don't know what it is. It's as though maybe in a very childlike way it's the way I feel the world should be. It's probably not a bit like that living there, but it just all looks the way the world should be. People strolling, cobbled streets, little shops selling all odd things, little fountains, doves and pigeons, it all seems like something I've been through and it stayed with me and in a way, moving to Sussex where I now live, which is way away from everything I've known, is going back to that.

CLARE: Because in fact you were brought up in the north of England?

LANE: Yes.

CLARE: What was it like? Where were you?

LANE: Well, I was in a fairly respectable part of Liverpool but of course you're never far away from the rest. My childhood in Liverpool was the streets, docks, the sound of the big ships, the overhead railway, the scouse accent, the sheer magic of Liverpool which I still love. It's deeply rooted in me without doubt and I suppose I can marry the two up. One is Liverpool, one is Rome, similar but one has the sun and the sun brings out fountains and doves, whereas in Liverpool it's cold and seagulls.

CLARE: So what are you doing in Sussex?

LANE: Right, well of course, I had this ambition, you see, that I wanted to open a sanctuary.

CLARE: When did you have that ambition?

LANE: Probably about ten years ago. And then a sanctuary that I supported went bankrupt and in those days I was quite well off, I was doing well at television and I was paying to keep all the animals because it had gone bankrupt. I was paying somebody else to feed them. Then I started looking for another house because I was restless, I'm always moving house, you know. They got bigger. I love a big house, not in a pretentious way. I like space and then I thought, 'Well, why am I paying somebody else? Now is the time.' So I started looking round, originally in Oxfordshire, near to London, but couldn't find anything. Broadhurst Manor was the only place that had what I needed. I rush blindly. I don't think things out at all. I thought, 'I'll buy it. I'll do it.' And in my life I've been lucky. Most of the things I've done have seemed to be disastrous but they've turned out OK, mainly because of my mother's spirit which leads me always to say, 'Oh well, what the hell! It'll be all right next week.' I don't worry about things most people worry about. The things I worry about mainly are people I love, or animals I love, being ill and dying. To me, anything outside of that is something you can manage.

CLARE: You were very conscious from very early on then about this issue of dying. You talked about the earwigs when you were four.

LANE: Yes.

CLARE: You were always aware of that?

LANE: Yes, I don't like the idea of dying. I don't only dislike it. It probably is a major worry. I don't think about it too often but sometimes I do and I can't believe that it is the way it is. But I think writers are like that. We tend, you know, to drone on about death, don't we, from what I've read, the few things I've read.

CLARE: When you say you can't believe the way it is?

LANE: Well, I suppose since I've had so many animals and seen some die, it always comes as a shock to me, you know. That a lovely thing – take a dove, because they're the ones that die most in the winter. This lovely flapping, cooing, bright-eyed thing suddenly looks nothing when it's dead. There's nothing there and it really does frantically worry me that because I can't help thinking, knowing it's one of the few things we're sure of. That one day I'm going to be like that and I find that quite horrifying, I really do.

CLARE: Do you find it horrifying?

LANE: I don't like the idea of our bodies disintegrating and I don't like what happens after death. And when my mother died, when I went to see her, I noticed that one of her eyes was slightly open and it was still very bright, she had dark brown eyes. And I remember that I was mourning mostly, she had gone and there was nothing I could do about that, I was mourning mostly about what was going to happen to her lovely face and the things I knew about her and her little hands which were so lovely. And I found myself worrying about that because the rest had happened and I realised that was it. But I didn't want the rest to happen, you know. I don't think this is an unusual thought, but possibly talking about it might be.

CLARE: Do you worry about the pain of death?

LANE: I'm not afraid of pain but I'm terribly afraid, because I'm claustrophobic you see. I had a wrong injection given to me in a hospital once and my central nervous system seized up and I couldn't breathe. It was a bit of a nightmare and it left me with claustrophobia, so the idea of losing my breath is the most terrifying thing. I won't swim because of it. I won't go under the shower happily. I prefer a bath. I don't like anything in front of my face. I have a cat that insists on sleeping on my face and I have to keep moving her. That worries me terribly and maybe that's why I'm so alarmed about death, because in the end that's what it's all about isn't it, losing your breath really. That does frighten me terribly.

CLARE: Do you remember the first death you saw? Was it your father?

LANE: No, no. I'd seen a few because I did nursing when I was quite young, when the children were slightly growing up and my husband used to take them two nights a week.

CLARE: You did nursing?

LANE: Yes, not in a very serious way. I was an auxiliary nurse. I saw a lot of death in the hospital in Liverpool.

CLARE: Why did you take up nursing?

LANE: I don't even know, to be truthful. Whilst I say I was thick at school, I really think I had an aptitude for that. Funnily enough, I could remember all the names of the drugs, of the illnesses. I felt as though I knew how the body functioned. I could understand what the doctors were talking about. It was just something I seemed to take to. It wasn't altruistic or wanting to help people, although I suppose that came into it. It was just something I knew I could be good at. But of course, I had two young children and I couldn't follow it through, so I just did what I could. And I saw a lot of death. I was on a ward where it happened frequently and at first, of course, I couldn't cope with it. I couldn't believe that, you know, old Mrs So and So, whom I'd grown to quite like, was dead. But of course you get used to it. I don't want to use the words 'used to it' but you do get to realise that it's part of it and so I had seen it quite a bit. I found my grandmother dead and I found my second grandmother dead. I was the first one to see them. They happened to be staying with me. I don't know what I did to kill off all these people but they were staying with me at the time. So I have seen it quite a bit. My father's was more distressing because he was struggling for the last 12 months and I didn't like to see that. I used to stand by the garden gate and watch him walk along the road on a sunny day and he had to sit down on a small wall. He didn't know I could see him and they were terrible moments, knowing him, the way he was, energetic, ambitious.

CLARE: Would he have difficulty breathing?

LANE: Yes, and I lost a stone during that year that my father was like that. I couldn't handle it at all. It was almost a relief when he died because I didn't want him to go through any more of that. So, you know, it's funny. It's my own death that worries me more because it's this lack of breathing, I suppose, this claustrophobic feeling of it.

CLARE: How much does that claustrophobia affect you? Would you avoid things like lifts?

LANE: I used to, for a while after the accident in the hospital, but I don't now, no. A room like this I couldn't have sat in. I'd have to have a window.

CLARE: This is quite a large room.

LANE: Yes, but there's no window.

CLARE: What about a theatre?

LANE: I wouldn't go and I wouldn't go in restaurants unless I was near the exit. My husband, my ex-husband, was very kind in those days. He understood it perfectly and he always used to choose a place where there was a window. But I got over it. I'm mostly over it. It's only water now that scares me.

CLARE: How did you get over it?

LANE: Just by making myself face up to various things and because I'm a quick decision maker and rush into things. I suppose I rushed into that. Here's a room without a window, get in there and shut up, that sort of thing.

CLARE: For you death is the end?

LANE: Oh, do you know, I keep changing my mind about this. I hope not. On the one hand, seeing my mother in particular, and seeing how empty she looked compared with when she was alive, I began to think that it had to be the end, there didn't seem to be anything there. But on the other hand, I don't really believe that we go through what we go through, all of us, for nothing, it can't be for nothing, can it? There's got to be something at the end of it. And yet I can't envisage what it could be. I certainly don't like these pictures of heaven with wings and all that rubbish. I couldn't do with that and nor could I live happily in a place that was so perfect and good. I'd have to have a bit of evil around me to give me something to fight against. So heaven doesn't appeal to me. So I don't know what I'd like to happen.

CLARE: Well, for all its faults, given that it generates a fair amount of anger in you, do you like life?

LANE: Oh yes, yes. I love life, I can boast about that. I get up each morning and I look out of the window and I'm thrilled. I don't care if it's raining, snowing, wind, I love it. The anger is just like a little cloud hanging above. I can call upon it if I want to and I can forget it if I want to. But it is always there.

CLARE: And is it always concentrated on this issue, which we'll come to in a moment, the issue of animal rights, cruelty, exploitation? Or are you someone who gets angry about other things?

LANE: I get mostly angry about what people do to other creatures. I can't bear it.

CLARE: To other people?

LANE: In some curious way, it's not that I don't care what happens to other people, it's that I have a comfortable feeling in my head that there are millions of people caring about people. And I feel I owe it to those that they are not caring about. Of course, I'm not very fond of the human race, I've made that quite clear, and yet . . .

CLARE: You have, yes, you have said some harsh things.

LANE: Yes, and yet curiously enough, I do know so many, good, nice people like the protesters in Shoreham, a new set of people for me. And so I say to myself, 'Where are these bad people that do these awful things?' and I don't seem to meet them, but I know they're there. We all know they're there. And so then I get suspicious and I think, 'Am I rubbing shoulders with them?' You know, the man who cuts the legs off frogs to serve frogs' legs and throws the frog in a bin bag – am I sitting next to him? The man who runs the factory farm in the way I know that some of them are run, the slaughter man who doesn't do it properly, I know they exist. Is he all round me, where is he? Because most of the people I know are great, so I get to think that the bad ones are dotted all over the place and silent about what they do.

CLARE: But where you live you'll certainly meet farmers?

LANE: Yes, yes.

CLARE: And they're busy farming the land and ...

LANE: I know.

CLARE: They've got herds and they're raising beef ...

LANE: Getting fat and with their big blue numbers on their side and their tags in their ears.

CLARE: You meet the farmers around?

LANE: Well, I think you ought to ask the farmers about that.

CLARE: What I mean is, you meet them, they are all around, how do you make sense of that?

LANE: I meet the fox hunters too. They come to my house and they're very pleasant to me. I say to them, 'Welcome, have a cup of coffee. I hate what you do.' I'll always fight it. I'll never understand it but not on a personal level.

CLARE: But some people get much angrier, don't they?

LANE: Well, you know this anger gets to a point where it turns to a deep, immovable sorrow. Anger becomes something other than anger after a while. Taking the live transportation of animals, watching those trucks, you feel anger but when they've got through and you know what the animals are going to, it develops into something else, something that is awful. You know, you walk round with it all day. And it's not anger any more is it, it's something else. It's something hard to explain. I know that I'm unfair and biased when I say this, but you see, what I can't understand is, when I'm sitting at a table, as I often am, with intelligent, sensitive, artistic people, to all intents and purposes lovely people, and they're all eating these animals and they don't even put a thought to how it got there. They even order veal, even now, I experienced that the other night. It's then I get angry. I think, 'Why don't you care?' You know they have things like little quails, roasted quails, and you could see the whole little thing on the plate. Well, you see, I know that it's almost unbalanced to say this ...

CLARE: Well, would you ask them?

LANE: I cannot understand them. They are beyond my comprehension. I cannot believe they can do it without a thought. And that's probably where my anger lies.

CLARE: Some people, clearly not you, but some people would turn their anger into violence. I'm thinking for instance of some animal rights activists, or I'm thinking of, say, the anti-vivisectionist movement putting bombs in people's post and so on.

LANE: Well, I think those people, I think you're talking about the ALF, those people. I believe that they began by being like me. I think they began by just caring about animals, by actually handling a sick animal. I think this is why, perhaps, people are cruel, because they've never handled a sick animal and seen the poignancy of it. And a lot of people, until they got their first dog, didn't know what animals were all about. This is a very common thing. So I think they began like me. And you do come up against a huge frustration because the government don't seem to care, you see, and these are the people who rule us. And they've now taken us into the EEC who care even less. So when you care about cruelty to animals you've no chance. There's no one for the animals. There's only you and you can't change the laws because they don't want to. So that promotes a sort of terrorism within the people.

CLARE: But my experience is a little different to that. I'm living in a country that has a strong agricultural tradition. In Ireland, and I think the same has been said of England, actually, the people who are, if you like, rubbing shoulders with animals, the farming community, the rural community, the rural areas of Ireland, people there would not be prominent in campaigning for animal rights. And yet they're very close to animals. They see animals born, they look after animals and they take them off, as you say, to slaughter. Or they cultivate horses, or whatever it happens to be. It tends to be city people, often one step removed, they may have domestic animals, cats and dogs and fish and so on, but they tend to be much more vociferous in arguing the rights of animals. So it's rather against the notion that it's because of people becoming close to and having contact with animals. It's almost the other way around.

LANE: I know what you're saying. Yes, I'm a city person. When I go up the lane by my house I'll say, 'Oh look, a pheasant.' There are so many of them. The majority of people in Sussex don't even notice they're there. I notice its colours, it's beautiful, the way it walks, the noise it makes and this is possibly because it hasn't been my pleasure to share my life with these creatures. I think city people, we get blamed for interfering in country life. I think we come into the country and we're filled with awe. I stopped my car the other day to look at these lambs that have just been born and I was just looking and looking and looking, and when I looked round, there were six cars behind me and they were all impatient to get on and I thought, dear God, I just wanted to watch for ever. Not in a silly, sentimental way, which seems to, I seem to be blamed for a lot, just the wonder of it, the amazement of it all. And so to the farmer, of course, to him it's his work. If you work in a sweet shop I imagine you go off sweets. It's a similar thing and I feel they don't care as much.

CLARE: What about the argument that Carla Lane's view isn't sentimental, it's a romantic view. That is to say, that being a human being, you're not particularly romantic about human beings, you know yourself, you know what we're all capable of and we're full of flaws. And we do things we subsequently regret and so on and we're a beastly species in lots of ways. We do terrible things to each other and we write about it and talk about it and we examine it and we go on doing it. Animals, however, there is about animals a seeming innocence in the sense that they have a nobility and a beauty and a purpose. We're not too clear what goes on inside their heads and we give them probably the benefit of the doubt and, in general, the picture that is painted by animal rights supporters would be of a fairly romantic view of the pheasant and the fox and the cat and the dog and the lion and the sheep and so on. But, in fact, taking man out of the equation, the relationship between animals itself is a cruel one.

LANE: A cruel one, yes.

CLARE: A harsh one – as you watch a cat play with the mouse, literally play with it, it's quite chilling.

LANE: I know what you are saying. I don't look at animals romantically. I see in them a purity which doesn't exist anywhere else. They're pure. They're not bad intentioned.

CLARE: Are you a vegetarian?

LANE: Oh yes, I've been a vegetarian for 30 years. I spent 30 seconds in a slaughterhouse and that was it. Accidentally, I got in there accidentally with a friend.

CLARE: How did it happen?

LANE: Well, funnily enough, it was in Liverpool and it was the Stanley Abattoir right in the centre of the city, and this friend of mine said, 'I'm delivering a television set to the pub,' which was the slaughterhouse pub next door. 'Come on, then we'll go and have some coffee.' And he and I went and something extraordinary happened. We went through a few doors looking for the manager of the pub and suddenly I was in the slaughterhouse and I didn't see any killing.

CLARE: What was it like?

LANE: Horrendous. I didn't see any killing. I just saw six little calves in a pen up to their hocks in blood just standing, and a young man came along and, as he passed he put, you know, this finger in the ear and went, 'Woo, woo, woo,' made funny noises. Every time he passed he did that and they all cowered and shivered and he just did it, adding to the noise and the smell and the awful awfulness of it. And yet I didn't see a killing. I have since. And I thought, it was just a blank thought, 'Do I want to be part of this? Can I ever be part of this? No.' Never ate meat since, not ever. But that is something else. I would never say, 'You must be a vegetarian.' That is dictatorial. All I wish is that these people would think about how it gets there. I am not fighting against eating meat. I'm fighting against cruelty. I'm fighting against what happens to the animal from its very moment of birth to the time it's cruelly killed. That's what I'm fighting about and I don't consider that to be a very odd thing to feel.

CLARE: No. So are you saying that it is possible to conceive of a system whereby animals were killed humanely or are you saying in theory yes, but in practice it's impossible?

LANE: It's not possible because unfortunately the men in this business are just desensitised. They have to be.

CLARE: Why then wouldn't you campaign for vegetarianism? Isn't that the only logical response to what you have described rather than saying it can be done better and cleaner and more humanely. You'd be campaigning, rather like many animal rights protesters are, that it shouldn't be done at all.

LANE: I think things like fox hunting shouldn't be done at all.

CLARE: No, I meant the eating of meat.

LANE: But the eating of meat I feel that, frankly, there's no hope for the animals in that department. I don't think there'll ever be a system in any country where any animal that is going to be eaten will be regarded at all by the people involved. The farmers are kind, some farmers are kind, but they still send their animals to the most excruciating deaths abroad. And these are the things that I get upset about.

CLARE: What about an individual, the farmer's wife, that customary rustic picture, going out and feeding her chickens and then one day wringing one of the chicken's necks?

LANE: That's fine. That was long ago though, it's not like that now.

CLARE: Oh, it still goes on a little, doesn't it?

LANE: Well, yes of course, and specially in your country but basically that's not what farming is about now.

CLARE: No, but you could live with that?

LANE: Yes, of course. Yes, but I couldn't do it.

CLARE: No, nor could I, I have to say!

LANE: But I understand it. Take the pig. I love the pig. He's so intelligent, he's beautiful, he's the cruellest treated of all. Nobody campaigns for the pig but he's on my mind. But, you know, in the days when the farmer took his pig on its final walk, after having a good grovelling life with good food, and he's nuzzling away and suddenly he receives a blow and he doesn't know what hit him. That is when I say it's fine, I'd like it not to happen, but I can accept that.

CLARE: You can live with that?

LANE: That is fair. But what I hate is the greed, the money that's made out of the cruelty. Unfortunately, I've acquainted myself deliberately with all the things that go on and most people haven't. The protesters down at Shoreham have done the same. What happened was when I was going to the ministers, and I've been to all of them, prior to Shoreham, they glazed over, not one minister cared a damn about what I was telling them, what I was saying to them about animals going to Spain and being killed with screwdrivers, horses being killed with sledgehammers. They didn't want to know. They glazed over and then they sent me a nice little letter telling me that they understood how I feel but that they were bringing the abattoirs up to scratch. I asked them if they were bringing the Spaniards up to scratch but they didn't answer. You see these people don't have the same feeling about animals. And these animals were going on the big ships, the big ferries, and they were going in at night and nobody knew they were there. A lot of people were travelling across the water, they didn't know that the animals were in the hold. And we started campaigning and our banners read 'For you it's a day trip, for them it's death.' Now, when the ferries gave up it was then that the dirty washing came out on the streets and you got it in little places like Shoreham, Brightlingsea, all those places. And it's not just me, it's the people, they saw it for the first time. That's all it's about. It's nothing to do with me, I saw it years ago. They've seen it now.

CLARE: And when you find yourself sitting with someone who is eating veal, what do you do with your feelings?

LANE: Oh, I ignore it. I don't talk to them about it, I have no right. It's not for me to tell people what to eat. I wouldn't dream of it. But most of my friends are vegetarians. The people I feel deeply about are vegetarians. I have some good friends who are meat eaters. That's fine. You know, I'd hate people to think that I go round pointing accusing fingers. I'm telling you what I feel deep inside but it doesn't come out. They don't know I'm feeling it.

CLARE: Now, you've said on occasions some pretty harsh things about humanity.

LANE: Well, I think the harshest thing I've said is that I prefer animals to people.

CLARE: Somewhere you said your pet hates include factory farmers, estate agents and government spokesmen. You can wipe them right off the face of the earth.

LANE: I didn't say that last bit.

CLARE: You didn't?

LANE: No.

CLARE: That was a misquote.

LANE: I wouldn't talk like that.

CLARE: No, I didn't think so now that I've met you and of course I realise that many quotes aren't quite true.

CLARE: I did say they were not my own favourite people but I don't believe in wiping them off the earth, for heaven's sake!

CLARE: All right. You're quoted as saying, 'I'm terribly romantic but I don't need a man to make me feel as if I'm the best woman in the world.' And then you added, mischievously, 'I prefer dogs anyway.' Now, what I'm really getting at is that often I am struck by the fact, it may not be a fact, we can discuss it, I'm struck by the impression that a profound empathy with animals is accompanied by a relatively profound dislike of human beings. I remember interviewing Professor Bernard Knight, the pathologist. Now you can understand a pathologist being pretty dispirited about the human condition when you think of what he's called out to see and so on. But certainly, and with a great deal of feeling, he did exactly what I suppose I was expecting, he made a fairly passionate endorsement of animals and a pretty vitriolic denunciation of man. And I wondered . . .

LANE: Well, you know if you walk the park with the dog, every single dog owner, and I mean every one, not just some, the conversation goes, 'Good morning.' 'Hi.' 'Everything all right?' 'Yes.' 'Oh God, why do we have to come out like this with these creatures?' 'Ah yes, but they're worth it, aren't they? They're better than humans.' 'Yes they are.' This is park talk. Most people who have animals do say they're better than humans.

CLARE: Now what are they saying? What are you saying when you say you prefer dogs?

LANE: Well, I have two sons and I have a brother and sister and I love them dearly and there's no one more wonderful. But in the beginning of my book, on the first page I've written, I turn to the company of animals when my spirit hangs its head. And I suppose animals to me, if things are going wrong with the human being, then they replace the faith that I'm losing. There is nothing more beautiful than sitting amongst animals and people won't understand it because not everybody is fortunate enough to afford to do it. I can do it. I look through my window, every window, and I see doves, peacocks, rabbits, every animal you can think, running on my land, free, unhampered, better from whatever happened to them, better than being shot, being run over, better staying with me on the estate, living. And it doesn't matter if you bite or sting or if you're ugly, I won't squirt anything at you and kill you. You can live on my land. I now have ten badgers, I have a fox on my land and I thought, what am I going to do with you, you're going to eat the rest of my animals. So I feed that fox to the point of bursting and she hasn't taken anything. So I just find it very peaceful. I love the way they behave, the way they look, they're unchangeable, they don't get moody. Well, sometimes they get moody.

CLARE: Your dogs don't chase the rabbits. I have a well-fed golden retriever and it does chase the rabbits and it usually catches them.

LANE: Well, I have a lurcher, would you believe, and he just sits there and lets baby ducklings walk over his face; cats abuse him. But I dare say if he was in somebody else's farmyard he may not be so nice. They do come to respect each other. The cats and the doves in my sanctuary feed out of the same dish.

CLARE: Is it that animals are simpler? You talked earlier about certain complexities of human mental processes. You referred, for instance, to things that have come out of the human mind, like computers, and sophisticated gadgets and machines, mathematics. After all, all of these things in the end are human productions and it's clear that that's an aspect of humanity and of human psychological function that you don't greatly warm to. Now, certainly animals are not notorious for their computer skills or their mathematical abilities. Is it the simplicity of animals, that they come straight through to you at the level of feeling?

LANE: No, I don't think they're simple you see.

CLARE: No, I'm using the wrong word.

LANE: Yes, I read the other day incidentally that a bee can do far more than any of our computers just by communication. No, I know what you're saying.

CLARE: Yes, I don't mean simple.

LANE: Yes, I know.

CLARE: It's much more fundamental, the contact.

LANE: But they are very complicated, animals, they have an enormous strength of personality and they don't let you do what you want with them. Try and put my dog in a room he doesn't want to go into! A lot of people say they like animals because they don't answer back – they do answer back in many ways and they're very demanding, even more than human beings really because you can let a human being wander off and be certain they'll be safe, an animal you have to keep looking for and caring for and wondering where it is and this sort of thing. So it's not they're simple, it's their purity, that's the word that gets me. They don't have bad intent toward you, they don't have evil thoughts, they don't live in our world. They're like a little nation of their own and we keep intruding upon them and trying to make them different. We domesticate them. They're just so different from us and I'm not clever enough to know the differences. I don't know when my animals look at me whether it's adoration or whether they just see me as a meal ticket and I don't honestly care. They are fascinating. They are totally fascinating.

CLARE: Right. I was struck in your comments about the ending of your marriage. Of course it lasted a long time, 27 years. You made an interesting comment which I'm paraphrasing and do correct me, I'm sure I'm not getting it absolutely right, but you implied in some way that having the responsibility of making another person happy was really a bit much.

LANE: Yes, yes I did. I said that.

CLARE: Because it impaired you as a person and your life. I was struck by that because of course running an animal sanctuary, that's quite a demanding task. There are heavy responsibilities. Presumably you have to get somebody to step into your place when you leave it and so on. Now, I anticipate that you'll say that you are not in the business of making animals happy. You're really allowing animals, you're facilitating them to live.

LANE: Yes, and of course a lot of them go free again, you see, when I get them better, they go away from me.

CLARE: But perhaps you might say more of that. What is it about humans? Humans can choose to do certain things. Their motivation is a good deal more questionable in many instances and I'll certainly concede you that. But there's more involved, isn't there, in the sense that relationships between humans are more complicated, even allowing for the complexities of animals, human relationships are more complicated than the relationship between humans and animals.

LANE: Oh yes, oh yes, this is why I write what I write. I am fascinated by the human being rather than in love with it. I'm fascinated by what we do, the nonsense of us, the way we hurt each other, love each other, hate each other. I love all that and I have a great feeling for it. And it could be that had I not got involved with knowing what people do to animals I might love people more.

CLARE: Because you do like people actually, don't you?

LANE: Certainly. Well, let's put it this way. I would never harm a person and if I see on television those children starving, I'm overcome so I don't even know why I say I prefer animals to humans except that I know I do. But maybe I'm saying I prefer their company, and that is quite different from preferring them. I think it's their company I prefer. The human being is an extraordinary thing, is it not? It's beyond all comprehension the thoughts we have, the things we worry about.

CLARE: But you write about human beings, you don't write about animals?

LANE: Yes, I think I write about human beings the way I see them and I don't think it's cruel, my writing.

CLARE: What pushed you into writing?

LANE: Well, the first poem I wrote, I was seven and I just wrote it because, I don't know, I just did it. I've tried to analyse why we write. I think the truth is we just can't keep our mouths shut really. I think we just have to go on about everything. You know, we go on about sunsets and nature and most people are probably having these so-called profound thoughts. They just don't go on about it. I think a writer just has to, we're just conceited really, arrogant in many ways.

CLARE: Do you have to write? Is it compulsive in the sense that if you don't, you feel just not quite right?

LANE: I have to write, yes. I don't take holidays any more.

CLARE: Why?

LANE: Mainly because I love where I am. It's still a holiday to me. I've only been there two years. I don't know. The holidays I've taken, I've always ended up sitting on a balcony writing or sitting on a wall somewhere writing. I love writing and I shall always do it.

CLARE: And is all your writing about people, about situations?

LANE: Yes.

CLARE: The way they relate?

LANE: Yes, because I am fascinated, I'm fascinated particularly in love and what it does to people. It brings out the best, it brings out the worst, it's sometimes a travesty, the tricks, the games.

CLARE: And what do you draw on?

LANE: I love it.

CLARE: Are you constantly observing? I'm sounding like people who talk to me – 'Are you reading my mind, Doctor?'

LANE: Yes, I'm sure they ask you these things. I suppose I am. If you were to send me out of here now and say, 'Write down what you saw,' I could tell them everything about you and what you wear and how you smile and how you move your hands and that clock and these walls.

CLARE: You remember all of that?

LANE: I remember all of that. But you ask me to remember a telephone number and, you know, my mind is wrecked.

CLARE: And how long might you remember it for? Might you forget about it and then ...

LANE: Always, no always.

CLARE: And you remember the way people speak to each other?

LANE: Yes, yes, yes.

CLARE: Phrases and mannerisms?

LANE: Yes, they are all like tunes in the head and you gather them. I can be driving along in London and I can spot one person who's no different maybe from the rest, maybe he's in a hurry, and I think, I wonder where you're going, I wonder why you've got that expression on your face, I wonder why you're in such a hurry. And I weave a story around them. But long after, I can think of them and I can tell you what colour their socks were. I take in so many things. But I don't say this in a boastful way because I'm absolutely hopeless at remembering names, numbers. But seeing things. I can remember dialogue but not numbers.

CLARE: Do you remember whether that was always something you had? When you were daydreaming at school, looking out the window, I noticed that when you described that, you actually did more than daydream, you actually described the whirling of the leaves, and you remembered the bricks and I wondered whether you could still see them?

LANE: Oh yes, that's a memory I will always have, looking out of the school window, because I was very unhappy in school and because I really couldn't keep up with it all but, gosh, I remember the colour of the leaves, the noise the leaves made, the way they used to get between the milk bottles, the bird visiting the nest and there were 59 bricks in the toilet wall.

CLARE: Did any teacher not spot that you had a writing ability?

LANE: No, they didn't cater for my kind in those days but they did put in my report that I was intelligent, which amazed me because I didn't do anything that pointed to that. They did say, 'She's an intelligent pupil, she has a fine sense of humour and she has an insight into things,' whatever that meant. And I've still got that report and I think to myself, well, it's not a bad assessment because they were nice enough not to say, 'But she's totally inadequate as a scholar and will never, ever get anywhere on that score.' They missed that bit out.

CLARE: Did I get it wrong? In reading about you, did I sense that the breakdown of your marriage and the rise of your career were linked in some way?

LANE: It was a very unfortunate thing, actually, because my husband was a naval architect and had a very good job and he was made redundant, which is always dreadful for a man. And we were having a bad time too and I was spiralling up and he was spiralling down and it made the whole thing very painful for both of us. I was never a domesticated person. I can't do with all that stuff of cleaning houses but I like nice houses so I pay people to do it. I can't cook. I can't even mend a fuse. I'm a pretty hopeless human being to be truthful. My only boast is that I can write and it's opened up doors for me to do other things.

CLARE: But you can love can't you?

LANE: Oh yes, I can love passionately. The people I've loved I've really loved but I don't appear to have loved as many as most, do you know what I mean. All of my friends have had about ten times as many men in their lives as I have. They could take the fun of it. I could never take just the fun of a man. I had to care, and care very deeply before I could, would, get really involved, and that doesn't happen all that often. In my life, twice. I love the concept of man and woman. I love the physicalness of man and woman. To me that is one of the most amazing things in life. But I cannot stand the ties that go with it. 'Where are you going?' 'Where have you been?' 'You're mine.' I couldn't live with all that you see. I was married to a very northern male and they are like that, undoubtedly. I am very Irish by the way. I'm half Irish.

CLARE: By northern, you mean possessive?

LANE: Yes. They had an idea of how you should be and where you should be and I am essentially a free spirit. I cannot have somebody expecting me always to present them with happiness. If I love them I'll make them happy in the loving, but it's the living with them, I found that difficult, I really did. I stayed with my husband mainly because it was the way I was brought up. I was brought up to love one man, to have his children and never glance left or right. That was the way I was brought up and I did that religiously for many years. And indeed I was separated from my husband before I even looked at another man. I played the game reasonably respectably. Not even in another relationship, I just found myself, I found one gets devoured by another person and I'm just selfish really. I'm just selfish. I don't really want to share my space with someone who's going to keep making demands on me. Maybe it's because I'm older and I've done all the demands. I was very young when I had children. My friends were still going out dancing. I was in with nappies and what have you and maybe, although I got it right for now, this part of my life, where I have two wonderful men who are friends and sons, I think at the beginning, probably it was a bad beginning because I missed a lot of fun, I went straight into the business of that precious cargo of children that you can't leave, you can't escape from, indeed you don't want to. But I'm all for love. I love love. If only the right man would come along and if he would say to me, 'OK, I love you, I'll have my breakfast with you, I'll have my dinner with you, I'm not going to worry if you disappear during the day, if you have to go to rehearsals, if you have to be in studios late.' No, I think the men of today are more like that, but in the days that I was married that didn't exist. We were not allowed. I used to go to the writers' club once a week and my God, if I wasn't home by ten o'clock, you know, there was a sulk going on. So, I'm sure I have the wrong impression of how relationships are now because I had 27 years of that.

CLARE: How much is that part of the writing as well? Was that a spur, the sadness? Because it must have been a sad time for you?

LANE: Yes. We all have terribly sad times. I lost a little grandchild, he drowned when he was three. My father died so young, my mother so quickly. Dogs, cats, you know. You go through losing so many well-loved persons that I think we're all equal in that way. But I suppose if you've got the kind of mind that I've got, whatever kind of mind it is, I don't know, these things linger and when I pick up my pen to write comedy, I never think in terms of laughter, that's the thing that is natural within me, my sense of fun. I really think in terms of misery. I never think what's funny, I think now, what is sad and can I look at it through what I call my third eye, which is a funny eye. It's like when something awful happens to you and you relate it to someone a year later and you're both laughing your head off because now you're seeing the funny, silly side of it. That's how I write, with a sad story but looking at it in retrospect.

CLARE: And when it's happening, when something pretty dreadful is happening, have you ever been in the situation of feeling you couldn't go on, it just wasn't worth it, there was no point?

LANE: No, I haven't felt that. I haven't ever felt that. I've never felt that tomorrow wasn't worth it. When you lose somebody, of course, grief to me, grief is the worst thing of all. Grief to me is the one excruciating thing that we have to endure and I'm not good at it but I get through it.

CLARE: What does being good at it mean?

LANE: Well, I say I'm not good at it in that, well, it's just the most awful thing, you know. I just can't bear it. It stifles the whole of my being, grief. I become a sort of moron for weeks. My whole being is shocked at the idea that I'm never going to see someone again. I really just become a nothing. But I know in my heart that I'm going to wake up one morning and think of them and smile, the way I do now. My mother, when she died last year, I was devastated. I walked round in some kind of dream. I would not believe she had gone. I wouldn't take it in at all. I could hear her. I could feel her around me and then, one morning, I woke up and I just thought of something she said, and I found myself smiling and now I do that all the time. So grief, like everything else, like anger, it drifts into something else and because I know that, I get through it. And I said to someone the other day who is grieving badly now, I said I know you don't feel it's possible, but I promise you, you will wake up one morning and feel different. They of course don't believe me and I understand that but you do, you just do. All I can say is, thank God nature has it that we only grieve over our own the way we do. It would be awful if we grieved about everybody the same way. Life wouldn't be worth living, would it? I have a little cat at the moment that's got a heart trouble and she's just going to collapse one day. She's been given six months to live. It doesn't sound much of a story. She's there and I'm watching her all the time and I don't cope very well with that situation. She brings sorrow to me even though she's preening, playing. I'm allowing her to be a cat. I could, of course, close her up and keep her still and she'll live longer but I don't believe in doing that. And she's, at the moment, that little cloud above me and I'm thinking, you know, I'm going to have to face it one day. She's just going to keel over and I'm going to have to be there and those things I'm not very clever about. I do get really hurt by them and agitated because she's young. And I think, why my little cat, why Pandora, why? A year ago, I was divested of a lot of money. But I am able to think, 'Oh well, next year, I'll make it up.' You know what I mean? So practicalities don't worry me but all this business of losing people.

CLARE: So who looks after the practicalities, because it's not chaos is it?

LANE: Oh God, a squad of people, a squad of people. I have to pay people to breathe for me!

CLARE: Do you?

LANE: Oooh, somebody does my VAT. Somebody does my books. Somebody accounts for me. I have a solicitor who looks at all kinds of other things for me. Somebody cleans the house for me. Somebody does the land for me. Somebody looks after the animals. But I touch the land and the animals. I get involved in that.

CLARE: And you are confident that you'll always be able to write? Do you ever get writer's block or sit in front of a page and wonder what on earth you're going to write?

LANE: I feel ashamed to say this but, no, my problem is that whilst I'm writing one thing there are arrows coming in with other ideas and I'm saying, go away, go away, I haven't time and my head is so filled with ideas and it's painful and I don't sleep. I don't know what a good night's sleep is. I'm going over things in my head. I'm writing plays, you know. I did my book in six weeks. Six weeks! People struggle for years doing a book. It might turn out to be the most awful book that was ever written. I don't know, but the point is, I don't have a problem that way and, oh boy, would I be afraid if I did. If that hits me that will be a new despair!

CLARE: Do you dream?

LANE: You mean dream as in sleeping and dreaming? Yes I do. Not sort of in an unusually often way but I often remember dreams. Obviously there must be many that I don't. I remember dreams quite vividly and I analyse them and I think, I know what brought that on. And sometimes I can go back and actually pinpoint why I dreamed what I did. And that fascinates me. They're so real and yet they're so unreal and you can go to bed and dream about somebody that you knew about 30 years ago, and their face appears in a dream for no reason, they just become one of the people in your dream. That means that there's something amazing going on in our heads, doesn't it, and I'd love to find out what it is.

CLARE: Do you think you're odd?

LANE: Oh yes, I am odd, I know I'm odd. I don't mind being odd. I used to get hurt when people called me a crank but now I'm quite happy about it. I don't know what the word is – odd, eccentric, mad, I don't know. I know that I'm not the norm as we see it but I don't think there's anything extraordinary about me, don't misunderstand me. I just feel that I'm going to end up, and I can see myself now, with long flowing clothes, a big hat, a basket on my arm with something in it that's real, like fruit or berries, and cats, and dogs, and that's how I'm going to be old, an eccentric old lady living amongst things that move and grow. I don't need too much company, you see. I'm quite happy to be on my own, as boring as I am. I just like to be on my own. I'm not a party goer or a socialiser. I really am the most awful person really when I come to analyse it, talk about it like this, which I have never done. I'm selfish, I think. That's my problem. I'm not selfish with money, I'm happily very generous in that way but selfish with my being. I think I just want to do what I want to do basically. That's not good, you know. It's not good is it? You're going to tell me off now aren't you?

CLARE: What if you used different words, if you said 'independent' instead of 'selfish'?

LANE: But I'm not independent, you see. You know when I lived in a flat I did nothing but borrow cups of sugar from my friend underneath.

CLARE: And of course you refer to this squad of people who look after you. So selfish – what do you mean?

LANE: I'm selfish. I think it's just growing older, valuing the time I have left, wanting to do so much and knowing I'm not going to be around to see the things I want to see. I want to see. So many things happen in this world and I know I will have been part of it happening, but I know I'm not going to live long enough to see it. It's going to take a long time and I suppose I want to use my time doing those things.

CLARE: Carla Lane, thank you very much indeed.

LANE: Thank you. You've been very brave putting up with all this.

Brian Masters

It is tempting to generalise and divide interviews into duels and explorations. Over the years, there have been a fair number of interviews in which discussing the possible influences and impulses signals an encounter of much skirmishing and scrimmaging, in which the subject sees the point and purpose of the exercise to be the keeping of even the most modest of inquiries at bay so that it ends as it has begun with little other than the facts, the biographical details of life, revealed. There have been some such engagements to relish – I think of interviews with Spike Milligan, Edwina Currie, Paul Johnson, Clare Rayner, Denis Healey and, in this collection, Martin Bell and Ann Widdecombe – which involved a fair amount of increasingly frenzied and inaccurate fast bowling on my part and some measured and elegant front-foot defensive batting on the part of the interviewees, to borrow an analogy from the world of one of the best duellists I encountered, namely Geoffrey Boycott. Then there have been others which have to a much greater extent resembled what might be termed 'clinical interviews', in so far as the subjects were willing to engage in a mutual exploration of what might have been, what seemed to be, what appears to make most sense of what is now happening in their lives, and here I particularly recall my meetings with Arthur Ashe, Derek Jarman, R. D. Laing and Sir Michael Tippett who have since sadly died, and with Alice Thomas Ellis, Ruth Rendell and, in this collection, Sir Kenneth Dover, Paul Theroux and Stephen Fry. Both forms of interview are enjoyable and revealing but in quite different ways. The interview with Brian Masters is, like the majority, a mixture of both.

It begins, it has to be said, as something of a struggle. I have to admit that I came to him a little wary of the motives which have led him to spend so much of his time as a writer dissecting, in graphic and explicit detail, some of the nastiest crimes and some of the most violent and disturbed personalities of recent years. His books, and in particular *The Shrine of Jeffrey Dahmer* and *She Must Have Known*, while admittedly very much better written and certainly more thoughtful than those popular pulp magazines devoted to gore and guts which are a feature of the racks of down-market newsagents, nevertheless seemed to me to appeal to similar prurient interest. Serial killer Jeffrey Dahmer's own conclusion concerning himself – 'It's just a sick, pathetic, wretched, miserable life story, that's all. How it can help anybody I have no idea' – seemed as reasonable a summary as any, including Masters's, that I had read. But it seems unlikely to inhibit the growth of a genre. Apparently the day after Dahmer was sentenced to life imprisonment in 1992, the prison received nearly 200 requests from authors and psychiatrists wishing to interview him.

So what did I learn from talking with Brian Masters? Well, first there is his mother – a woman who only learned in her adult life that the 'aunt' who brought her up was no aunt at all but was in fact her real mother. Her own upbringing was wretched and emotionally deprived and her mothering skills were, not surprisingly, seriously stunted. His father is a nervous, anxious man, crippled by a stutter and perplexed by his seemingly weak, effeminate elder son and eventually develops quite a severe paranoid illness. The family atmosphere in the early years, as described by Brian, is not so much poisoned by hostility or cloying in possessiveness as rather empty and undramatic. Communication is somewhat sparse. The net effect was to exacerbate his own tendency to stay on the margin, to develop a detached, disinterested manner and to observe rather than participate.

And then there is his school. Though from a Protestant working-class background, he goes to a Catholic school and identifies with the contrasting, colourful Catholic drama of sin and redemption, of guilt and transformation. He becomes an altar boy. His parents are the first objects of a redemptive desire which, in adult life, becomes a driving force behind his writings on such fallen sinners as Myra Hindley and Rosemary West. He finds a talent in writing and the confusions, the emotional conflicts he experiences in his late adolescence, he begins to articulate through his literary skills.

The interview unfolds. But there is a growing and considerable resistance. The man who has made a substantial literary reputation out of his efforts to make Jeffrey Dahmer and Dennis Nilsen somewhat more comprehensible baulks at a similar effort being made to understand him. He is clearly uneasy at connecting what he is doing now with his life to anything that happened to him in the course of his childhood and family upbringing. He attempts to shrug me off with a reference to 'spiritual explanations' for his redemptive impulse, an impulse which led him when he was already 38 to adopt a violently disturbed 13 year old called Gary, who had been abandoned by his father and had lost his alcoholic mother by the time he was ten years old. For the next five years Masters was to act as Gary's surrogate father, mentor, guru and saviour. He introduces the boy to a whole new life, a new set of values, a new way of behaving. Gary goes to school, learns about literature. Masters becomes Professor Henry Higgins to Gary's Eliza Doolittle. It is a curious echo of a relationship in Brian Masters's own life which is not discussed in the interview. When he was aged 15, he met the television performer Gilbert Harding who became something of a surrogate father to him, teaching him grammar and social graces and encouraging him to go to university. Harding died before Masters obtained his first class honours at Cardiff University.

And there is something of the Professor Higgins about Masters's lack of emotional involvement. At one point in the interview, when we are discussing the motivations behind his writings on serial killers, he says, 'I do not want to be poisoned by the feeling of anger and resentment and bitterness and vengeance all my life.' There is an intriguing reference to unresolved feelings about his mother and he then reveals that when he was writing *The Evil That Men Do*, a book which is preoccupied with the saintly and dreadful things that human beings do to each other, he began increasingly to think about her and in particular his childhood judgements of her which were largely based on anger and resentment. Earlier he has described examples not merely of physical but of emotional neglect but without feeling, without rancour. He who can speak and write with controlled detachment and a wry urbanity about the vilest of behaviours manifests a first real flash of anger when I remind him of something he has said about the morally self-satisfied. Why does that bother him? Is it to do with his homosexuality? And why too is he so fearful of emotional closeness? He denies he is but I remind him of something he wrote himself at the end of his book on Gary, where he concludes that human relationships are inherently dangerous. Clubbable and gregarious in social life, Masters is more than a little wary about closer, personal ties because, as he puts it, with possibly subconscious reference to a child's universe, in close relationships there are bound to be 'tears before bedtime'.

At this point the interview changes gear. Masters acknowledges that his benign, positive, Christian view of human beings as essentially decent if flawed may be no more than a cloak, a cover-up behind which lurks in his innermost psyche a much more pessimistic and paranoid vision. He fears involvement. He is drawn to destruction. We return to the notion of intimacy, of dependence in personal relationships. He admits that it is something he 'very carefully' avoids without always being aware that he is doing so. For him dependence involves being trapped. Anyway, he declares, he has been independent for so long, certainly since the age of four! And he who has found it so difficult to describe his relationship with his parents now provides a vision of those years in which he has had to get on without emotional support, to be self-reliant and self-sufficient, to be in control. He could not be what his father wanted and his mother was too preoccupied sorting out just who she was to pay much attention to little Brian's problems. The one person who appears to have made a difference, Gilbert Harding, dies. And he makes the connection between this kind of independence and his seeming preoccupation with people with whom no one in full possession of their faculties would get too close without a very careful, rational analysis as to what they were about. He quotes Dennis Nilsen who accused him of writing about the victims of Nilsen's violence in an overly objective and reductive way. At the end of the interview he seems to be suggesting that he could adopt and relate to Gary and could engage in a cool, rational and, at times, seemingly intimate, analysis of people like Jeffrey Dahmer and Dennis Nilsen precisely because it enabled him to enjoy the illusion of relationship without the dependence, the intimacy without the involvement of genuine personal relationships.

The interview ends with Brian Masters musing on the fact that he is largely afloat, unencumbered by relationship baggage. He doesn't know his grandparents. He has no children. As he puts it with refreshing candour, 'in a sense I have no past and no future'. The independence he so enthusiastically endorses in the interview is his.

CLARE: Brian Masters was born on the 25th May, 1939, in the East End of London to working-class parents. He was educated at the local Roman Catholic primary school, at Wilson's Grammar School and at University College, Cardiff, where he read Modern Languages. He began his writing career with critical studies of French literary figures, followed by books on subjects as diverse as dukes, great hostesses, dreams about Her Majesty, the Queen and the mistresses of Charles II. But Brian Masters is best known for his chilling study of the mass murderer, Dennis Nilsen, *Killing For Company*, which won the Gold Dagger Award for non-fiction in 1985. He has written a similar study of the American serial killer, *The Shrine of Jeffrey Dahmer*, and a compelling account of the Rosemary West trial, *She Must Have Known*.

The title of his most recent book, *The Evil That Men Do*, reflects his continued preoccupation with the nature of good and evil.

Brian Masters, you struggle to make sense of the motives and actions of others, are you as curious about your own?

MASTERS: I've become more curious now, yes. I didn't used to be at all but certainly when I was writing *The Evil That Men Do*, in trying to explain and comprehend why some people behave well and others behave badly, I found myself looking at my own memories and trying to reinterpret them with maturity.

CLARE: This making sense of evil, or explaining it in some sense, are you any clearer about the origins of that particular impulse, where does it come from?

MASTERS: Well, there can be a variety, a confluence of different adverse influences which can make evil reveal itself, show itself. I suspect it's always latent.

CLARE: Adverse influences on you?

MASTERS: Not necessarily on me, I was talking generally. Adverse influences on somebody who does behave badly. They may be genetic, they may be to do with upbringing and environment or bad moods or bad food. All sorts of things can interfere and most of us are strong enough and resilient enough to resist them when they come singly, not in battalions. But if you are hit by four, five or six of these adverse influences all at the same time, you may not stand much of a chance.

CLARE: But when I was reading about you and your antecedents, your parents for example, I was struck by the fact that in your immediate life, there is a figure to whom all sorts of things happened. Your description just there of a battalion of adverse experiences is a very good description of what seems to have happened to your mother. And yet, I'm not clear really at the end, what sort of person emerged from those experiences. You describe them in things that you've written. One would have anticipated, given what you've said, that she might have turned out to be an evil monster, but she didn't.

MASTERS: Absolute saint, in fact. She withstood all those adverse influences, which were mostly to do with health. She didn't know her own parents at all. They died of consumption in their twenties. She was brought up by other people whom she thought were her parents and only discovered at the age of 17 that they weren't. Then she was told . . .

CLARE: Yes, she was brought up by an aunt, Lottie, wasn't she, who she thought was her mother.

MASTERS: And I thought was my grandmother. But, in fact, I never knew any of my four grandparents.

CLARE: And she was told in fairly brutal or tough circumstances the truth.

MASTERS: Yes, she was. The doctors had said that she wouldn't live to 21 so Lottie and Nobby told her that she might as well know the truth, 'We're not your parents and, by the way, you've got a brother.' And they opened the kitchen door and there was a strange man. She spent most of her childhood in hospital, having inherited poor lungs, you see, and she also coughed for about two hours every day. I remember that my first sound that I ever made, as children do learn to talk by imitating what they hear, my first sound was to cough, and that must have been mortifying for her. But, of course, I was perfectly innocent about it. It's looking back now I wonder what she must have felt.

CLARE: But just that phrase, looking back, there's a number of descriptions of her that you have given that suggest that you didn't always regard her as a saint.

MASTERS: Oh no, I don't think I've ever looked upon her as, as somebody who behaved badly. When I say looking back now, I now look back and see and try to comprehend how I must have felt at times, when I was an infant, when I probably did think she behaved badly. I remember very clearly being in my cot. I remember the bars of the cot and being covered in excrement because I'd shat myself while I was lying there, and it was all over, it was in my head, it was everywhere. I must have been left there for a long time and I suppose as an infant I must have felt alarmed and angry and neglected. But of course, I now realise, if I did feel that, and I'm not sure that I have recovered the memory accurately, but if I did feel that, I now realise that it was quite unjust because she was a very ill woman and she was probably struggling to gain her own breath.

CLARE: But, that memory is clearly a vivid one. That was when you were around two or three. But there seems a huge gap. I read about your adolescence but don't you have any other memories? You seem to say, 'Well, I may have been angry, I probably was angry, but as I look back now I'd no reason to be angry.' I still don't get a feeling of what were you like as a child. What was she like? How did you both get on?

MASTERS: Well, it's interesting you should ask because I wonder myself. We had a perfectly ordinary relationship in the sense that she made the meals and I ate them and she made sure I got up and looked tidy when I went to school. But we didn't have much to talk about to each other. I remember her telling me when I was 19 or 20 that for two years, between the ages of 14 and 16, I hadn't said a word to her. But, of course, that's when one goes into the privacy and mystery of adolescence. But you're asking about earlier. Infancy I don't remember.

CLARE: Your childhood? You're the elder son of two boys.

MASTERS: Elder son of two boys. There was a six-year gap.

CLARE: So, again, you would have been, as the elder of two sons, closer maybe to your mother?

MASTERS: I remember her being very proud of me that I always did so well at school. That pleased her no end. I don't remember her chastising me for anything. I remember my father wasn't proud of me on the other hand.

CLARE: Wasn't?

MASTERS: No. I wasn't the boy he rather expected.

CLARE: In what way?

MASTERS: Well, you know, if he gave me a cricket bat to hold I'd hold the wrong end of it and if he kicked a football at me I'd run away from it, so I think I disappointed him. But Mum seemed to be perfectly contented with me.

CLARE: Do you remember your sense of disappointing your father?

MASTERS: Oh yes, most surely.

CLARE: Painful?

MASTERS: Yes. How on earth was one going to achieve his approbation? There seemed to be no way.

CLARE: And was your brother Colin's relationship with him any different?

MASTERS: Quite different. They were much closer. Colin still is very close to my father in memory. He still visits his grave every year.

CLARE: What does Colin do?

MASTERS: He's in business. He's a marketing manager.

CLARE: What did your father do?

MASTERS: Well, my earliest memory of him is in the Home Guard wearing his little khaki cap. He couldn't go to the Front I think because his eyesight was too poor. But I remember him first as a soldier, then for a period he was unemployed, and then he was in charge of the laundry department at an hotel. But there again, it's odd when I think of it now, there must have been some distance between myself and both my parents, because I never really interested myself in what he did and he didn't bother to explain to me what he did. The periods I remember of closeness in the family were when we sat in the corner of the living room around the wireless to listen to particular favourite programmes on the radio. That's the only time when the family was all together. Apart from holidays in Herne Bay, I remember those as well. Otherwise we were separate people.

CLARE: I've been reproved by critics by sometimes becoming too preoccupied with the family as an influence and you're a good person to bounce that off in a way, because, in one sense you're a very typical, if you like, the product of a nuclear family of the mid-twentieth century, two boys and two parents living in the East End and then later in Barry in Wales. Incidentally, why did you move to Wales?

MASTERS: Because there was a terrible smog in London which killed 20,000 people or something and my mother's lungs were so poor, she was told by the doctor she had to move. And so we exchanged with other people in council houses and they moved to Barry. I stayed in London. I was living in digs at the age of 16.

CLARE: Do you think your family, your parents are an important influence?

MASTERS: Yes, I'm sure they are. But if you ask me to delineate exactly what influence that was, it's very difficult. There was no unhappiness and there was nothing monstrous to tell. They didn't do anything terrible and nor did I, I think. But somehow we were islands drifting around in the same house. We weren't cosy in a funny way.

CLARE: But, let me push you on that. There was a suggestion that Colin and your father were closer.

MASTERS: Yes.

CLARE: And I don't know what Colin and your mother were like. Is it that you drifted around a bit? How were you in relation to the other three?

MASTERS: If from a very early age one feels that one is somehow inadequate or wanting in some measure, that one's not quite what was expected, then you tend to retreat into privacy. I suppose it's all my fault. Yes, I did become very, very private and it was impossible for my parents really to connect with me as much as they would have liked.

CLARE: And sometimes it has the effect too that the person who retreats develops some particular aspect of themselves, makes that their marker, if you like, which sometimes separates them even further from the others. I wondered did you do that? I'm thinking of your academic success.

MASTERS: Yes, I suppose so. Being good at school gave me some reason to feel, well, there is something I can do after all. But I did it for myself. Of course, I wanted them to be pleased and happy and, as I said, my mother was, my father too. I remember he was rather bemused that I should do so well, as if he didn't expect it.

CLARE: Did it distance you from him, your doing well? Did he see you as a sort of intellectual?

MASTERS: Yes, as a swot. But I think even at that age I had realised that there was no way that I was going to become the sort of person that he might have wanted, so the best I could do was follow this other path and see if I could do well in that.

CLARE: What sort of man was he?

MASTERS: He was insecure. He had a terrible stutter.

CLARE: Even at home? Did he have it at home?

MASTERS: Yes, even at home. Of course, when I entered adolescence his stutter grew worse because he found it more and more difficult to say anything to me. He was decent, good, kind, but not thoughtful, and there's a difference between kindness and thoughtfulness.

CLARE: What is the difference?

MASTERS: Oh well, thoughtfulness requires imagination. It requires putting yourself into somebody else's position and wondering how you could please that person. Kindness is being kind from the inside out, as it were.

CLARE: And how did he and your mother get on?

MASTERS: Very well, as far as I could make out. There were no arguments. I never saw them fight or row or squabble. In my childhood there was nothing untoward that I can recall.

CLARE: Later on?

MASTERS: Later on, when I was already grown up, my father went through a terrible bad patch where he became insanely jealous. He imagined that my mother was flirting with the milkman and the postman and everybody to such an extent that he would telephone her about every ten minutes throughout the day and ask her where she was and which room she was in. He would make her draw the curtains so that nobody could look in.

CLARE: You'd left home at that stage?

MASTERS: I'd left home by then but it's interesting because that kind of illness, and it is a kind of illness, it appears to erupt suddenly but it always has a long period of preparation. The potential for that jealousy must have been very early on.

CLARE: You used the word insecure – was he insecure about her?

MASTERS: Yes, I think so, I think so. You see, his stutter had a tremendous effect upon him and I think he probably felt that it would make him an unworthy person to be with. Although he was wrong, I mean, he wasn't unworthy to be with at all and he was actually quite an attractive-looking man as well, and he worked hard, for heaven's sake. He did work hard to give us some kind of life. There wasn't much he could do because one earned very little then. But I remember on one occasion he won the pools, and this is what I mean about kindness, he won the pools and spent the entire money, it was £120 which in 1948, 1949, was quite something, spent all of it on Colin and me. It was our first Christmas where we had real presents.

CLARE: I'm interested in this issue of speaking and not speaking. He had a stutter. Your mother said you didn't speak to her for two years. You say yourself, communication between your father and yourself was actually quite difficult. When your mother said to you you didn't speak for two years in your adolescence, did she feel that it was some kind of attack, or that it was bound up with some feelings you had about her?

MASTERS: Yes, I think she felt that I must have been angry about something or other, but she didn't say it in any chiding way. She wasn't trying to embarrass me or reprove me. She seemed bemused by it. Of course, it's an exaggeration – one did say hallo and goodbye.

CLARE: Sure. But somewhere I saw that you said that now you feel you regretted some kind of misjudgement of her. That suggested to me that somehow you have a recollection of being angry about her. I wonder the extent to which, as you reconstruct so many people's lives, you find yourself reconstructing your own. I don't mean reconstructing in an artificial sense. I mean re-examining rather than reconstructing. I sense that as you describe your father and your mother, you're reinterpreting them as if they were cases.

MASTERS: They're characters. They're people whose biography I'm trying to write.

CLARE: Yes, that's right, that's right. But at the time, when your feelings were more intuitive, more instant, your feelings would have been more turbulent?

MASTERS: No, I don't recall that at all.

CLARE: You don't?

MASTERS: At the time we seemed to be slightly distant, not in any unpleasant way but as if we didn't have much to say to each other.

CLARE: What about another point, that you are unusual. You come out of a working-class home, very simple people, not particu-larly intellectual, not particularly articulate, and here's this little boy and he does very well I take it. You went to a Roman Catholic primary school. Was that the local school?

MASTERS: It was next door so I just rolled out of bed into school. That's the only reason I went there.

CLARE: And then you went to a grammar school, Wilson's.

MASTERS: Yes.

CLARE: And clearly did well. And then you went to university. Now, the point I'm making is, as you proceed through those steps, did that take you away from them? Did that open up a gulf, precisely as you succeeded, so that that which you had to say to them and that which they had to say to you became less and less?

MASTERS: I remember when I published my first book my father wouldn't believe that I'd done it. He couldn't conceive how anybody could write a book. We had no books in the house. It was a prefab where we lived when I was a child so, yes, it seems to have made the distance ever greater which is a terrible paradox because, of course, one was really doing it to some extent for them. They were, of course, very, very pleased but they didn't understand why. They didn't understand what it was about. They didn't understand what I was about.

CLARE: And did you know what you were about?

MASTERS: Not really. It was trial and error. It was feeling one's way. One comes to grips with things far too late in life. I feel like saying to God, thanks for the rehearsal, I'm ready to start now. But no, I wasn't very introspective then, and didn't understand things properly.

CLARE: When did you start becoming more introspective?

MASTERS: When I started writing, I suppose, because my writing career is based entirely, it seems to me, on one principle purpose and that is to clarify and to explain. And so precision of language is important for that. If you are writing a biography, it is important that you should understand exactly what that person was and what were his or her motives and impulses. And in so doing, one is bound to understand oneself better. But that always comes later, I haven't started thinking about myself until very recently.

CLARE: But, as you know, and I certainly find this, as you start to put flesh on the bones of someone, as you, in a sense, try to explain them, in a funny kind of way, the more you get to know, the less easy it is to explain. I'll give you an example. There is a simple description of Brian Masters through a number of interviews and newspapers and sketches and so on, there's a simple description of a man. There's usually explanations of why he is the way he is and that's it. But when you actually meet him, and when you start to burrow and look and get more inputs, initially you are convinced that you may know more. But then you do not find that. You if anything, understand less. Even as we talk and you start to think about your mother and your father and Colin and the family, you can describe everything but it then becomes even more mysterious.

MASTERS: Well, that is certainly true. But one has to try to disguise it from oneself otherwise one would never do anything.

CLARE: You are interested in explaining?

MASTERS: I want to go beyond description. A biography which merely describes, the nineteenth-century biographies did that, just chronological accounts, it's not even worth turning the pages. I think I do want to go beyond description. Of course, one is aware that one will never completely succeed, but one can't live one's life on that assumption otherwise one wouldn't do anything.

CLARE: Your writing career, did this start while you were at university or afterwards?

MASTERS: Yes, I wrote newspaper articles while I was at university.

CLARE: But in your writing career there is a change?

MASTERS: There is an evolution. There was no conscious decision to change subject but the subjects are all very disparate, as you've noticed, and I think that's a professional reason. I like to be enthusiastic about what I'm writing and the best way is to start from a position of ignorance so that your enthusiasm in discovery transforms itself into the words you use and may in fact enthuse the reader. If you stay on one subject and become an expert, you'll become bored and your writing will become boring, so I've tended to jump from one subject to another for that reason. But there's probably other reasons beyond that which I may not be entirely aware of.

CLARE: Well, you're most intrigued by, and seem to me to be most intent on, trying to clarify this crucial question about human beings, and that is, the goodness and the badness of them. There's a recurrence certainly in your most recent writing of this contemplation of what you see as a sort of split. Indeed you quote Versilov in Dostovesky's *A Raw Youth*, 'I am split mentally and horribly afraid of it. It is as if you have your own double standing next to you.' Now, I know that you're interested in this in relation to some of the extraordinary people that you've written about and one or two that you've met but what about it as it applies to you?

MASTERS: But it doesn't. I used that quotation as a way of explaining the character I was writing about. I wasn't writing about myself. If I were to write about myself, and who knows, I might do one day, I wouldn't use that at all.

CLARE: You don't think it applies to all of us?

MASTERS: No, horribly split is a pretty dramatic way to put it. What does apply to all of us is that we are capable of being sweet natured at one moment and possibly malicious at another. But that's not a horrible split. It's a kind of overlapping of different moods which occur to most of us in any week of our lives. But the character in Dostoevsky was horribly split in that he was aware of something deeply malevolent which he couldn't control. I'm not aware of that.

CLARE: No, but there's a paradox here because on the one hand, the people you write about, the Jeffrey Dahmers and the Fred Wests and the Dennis Nilsens, of course, they're right out on the edge, they are extremes and some would say they are mutants, there don't seem any relationship between what they stand for, think of and do, and the rest of human beings. Now, I don't know where you stand on that notion of a continuum or some kind of categorical difference, but I did understand that one of the motives that you have for writing about such people and events is to try and hold it all within the confines of human experience. That even this has to be understood in terms of human beings and humanity. So, in one sense, they have something in common with us.

MASTERS: Yes, in one sense.

CLARE: Well, what is that sense? In the sense that we all have a dark side, a shadow?

MASTERS: Yes, we all have a shadow. But theirs is a shadow which has grown and consumed them. And I suppose what I mean is that by considering people whose personalities have disintegrated to such an extent, we are perhaps better able to understand those of us who haven't yet disintegrated, or perhaps never will disintegrate. Certainly not to that extent.

CLARE: And, in your case, or in mine, the reason, assuming that we haven't disintegrated? There's no single reason, I anticipate you will say. I know you will say that. None the less, can you conceive of even a multitude of reasons. Let me look at it in a slightly different way. There's a very interesting account by you, somewhere, I can't remember where now, of your time as a head boy.

MASTERS: Oh yes.

CLARE: In Wilson's, and, like many a school at the time, the head boys and prefects were themselves required to inflict punishment for misdemeanours by the younger boys and so on. And, you were a head boy there, so clearly your academic career was matched by a sense of achievement and discipline, and you write of that time, 'I remember thinking clearly there I ought to be able to bring the arm down with force enough to inflict pain, but unaccountably being unable, perfectly unable, to do so. I was not weak, I was unwilling.' And then you did something which I felt let it go. You say, 'Some invisible power seemed to stay my hand before the cane reached its object.' I read this and I read this of a man who himself has written about, analysed, people who have done the most terrible things to other people, and I wondered, 'Well, what stayed your hand?' Here's a very good example. The issue of violence can begin that early, an adolescent boy given control of other boys. You can beat them. You didn't. I'm not going, on this programme, to accept for a moment the invisible power, although many of my listeners may say that's exactly what stayed him. So, what is it? Because your background at that stage, Brian, there was nothing particularly unusual about it, but sometimes there's nothing particularly unusual about the background of people who go on and do some rather odd things.

MASTERS: Oh I know.

CLARE: So here's a moment that you might have crossed the boundary, but you didn't, and you reflected on it.

MASTERS: I reflected on it and when I described that I can remember very clearly being in the prefects' room and having the cane and thinking, well, I've got to hurt this kid.

CLARE: Yes, you remember that.

MASTERS: I remember that and going through the motions of bringing the cane down and it just wouldn't work somehow. And, of course, it became famous in the school that if you get run in you go to Masters because he doesn't hurt. So what was that? What stayed my hand because I wasn't then a mature, introspective fellow? I was a 17-year-old boy who wanted to do what other 17-year-old boys do in that position, which is to inflict the cane properly, and I couldn't do it. Fear, perhaps, fear of the consequences, fear that you might actually, it might be painful and I wouldn't want to do anything which created pain in another. But I couldn't analyse it then, I'm doing this retrospectively. But that might be what it was. It was a fear of actually hurting.

CLARE: Were you sensitive to pain yourself? Would you have taken your punishment like any of the others?

MASTERS: Oh yes, and as a young boy I had taken punishment, yes. We all did. We put exercise books down our trousers.

CLARE: Elsewhere, I think, you talk about that something in us can turn us into a despot or a murderer by tapping into that kind of potential that is in us. But clearly, we're no further on when we start to try to analyse it. The attempt is understandable, the detail with which one analyses some of the greater ferocities, but we're no wiser. You cannot explain to me why you held back your hand. It is as difficult really to explain as to explain, why another serial murder?

MASTERS: Yes, in a sense, that is true, but I repeat what I said earlier. The fact that the explanation is difficult should not cancel out the attempt to explain.

CLARE: Are you drawn to horror?

MASTERS: Oh, Lord no. Absolutely the opposite. I cannot sit through a film in which nastiness occurs.

CLARE: But can you read your books?

MASTERS: My own books are not horrific in that sense.

CLARE: There are moments in your books that are horrific.

MASTERS: Are there?

CLARE: I think so, yes.

MASTERS: Well, I'm not aware of that.

CLARE: You said a very interesting thing. Indeed you're the only person I've seen write this and I immediately empathised with it. You wrote somewhere that in your decrepitude, some of these things, these memories, these things, would come back unbidden, and haunt you. Well, let me share something with you. I was once asked by a publisher, to look at a book that had not yet been published. It has since been published but I won't tell you what the book was. And they asked me whether I thought, as a psychiatrist, that it would stand up if there were a trial about it in relation to obscenity. There are moments in this book of extraordinary cruelty. Well, I wrote to them and said I think it probably would pass the obscenity laws because the obscenity laws are so defined that it's very difficult to see how something wouldn't pass them in a way. But that's not the point of what I'm putting to you. What I'm putting to you is, that I said to them, the problem with reading this book is, that afterwards, having read it, it is very difficult sometimes to get some of these ideas out of one's mind. They are there and every so often, re-emerge, sometimes unbidden. Many people will turn away from reading about violence for that reason, not because they want to live a clean and bourgeois life and want not to believe that such things happen, but because they fear that they will be altered, that it will enter into them, in the way horror does, they feel the horror of what they have read becomes itself a kind of incubus. I thought you were referring to that, I thought you were hinting at it when you wrote that interesting observation that maybe in old age it would come and haunt you, and I thought, well why does he have to wait until old age, doesn't some of this haunt him now?

MASTERS: It doesn't haunt me now. But in decrepitude, perhaps in very old age, some of those images might. I would be less able in senility to control their effect upon me. That's the danger that I sometimes worry about. But I would be very alarmed indeed if I thought that anybody who'd read my books had been haunted by images which he found therein, because the point of the books is precisely to rid the subject of its intrinsic horror and enable the reader to reflect upon it. Once you start reflecting, because knowledge is always preferable to ignorance, once you start reflecting upon it, then you are able to grasp it better and not allow it to infect you emotionally. This is what I hope I can achieve. If you tell me that readers walk away from my books feeling miserable and worried and hurt, then I would not be pleased at all.

CLARE: Well, I don't know what readers will do. I'm talking about myself. In one sense, professionally, I'm right alongside you. Your work is about making sense of the irrational. Even the most appalling and repulsive has to be examined. It's part of humanity. That's at one level. But at another level? I asked Bernard Knight when he was here on this programme, the forensic pathologist who was involved in the Frederick West trial, I asked him how he coped with the horrors he confronted when doing his job? It may be easier when you're writing it, when you're in one sense professionally detached, as I might be detached when clinically interviewing somebody who's done something. But when I go home and for a moment that awful thought of what Brady did to Leslie Ann Downes or what Fred West did to his daughter, sometimes that comes unbidden into my mind, if that happens without an emotional response, if I remain calm and detached, surely something awful has happened to me then?

MASTERS: What has happened to you then?

CLARE: I've become, I've become, emotionally dead.

MASTERS: Complicitous?

CLARE: Well, is it? Is it complicitous?

MASTERS: Is it complicitous? I certainly hope not.

CLARE: Well, why do you hope not? In one sense don't you want people to remain appalled. Don't you want both, to understand and to retain their emotional responses?

MASTERS: Of course they should, they must be appalled. But you used the word detachment, you must be appalled intellectually, you must recognise that this is an appalling thing to happen.

CLARE: But they do anyway, Brian, in relation to the things you've written about. There's absolutely no need to write the account of Jeffrey Dahmer or Dennis Nilsen so that people will be appalled, because just reading about what they did in the newspapers appals people.

MASTERS: Well, my books and books of this nature want to go a bit further to examine why you were appalled and whether you have every good reason to be appalled or whether, in fact, there might be something that is worth comprehending which goes beyond the position of being appalled.

CLARE: But then we are brought to that awful statement of John Major's – there's too much understanding and not enough condemning. Isn't this the problem there, you saying that if I were to understand more, I would I be appalled less. Would I?

MASTERS: That is a danger but it's a danger I think I am at least prepared to run, at least I will say something, I'll stick my neck

out and say yes, you might be appalled less and it's probably
proper that you should be. Although the evil act that you have
been examining remains an evil act. You must at least have the
humility to recognise that it was committed by a human being
who is as human as you are. But it's very hard to do and it's a
very unpopular point of view to take. But, I suspect that if one
reads the sort of things I've written on the subject, that may be
the conclusion you will tacitly draw.

CLARE: But I'm not criticising you for what you're doing, I'm
interested to know what you think happens to people who read
what you have done. And I don't have the answer to this. That's
why I wanted to interview you. I wanted to explore my own
feelings to this. I'm not clear myself. On the one hand, I am
about my own business, I would be one of those psychiatrists
who saw some of these people. That's what motivates much of
what you do, you're trying to see what lies behind an
extraordinary story at first hand. Rather like, what lies behind
Brian Masters? The problem is that no matter how it is
explained, certain kinds of activity like Dennis Nilsen's serial
killing or the terrible deeds of Fred West, remain, by definition,
extraordinary.

MASTERS: Of course it is, by definition, extraordinary, but because
it's extraordinary there's even more of an imperative that we
should try to comprehend it. Otherwise one just acccepts that
this kind of evil behaviour is random and doesn't need
explaining and just accept it, enjoy reading about it. You asked
about the effect it might have upon the reader.

CLARE: Me.

MASTERS: Or you.

CLARE: No, yes. I'm going to be honest about this, I'm not going to
talk about the readers out there in some kind of patronising way,
I'm talking about me.

MASTERS: All right. You.

CLARE: People are always going on about corruption. I'm talking
about this notion that on reading in full detail, which incidentally most of us have been spared in relation to some of these
crimes. I don't think anybody's read the full details of Ian
Brady's crimes, for example. I'm not absolutely sure of that but I

certainly haven't, there is this notion of being corrupted by contact with it. Well, let me turn it round to you. You've actually said it yourself. Trying to understand, you said, requires a degree of identification which is pregnant with danger. I thought that you're getting at what I'm on about but maybe I mistook you. So I'll ask you. What was the danger that you thought it was pregnant with?

MASTERS: Well, of course there's a danger. If you are going to try to work out what happened to Dennis Nilsen to make him do those dreadful things 17 times, the moment you do, you've got to try to do it from the inside, you've got to try to see the world through his eyes in order to see what murder means to him, not what it means to the reader, what it means to him.

CLARE: He may himself have the same difficulty that we have of making sense of anything. He's in turn bound up with giving you a picture that he's trying to make that other people have fed him, defence lawyers and so on.

MASTERS: That's right, and which I then have to interpret by weighing what is plausible and what isn't and what I understand and what I don't.

CLARE: OK. So you get inside his eyes and look at the world the way he looks at it and …

MASTERS: Well, that could be dangerous if I succeeded entirely. If I do succeed in seeing the world as Dennis Nilsen saw the world then don't I, to some extent, become Dennis Nilsen. Now, I present it only as a danger because it hasn't happened and I've never felt that I could possibly understand a murderer's motive to that extent, but that doesn't obviate the fact that there is a danger.

CLARE: That's one danger. A second danger, one you don't seem to be acknowledging and I'm not terribly sure I buy it much either, but I'll mention it, there's the danger that by getting inside the skin of somebody like that and trying to make sense of it, it becomes understandable in the sense that we then start asking the question, why doesn't it happen more?

MASTERS: I don't see the sequence of that at all.

CLARE: Well, in the sense that, if you put together a number of factors in explaining the emergence of a figure like West or Nilsen, and those factors are actually not all that uncommon …

MASTERS: Yes, I see. Well yes, indeed one wonders why it doesn't happen more and then one has to fall back on abstracts, on the notion of grace and of spiritual salvation, protection of some kind, whether it's protection within one's own character or protection from the circumstances which one encounters in life.

CLARE: But then Brian, you're back to where the reader started.

MASTERS: Yes, I know.

CLARE: That's how the average man and woman make sense of it anyway.

MASTERS: I would never say for one moment that I've solved the problem, that I've answered the question, I just say the question is worth asking, and it must continue to be worth asking, although whatever I write, or what anybody else writes, will never stop another serial killer coming upon the scene in a year or two and creating mayhem all over again. We can't stop it happening but it is very important that we see it as something rather more than just garish headlines in the newspaper.

CLARE: What about the third motivation, that it's about some kind of redemption? I think you came closest to it in Nilsen's case when you seem to feel that by making sense of it for you and me, you make sense of it for him. He doesn't become totally wasted. There's a bit of that in Longford's treatment of Myra Hindley. The notion that the redemption is important. But to whom is it important? I feel it's important to you.

MASTERS: Yes, well, certainly it can't be important to Nilsen.

CLARE: Oh it could be important to Nilsen.

MASTERS: It might be important to Nilsen.

CLARE: Well, it might make his life worth more than clearly the life is. But we'll come back to that. So you will agree that it's of importance to you?

MASTERS: It's important to me.

CLARE: But why is it important to you? Why do you feel the need to redeem these people?

MASTERS: It's not that I feel the need to redeem these people. It's that I feel the need to point out that redemption is always possible. I would hate to live in a world in which vengeance was the only motive which mattered, vengeance was the only emotion which conquered all others and that the notion, the idea, that one may redeem oneself by one's works is smothered. That would be a horrible world. In fact, to some extent it does exist now, and I suppose in a way I'm trying to redress the balance against that. It's not the person that I wish to redeem but I want the reader to recognise that redemption is possible.

CLARE: But, of course, redemption is possible but, in a way, it is rather like forgiveness. The only person who truly can forgive another person is someone who has been affected by that other person. The notion that you and I should forgive, say, Myra Hindley, is meaningless. She has a problem and the people she's affected have a problem to resolve in that respect. But, likewise, I'm not sure there's much you or I can do about the redemption of other people. That's for them surely?

MASTERS: No, no I wouldn't suggest that I have the right or the ability to redeem anyone, but I am merely suggesting that I want the reader to recognise, or any person, you, to recognise that redemption is possible.

CLARE: And what would I do differently if I recognised that, in relation to any of these people?

MASTERS: Well, you might be more tolerant. Going back to Mr Major, you would understand more and condemn less. Let me give you an example. There was a murderer back in 1932, I think it was, Leopold de Loeb, who kidnapped a neighbour's boy and with a friend murdered him just to see what it would be like. They were convicted, quite rightly. They were sent to prison. One of them died in prison, the other one lived on, and on, and on and while he was in prison he studied medicine, he became a doctor, he helped find a cure for malaria, he wrote a textbook on mathematics which is used in American schools throughout the land, and he came out of prison 50 years later and became head of a hospital in Puerto Rico. Now, his crime remained vicious, foul, evil, back in 1932, but his subsequent life did redeem him to some extent. I would like people to look at that and see that it is possible, because there is hope then, there is hope that goodness may, can, prevail.

CLARE: That's a strong impulse that goes back. You once felt that about your parents, when you were in adolescence, you once were thinking of being a priest and converting them.

MASTERS: Oh yes.

CLARE: Do you remember that? I thought that you actually wanted to convert them, you felt that in some way they were in hock to the devil?

MASTERS: Ah yes, yes, but that was infantile.

CLARE: It was adolescence!

MASTERS: No, it's a bit before that, it was at the age of 11.

CLARE: You wanted to be an altar boy.

MASTERS: Yes, I was an altar boy at the Catholic school and they were all Catholics there apart from myself. But I obviously wanted to be like them, so I became an altar boy and was very keen on it and wanted Mum and Dad to convert to Catholicism. And they said, 'Oh come on, don't be so bloody silly!' And I felt sure that they were condemning me to hell. But that was before the cognitive age, that was at the age of 11.

CLARE: Maybe, but that last story you gave me was a direct echo, it was of a man who redeemed. I was Catholic educated. That's the sort of story I would have been reared on by my Jesuit teachers. It's the story of evil and redemption and you told it again. It is the story of Ignatius Loyola, the founder of the Jesuits. It is the story of all the great Christian saints. It's the story of evil being redeemed.

MASTERS: So you see an echo there.

CLARE: Don't you? Well, I'm intrigued where it comes from in your case. Maybe the critic who said I've got family on the brain is right. In your case the crucial influence is not so much your family as that school experience. What was that like? I'd forgotten you were not a Catholic but you were in a Catholic school.

MASTERS: That's right. Well, that was at first a bit alienating. I felt that I was not one of them and didn't belong and it was very odd and awkward but I got over that pretty quickly and assimilated myself and I became more Catholic than the Catholics, but only for a very brief period. When I went to Wilson's Grammar, which is Protestant, I then realised that the Catholics were the ones who were sending me to hell, so I said a plague on both your houses very early on.

CLARE: But what's interesting, Brian, in this dialogue is that, thinking about yourself, you say, 'Well, I don't know, maybe that's a factor, maybe,' but if you were writing this about yourself as a case study I can see you chasing these factors, and maybe looking at the issue of wanting to be a priest and writing a very interesting chapter on Catholicism and adolescence.

MASTERS: All, all the profound influences that they had.

CLARE: That's right, that's right.

MASTERS: Oh dear, oh dear!

CLARE: But with you you're very reluctant. You feel of that time with your parents, 'Oh, I don't know about that, it was only a passing moment.' But was it? I do feel in this instance, I'm not making too much of this, I'd forgotten that you were in a Roman Catholic school, but I was very struck, in reading your books and one or two interviews with you, that you did speak a language I was instantly familiar with, the language of evil, redemption, sin. You did it a second ago when you said, 'Well, then I have to reach for spiritual explanations.' I have to reach for non-psychiatric, non-environmental, non-genetic factors, to explain why someone with a pretty ordinary background, or maybe not so ordinary, maybe a rather miserable background, but one shared with so many millions, why such a person turns out to be a monster, or does monstrous things, I should say. But, in your case, the reference is to a spiritual explanation. That's what a Christian says.

MASTERS: Yes, yes, perhaps.

CLARE: Yet you've been pretty critical about that.

MASTERS: I'm not Christian myself but I have many of the same impulses as Christians do and the best of them, you mentioned Frank Longford earlier, he is a very fine Christian it seems to me and I share his impulses but I can't . . .

CLARE: My only criticism of Frank Longford though, and I've said it to him when I met him, is, and it's a slight criticism I may have of you, I don't know, is that he has a tendency to forgive other people for things that they didn't do to him.

MASTERS: No, no, no, I certainly couldn't forgive, I have no right to forgive Nilsen for what he did to, well, one name springs to mind, Billy Sutherland, he was one of the men he killed. It's for the supplicant family to forgive him if they wish to. It's not for me. But since you're on to forgiveness. I am very, very keen indeed to forgive people who do me harm. I do not want to be poisoned by the feeling of anger and resentment and bitterness and vengeance all my life.

CLARE: Is that because you once were?

MASTERS: That I was myself vengeful, and angry?

CLARE: Yes, yes.

MASTERS: Don't remember any of it. I'm not being evasive, I really don't. I think I've had a very equable life.

CLARE: You said you never want to misjudge anyone like you misjudged your mother.

MASTERS: Yes, well, again, when I started writing the book, *The Evil That Men Do*, which meanders all over the place in examining why people behave well and behave badly, it was then that I started thinking about my mother more profoundly than I ever had before. It's not that I've spent my lifetime misjudging her, but I now think, at my age now, looking back, that I might have misjudged her when I was young. I don't remember having misjudgements on my mind as a youngster, but I think I probably did. She must have felt it.

CLARE: What is it that causes you to decide that redemption is an important message for people to believe in? Someone else wants justice to be right at the top, someone else wants equity. Maybe there's no explanation, any more than there's an explanation for why Nilsen did what he did. I struggle, as you do, to try and make some sense of it. You're a man who says I don't want vengeance. You want forgiveness and you want redemption.

MASTERS: You see, all these abstracts have positive influences.

CLARE: Of course they do but they also have positive origins. You once wrote, 'The moral self-satisfaction of those who see the world as an ordered balance of right and wrong, in which one has simply to elect which way to go, makes me want to vomit.' And I've just been reading one or two of the things that you've written about what people had done to each other, which certainly made usually sensitive souls want to vomit as well. I thought, that's interesting, that here is something that really gets Brian Masters going, he can retain a degree of detachment when he's discussing certain awful aberrations, but there's one thing that really makes him 'want to vomit', and what is it, you call it the moral satisfaction of those who see the world as an ordered balance of right and wrong. Now, I know what you mean and I sometimes get impatient with these people, but, that they make you 'want to vomit'?

MASTERS: Don't press that too far, it's a choice of words.

CLARE: Yes, although a choice of words is interesting, but I'll let it go. So what is so awful about people who want to see the world in terms of right and wrong?

MASTERS: Because they don't think. It's self-righteousness. It's self-confidence to such a convinced degree that they're blinkered and will not see the world as it is, they only see it as they want it to be.

CLARE: Even though I know that you would probably not disagree if somebody said to you, at the end of the day, one of the most powerful things that you can say about what Nilsen and West and Dahmer and others did was, it was wrong.

MASTERS: Yes, of course. I'm not going to say no, it was right.

CLARE: No, of course not, no, no, but the notions of right and wrong, I sound like your Catholic master going on about this, that ordered balance that you talk about, the notion that it's all clean and precise, that clearly does get to you.

MASTERS: It isn't all clean and precise. It's subtle and complex and difficult. But people who don't see the subtlety and the complexity and the difficulty of it simply are prepared to condemn and, and be angry without thought and it's that which offends me, I think. But that there is an order I think is perfectly clear in the words that people use in your profession. You talk about personality disorders, which presupposes there is an order, and doctors talk about chemical imbalances, which presupposes there is a balance.

CLARE: In your struggle to make sense of and redeem, pull back into the community of humanity even those most on the edge, in your attempt to make it understandable, has that made you feel differently about your fellow human beings?

MASTERS: Oh, in a very profound sense, yes, and in a very paradoxical one too. I am now much more able to see the goodness in people than I used to be. Having had to contemplate such wickedness I am now joyfully aware that most of the people that one encounters in life are essentially good. One took it all for granted before. It's not that I went around thinking the world was wicked and against me or anything but I took it all for granted. One didn't think profoundly about it. Maybe my thought isn't very profound now. I'm very much second eleven but, nevertheless, as a result of writing about the West case and Nilsen and so on, I have had to contemplate some of the most vicious things that people have done and it has made me, as I say, very thankfully and gleefully aware that most people are good. And that is something really nice to take with me to my old age and deathbed.

CLARE: So it hasn't made you cynical?

MASTERS: It's a paradox. No, it hasn't made me cynical.

CLARE: Or wary of human beings?

MASTERS: No, absolutely the opposite.

CLARE: There was one example in your life when it wasn't the redemption of notorious people that you studied and wrote about, there was an actual personal example. You fostered, adopted, a young man called Gary whose life was in a mess and you've written a book about it, a very interesting book it is too. It is about the impact he had on you, and we'll come to that in a moment. But was that motivated by some kind of desire to save him?

MASTERS: Yes, I suppose it must have been, but motivated presupposes or suggests that there was a plan afoot. Well, there wasn't. It happened by accident, most of the things that happen to me in my life seem to have been by accident.

CLARE: Most of the things that happen to most of us ...

MASTERS: Well indeed, indeed. This wasn't something that was intentional at all. There was a chap who was going to take my students around London one day. He said he couldn't do it because his wife's grandson was off school and he had to look after him. I said, 'For God's sake, I can't get anybody else, send the boy over to me. I'll look after him for a day.' And so that's how it occurred. The boy came over and it was immediately apparent to me that he was in dire need of some parental influence on his life. He wanted to matter in some way. He had played truant all his life. He was virtually uneducated. His grandmother didn't care whether he came home or didn't come home and after he'd spent the day playing draughts, watching television, he said, 'Can I come back one day?' And I said, 'Sure, if your grandmother agrees.' Gradually it was clear that he needed, he wanted very much, I'll go back to a word you used earlier, since you introduced it, he wanted redemption. And I said earlier that it's not for me to redeem other people, I have no right, but in that particular case, I did try on a personal level to make somebody's life better and to make him forgivable for all the terrible things he did.

CLARE: And what happened?

MASTERS: Well, again, we go round in circles. It didn't succeed in the long term. It did in the short term. He was able to see a different set of values. He was able to recognise the worth of them and how they could improve his life. He did go to school. When I became his official foster father he went to school in order to earn my approbation. I had to learn very, very quickly how to do it because, of course, I had no experience. But in the long term, I don't know. He left when he had a girlfriend and his girlfriend's parents said that he could go and live with them and I thought, 'Well, this is waving a magic wand, that's not what life's about. He shouldn't really do it.' But, I went to see the girlfriend's parents and explained to them what a handful he would be, but they were keen on doing it. I remember his saying to me something, and he wasn't a very articulate youngster, but he said something to me that day, or the day before he left, he said, 'Look, I know you've tried to be mum and dad to me but you can't really. Now I've got a chance to have a mum and dad, both, male and female, as an influence on me and I must take the chance now or it will be too late.' And I realised he was right.

CLARE: And his effect on you, how did he change you?

MASTERS: Well, again, it had the effect that I mentioned earlier of making me much more tolerant and much more wise, perhaps, much more affectionate for humankind, with all their difficulties and pains and anxieties and bad behaviour. It opened a window on motive very much to me and I could see what was going on behind the things that he did more clearly than I had ever theretofore done. So it changed me in the sense that it made me more human, I think.

CLARE: I was cheating a little bit when I asked you that, because you'd actually answered the question. You write at the end of the book about Gary's influence on you: 'He made me see the world through his eyes, not with reason and argument but by affective, i.e. emotional, identification. And what I saw troubled me to such an extent that I began to feel, and still do feel, that human relationships are inherently dangerous. This was the very opposite of what I had intended. Gary's legacy with me is palpable, mine with him probably effervescent.' And I'm again rather intrigued by that because here again, touching on what we were talking about earlier, is this sense that actually, as you came to look at life through the eyes of somebody like Gary, you may be right, you may feel better about human beings, but that's not what you wrote. Here if anything you feel very, very wary. There's a danger. In fact you say, 'Human relationships . . .'

MASTERS: Are inherently dangerous. Yes, I'm saying the opposite now and I wish I hadn't written that really.

CLARE: Well, there's some truth in it though. Why do you wish you hadn't written it?

MASTERS: Because it's so negative and it's essentially unhelpful. Of course human relationships are inherently dangerous but one mustn't therefore avoid them.

CLARE: Do you?

MASTERS: I think on a certain level, absolutely not because I'm very gregarious and I like social life and I like dinner parties and clubs and so on and so forth. But I suppose I do avoid an intimate closeness because there will be tears before bedtime.

CLARE: And it would be painful?

MASTERS: It can be. Look, well, it's almost bound to be.

CLARE: Why is it bound to be?

MASTERS: Because people don't really know each other. They think they do but then they realise they're on parallel lines and are likely never to meet and that creates frustration and anger and, how can I put it, disappointment. Disappointment, yes, not anger perhaps, disappointment. That is a very, very much stronger word for me than it is for most people.

CLARE: Based on experience?

MASTERS: Well no, I don't think so. I wasn't disappointed in that experiment of looking after the boy and I haven't been disappointed in my friendships. I haven't been disappointed in my career and I'm not, despite your probing, disappointed in my parents. So I feel quite blessed. But I certainly wouldn't want to be on my death-bed thinking, 'Well, I'm disappointed in what's happened in life.' And perhaps if one got very, very close to someone, one might risk that. Perhaps I'm afraid of risk, I'm not sure.

CLARE: Have you ever got that close to someone?

MASTERS: Oh yes, it has happened.

CLARE: And then what happened?

MASTERS: Well, it dribbles on after a period. No, I mustn't be, I've already chastised my early remark there with being negative so I mustn't be negative now. The relationships which are close can be extremely rewarding and have been in my case. But they do present one with extra problems and perhaps one or two problems is enough without having to add to them.

CLARE: I don't disagree with you. But you would expect me to think that human relationships are inherently dangerous. It's you who talk about human beings in a rather more positive way than I think I do. I accept that they're inherently dangerous, but it doesn't stop many of us engaging in them.

MASTERS: No.

CLARE: Unless of course we're so burned or we don't need them, or we seek that kind of danger in other ways.

MASTERS: Well, I certainly don't seek danger. I spend my life trying to avoid it. I really don't like situations which are painful. I don't like pain, going back to being a boy at school, not wishing to inflict it.

CLARE: But you're drawn to the horror.

MASTERS: I don't think so. It's not the horror which interests me.

CLARE: Oh I know that. I'm not necessarily saying it's the whole sum total that interests you, but at the heart of it what makes Nilsen, Nilsen, what makes West, West, what makes Dahmer, Dahmer, what makes them of interest to the average punter, the reader, is what they've done. That's what makes them interesting. It's what they've done. They've done things that monsters do. You talk about the danger of the identification, you talk about it being 'pregnant with danger'. So you, there's a danger you don't seem to fear, but real live people, that's a danger you prefer to avoid?

MASTERS: Yes, well it's quite possible that when I talk about the essential goodness of humankind, I'm fooling myself. You may be right. I mean you seem to have detected in what I've written various strands which create an image of a person that I don't see, I don't think of myself as being. Now the question is, which is the correct one, or are they both correct? Am I pulling the wool over my own eyes and yours by saying that I think that everybody's lovely really, where I seem to have written several times that you mustn't get close to people because they're not lovely. Which is true? Both. So one must tread a path which attempts to be truthful in recognition of both.

CLARE: When you ruminate on good and evil, do you, in the classic Catholic sense, do it in relation to yourself?

MASTERS: You mean look at my own behaviour?

CLARE: To help the listener who isn't familiar with this strange sect, so much of Catholicism, certainly in its orthodox glory, was to do with personal sin and personal redemption and the confessional and the notion, which is very powerful in certain kinds of Catholic thinking, that there but for the grace of God go I. Some, I suspect Frank Longford would articulate this, because there is something of the sort of mad saint about him, he would be prepared to brave the wrath and say, in certain circumstances, even I could do that. Maybe I'm wrong, maybe I'm wrong, I shouldn't quote someone who isn't here, but there are people who, given the philosophy of Catholicism, analyse sin and guilt and innocence in personal terms. Nothing is outside the pale because, given God's grace or the absence of it, you could be a saint or a Gestapo gauleiter. You could be Dennis Nilsen.

MASTERS: Well, on one level, I think that is inescapably true. You talk about the Gestapo. One only has to remember the historical truth of what happened in Germany from 1933 onwards to know that most of those people, who delighted in torture and dismemberment and humiliation, were ordinary greengrocers and bus conductors before they were given the sanction to behave in that way. So, if so many of them, and there were thousands, can suddenly become monstrous in their behaviour, the possibility must always be there, and that is a bit frightening.

CLARE: But in terms of yourself, when you are wrestling with such issues, as you did in that book on saints and sinners, *The Evil That Men Do*, where you looked at people who did amazing things in a self-sacrificial way for others, and then people who did amazing things and were terribly brutal in a self-serving way, I'm interested to know how much is this happening to you now? As you've written about them, how much you're reflecting back on what makes you the person that you are and whether some of the things you've done, let's take something like the redemption of Gary, do you think, well, maybe in retrospect, my attempts in that way were motivated not at all by the purist of motives but by murky ones?

MASTERS: I don't think that at all because I remember very clearly what I was thinking at the time. I remember thinking, this lad needs attention and if that's what he needs, that's what he's going to get, from me at least.

CLARE: But you teased as well. There's a sentence somewhere, 'Were there no homosexual elements in my emotional furniture it's doubtful I would have noticed the boy at all.'

MASTERS: That's quite possible too. Those of us who are capable of homosexual affections are more likely perhaps to notice a man, a young man, who is in need than those of us who don't have such capabilities, that's all.

CLARE: You see, the reason I'm interested in this is that when one starts to analyse and explain evil, not explain, but certainly make it more comprehensible, a funny thing happens to good as well. Psychiatrists are for ever accused of this, that virtually anything a person does, St Francis of Assisi, Brian Masters with Gary, has murky motives. By definition we do that which satisfies us and it is the world that decides whether what we do is good or bad.

MASTERS: I quarrel with that. We don't always do things which satisfy us. We do things sometimes which satisfy other people and are designed to be beneficial to other people which may not satisfy us. If I wanted to satisfy myself I would have gone to the boy's grandmother and said, 'Look, I just can't cope with this. He's throwing furniture about. He's being impossible.'

339

CLARE: But then you would have been admitting failure. You wouldn't have redeemed him.

MASTERS: No, I wouldn't. I would have failed but I would have looked after myself more.

CLARE: But maybe it's more important not to fail than to look after yourself.

MASTERS: [Laughs] Now you really are being dialectic!

CLARE: But as I struggle to make comprehensible anything from the latest IRA outrage to Dennis Nilsen, my wife would say, 'But where does that leave good?' And I think it's a good question. I'm not saying I have an answer to it. I'm interested, I ask you because you've thought about these things in a way that an awful lot of people haven't bothered. But where does it leave good? Some evil becomes comprehensible because you can see why the person did it in a way that fulfilled or met certain profound personal needs, which we regard as abhorrent and appalling, and rightly so in most instances. But likewise, people who do good, you're pretty harsh on some of them yourself. St Theresa gets a bit of a battering, St Theresa of Lisieux, I hasten to add, not St Teresa of Avila. The fact remains that you're pretty sceptical, almost anyone who gets involved in this business becomes sceptical about motivation and I'm sceptical about yours. And I'm asking, are you sceptical about yours?

MASTERS: No, I don't think I am. Perhaps I should be but I don't think I am. You say, where does it leave good. I go back to what I said earlier, that contemplating this abhorrent behaviour makes one more and more aware of decency and saintliness, if I may use the word, in the vast majority of mankind. Now, the best text I know on an addictive and repetitive murderer is Shakespeare's *Richard III*, and there you see very clearly an analysis of what made this man become so ghastly and vicious and malevolent and harmful. But at the same time you see in the same play the saints, Clarence, for example. You're much more likely to be obsessed with these people if you simply read what they did in, in the more shabby of our newspapers, which don't want to go any further than a list of the bodies and what condition they were in. If, like Mr Shakespeare, you do want to go further, then you will open a light on something finally much more satisfying because you see the goodness as it's thrown up against the wickedness. If you just rely on the newspaper reports, all you'll see is the wickedness, and that's far more dangerous really. It doesn't lead you anywhere.

CLARE: No, it doesn't. But where has it led you? You feel you understand more of what makes human beings do things?

MASTERS: I am constant in the attempt to understand more. Whether I succeed or not is another matter but I think one must try to understand, yes, one must. One is beholden to. It is one's duty. One mustn't go through life eating marshmallows.

CLARE: So you feel all in all that understanding is usually beneficial?

MASTERS: Always.

CLARE: Always?

MASTERS: Always. Because the opposite, not understanding, being ignorant of anything, and it doesn't have to be a serial killer's career, but being ignorant of motive is blinding yourself to the possibilities of goodness.

CLARE: But then if I were to say, having read the books that have been written about, say, Jeffrey Dahmer, the multiple murderer in the United States, who did all sorts of dreadful things, if I were to say, I don't in the end understand that. What is my loss? I don't understand how the atom is split. I don't understand how Einstein evolved his theory of relativity. There are things I'm in awe of and, in a sense, I am in awe of some of the things that human beings on the very edge of sanity do.

MASTERS: What you're saying is why should I bother? Well, it's your job to bother. You professionally should bother anyway, but even if you were not a psychiatrist, one must bother.

CLARE: Why? I'm asking why, why does the ordinary person have to bother? They've enough to bother about. There's that famous remark in a Woody Allen movie, 'I don't understand how a tin opener works, don't ask me to explain the Holocaust,' and I empathise with that. And certainly everybody in the cinema did, and knew immediately, there's so much to understand. OK, leave Dahmer and Nilsen and the rest to the psychiatrists.

MASTERS: Yes, yes, leave them out.

CLARE: Because if you write about it, with the best will in the world an awful lot of people will reach for the book because of the titillation, because they're going to read horrors here like Bluebeard's Castle, and it's going to be horrific and it's going to titillate and it's going to excite them, and then they go home and put on the kettle. And they're going to be no wiser.

MASTERS: Well, then one would have failed. But if I may give myself a little bit of satisfaction for a moment, I have had letters from people who have said that they bought my books precisely for the reasons which you've just enumerated, they thought it would be exciting and a jolly romp through murder, to find that the books made them much more reflective than they ever believed that they would be and it's turned them on to go and read something much, much better and much more profound, like Dostoevsky, for example. I have had such letters, I'm not inventing them. So it is possible that wisdom, knowledge even about such terrible subjects, may ennoble you to some extent. If you don't want that, if you simply want to have the satisfaction, the comfort, if you like, of ignorance, the comfort of knowing that these terrible acts are simply evil and are not worthy of comprehension, not worthy of inquiry even, then you will buy the shabby newspapers and read them and stick at that, go no further.

CLARE: Has your experience, has it affected your attitude to religious belief?

MASTERS: That's a difficult question because belief is a word I try to avoid. Obviously, you don't believe anything which is correct. Belief wouldn't be necessary if it is a fact, if you can know it. I am no closer to that than I ever was before, but I am very close to the recognition of the power of prayer which came upon me as I was getting to the end of *The Evil That Men Do*, which is a kind of rumination on why some people behave badly and some people behave very well. And I didn't know how the book was going to end but when I saw the end coming in sight, I realised what it was. It was an appeal to the reader to think very carefully about things before you do things, before you say things, before you explode into rage or before you do something which you know is going to be harmful. Think it through, think very carefully about it. Spend an hour in contemplation thinking about it, and you will end up by doing the right thing. And that is what prayer is. I mean, people who pray think they are praying to God. I say they're talking to themselves, and it's talking to yourself, quietly and deeply and logically, which will produce the final benevolent result. It's when you act according to impulse and don't think and don't pray that you will have the wrong result.

CLARE: I'm still thinking about that issue that you talked about which I think is an intriguing one, the notion that human relationships involve a kind of danger. One of the dangers which, I was struck that you didn't worry too much about when you took on board Gary, though others warned you of it, is the danger of dependence. That you might have become so important to Gary that he would have come to depend on you in a way that people do. It is rather like your poor father who got completely out of kilter in relation to your mother, he was so anxious about all sorts of things. Is that in there somehow? Is that bound up with your wariness of human relationships?

MASTERS: No. When he was dependent on me I recognised that the dependence was a kind of gift. It was something, a responsibility one had to accept and turn to good if one could. A lot of people don't have this opportunity. I was given this gift, if you like.

CLARE: But you didn't worry that he would become emotionally dependent on you?

MASTERS: Well, there was that possibility but I managed to avoid it by making it perfectly clear that he had his own life outside of the house and at school and with his chums and so on. And so to return to the story that I told you earlier, when he came to me and said that he wanted to go and live with his girlfriend's parents, I realised that the danger of his being too dependent on me had been, thankfully, avoided.

CLARE: You had been aware of it?

MASTERS: I suppose I had been aware that it might have been dangerous. At the time I expected him to stay there until he was old enough to get a job and go and get a flat of his own. I expected him to be there until 18 or something.

CLARE: But you have never become dependent on someone else?

MASTERS: No.

CLARE: No?

MASTERS: Why, I don't know.

CLARE: You've been candid elsewhere about your homosexual or bisexual tendencies, because men and women have figured in your relationships, is it related to that? Is that the danger, in a sense, that you're too complicated?

MASTERS: I don't think dependency has necessarily to do with sexuality, with sexual inclinations one way or the other. So I think that's a red herring. But dependency is a very interesting subject, and it's something I've never thought about until you now point it out, that in fact, I am crucially and horribly self-sufficient and I wonder why. This dependence is something which I very carefully avoid, even perhaps not knowing that I'm avoiding it. I've not looked at it before. Now what is the danger of dependence? The danger of dependence I suppose is that one is caught, trapped, can't live, one can't flutter out of the cage and live a life. So now I'm thinking without prompting, is that because I was dependent upon my parents? I don't know, I really don't know.

CLARE: Or that you learned very early to be independent?

MASTERS: Learned very early to be independent? I think that's more like it. I learnt very early to be independent. Going backwards in time, I was independent at 16 because they moved to Wales and I stayed on in London and then, going back even further beyond that to the position we started when we launched this conversation, I was independent as soon as I realised at about the age of four that I was not what my father expected or wanted, so I made a life for myself. And I've protected myself ever since, by being independent and, even writing about such dreadful people as Jeffrey Dahmer and Dennis Nilsen, I have been detached and independent of them. I don't need them and I write about them as a subject. In fact, Nilsen, because he's not a stupid man, he once chided me and said, 'You're writing about the victims of my crimes in a way that is so objective, you're reducing them to objects in a way that I reduced them by killing them. You shouldn't do that!' he said. I remember what I had done was to omit their names. I thought I was doing the right thing because I didn't want their families to read exactly what had happened, so I gave them numbers rather than names and I scrambled the order in which the deaths had occurred, and it was at that point that Nilsen said, 'No, you must give them back the humanity I took away from them. Give them their names and you will give them back some respect.' I'm meandering a bit now. I forget why I've got on to this point. But we started with dependence and I don't know how I led there.

CLARE: To detachment.

MASTERS: Detachment, yes.

CLARE: Objectivity.

MASTERS: Detachment, objectivity, is a way of asserting one's independence of everything, and that's perhaps more dangerous than human relationships, which I said were inherently dangerous. So I possibly have done exactly the opposite of the right thing!

CLARE: How would you like to be seen? Does that worry you? We've talked about making sense of other people. Does it matter to you what people make of you when they write about you, or talk to you or talk about you?

MASTERS: If they know me then they'll know that I'm a fairly cheerful and jolly person. If they don't know me, they'll think I'm weird and they're quite welcome to that, it doesn't matter. I'll tell you why it doesn't matter. Again, it's a question of dependency – on time. I told you earlier that I don't know my four grandparents. I have no children so in a sense I have no past and no future. All that I am is here now, so it doesn't matter what people think of me after I'm dead. If there were children and grandchildren, then I would want my image to stay with them and I would want it to be a good one, but it only affects people who know me now, and I can control that.

CLARE: Brian Masters, thank you very much indeed.

Yehudi Menuhin

Before I ever met Yehudi Menuhin I read his own autobiography, entitled unrevealingly *Unfinished Journey*, and his wife Diana's autobiography, more tantalisingly entitled *Diana Menuhin: A Glimpse of Olympus.* Lest some, unfamiliar with the Menuhins, might think that Diana's reference to Olympus reflects an appropriately awed view of her prodigy husband, I should point out that Diana Gould, as she was before she married him, was herself an exceedingly gifted artist. A superb ballerina with the Marie Rambert Ballet School, she was picked out by Sergei Diaghilev to join his company when only 14 and later she was asked by Anna Pavlova to become a soloist in her company. Her entire training had been with great Russian ballet teachers, but both Diaghilev and Pavlova died before Diana's dream could be realised and she sacrificed her own remarkable career as a dancer when, aged 35 years, she married Yehudi Menuhin in 1947.

Of his wife, Yehudi Menuhin has this to say in a preface to her own book: 'I always have the feeling that surrounding me with her love and beauty, creating most liveable and wondrous homes for us and for our children – from California to Greece via London and Gstaad – she has still denied herself and cheated the world at large of those radiant and in their turn creative fruits which were meant for a far larger stage and a wider public.' While he readily admits to the happiness and tranquillity and, indeed, freedom that marriage has afforded him, she is a good deal more brisk and sceptical. Marriage, she has declared, is a service and, 'If you don't know that you shouldn't be married.' Reading her autobiography, it is difficult to avoid the conclusion that she could have as easily survived without Yehudi as with him. Reading his autobiography, it is impossible to conclude that he could have survived without her.

But that, it could be said, is the story of Yehudi Menuhin's life – an ability to navigate a life secure in the knowledge that there are concerned people around who will always look after him, who will place him at the centre of *their* lives and who will understand the purpose of *their* lives in terms of caring for and protecting him. It had been thus from the beginning. Early in this interview, after he has talked eloquently and movingly about his loving relationship with the violin, Lord Menuhin describes himself somewhat tentatively. He selects the adjective 'serene'. It is an understandable choice. He started his life at the very centre of his parents' 'undiluted affection' – undiluted, that is to say, by any particularly negative feelings towards him, their only son, and undiluted too by any intense feelings they might have felt towards each other. Twice his father abandoned his own career on Yehudi's account – in 1917, one year after the birth of his son, when he gave up his university studies to earn the family's livelihood by teaching Hebrew, and ten years later when he gave up education altogether to manage his son's growing musical career. The young Yehudi was not unduly aware of his father's sacrifice until very much later. He was the first-born, the apple of both parents' eyes and beloved too by his two younger sisters, Hephzibah, four years younger, and Yalta who completed the family a year and a half later. 'To have sisters, especially loving and admiring ones,' Yehudi Menuhin has written, 'is an experience I unreservedly recommend.' He adds, not unreasonably, that a brother 'would perhaps have challenged my position'.

Indeed a brother would but none did. If there were divisions between his parents they did not concern nor affect the growing prodigy. Much more likely is the possibility that Yehudi's talent served to give his parents a joint focus and purpose. When he was two, for example, they smuggled him into a matinée concert of the San Francisco Symphony Orchestra and apparently continued this undercover operation until he was old enough to have a ticket on his own account. Both had a refreshingly wise, sane and balanced attitude towards their son's ability as is evidenced by his mother's refusal to be overawed by invitations from royalty for her small son to play for them. A childhood 'guarded but also stretched to fulfilment', in George Steiner's phrase, certainly served Yehudi well – he was able to grow and mature at a sensible pace. And, as with Tony Benn, Yehudi at an early age was in contact and at ease with, and in receipt of, the plaudits of the great and the famous. Where Benn met Ramsay MacDonald and Oswald Mosley, Menuhin met Edward Elgar and Béla Bartók; Elgar declared in a letter to George Bernard Shaw that the young Yehudi was 'a wonder boy', while Bartók wrote the Solo Sonata specially for him. At the age of 11, Yehudi Menuhin made his Carnegie Hall debut playing the Beethoven Violin Concerto and the critic Olin Downes in the *New York Times* wrote of the occasion, 'It seems ridiculous to say that he showed a mature conception of Beethoven's concerto but that is the fact ... A boy of eleven proved conclusively his right to be ranked with the outstanding interpreters of his music.'

Rare indeed is the person who says to me, 'I cannot tell you how happy my childhood was,' and writes, 'I am one of those privileged people whose early years shine in retrospect as a time of unblemished happiness.' When such a claim is made I often have reason to doubt it. But in Yehudi Menuhin's case I believe it. There is, for a start, an extraordinary consensus concerning descriptions of the young, adult and now ageing, man. His childhood is disciplined and serious with streaks of normal, boyish impishness and cheek. His adult persona, as described by his wife, manifests a freshness of spirit, a 'chronic' optimism, a never-waning appetite, a searching mind ever on the ramble, a willingness to trust others bordering on the naive. Those who meet him, even the most sceptical, remark on his gentleness and his integrity. He has never suffered from stage fright. His physical and mental health are excellent. His blood pressure is low not high. He has the enviable ability to relax and sleep in the most unlikely places. While his wife frets and fusses waiting in airports, rushing in taxis or 30,000 feet up over the Pole, her husband, more often than not, is dozing in a tranquil nap. The only stimulus likely to make him angry is other people's inhumanity. To some, such as one of his protégés, Nigel Kennedy, this lack of anger can seem to be a kind of passivity and at times that most certainly is what it is. At other times, it exudes an aura of indifference, what Menuhin refers to as an 'inbuilt selfishness'.

Would Yehudi Menuhin describe himself as a happy man? 'I don't think I could describe myself in any other way. As a very blessed and a very happy man, a very lucky man.' 'To find genius and happiness united,' writes George Steiner in a preface to *Unfinished Journey*, 'is nearly a scandal.' We are accustomed to thinking of genius as tormented. Yehudi Menuhin finds his happiness in his career which, more accurately, should perhaps be called a mission. In so far as there is a stumble on the inexorable path upwards and onwards, it relates to his first marriage. He appears to have been in the process, not so much of maturing out of his own family and into an adult relationship, as exchanging one family for another – note the extraordinary double marriage involving himself and his sister marrying a sister and brother and his desire to have all three Menuhins married at the same time. His first marriage was the mistake of a young man suddenly independent – after all he had never even gone to school but had been educated, tutored, at home. But whether, in one sense, Yehudi Menuhin can ever be said to have 'grown up' is perhaps a moot point – with his second marriage, he found a woman prepared to do what his mother, and indeed his father, had done, namely subordinate all her talents, desires, ambitions to his needs.

In his autobiography, he mischievously suggests that there is a tendency for ugly violinists to marry beautiful wives. In the case of the Menuhins, the tendency is only half-fulfilled. Diana Menuhin is indeed a very beautiful woman but Yehudi Menuhin is no ugly man, indeed, particularly when younger, strikingly handsome and sensitive. But he goes on to make a number of perhaps more pertinent observations concerning the typical violinist. He suggests that the violinist is more sensual than intellectual, somewhat narrow in outlook and probably vain. He takes a pride in the sound he produces equivalent to the pride his wife takes in her good looks. He is romantic in the sense of having sentiments to express but he is not all wings and freedom and unfettered impulse.

'On the contrary,' he writes, 'he is an animal shackled to a treadmill of his own devising, on which untold hours of labour grind out grudging rations of satisfaction that may, if he plays well, last the length of a performance but are exhausted almost before the applause. Given that most of mankind wear out their days on one treadmill or another, for lesser reward or none, the violinist is, finally, privileged.' And so are we privileged who have enjoyed and continue to enjoy the greatness of one of this century's finest interpretative artists.

CLARE: At the age of 80, Yehudi Menuhin, Lord Menuhin since he was made a life peer in 1993, can look back over a truly extraordinary life story. By virtue of his gift for playing the violin, he has become not only one of the great musicians of the twentieth century, but also a kind of living legend, with influence and interests far beyond the world of music. Citizen of the world, campaigner against injustices, enthusiast for ecology, yoghurt, organic food and generally all things wholesome, he is a celebrated student of yoga, who has been known to conduct orchestras and carry on conversations standing on his head, with Pandit Nehru and Ben Gurion, to mention but two.

He was born on the 22nd April, 1916, in New York, and was brought up with his two sisters, Hephzibah and Yalta in San Francisco by devoted Russian-Jewish parents. He first picked up a violin when he was barely three years old and by the age of four he knew, or instinctively felt, that to play was to be. Since then the miracle boy, as Albert Einstein called him, has played with the world's most famous orchestras and conductors to almost unparalleled international acclaim and adulation. As a music critic once remarked, 'Even when he plays out of tune, it's worth listening to.'

In addition to a British knighthood, peerage and Order of Merit, he has been showered with innumerable international honours, and yet, one of his proudest achievements is the Yehudi Menuhin School for Young Musicians in Surrey.

He has been married twice and has four children. His second wife, the former ballerina Diana Gould, has been the mainstay of his life for nearly 50 years. She describes him with affectionate irreverence as, and I quote, 'A unique, unworldly character who prefers to live on cloud nine. He is not really a man, he is an institution.'

Lord Menuhin, when writing about, I think it was the composer Ernest Bloch, you said, 'The difference between what someone appears to be and what he imagines to be is sometimes wide.' And I've been wondering to what extent this is true of you.

MENUHIN: Well, I think you must ask Diana. She would be, I am sure, prepared to give you a very precise analysis of that difference. In fact I've often wondered and last night I had the occasion to speak with the headmaster of my school, who is the son of a priest, of a vicar, and I said there must be moments when it must be extremely difficult for a vicar's wife, and for the vicar himself, the physiognomy he presents to the congregation and the wife knows a quite different one at home. And obviously there are dichotomies there but I fortunately am very aware of, how shall I say, of myself as a man just like others, full of all kinds of weaknesses and lacks and gaps and so on and so forth. From my very earliest days my parents have always inured me against any kind of flattery, or, you know, adulation. It really does fall off me, like water off a duck's back.

CLARE: How did they do it, your parents? What would they have said to you? Because, of course, from the earliest of ages, you would have known that people around you thought of you as special.

MENUHIN: Well, you know, not necessarily so. I was determined to play the violin as well as I could and I measured my worth purely by my capacity to somehow get near to my dream, to my goal. So that whatever people said had nothing to do with the facts of my own assessment. My parents also saw to it that I didn't waste my time on reading reviews or on seeing people. I never look back in fact. I always look to the next challenge, to the next obligation, to the next effort to learn a new work or to conquer some difficulty. So that I have never sat back and said, 'Oh, wasn't that good?' Perhaps at the end of a good performance, I may feel a moment of satisfaction, but that is a very ephemeral sensation. It's not even like an artist, painter or a sculptor, who can look at his work for ever and say, 'Now, that was wonderful.'

CLARE: When you're actually playing, is there a sensuality about that?

MENUHIN: Oh yes, oh yes, definitely.

CLARE: Can you describe it for me?

MENUHIN: Yes, yes. It's a sense of fulfilling a dream, an image that one has carried of that particular music in terms of its coherence, structure, its shape, its proportions, its quality of emotional content, its perfection in terms of economy of effort, of smoothness of technique. There are many criteria, and if they are fulfilled, then there is a deep satisfaction, of course.

CLARE: As it's happening?

MENUHIN: As it's happening, oh yes, very much so. No, it's not something that I relish in the armchair afterwards. Oh, perhaps, you meet a few people, a few musicians who come back and comment on it favourably. That is pleasant, but I'm immediately taken up with the next performance, whatever that may be.

CLARE: Do you have a violin that you have had for many, many years?

MENUHIN: Oh yes. My first great violin I had, let me see, I received it at the end of 1928.

CLARE: When you were 12?

MENUHIN: Yes, when I was 12. And I had it until I went to Japan the first time, in other words, around 1951 or so. And then I bought another Stradivarius which I had for another 35 or 40 years.

CLARE: And would you have kept both of those?

MENUHIN: No, I kept my very last one, a Guarneri, the Lord Wilton, which is the most beautiful Guarneri perhaps in the world. And no, I wanted a beautiful house in London so I gave up one of the fiddles.

CLARE: What is the relationship between someone like yourself and a violin?

MENUHIN: A very close relationship. It's a life's companion in fact, and it receives and gives like a companion does and has to be handled in a particularly considerate way, and to evoke the ready response, the return vibrations, as it were and to hear a voice, it is a voice that one coaxes and makes. It's one's own voice but it's also the voice of the instrument and it's a beautiful instrument and I've had the good fortune to have only beautiful instruments since I was eight.

CLARE: It's something alive?

MENUHIN: It's something alive, exactly. It's so much more than a toy for a child because it speaks and you make it speak. I can well understand they speak of prodigies but it really is a real desire to have with one, next to one, vibrating with one, something which, as you say, is alive.

CLARE: Would you worry about it and its health?

MENUHIN: Oh yes, yes, absolutely.

CLARE: Can you give me an example?

MENUHIN: Well, it is a very fragile and a very responsive, a very sensitive instrument. Changes of temperature, extreme dryness, extreme humidity, extreme heat or cold, all affect it and one has to keep it sheltered from these extremes if you only can. It's like much more, it's like furniture but much more than that, of course, because it's the most beautiful craftsmanship, but it's crafted to have a voice as well, and that voice suffers. It's perhaps as sensitive as a singer's larynx.

CLARE: Did you ever lose it?

MENUHIN: From time to time, I'd take it to the violin maker or repairer. It has to be adjusted sometimes. It comes open in cases of humidity because they never glue it with that kind of glue that never gives because that would be the end of the violin, it would crack then. So it has to give – between the table and the shoulders, for instance. And sometimes it used to come open, any violin comes open, and had to be reglued. Then other times the table also moves with relation to the back and therefore the sound, what the French call *l'âme*, the soul, the sounding stick, which is a little piece of wood, which connects the table with the back, may get loose. Or other things, like for instance, tuning the strings down when I'm not playing it, not all the way down, just a little bit, enough to relieve the table of the violin, as it were, of that very great pressure. Especially with metal strings which they didn't have in the old days. Metal strings are in a way an abomination.

CLARE: Why?

MENUHIN: Because they impose a strain on the violin and increase the brilliance no doubt and, of course, the string lasts longer, but a violin with gut strings, or wound gut in silver thread or gold thread, is a much more relaxed instrument. So instruments are now all, almost all, played with metal strings, which should be tuned down about one or two tones so as to relax the violin.

CLARE: I assume there would be times when the violin would not be on song, so to speak?

MENUHIN: Oh yes, yes there are such times and they are difficult. One waits until one can get to someone who really understands the violin and knows how to move the sound posts, or the bridge may have moved slightly. It can depend on so many different factors. Sometimes, under certain climatic conditions, the fingerboard tips down towards the body of the violin, the angle changes and one inserts sometimes a little form between the fingerboard and the table to keep that from happening. But it's a constant vigil.

CLARE: Yes. One of the reasons I wanted to interview you, and it was echoed in George Steiner's preface to your book ...

MENUHIN: *Unfinished Journey?*

CLARE: Steiner muses in that preface on this very interesting conjunction in you of an extraordinary talent, genius, and seeming happiness, contentment. I'm a psychiatrist and I see a lot of people who are not very happy for all sorts of reasons, some outside their control, some on the margins. But it raises questions about the notion of happiness. What are the constituent elements that go to make up a contented person? You do appear to be – now you may tell me you're not and this is a misreading of all that's been written about you and so on – but you do appear to be someone who has a serene temperament.

MENUHIN: That is true. I'm serene except when I'm faced by officials who become officious and want to exercise their little power, or when I see abuse of power, or when I read about man's horrid side, evil side and the way he can behave to his fellow men.

CLARE: That would upset you?

MENUHIN: That would upset me very much. But normally I am indeed quite serene. I think I've inherited that equally from both my parents. I have inward great passion, without which one could hardly play the violin or make music. On the other hand, that has had its outlet, so that there are few frustrations that have been built up over time. I imagine many, many people are living with so much that hasn't been satisfied. From the very beginning, I see it with children when we go into the violin schools, schools where there is violence and prejudice. I have a project that goes into a school, one school in each of nine countries, and we come with singing and dancing, folk music and the children getting to know each other's folk background and traditions. All these prejudices and resentments and frustrations disappear. At least the social ones. And then when I think how many children are deprived, not only of their birthright but in terms of satisfaction of their curiosity, their desire and need to sing and to dance. A child is made to move and to satisfy first of all the senses and by example, and not from books. Teachers so often don't give the example. And I think anything that's taught by example as the violin can, must, be taught by example, or horse riding rather than from a book, when you have the right teacher, then you have a guide and someone whom you revere and to whom you are indebted and full of love and respect, that's important.

CLARE: As your parents are described, neither of them was particularly like you. Your father is described as spontaneous, exuberant, loving and hating, feeling intensely. There's a lovely quotation where you, in an interview, you described his sensuality, you say he once told you that he knew every inch of your mother's body. You said he thinks in absolutes of black and white. So that's your father. Your mother comes across as a remarkable woman: self-sufficient, dutiful, purposeful, an enormous sense of right and wrong, emotions strongly under control. She's 100 and she swims in icy cold water periodically!

MENUHIN: No, not quite but anyway . . .

CLARE: Not quite. Well, they come across as very emotional and fiery people. I'm not suggesting you're not emotional but I don't think I saw the adjective 'serene' applied to either of them, and yet it's the commonest adjective applied to you.

MENUHIN: Yes, well I think it comes from a balance perhaps between them. I don't say that I'm always serene, but I do have a sense of proportion and perhaps I'm very selfish. I mean by that, that when I feel healthy and well and I've been blessed with good health, I look after it too. It's not absolutely the good health of, shall we say, a karate expert, but within its limits it's very reliable, if I look after it. I've had an operation on my back in 1950 in South Africa ...

CLARE: But otherwise?

MENUHIN: Otherwise, ever since then, I know what to do to, to keep myself flexible.

CLARE: You've used the word selfish. Say more about that.

MENUHIN: I feel that so much of people's frustrations is of physiological origin and comes from suppression of movement, of a feeling of elasticity, of lightness, of balance of the muscles and the nerves and so on. I've had very little pain in my life, very little, other than that which preceded the slipped disc and so on.

CLARE: Physical pain. What about emotional pain?

MENUHIN: Emotional pain? Yes, I have had emotional pain. But, again, there was the music on the one hand and the obligation and then, on the other hand, a certain selfishness in terms of keeping myself. I didn't break down in the sense of, you know, taking to alcohol or to cigarettes or to any escape. I never escaped in that sense. I like the feeling of self-reliance. Nor would there ever have been justification in blaming others or circumstances for my, shall I say, bad mood, because there was no one to blame and there could be no one responsible except myself.

CLARE: Would it be unfair to say that that can be traced back to the fact that you started out in life with really the undiluted affection of your parents?

MENUHIN: Absolutely. I think that is one of the chief factors. I cannot tell you how happy my childhood was. Even when the difficult moments came, when my father had to decide whether to leave his work or look after the family, as it were, and stay with me, this was between Paris and his leave of absence from his work in San Francisco.

CLARE: When you were developing as a musician?

MENUHIN: Yes. Or the fact that my parents often had, what would you call them, kind of misunderstanding, they weren't really exchanges. They weren't made for each other and yet they were perfectly complementary for me, for the children. And my mother must have suffered a great deal.

CLARE: Why do you say that?

MENUHIN: Because she was longing for her Crimea. Only three years ago, at the age of 97, and she's been in the United States living in Los Gatos, surrounded by friends, loving friends, young people who adore her and care for her and doctors galore who take pride in her, although she is very wary of medical advice and knows exactly what's best for herself, she confessed, she said, 'You know, I am an exile.' I have lived in exile. And that's from someone who had not seen the Crimea in, well, 85 years. Which is quite, quite remarkable. She is really a piece of that earth, of the wild Crimea. And, of course, India filled a great yearning, a great hunger that I was almost unaware of but I was drawn east, ever since I heard my first gypsy in Romania, that has been part of my life and that is my mother's life. My father was a very careful man. He didn't want to take risks, he always prepared everything. And my mother used to make fun of him and she would always take a certain nasty satisfaction in the fact that, for example, he would tell her about his plans for a cruise, you know, he'd take her to this or that place and tell her that he'd got the best cabin and so forth. And a few days before the cruise she would say, 'Well, I really don't feel like going,' you know, that kind of thing. Very cruel in a way. But she is capable of cruelty, and especially cruelty to herself. She has a kind of satisfaction in seeing how much pain she can take, even, I believe self-inflicted. She has incredible discipline. And, as my yoga guru who used to come every summer to put me through my paces, when I told him about my mother's hundredth birthday, I wrote him the other day, he answered, he said, 'Only a person of real discipline can reach the age of 100.' And that is certainly true in the case of my mother. Her far-sightedness is quite remarkable too. She wanted me to grow up without any burden, Jewish burden or any sense of restriction of any kind. And it is no doubt thanks to her that I feel at perfect ease wherever I may be.

CLARE: How did she do it?

MENUHIN: Simply by choosing very carefully who were our friends, who was allowed past the front door, and only seeing the people who we could, and she could trust, Jews and non-Jews. She named me Yehudi after all, out of protest at the landlady who proudly told her that she didn't take Jews.

CLARE: Really?

MENUHIN: Yes, yes.

CLARE: How do you mean? Tell me about that. I didn't know that.

MENUHIN: Oh, that's an old story. They were looking for an apartment before I was about to be born and they came upon a very pleasant, sunny, light place in New York, somewhere in the Bronx I think. And my mother went up and looked at it and was delighted and then the landlady, wanting to oversell, told her that she'd be glad to know they didn't take Jews. And, of course, my mother said, 'Well, in that case we can't take it,' and came down to my father who was waiting outside and said, 'Well, if it's a boy his name will be Yehudi so there's no mistaking.' And yet, she was very anti-ghetto. She didn't want any kind of feeling of belonging to or any possessions. No one possessed me. I was free. And I still am free and I feel very close to fellow Jews but I'm totally free.

CLARE: And you're free also, are you, of any sense of duty, you know, that burden that sometimes a son with talent who has a mother with great expectations feels?

MENUHIN: Oh, I feel very dutiful in that I'll do anything I can for my mother, my parents, my father and towards Jews too.

CLARE: But there isn't a sense of, I'm trying to think of the word ...

MENUHIN: Of compulsion?

CLARE: Yes.

MENUHIN: No, and my mother has been no burden at all in that extraordinary way of hers of never demanding anything, never saying I should be close to her, never saying, come to see me more often, an extraordinary sense of self-sufficiency.

CLARE: How did she explain to you, this little boy growing up, this talent? What was the explanation?

MENUHIN: There was no explanation. I wasn't particularly talented.

CLARE: As a violinist?

MENUHIN: She may have thought highly of me but never in terms of outside assessment. I was a boy who had to be taken seriously and all my studies done fairly well. I was never punished, never, for anything. Even when I misbehaved which I did twice at home, very badly.

CLARE: Twice! You can remember 80 years later?

MENUHIN: But you see, without being punished. I remember that!

CLARE: Can you remember what they were, those misdemeanours?

MENUHIN: Exactly.

CLARE: Tell me.

MENUHIN: Yes, I was about four and we were walking in San Francisco, I know where it was too. It was on the street going off on an angle from Market Street. I had made up my mind, one of those terrible Greek vows, that I would stick my tongue out at the first person who we may meet, you see. Now, I couldn't go back on an honourable vow and that happened to be a great friend of the family, and I realised it was a friend but what could I do? After all I'd decided I'd do that and it was a test of my own resolve. So out came my tongue. And it was totally wrong and my parents said, 'Why did you do that?' I said, 'Well, I had thought it was something I had wanted to do and I'm terribly sorry.' And then the other time was when we sat at table, one of the first times I sat at table. My mother had prepared a big elegant table with lace and lovely glass and so on and so forth, at 1043 Steiner Street, that was where we lived. It was a nice house, paid off by renting garage space which my father rented at seven dollars a month and, as it was only 50 dollars a month instalments, that paid for the house. And, it was a very nice house with a nice garden and my mother gave, from time to time, these parties. She'd just come back from hospital with my youngest sister and we had a tenant in the house, she rented a room, the upper rooms. In the front were two Russian ladies who belonged to the house, as it were. And once a year we celebrated Russian Christmas or something with them. And at the back of the house was a young man. And my mother had a very pleasant nurse at the hospital and my mother had this in her blood, she always liked to bring young people together in the hope they might stay together. And so I knew of the plot. And we were sitting at table, quite a number, there must have been about 16 of us, and I pipe up suddenly and say, 'Mr So and So', I've forgot his name, 'You know why you are here?' And he said, 'No, I'm having such a lovely party,' and so on. And I say, 'No, no, you are here to marry this girl, you see.' And, of course, a terrible thing to say. But I said to my mother next morning, I said, 'But it's the truth, isn't it?' And then she tried to explain to me how sometimes one had to tell white lies and I learnt about white lies as a result of that. How to be courteous and not to offend people or embarrass them.

CLARE: Which she explained to you?

MENUHIN: She explained it, yes.

CLARE: There was no punishment?

MENUHIN: No punishment, no.

CLARE: I understand you never went to school, or you did for one day, I think?

MENUHIN: Not even one day. One morning I went to school.

CLARE: What happened? Why did it only last one morning?

MENUHIN: We were living in America and my parents felt we must do it the right way and so I was sent to school, a very nice school on, above, on a hill, San Francisco's full of hills, with a park in between, and my mother knew the headmistress. And when I came back from the morning, it was just a morning, my mother asked me what I'd learnt, how I felt, and I said, 'Well, I really didn't learn anything.' I sat somewhere in the back of the class and there was a little window on the wall, pretty high up on the wall, through which I could see a few branches, tree branches, and hoped that a bird would alight on, on them. No bird alighted but I kept hoping and looked at the branch and that's about all I could report from the morning at school. So my mother promptly said, 'Well, we'll educate you at home.' That was that. And you could do it in those days, thank God. There weren't laws and regulations whereby people had to conform to every kind of convention. And then my mother sent my sisters several years later to the same school, and the same headmistress asked for an appointment to see my mother at home, and reported that both my sisters were mentally somewhat backward and defective, so my mother took them out of school, and of course, no children could have been more brilliant than my two sisters. But it just shows they weren't cut out for that kind of education. They had their own mind and didn't know what they were doing in the school. Now, this is not to decry schools because I have a school of my own, but it is I think a slightly different place from the place I was sent to.

CLARE: There was no competition in your early years?

MENUHIN: No, no competition at all. And my parents realised it would be wrong to tell me, you know, this other little boy is making a great success, you should work harder. And they spared me that. Only once they mentioned it, a boy called Rigero Ricci, who was about my age and became a wonderful violinist, studying with the same teacher, and I resented that and they must have felt that. I didn't want to proceed on the basis of competition. That's not a musician's life, it's not an artist's, it's not a creative approach. I wanted to proceed on my own, at my own pace. That's instinctive, I didn't formulate it that way but I didn't want to be bothered with other people, whether they did well or badly, it wasn't my concern.

CLARE: When you look back at these years, do you feel that it prepared you for life?

MENUHIN: In some ways it did, in other ways it didn't. There was plenty of adventure in that we travelled a great deal and met any number of interesting people and saw fascinating landscapes. I remember staying awake one night travelling by train from Sydney up to Brisbane in Australia and seeing these wonderful white eucalyptus, like ghosts under a full moon. It was bewitching. I would love to have got out of the train and walked. I had any number of wonderful experiences on the high seas and everywhere, and in Paris. So that there was no lack of adventure. Nor was there lack of physical play. My sisters and I played tag and ran wildly in the local park and even played a bit of tennis and later on quite a lot of badminton. But there was no assessment, personal assessment of people under negative circumstances. Later on, I had to see that there were circumstances when you had to learn to assess people and what you expected them to be. Still my attitude is to trust everybody and wait until they prove they're not trustworthy. And even then, understand them and just remove the cause of the untrustworthiness.

CLARE: And that presumably is where your wife, Diana, would say you're vulnerable, you have to be protected because, of course, by the time you find out they're not trustworthy they'll have exploited you?

MENUHIN: I know. On the other hand, I can't waste time brooding on it. Certain people I trust absolutely. Others I reserve. But spending my time assessing characters and wondering and suspecting the possibilities of being let down, I can't do that. I take reasonable precautions but beyond that . . .

CLARE: But she does, doesn't she, regard you as 'hopelessly naive'?

MENUHIN: I think she does and yet I don't know. I certainly give her justification!

CLARE: You've sustained this second and very successful marriage of many years, but I wondered whether the first marriage came adrift because, in a sense, you weren't streetwise emotionally?

MENUHIN: Because I couldn't assess the person? I fell, naturally, for the first opportunity to be free.

CLARE: To be free from?

MENUHIN: To be free from the family. It was partly the fact that we were so close that the three of us burst out. In fact, it was very curious, because my sister and I married brother and sister.

CLARE: Your first marriage was to the sister of your sister's husband?

MENUHIN: Yes, exactly. Lindsay and Nola Nicholas were a charming couple, Australian, full of life, full of freedom, full of well-being and sport and it was really very attractive. Lindsay, he had a great sheep farm and Nola had red hair, and it was what had to happen at that particular juncture. And when my sister Hephzibah and I decided to marry Lindsay and Nola, brother and sister, we felt sorry for Yalta.

CLARE: Your other sister.

MENUHIN: And so we rang the most likely person, Bill Stix, a friend of the family's, who wasn't married, a young man, and explained it to him that he should really propose to Yalta and we arranged her marriage, which was not successful.

CLARE: And the marriages all happened around the same time?

MENUHIN: Exactly, very nearly the same time. Mine happened on the 26th May, 1938, in London, Caxton Hall and my sister Hephzibah's followed about a month and a half later in Los Gatos, at the house where my parents lived at the time, with Nicholas's father present and his young wife, who was about as young as my betrothed. And although there was natural attraction and very strong attraction, it, it had no real basis. In fact, Nola was the first to say that we were really not destined to be together. But the result is a lovely daughter, Samira, my only daughter. The three other children are boys and very fine sons. So I cannot regret. She had a very sad ending. She took, you know, to the bottle but not as a result of me, I am glad to say, not as a result of me. She had several affairs during and after.

CLARE: What did you learn about yourself through that? Did you have to learn about other people outside the family, about other people and their complexity?

MENUHIN: Well, that came pretty naturally. Actually, I've almost never suffered from other people.

CLARE: Have they suffered from you?

MENUHIN: Yes.

CLARE: In what way?

MENUHIN: Sometimes just the desire to do the right thing which would be good, and sometimes it can be as injurious as deliberate, wilful injury. It's very curious how very often good intentions can be that. I'd learnt, that one must be very careful in trying to improve or help. Helping people is one of the most difficult things in the world because very often it doesn't apply, it cannot be absorbed. It's easier to help strangers than family. Oh, I've done many things of which I would rather not do, but . . .

CLARE: Such as?

MENUHIN: Well, I can only go a certain distance to satisfy you but the years between the breakdown of my first marriage and marrying Diana were very, very hard years, for her, very tragic years, and for me very difficult too.

CLARE: These were the years when you were disentangling your first marriage and you have written about that. Would you say of yourself that you need somebody? You talked about your self-reliance, and you talked about the first marriage as a sort of act of freedom from the family. I wondered whether when you look at yourself that you note that you've always had some-body. After Nola came Diana. I know there was a difficult period while you were sorting out the first but there always has been somebody, and therefore the question is, are you self-reliant?

MENUHIN: I'm not sure. I'm not sure. I've a thousand interests in things, in music, in social work, in politics, in the school, in projects, in books. I want to read and there are things I want to know. There are a thousand things but I don't think I'm that self-reliant that I wouldn't need support. I don't know. There are many things I've never tried. I've been spared, that's one thing about my life, I've been spared so many catastrophes and tragedies that other people have had to go through that I cannot really assess how I would stand up to them myself.

CLARE: You wonder?

MENUHIN: Sometimes I wonder, yes, I don't know. And part of my life has probably been not only doing the best I can to pay for the blessings I've had in my life and try to secure them in a way that justifies my having had them, often undeservedly, but I've had this extraordinary fortunate life, but it is also perhaps an investment for the future. I don't know. The motives are very mixed. There is always an equal amount of instinctive self-preservation, a balance, and I don't think any motives are totally pure but they can be pleasant or unpleasant.

CLARE: Was your ability ever a burden in the sense that you felt this has been bestowed on me, I must do something with it?

MENUHIN: No. It had been a burden under certain circumstances when, for example, I had played so much during the war and kept on playing and had lost any, how shall I say, preparation, care, practice and, and I just played. It's like using a machine without looking after it. There was a time when I felt I really did have to start polishing and learn again. And I had enough talent to play very well, and I hear my recordings, and obviously, from an early age, I played without really having gone through the preparatory stages. And no doubt my wise teachers, and no doubt they were wise, felt better leave good enough alone. So I was left with wonderful examples and an analytical mind, probably Jewish mind, wanting to understand, analyse, justify, legalise, everything I was doing, including the interpretation. I can tell you exactly why I interpreted a work in a particular way. I can defend it. I don't have to say like they used to in the nineteenth century with full justification, 'Well, that's the way I feel it.' That was sufficient. Well, they had probably good examples and traditions so they didn't go too far wrong. I think it's a balance of this mind, my mind and feeling. I could have lost my way several times and thank God there was always a margin. Always I played well enough, even at my worst. It was still like the man you quoted, the man who said 'even when he plays out of tune it's worth listening to'. I hope I didn't play out of tune too often. But, anyway, there was sufficient in life to keep it interesting, fascinating. I was never actually, excepting *vis-à-vis* Diana during those very difficult years, in despair. But I was in despair a few times.

CLARE: Were you?

MENUHIN: Yes. But that was that period.

CLARE: Ever to the point where you would have thought I can't go on?

MENUHIN: No, no, never to that point.

CLARE: As I read it, your wife, in a sense, protects you. She ensures that you can do what you have to do best. She describes marriage, she's got a couple of wonderful quotes ...

MENUHIN: A service.

CLARE: Yes, marriage is a service, I think she says that anyone who doesn't know that, if you don't know that, you shouldn't be married. Marriage is a service. Now it's not very politically correct these days to say that because clearly she's talking about it from her perspective. She's not assuming that for you marriage is a service?

MENUHIN: No, no, although I want to serve and try to serve but for her it is. And she is keeping that up. She's a perfectionist.

CLARE: Is she?

MENUHIN: Oh, incredible perfectionist. And whatever may be wrong, whether it's a button or it is a move, a political move, or it's something I've written which may have been and very often is written very quickly, she will work on it until she gets the sense out of it. There's no one else who can do it as she does. She's always fascinating but now she's finding it difficult to move as she used to, you know. She used to move like a gazelle. Now it's no longer that way and that's very, very sad. But she's so lively and so alert and needs so much encouragement and stimulus and very often the life I led when she came with me everywhere was a life of service, rather than of stimulus.

CLARE: Really?

MENUHIN: Yes. But today she needs a great deal. I think the book did a great deal for her.

CLARE: Her book – *Diana Menuhin – A Glimpse of Olympus*?

MENUHIN: Yes, her book.

CLARE: Reading her book, I got this insight and I want to test it, that in a sense, she provides the salt for this nutritious soup that is you? Being devil's advocate for a minute, I think your upbringing is quite remarkable. It gave you certain things that many of us don't have. It gave you a sense of acceptance of what you are, confidence, such that you don't really bother analysing it. You are this person. You've got a great talent but again your relationship with it isn't particularly neurotic. You accept it. You express it and you exult in it. The weakness, there's always a weakness, is that in relating to the real world, to the world of competition and organisation and money and commercialism, there are certain deficiencies. You've said it yourself that you will wait, that somebody has to prove their shortcomings.

MENUHIN: It's true.

CLARE: You need a skin, a tough skin, which I feel she provides.

MENUHIN: Yes, but she is, how shall I say, she's much higher than that. She also is very discreet and never interferes.

CLARE: She's very subtle?

MENUHIN: Very subtle too.

CLARE: With you?

MENUHIN: Very subtle.

CLARE: But she's pretty blunt with the rest of the world. She has this wonderful phrase with which she describes herself, 'awfully frank, frankfully awful'!

MENUHIN: And fortunately, even she is, as I am, shedding to a certain extent, the caution, which I think is a good thing. Because at our age we should be able to say what we feel. When I was a boy, money was never, never mentioned in the house. My father looked after my affairs and he gradually, as I grew up, introduced me to the world of concerts and things, so I became fairly well acquainted with agents and so on and so forth.

CLARE: Fees and so on.

MENUHIN: And I've kept the same agents all my life until they died, three generations of agents in France.

CLARE: Have looked after you?

MENUHIN: Yes, yes. I've been very loyal and they've always treated me well. And finally since, thanks to Eleanor Hope, she's found an excellent man to look after my affairs which were very complex. You can imagine – earning money in various countries. It created complications in every respect and she's brought it all together and one person is looking after it so I am delighted. I don't have to worry about that. All I have to worry is to see that I remain healthy and can do my concerts.

CLARE: If we think of your relationship as a synchrony, what is it your wife brings?

MENUHIN: She brings the comfort of a human being who is totally dedicated, totally trustworthy, able to help under all circumstances, in all conditions from literary to social, you, you name it. My wife is, above all, aesthetic. She is herself beautiful and so is everything she touches. Any woman that comes into the house, whether it's a maid or a cook, or a secretary, improves in looks within months, and dresses differently. Diana is a presence which is as solid as a rock of Gibraltar even when she isn't well. She's gone through much pain in her life from her early training with Ballet Rambert, and throughout her life she speaks of a black fairy which you read about in the book.

CLARE: A fairy, yes.

MENUHIN: Yes, always ready to throw her back a few steps from her ambitions.

CLARE: You have a role to play in dispelling that black fairy, don't you?

MENUHIN: Exactly, and I don't always succeed and that is what bothers me. In fact, I probably do many things that satisfy the black fairy! But it is my effort to assure her that the fairy isn't that black. But it's sometimes difficult to persuade her. But certain things do. She adores her grandchildren and her book has done much, and she does so much, and she can do so much.

CLARE: She very largely reared your children. I think you said of yourself, I may be quoting her, I may be quoting you, that you saw less of your children than if you'd had life imprisonment.

MENUHIN: Something like that. But she has been with the children from the beginning.

CLARE: Do you regret that?

MENUHIN: I regret that. I do. Because I think that had I been at home and been with her, and with the children regularly, daily, instead of being away for months, I could have made her life easier and the children's life perhaps more balanced.

CLARE: Would you have been away for months?

MENUHIN: Well, you see on tour I would go away and Diana would share the time between the children and joining me on tour.

CLARE: And the tours could last months?

MENUHIN: They would last months. And that is the penalty. And the children pay for that penalty.

CLARE: How?

MENUHIN: Well, although I'm now very close to both of them, I think that my absence and the fact that I couldn't balance the parental influence, was probably the cause of, well maybe resentment, maybe disappointment, maybe actual disorientation. Fortunately, Jeremy loves his music and is a wonderful musician and Gerard is a wonderfully honourable, honest character. He is inclined to be very critical of people, too critical. That's something that goes against my grain.

CLARE: Would he be critical of you?

MENUHIN: Sometimes, but on the whole no. On the whole he has taken it out on his mother, curiously enough. He was very cruel to her. But he's a wonderful boy and we generally now get along very well. Although sometimes when I feel he is critical of other people, or of me, feeling that I may be more naive than I am, that he could protect me, there are points of friction, yes.

CLARE: When you look back and say, 'Well, I was touring for months and so on,' the question I always want to ask somebody such as you is, do you think that it is inevitable, that's the nature of it and it has to be so? Or do you think it reflects this thing about the artistic spirit, that it drives, and that's why it's often equated with a kind of selfishness. It takes absolute priority. For instance your wife, when she says, marriage is about service, is acknowledging that. She is saying, look, when you are in the presence of someone like this, with this kind of talent, you've got to accept everything else will come second.

MENUHIN: Yes, well she certainly has lived up to that incredibly.

CLARE: Do you think it's true? Do you think that that is the nature of an artistic essence?

MENUHIN: I think there is a certain great, inbuilt, I suppose it's an inbuilt selfishness in that you're committed to something. But I don't think it's only the artist. I'm sure the politician feels that he is going to save the world and ...

CLARE: The difference I've often felt, and maybe it's about how art is now seen in the twentieth century, is that perhaps only in art and perhaps one or two other fields, such as medicine, where the servant, in your case your wife, feels they can't really interfere. The politician pursuing his politics looks nakedly selfish and it's about something like power ...

MENUHIN: Yes, exactly.

CLARE: It's a bit smelly to be honest. Whereas in a career like medicine, the doctor can say of his unavailability at home, 'I'm out saving people. So your feelings of resentment are really unworthy of you.' And the artist says, 'I am serving the muse. This isn't selfishness, this is something else.' So in, in both instances, the spouse, usually the spouse or the family, they're made to feel bad if they make too many claims on this person.

MENUHIN: Yes, yes, it's true. And Diana's made the minimum of claims on me. But it doesn't prevent the fact that I feel sometimes very, very guilty that I couldn't give her more time and the children more time. But her devotion is unbelievable. It's so touching and so wonderful and, under the worst circumstances, she's never failed.

CLARE: What does she mean about that reference I made in the introduction to the fact that you're on cloud nine? I'll put it in another context. Sometimes, I gather you may have experienced this when you were quite a child in that you sometimes felt in another gear from the rest of the world?

MENUHIN: Quite, quite. I retire into a strata of my own where I remain somehow untouchable, untouched, unreachable.

CLARE: Do you recognise that yourself?

MENUHIN: Illogical. Well the fact is that if I do look at a score and am entranced with, how shall I say, the strategy, the structure ...

CLARE: The elements?

MENUHIN: The elements, how they fit and how they succeed each other, the links and so on, I can be lost and I do make life perhaps difficult for someone who is concerned with the daily mechanics of living. I must confess, and I do actually relish it, that I can administrate fairly well by shoving off responsibility on other people and if they do the job that's fine. So that I keep the essentials that no one can do for me. Today, for example, it's a whole lot of letters that I must write by hand, not only dictate, congratulatory eightieth-birthday anniversary letters from various people whom I'm very fond of and so really I must write the replies by hand. So no one can do that for me. And I'm looking at a score for tomorrow's rehearsals in Malvern. I've got to look at those scores, no one can do it for me. And as far as possible, I am glad and terribly grateful when somebody does everything that I don't have to do myself. There's a motto in life I think which is very good – 'Never do anything that someone else can do for you, someone else can do better.'

CLARE: Yes. But you have this ability to switch off? To switch off the distractions?

MENUHIN: I do, I can.

CLARE: You can?

MENUHIN: I can.

CLARE: You've always had that? It looks like it goes back quite early?

MENUHIN: Up to a point. Unless there were distractions of a personal nature, yes, but otherwise I can.

CLARE: And when you're in that kind of state, would I know, if I came into your presence, would I know that you're in, you know, one of those not-to-be-disturbed moments?

MENUHIN: No, no, no. You probably wouldn't know because I'm always ready to respond. Diana's been very respectful of my work and so on and so forth and the children too.

CLARE: But you would actually be abstracted? You would be thinking of something else?

MENUHIN: I'd been thinking of something else, but I'd go back to that probably. My best moments of thinking are early morning, that's when I'm at my clearest, or at least I imagine I'm clear.

CLARE: Yes. Would you say you have this ability to relax?

MENUHIN: Yes, yes, on the whole I do. I can sleep almost anywhere at any time.

CLARE: Do you dream?

MENUHIN: Yes, I have dreams but I always forget them. Once or twice I didn't forget them and now I've forgotten them, and they were very interesting dreams.

CLARE: But you sleep peacefully?

MENUHIN: Yes, I do, I do.

CLARE: Do you think much about what's after life?

MENUHIN: Well, yes, naturally from time to time, one wonders how I'm going to take the moment of death. And I think if it happens in the natural way, without disease or pain or so on, and it happens at the right time, not prematurely which happens to such a great extent today and cruelly and horribly. If it happens at a natural time, I think it must be a release and a very welcome dissolution.

CLARE: What would be a natural time?

MENUHIN: There is a natural time. I think when one has reached the maximum of one's physical and one's mental capacities. After all, if there were no death there would be no life. It's part of the cycle, it's got to be. And there's no point in not respecting that, that cycle. And when it happens, as I say, not by stupid accident, or by cruel fate, or by the horrible death that people have to face in countries, in dictatorships in Iran or Soviet Russia or the Jews in Germany. Man's life is so subject to these unnatural, we call them unnatural even though they are in the majority, unnatural endings.

CLARE: How did your father die?

MENUHIN: He died from, I think, cancer of the kidneys.

CLARE: Was that some time ago?

MENUHIN: Yes, about 15 years ago. He loved life, I must say. He ceased travelling with me which was his great delight and after that life became rather difficult, just my two parents living alone in Los Gatos. But still he kept an eye on my life and my affairs. Eleanor Hope, she was my secretary, now she's much more, agent and everything, she has some letters of my father, written in passionate typewriting with red letters and underlined about what she must do to look after me, and so on and so forth. It's very touching. She keeps those letters.

CLARE: He took a great delight in your success?

MENUHIN: Yes, he did. But where my father wanted to be part of it, my mother makes a point of being apart from it.

CLARE: Though she takes an interest in it?

MENUHIN: Yes, but I'm to her her first-born, her beloved, and am treated like the infant Jesus. But, you know, she never lays on any kind of flattery or anything.

CLARE: But you've lots more you want to do?

MENUHIN: There are many things I'd like to get on with. And mostly musically. I love conducting, that is the joy of making beautiful music and exploring the repertoire of the orchestra, which is so much greater than the repertoire of the violin. But, in other fields as well. For instance, in Europe, I feel that the cultures should have a political voice, not only the States. And I'd like to see the cultures have a direct connection with the community, like grandchildren with grandparents.

CLARE: Talking of your father and given what you describe him as, a man with an enormous appetite for life and given to thinking in terms of absolutes, of black and white, I think you said that you prefer to think in terms of grey, would you and he have clashed? Your temperaments were very different.

MENUHIN: No, no, never clashed. Our tours were always so close and so amiable. He always filled my mother's injunctions as to what I should eat and what he should order.

CLARE: Your mother would, would lay those down, would she?

MENUHIN: Oh yes, yes, she did.

CLARE: She wouldn't come but she gave him the instructions. Why did she not come?

MENUHIN: Well, she was with the children, with my sisters.

CLARE: It's interesting in that it's not typical is it, a mother not involved, detached, was the way you described it?

MENUHIN: She came to New York for the American tour and kept house in New York for the daughters, I mean for my sisters, and we'd come together in New York or they'd come to San Francisco but the rest of the tour, the stands, you know, every three or four days of concerts, that kind of thing, she couldn't do. Besides my parents had drawn up a very clear understanding over which departments were whose. My concerts and my travel and all the business were my father's department. The education, the home, the daughters, were my mother's department. And the two were kept quite, quite separately.

CLARE: You talked earlier about the fact that perhaps one of the reasons that you are not a particularly malicious or negative person, you talked about from the earliest age, your emotions would be, I hope I do credit to how you described it, they'd be expressed through your music, through your playing. Does that mean that prior to playing and after you've played are very different emotional states?

MENUHIN: That's a very interesting question. I wasn't aware of a change. I was just aware of the satisfaction of expressing my emotions and I did that continually. So I think it was like the flow of a river. It wasn't a change of gear. It was more or less the emotions would continue there and the music was the continuing means of expression. And nor was any expression barred. I mean I was free to say what I wanted and to entertain, to talk as I wanted, and I had long conversations with my sisters who thought that everything I said was gospel.

CLARE: Did they?

MENUHIN: Yes, yes, I was spoilt you see, I was spoilt from every point of view, excepting the fact that I realised the dangers of self-indulgence or flattery or, you know, getting the wrong idea of what I was about.

CLARE: And your mother held the key to preventing that happening?

MENUHIN: Yes, that's right, yes.

CLARE: So there was an extraordinarily subtle mix?

MENUHIN: I suppose, but very natural too. She didn't hold much of other people's opinions either. I mean she knew very well when people came and were just there for the er, or, benefactors for instance, she shooed them off. Anybody who wanted to ask me to play at a private home or so on, even when we were in Sophia, when the queen of Romania asked if I might come to the palace and play, mother refused. Ernest [Bloch], my great teacher who was the favourite of the court, asked her to come to his villa, where she listened in a room adjacent to the studio.

CLARE: The queen did.

MENUHIN: And where I met her afterwards. Yes. All people, who might wish to exploit me, as it were, or to whom I'd be under any obligation, were kept totally away.

CLARE: Remarkable.

MENUHIN: I remember in London we were asked, I forget by what great hostess, at one time, if we would play. Those were accepted, how shall I say, conventions in England. The artist would be invited and paid a big fee. I think in those days it was £5,000. And my parents discussed it and I remember they decided no, it wasn't that kind of performance, a performance in the ancient tradition of playing for your supper, which used to be *de rigeur*. Of course, that has changed now. I believe they wouldn't think of not inviting the artist to supper. But in the old days, still between the wars, artists were invited to perform. There was the old story of Kreisler who was invited by a great lady in London and asked if he'd bring his violin. He said, 'My violin doesn't dine.'

CLARE: What I was about to ask you, because it suddenly crossed my mind, was how did your mother and your wife get on?

MENUHIN: You know, quite remarkably, and that is largely thanks to Diana, to both. Diana has meticulously tried to keep her end up. She writes, even now, every two weeks. In fact yesterday she said, 'It's my day, I must write your mother.' And my mother's come to respect a person of such integrity. There was a rough period when the first book about me came out and the writer, what was his name, a nice Russian man, had said a few things which I had said about my mother which were not totally complimentary, and my mother was sure, both my parents were sure, it was Diana's work.

CLARE: Oh I see!

MENUHIN: So you can imagine.

CLARE: They didn't think it came from you?

MENUHIN: It came absolutely out of me, I was as honest as I am to you, you see. But my parents had led, in their way, such a sheltered life with the children, that when the first, when my younger sister came adrift, as it were, and felt rather strongly and spoke about my parents, they couldn't believe it. They couldn't believe it. It was very, very hard on them because they had done

374

everything with the full goodwill of their devotion. But Diana's been absolutely wonderful, and the two, my mother and Diana, are the closest of friends with tremendous respect for each other.

CLARE: You have talked about music as the most revealing, the most moving of all the arts, and music, of course, is very direct, music goes straight from you to me, there's no linguistic barrier. A friend of mine, who was a remarkable literary figure, he always mistrusted music. He died rather tragically. But one of our last conversations was about music. He had no interest in music. He had no ear but he rather powerfully argued, as was his wont, the fact that there was a danger to music too, precisely because it could go straight across without any filters. Music could do devilish and demonic things to people. I never really thought too much about it but I thought I must ask you.

MENUHIN: It could release emotion and could either strengthen or weaken people, according to what that release occasioned. And certainly Plato had his ideas about music and the Chinese must have had something like that because they adopted a pentatonic scale, which avoids every kind of dissonance, or chromaticism, every kind of note that can cause pain or emotion. And yet they knew about the twelve-tone chromatic scale 12, 3,000 years ago, at the same time as Pythagoras, because I've seen dug out of graves wonderful series of bells, 12 to an octave, six octaves, six or seven octaves from the smallest bells, perfectly tuned. Quite amazing. So they knew about chromaticism. I have a suspicion that their folk music must have used chromaticism, and their songs. But, officially, the pentatonic scale was the only one recognised because it was the only safe scale in musical terms. But I think your friend may have a case. If you want to keep a population free of, how shall I say, public manifestations and that kind, but, certainly now, with this awful piped music, the muzak, which also attempts to put people in the right mood to buy. It's like, say, music played for cows so they give better, more milk. The customer in the store gives more money out if there's more music going on, presumably, otherwise I don't know why they do it, because I don't like to have my mood dictated to me by music I haven't chosen. And, sometimes there's been music in films and plays of the most ghastly air fights from the First World War, you know, planes coming down in flames, and certain of the music that's chosen for in-flight entertainment is, I think, totally inappropriate.

CLARE: When you look back at your life, is all that has gone to make it a great surprise to you? Is it a great adventure, or is it more or less as you would have imagined it would be when you thought about it, when you were nine, or 18, or 27, or whatever?

MENUHIN: Well, I certainly couldn't foresee the details nor could I see the fact that I could enjoy a dream coming as it has come true of the school and seeing, meeting the children and the staff and the governors and so on. I couldn't have foreseen that but there has been a main direction to my life and everything I'm doing today is related to some seed that was planted when I was young. One of the funniest things is, or rather curious things is, that I prepared my speech or began preparing it, which I would give when I was given Swiss citizenship, I began preparing it already when I was 13 in Basle. It's, it's a very curious thing. It was something I liked, I admired Switzerland. I thought it is so well run, it has kept out of wars, neutral, there's nothing that has been destroyed there. It's a different country to any other country I know and I think it's administered well, those people know all about how to handle democracy. They really do. You go to any little town council and you have a much higher standard of behaviour than in almost any other congress in the world. Because they know how to give and take, they know they've got to resolve their differences. They're villagers, they're not professionals. They haven't been elected, they run their own little village.

CLARE: And at the age of 13, you thought, 'I'll be a citizen'?

MENUHIN: I must be one day a citizen and I prepared my speech, how I would accept it as it were, because I couldn't bring it about. And I confessed to that when they made me a citizen about 20 years ago. It's very curious.

CLARE: You've said, I think, that you lived your life the wrong way round. You were born old and you're growing younger. Say something about that.

MENUHIN: Well, I feel it might apply to a great many people if they led the kind of satisfying life I have. And that is that you are born with your life ahead of you, the burdens are unknown, the fears are there, the questions; how will you survive, what will you do, how will you support your family? I mean it's quite a burden and young people live under that burden today more than ever because their future is quite unassured. I'm the other way round. I compare myself to the airplane towards the end of its journey, getting light, having spent its fuel and being able to travel higher and faster than ever before. And so in that respect, and also in the respect that I had talent and a certain amount, a certain degree, of instinct and foresight, as life progresses there is that satisfaction. But also, the fact that I had talent, that I started off at a young age with great success, you can compare that to a balloon with just a mooring but to support that height I had to go about building the tower and build it from up to down, as it were, which is a very curious experience, of manufacturing bricks at 5,000 feet and then putting one underneath the other to finally reach earth. And, in that respect, I suppose I started at many levels very high, the dreams, ideals, concepts, abstract philosophies, and then had to put them into practice and apply them and see how they worked. Whereas ordinary people are geared into life. I wasn't geared into regular life, ordinary life. Even now my work and my thoughts, my music, my activities, protect me. I often wonder if I found myself in a town without any resources whatsoever, without a violin, where I was totally unknown, what would I do, what would be my first step. I don't know that I'm one of those who, if given one dollar, would make a million in the course of a year, you know, one of these wonderful whiz-kids who can make a fortune out of nothing, I don't really know how I would proceed. I would be sore put to it.

CLARE: Would you describe yourself as a happy man?

MENUHIN: Yes, yes I would, I don't think I could describe myself any other way. As a very blessed and a very happy man, a very lucky man. I certainly have no concept of what would make me happier or luckier than what I already have.

CLARE: Yehudi Menuhin, thank you very much indeed.

Paul Theroux

In an elegant essay entitled 'On the Pleasure of Hating', William Hazlitt observes, 'Nature seems (the more we look into it) made up of antipathies: without something to hate, we should lose the very spring of thought and action.' He might well have been writing of Paul Theroux. A prolific novelist, short-story teller, essayist, Theroux has earned quite a reputation as a scathingly dismissive, truculent and aggressive man, particularly as a travel writer, a form of which he is an acknowledged master. Consider some of the comments attributed to him. On the French: 'The French are entirely frank in expressing their racism. I wondered whether this lack of delicacy, indeed stupidity was an absence of inhibitions or simply arrogance. Their public offensiveness ranged from smoking in restaurants to testing nuclear bombs in the Pacific.' On Greece: 'A cut-price theme park of broken marble, a place where you are harangued in a high-minded way about Ancient Greek culture while some swarthy little person picked your pocket.' On the Chinese: 'Unclean, evasive and bad-mannered.' On the Japanese: 'Little bow-legged people who can't see without glasses.'

He has had a notorious public row with his older brother, Alexander, who wrote a savagely critical piece about him which declared, 'We in the family don't mind his affected gentility, his smug and self-important airs ... No one I have ever met in my life is a worse, almost pathologically unsympathetic listener.' Paul Theroux's response is, first, to point out that literary spats between brothers are not exactly rare in the history of literature. Just think, he reminds me, of William and Henry James, Lawrence and Gerald Durrell, the Shaffer twins and so on. Later in the interview, he challenges this public image of him as 'a difficult person, a cantankerous traveller, a grumpy man, someone who's always poking fun, looking for trouble.' But, anyway, he insists, writers, particularly writers of fiction, are not normal people. They are incomplete as is the world they inhabit. The beauty of writing is that it can give the writer a second chance to live out life. The writer is about the remaking of a world that was never properly designed in the first place.

In his case, the trouble started right at the outset – the size of his family. He is the third of seven children and both his older siblings are male. 'I think large families are very problematical,' he tells me. 'People say there's a lot of love in a large family and that's true in many cases, but I think it's more true to say there's not enough,' and it is difficult to avoid the suspicion that much of the truculence of the relationship he exhibits towards the critics, the general public and, indeed, large swathes of the world, wells up from a reservoir of feeling originally filled by repeated small streams of sibling jealousy, resentment and rage.

Theroux is interested in the extent to which birth order and family size might explain his own particular preoccupations and behaviours. What do we know of the impact of birth order? According to Frank J. Sulloway, author of *Born to Rebel*, an exhaustive and systematic examination of the relationship between birth order, creativity and family dynamics, the most consistent predictor of rebelliousness is indeed order of birth. 'Compared with firstborns,' he concludes at the end of a monumental work which took him 26 years to complete, 'late-borns are more likely to identify with the underdog and to challenge the established order.' Whereas first-borns are more likely to identify with parents, authority figures and established institutions, individuals born further down the family line are much more likely to rebel, break out, assert their independence and challenge the family status quo. They are more likely to question authority and to resist pressure to conform. They are also more likely to take risks. First-borns, after all, through most of their childhood enjoy being bigger, smarter and stronger than their siblings. It is hardly surprising, therefore, that the probability is high that first-borns learn to feel more secure and self-assured than those who come later in the pecking order.

Siblings having intermediate birth ranks tend to adopt intermediate degrees of radicalism. And birth order seemingly influences our reception of new ideas. Theories that have socially radical implications tend to be taken up and advocated by later-borns and rejected by first-borns whereas theories that have socially conservative implications display the opposite trend.

It is interesting to compare these probabilities with the individual circumstances of the Theroux family as told to me by Paul. The first-born at one stage flirts with the idea of becoming a painter but ended up a lawyer – no great rebellion there. The second son, having briefly considered the priesthood, became a university professor but he also writes. Now younger siblings are especially sensitive to adverse comparisons with their older siblings, which is one reason why they tend to be drawn to interests and careers that older siblings have not already chosen. Alexander and Paul, however, have chosen the same interest, writing, and inevitably there is trouble. Paul, the third son, to be followed by the first girl of the family, is the one that appears to have been the first to make a clean break. Much of the interview is concerned with how Paul is seen by his family, how he perceives its influence and indeed by a consideration of the role of the family as an influence on personal development in general.

He is quick to take me up on my suggestion that he is aggressive. He disputes it. He reminds me that his reference to burning down his brother's house is a joke but then he confesses to considering writing 'a withering reply', and there is scattered amongst his prolific prose a fair amount of anger and lashings of contempt. One critic, Peter Walker, reviewing Theroux's travel work, *The Happy Isles of Oceania*, observed that stopping to chat to Theroux is 'a risky business: there are so many things – your grammar or your jumper or your political views – that may suddenly enrage him and then, there you are, impaled on the page among all other oafs and dimwits who abound in Theroux's travels.' One of his novels, *Dr Demarr*, which was published in 1990 but which I only read after our interview, is intriguing in this regard and, given his argument with brother Alexander, intrigues me now even more. It is the story of twin brothers, George and Gerald, who are bound together not by love but by hate. Eventually George is murdered to the scarcely concealed satisfaction of Gerald. It is a chilly, smoothly told tale full of sibling rivalry in its most ferocious, most destructive, form.

What are we to make of Theroux's fiction? How revealing is it of him? He plays a tricky game – in the introduction to his collection of short stories he writes, 'I am the shadow, the fiction is the substance.' In 1996 he wrote *My Other Life*, which he calls a fictionalised autobiography and which is full of blind alleys, red herrings and deliberate distractions to mislead and deceive. Elsewhere he is reported to have described it as a fantasy of the life he might well have led – echoing again his view of the writer as someone able to get a second, third and further chance at living life, or perhaps it is just another example of the 'wildly gesticulating for attention' pattern of behaviour which he attributes to his position in his original family. Whatever the truth, interviewing Paul Theroux serves to remind me why I am always a little uneasy when I interview a writer, be it inside or outside the psychiatric clinic. Such is the skill of a great writer at creating a life which might have been, or could well be, that I can never ever be terribly clear about the life that is. Theroux talks evocatively, movingly, tellingly of his exile, his home in Massachusetts, his first wife, his children, his need for space and time and perspective. He ruminates thoughtfully on his role and performance as a father in the light of his experience as a child from a very much larger family. I leave the interview ruminating on the man I have met, urbane, shrewd and forthcoming, and yet I feel I have only been given a glimpse, a hint, of what is going on in the Theroux mind. Perhaps I have indeed encountered but a shadow and it is the case that I am more likely to find what makes this particular subject tick by going back to the search within his substantial and formidable body of writing, wherein his own world and the worlds he freely and marvellously creates are so fiendishly juxtaposed.

CLARE: 'You'll either love him or hate him,' writes Paul Theroux, of a character in the opening sentence of *My Other Life*, his much quoted and analysed imaginary memoirs. The same might be said of Theroux himself. He's been accused of parading 'in your face' prejudices and of scathingly dismissive, gratuitous, nastiness in his highly successful travel books. In fact, he was known as Mr Nasty when he was living and working in London and even one of his brothers described him recently as 'small, surly and spiteful'. On the other hand, his devotees say that it is precisely Theroux's bad temper that distinguishes him from lesser writers. As Jan Morris and other distinguished travel writers have said, 'We do not want Theroux contented, we want him truculent and resentful.' Reviewing *Kowloon Tong*, his latest remarkable novel which is set in Hong Kong just before the handover, the *Sunday Times* has described it as 'the work of our most compulsive storyteller on peak form'.

Two of his 36 books, *My Secret History* and *My Other Life* are fictitious autobiographies in which Paul Theroux cleverly keeps you guessing about his real self and his real life. What seems to be reasonably certain is that he was born in 1941 in a suburb of Boston, Massachusetts, into a large Roman Catholic family. His first ambition was to be a doctor. After university, he began to travel and to write. Avoiding the draft in Vietnam, he went to Africa as a Peace Corps teacher, later lectured in Uganda and Singapore, and in the early 1970s came to England with his British wife and two children. The many books he wrote during his stay here, include *Picture Palace*, which won the Whitbread Literary Award in 1978, and other prize-winning novels and travel books, such as *The Mosquito Coast*, *The Great Railway Bazaar*, *Pillars of Hercules* and *Riding the Iron Rooster*. After 18 years and following the break-up of his marriage, he returned to his roots in America, where he now lives.

You said somewhere, or you were quoted as saying that people who are normal don't become writers. In what sense do you feel that you are not normal?

THEROUX: There's a leading question! I said that I felt that writers were dysfunctional, there's something missing, something that was filled by the act of writing. Virtually all the good writers that I am aware of, ones that I've read, have expressed a deep sense of unease, disquiet, loneliness and I think that loneliness is almost the informing emotion. In what way am I not normal? I don't know. I suppose it has something to do with coming from a large family, where I was looking for a space, looking for a space to occupy. No matter how large a house a large family lives in, still you feel overshadowed.

CLARE: Overshadowed?

THEROUX: Yes. I came number three in a line of seven children and I think there's something in birth order, I suppose. And then there is sibling rivalry, something like that.

CLARE: But the first two brothers?

THEROUX: Yes, the first is the classic over-achiever, pleasing the parents. The second one was actually overshadowed by him. I was overshadowed by both but because I think they were ahead of me. I also missed a lot of scrutiny but I also felt, I suppose, some lack. So this wildly gesticulating for attention is character-istic of a lot of writers and may have been a characteristic of mine when I was growing up. I certainly felt a desire to get away.

CLARE: Was there a gap between you and the boy above you and the child who came after you?

THEROUX: Yes, the child that came after me is my sister. She was the first daughter so she had a different sort of attention, being female. I had two older brothers. You were asking in what way do I not feel normal. I think there's something to that. That, if I were not dysfunctional in some profound way, why would I ever have had the desire to be a writer? Why would I ever have had the need, which is an intense one, and the intensity, the imaginative intensity to want to write a book, which is a lot of trouble. I must find, or I must have found, some fulfilment in the act of writing, in the creative act.

CLARE: But I am interested in the link between those two things. You're talking about some kind of loneliness, detachment, separateness, and the process of writing. What is it that writing does, that in any sense fills a gap or makes up for a need or corrects a disjunction? Why writing? You might have gone off and, I don't know, done something else and you'd be sitting here saying that's why I was a mountaineer or a, a hermit or a missionary in Africa. But you've made the link between this sense of disjunction and the process of writing.

THEROUX: Yes, but the people that you just mentioned, the mountaineer, the missionary, the adventurer, aren't making anything. They're making journeys, they're not making anything. A writer is actually creating something that's not going to go away. He's remaking the world. I've often felt, you know, *esprit de l'escalier*, this wit, staircase wit. I wish I'd said that, the writer is someone who, in his heart, is always saying, you know, is in a position of wishing he'd said something and then has a chance to say it. Fiction, I said once, a character said this, fiction gives us the second chance that life denies us. Afterwards I wondered, why did I say that? What is it that I've been denied? But these are all a way of exploring the things that you lack but certainly you have this, this chance to order the world, to see it more clearly, to examine a motive. Or if you have a bright idea to put that down and be rewarded for it. You know, you put it down, you say, there it is. It has symmetry, harmony, brilliance, all those things that Joyce mentions in *Portrait of the Artist*, I think he's quoting Aristotle but you have that thing. 'Look, look what I made! Look what I did!' And I'm relating to the family so I'm giving you a lot to go on when I immediately relate it to my family and saying, 'Look what I did, look what I did.' I'm sure that's a factor.

CLARE: You were quoted as saying in one interview that your mother hadn't liked your first book?

THEROUX: Right.

CLARE: And your father never read anything you wrote?

THEROUX: My father read certain books. My father chose the books carefully. He read my first few books and I think, though he never told me this, my father passed away two years ago, he never told me that he really didn't want to be upset by anything that I wrote so he waited a while. He read *The Kingdom by the Sea*, *The Mosquito Coast* and I think one other. Of *The Kingdom by the Sea* he said, 'I'm amazed, every morning you get up and you walk 20 miles, that's incredible.' He never made a comment on England but the idea of getting up and walking 20, 25 miles, he thought, 'That's amazing, did you do that?' Well, I used to go paddling and he'd say, 'Let me feel your hands,' and he'd feel my hands and say, 'God', so that impressed him, effort, physical effort. And then *The Mosquito Coast*; my father was a bit of, you know, had a lot of Yankee ingenuity so he could relate to the main character in that book. My mother wrote me a letter which I still have, on receipt of my first book, in which she said she was disappointed by the book. She said, 'I think this book is trash.' And she actually wrote it in capital letters: 'I THINK THIS BOOK IS TRASH. Would you be proud to show this to our friends?' and then she named the friends. And I thought, this is interesting. A lot of people have said, 'God, that must have been very discouraging to you,' and I said, 'No.'

CLARE: And painful?

THEROUX: But it wasn't, it wasn't. No, no, no. Then I saw that I'm not trying to please her. I'm not saying, 'Look what I did.' I realised then that I'm on my own because I had good reviews for it and so the idea of settling a score with the family or getting approval from them wasn't that important. I think what I wanted was a place of my own, a place to make my life, to be given a chance to make my life, which is probably why I left the States, left the family, went to Africa and stayed away.

CLARE: It's difficult being in a large family. There's this mixture of, of loneliness you mention, but also not having much space, it's a sort of contradiction really.

THEROUX: I think large families are very problematical. People say there's a lot of love in a large family and that's true in many cases, but I think it's more true to say there's not enough. There's not enough attention, there's not enough time, there's not enough to go around, so what often happens is you depend very much on your little cluster. You have a little clique. It's more like a tribe living in the jungle where there's a little cluster over here, and a little cluster over here, and the girls in the family get on and they commune with each other and the older boys, and then the younger ones are like the nephews of the older ones. And when you got to a Third World country, say you go to Guatemala, children, young children aren't raised by father and mother. You see the girl in the family carrying the baby and usually feeding the baby, and I can relate to that. When I go to Africa and I see the 12 year old carrying the three year old, I understand that. It's clearer to me.

CLARE: Because once you did it?

THEROUX: That's what happens in a family, yes. The youngest in the family is like my nephew and I'm like his uncle and an uncle–nephew relationship is a very strong one. So I think that's the pattern in a large family.

CLARE: And within your family then, there would be bonds between you and some of your siblings that would be positive and strong, others would be more detached, distant, even negative?

THEROUX: Yes, I think that's normal in a family. The idea of creating the illusion that it's all love, all harmony, is really not accurate. If you're looking at a large family you're looking at a different magnetic field, where there is, as you say, some of the bonds are very positive and, and there are a lot of rivalries. A very important person in my family is my mother and my mother is someone that has always fascinated. One of my older brothers used to call her Queen Lear, and my children used to say she's like Volpone, a sort of female Volpone. My mother's a lovely person but a very strong personality, a very needy person. To understand my mother you have to understand her family and we've anatomised her family. We used to do imitations of our uncles and aunts, her brothers and sisters, and of my grandmother. One of my brothers did a terrific take off, he had a little skit about my grandmother, who's an Italian, meeting a Black Panther. It's probably not for family entertainment, but I remember it was my grandmother, this is the 1960s, my grandmother, Angelina, meeting Eldridge Cleaver. It sounds probably Monty Pythonish here but it's the sort of thing in a large family. There's a lot of mimicry. One imitates another, speaking, acting, the way they walk. My younger brother used to do imitations of my father putting his pyjamas on, hilarious, absolutely. And you'd have an audience. If you're an only child or there's two of you, that doesn't happen. In a large family everyone's mimicking everyone else and sometimes it's savage.

CLARE: And sometimes too a large family can become very turned in on itself. It's got a full audience, it's got relationships to analyse, it's got shifting alliances and so on. Was that the way it was?

THEROUX: Yes, I think that's the normal part of a large family. Although I wouldn't have said so at the time. When I was growing up if you suggested to me that there are shifting alliances, there are rivalries, that not everyone is equally happy at the same time, I would have said, 'No, no, no, the family that prays together stays together, we're a happy family, we go to church together, we eat together,' which is what we did. That's a big thing, meal time in a big family. It is a real scrimmage! And I would have said, 'No, no, no we're happy, it's not like that.' Later I realised, no, it's normal to have rivalries, it's normal to have cliques, it's normal when one leaves the room for the other to whisper and nudge and say, 'Did you hear what he said, did you hear what he said? He said ...' do that sort of thing or mimic my grandmother or my grandfather or my father, for that matter. My father on the telephone, the way he talked on the telephone, we used to laugh up our sleeves. My father passed away two years ago. We miss him very, very much and realise how he was the still centre of the turning world. He was the strong person whereas his love for my mother was so strong that he made my mother out to be the strong one and I realise that it wasn't a sacrifice. He came from a very secure, happy background. He was a much loved person, my father, and so he was very, very strong in that.

CLARE: What did he do?

THEROUX: My father had a number of different careers, starting with being in the leather business and doing quite well. Then his business went into liquidation in the late 1940s and then he became a shoe salesman and so he went from dealing in hides and skins and doing all right to being a salesman, putting on shoes, selling shoes to a person. And I've always felt that's a tough profession actually, because to fit a pair of shoes you're in a sort of kneeling position. And I loved it when he retired because I thought, 'Here's a man who has a lot of different careers who ended up being a salesman.' Although he didn't mind it. He sort of did it. He was a great reader, an amateur historian and he would have said, 'What do you mean? It's a living.'

CLARE: And was it a living? There were seven of you after all.

THEROUX: Yes, it was strangely enough. We seemed to do all right. I never felt that we lacked anything but he emphasised it and my

mother emphasised it that it was up to us. That as far as money
or any sort of material things, 'It's up to you,' they'd say, 'You
want something? Get a job.'

CLARE: Did they have expectations of their children in terms of
what you were going to turn out to be?

THEROUX: Yes. In the 1950s people had a very programmatic sense,
I think, and certainly in America, of what the professions were
and I remember the eldest had artistic ability and he was going to
be a painter. The second one was very funny and related very
well to people and so naturally, although this sounds a bit
strange at the time, he was going to be a priest. I had an ability in
the sciences, I loved the biological sciences and related all right
to people, I guess, and I was going to be a doctor. My sister was
going to be a nun.

CLARE: Really!

THEROUX: Yes, well because she was a girl. Now of course it didn't
work out that way. The artistic brother became a lawyer. The
priest brother tried it for a while and it didn't work out, he
became a professor, a university professor and a writer. I gave up
the idea of becoming a doctor, although I did a science degree.
And my sister, of course, became a teacher, not a nun. It was the
idea of fulfilling a role, that this role was, you know, 'You can
draw very well, you're going to be a painter.'

CLARE: But shifting from the role didn't cause too much heartache?

THEROUX: Not at all, not at all. My parents eventually came round
to the view, sensible view, that whatever you did mattered a lot.
As long as you were happy in what you did and you did it well
and you were proud of it, that was what mattered. You didn't
have to fulfil a role. Although all of us wanted to please them to
a greater or lesser extent and my almost priest, priestly brother,
the one that was going to have a vocation, I think was trying
hard to please them. Not going to medical school is one thing
but dropping out of a seminary is a tough thing because you've
been marked by that thing.

CLARE: That's why when your mother said what she said about
your first book, you felt, 'Well, you know, I accept that. I'm on
my own, it's my own situation.'

THEROUX: I felt I can tell you, I actually felt liberated by it.

CLARE: Did you?

THEROUX: Yes, yes.

CLARE: Genuinely?

THEROUX: Yes. I've told people that I felt liberated. I realised that I wasn't writing this book for her, I didn't want my mother and her friends to be my reading public. I knew that it's inconceivable that they ever would be. It's silly, but my mother was doing me a favour by telling me that. But when I tell someone who has one sibling, or who grew up an only child, that my mother said my book was no good, they say, 'That must have been such a blow.' I say, 'No, you don't understand. If you came from a large family, you would understand. This isn't a problem.'

CLARE: And likewise it didn't affect the rest of your relationship with your mother?

THEROUX: Not at all, no.

CLARE: Which was what? What was it like?

THEROUX: My relationship with my mother?

CLARE: Yes.

THEROUX: Obviously oblique because of that. I felt I probably would never be able to please her. I could never be the person that she wanted me to be precisely because she didn't know the person that she wanted me to be. She wanted, I suppose, me to be, to turn into a respectable person, in a vague sort of way. But I would not be able to please her because she didn't really have a notion of what it was that it would be. And if you're a writer, you know the people who are impressed by you are people who are told to be impressed. So some people often say to me, 'I met someone who really thinks the world of your work' – it might be someone I've known for years, and they say, and you know there's a sort of gleam in their eye and they think, 'God, all these years I've known you, and I've just met this person who says he collects your books and everything,' and you think, this person has just been told that but he didn't have any notion of what I did for a living.

CLARE: And as you wrote more and you did become recognised and you won the Whitbread Prize and so on, what effect did that have on your mother? Presumably people said to Mrs Theroux, 'Your son Paul, he's some writer.'

THEROUX: Yes, of course, they must have said it at some point but you're asking did it matter to her?

CLARE: Yes, what did it do to her?

THEROUX: No. If someone praised me my mother would be very proud, but she would need to know, to have the assurance that they were praising me in the right way. She wouldn't want anyone to say, 'Your son is some writer', or 'Does he have a vocabulary that he can swear up a storm?' Well, you know, you'd have to be praised in the right terms, I suppose.

CLARE: But did the view that she conveyed to you about your first book, were they more or less the perceptions she had of you, her son, as a writer?

THEROUX: No, it changed because later on she said, and still says from time to time, 'I love your travel books,' which is a way of saying, 'Enough with the novels,' or 'Watch what you're saying', because it is a disreputable thing to write novels. You're writing about the human heart. It's a sordid business delving down there, it's a messy business. You're dealing with things that are not spoken of in a respectable household and although my mother is a creative person herself, she's actually quite a good painter, still the idea of the eyes of the public, you know, the notion of esteem, matters a lot if you live in a small community. To me it never mattered a lot. As a matter of fact, I've always rather liked the idea of literary outlaws. People like, I don't know, Henry Miller and William Burroughs, wild men, those are the people that I felt personally liberated by. I felt, 'Well, they're doing it.' Now, Henry Miller was a hen-pecked husband, William Burroughs had a private income. I didn't know that at the time. The image of a writer to me when I was growing up was of someone who's really quite glamorous and wild and dangerous.

CLARE: Did you ever want to become a priest?

THEROUX: No, never, no. The thought scared the hell out of me. The idea of missing the company of women. Growing up in the 1950s and coming of age in the 1960s, just the curve of a woman's leg, you know, a woman's form. To be denied that! I remember in fact, walking down the beach with one of my older brothers, and we were talking about someone who was gay and there were two young women lying on the beach, and I remember him looking at them saying that so and so is gay and how can he do it. And he was looking at these two and just the curve of their behinds, you know, just lovely, lovely *derrières* and saying, 'How can he do it?' And that's how I saw it. I'm not talking about chasing women but a priest seemed to me a man in a prison, not a spiritual person at all.

CLARE: You served mass?

THEROUX: Yes, I was an altar boy.

CLARE: You were an altar boy?

THEROUX: But even then I remember my father saying, he used to quote an Archbishop in Boston, who was at a seminary speaking to some newly ordained priests and saying, 'You'll never have to worry about the price of a pork chop,' and my father used to say, 'What does a priest know?' My father wasn't anti-clerical but he'd say, 'What do they know about a large family, what do they know about marriage, what do they know about the stresses and strains, the price of a pork chop?' So in his view, it was a complete unreality. In mine, it was a kind of denial and fear. I wasn't frightened by the thought, but I thought, you know, wild horses couldn't get me to do that. What I found interesting about being an altar boy was my first swig of wine in the sacristy, in the sacristy, mass wine. I remember pulling out the cork in the mass wine and swigging it. Most altar boys have had their first drink of alcohol in the sacristy before the priest shows up and puts on his cassock and surplice. We all tasted it, that grapey, lovely grapey taste and the people howling at funerals, people weeping at weddings, getting money for a wedding, the smell of beeswax and a candle, the incense – those were the things that attracted me to being an altar boy and then I was bored stiff by it and gave it up. I'd had enough of it. And I think stopped, around about then I lost my faith, or, I don't know even whether I even had any deep faith.

CLARE: And now?

THEROUX: Now I think, well, having faith is different from having a spiritual sense. So I have, I suppose, a sense of spirituality, let's say, but I don't know, I've never looked deeply into it. But seeing some sort of kinship with, you know, the rocks and stones and trees whirling around in a Wordsworthian way, does mean something to me, yes.

CLARE: What was it that, in addition to your interest in the science, was there anything else that drew you to medicine? You were in premed for a while at the University of Massachusetts. Now, when you think back, what do you think was going on there?

THEROUX: Two things, I think. One was the vocabulary. The vocabulary of science I have always found much more vivid than the vocabulary of literature. So, for example, is it in the pancreas, we have the islets of Langerhans. Well, the islets of Langerhans in the pancreas always struck me as places I want, you know. Forget the British Isles, forget Tahiti, the islets of Langerhans, that's what you want. The bones, the names of the bones, the names of the organs, the processes, scientific names, I must say, I found thrilling and memorable. Understanding the process of science but also remembering the lexical items, the language of science I found attractive. And, then, I suppose, repairing, the idea of repairing a body, or not so much fixing a mind but delving, so delving in a body, delving in a mind and being useful. You know, when I was in Africa I was a teacher so I felt, I was teaching English, I felt pretty useless.

CLARE: This was when you were in Uganda?

THEROUX: I started off in Malawi and Nyasaland became Malawi and then Uganda and, you know, teaching 'it's a dog, it's a dog, it's a duck, it's a duck, it's a dog, it's a dog, it's a duck, no it's a dog, it's a duck. It's a duck, it's a dog . . .' That. Then I would go down the street and see a friend of mine who worked in the hospital and I'd say, 'What are you doing?' 'Oh, he had a strangulated hernia.' 'Really. And what is that?' 'Gonorrhoea.' 'What do you do for that?' Fascinating. And I had to say, 'It's a dog, it's a duck, it's a dog, it's a dog.' And this guy seemed to be doing something that was really useful. You know, injecting people against smallpox, yellow fever, elephantiasis, yaws, beriberi or whatever. He seemed to be doing something really useful or just pulling someone's sore tooth. And I thought, 'What am I doing?' Just irregular verbs, or whatever it was. I used to fantasise about having this big lorry, with Clinic on the back and you'd let people know in advance that you were coming and you'd stop at this crossroads and people would queue up and you'd come in and say, 'What's wrong with you? Sore foot, fix him, sore tooth, pull it out.' Pregnant, examination, blood test, just fix them all and then move on and go up and down the country with a movable clinic. Still it's something that I would be happy to finance if anyone wants to do it. But there are certain practical things in a Third World country which are really, really valuable and I never found the teaching of English that way. Well perhaps, perhaps it was useful, I don't know.

CLARE: Do you sometimes wonder about the usefulness of what you are doing?

THEROUX: Yes, I have questioned it at times. It seems pretty self-indulgent sitting around all day writing something, but it's the only thing that I found that I can do well. Somehow it's such a part of me, has been a part of me for, you know, more than the 30 years that I've been publishing. I think probably for 40 years it's all I've thought about even though I've pretended to be interested in other things. I talk about my work. I dishonestly complain about it. I mention it as though it's, you know, nine to five because that's the language that people understand but I know that it's a process of life, it's something that, that I do and I can't separate it from my existence and probably I'm lucky I've published the books. But I can relate to people who after their death they find, they open, an attic and they find a lot of unpublished manuscripts, something that they did. I can relate to someone who does it. I can relate it more to a painter, a man who sketches pictures, draws pictures, paints pictures. The big canvas, the small canvas the sketchbook, I can completely relate to the traveller, painter. Edward Lear, Turner, Stanley Spencer – someone who goes to a place and comes back with the sketches, half-done things, ideas for big canvases, rather than the writer who writes a book, five years pass, writes something else, few years pass, writes something else. At the end, you know, the four-book person.

CLARE: And then there's the fact that not only are you writing but you're writing and being read. I pick up in what you've said about this in relation to readers and people coming up and telling you what they feel about what you've written and critics and so on. It doesn't take a psychiatrist to know that you're ambivalent about this process of the reading. You make your writing sound like it's just part of your living, rather like breathing and, and eating. Of course, it's also one of the things that you do that involves other people. They start to read it and comment on it and interview you and an extension of what you're doing becomes a major part of your life. The going round and talking about it, or not talking about it, and at times you've said some pretty harsh things about people who say to you, 'I liked this' or 'I didn't like that,' or 'That was trash.'

THEROUX: People say, 'I didn't like it.' I thought why should I be interested in your not liking it?

CLARE: You're not interested?

THEROUX: I'm completely uninterested in people who say, 'By the way, I like this but I didn't like that,' and 'I don't like this and I don't like this very much.' And what do I care?

CLARE: What do you care? Do you care at all?

THEROUX: Yes, I care. A writer's a fool who says he or she doesn't want readers. You want readers. I don't want unqualified praise necessarily, but I'm not interested in notices, in being reviewed, let's say. That's not where it comes from. Someone who writes a letter from Winnipeg, from some little town in Australia, from America, a student, a prisoner, someone who has bought a book, who has read the book, who writes a letter.

CLARE: Even if within that letter he might say, 'But there was this I liked . . .'

THEROUX: That's all right, I don't mind that. I'm curious about people who live by books, not someone who's paid to review a book. Not the literary journalist – that's part of the job. But someone, usually it's a woman, usually it's someone home with children, it's usually someone in a remote place. It's usually someone who just has that, a hankering to leave but can't.

CLARE: Why do you think it's usually a woman?

THEROUX: Women are much more committed to books, to buying books and to living by books than men. Men, there's something about the machismo of maleness that prevents them ever from allowing themselves to praise a book. Men are natural competitors. Women tend not to be. I realise I'm generalising here but women are home. Traditionally, how have women managed to know the world? Through literature and men. I'm thinking probably about people that I grew up with, people in America. How many men have said to me, 'What do you do for a living?' 'I'm a writer.' 'What do you write?' 'Blah-di-blah.' 'Never heard of you. My wife's the reader, my wife's the reader.' And the letters, eight out of ten are from women, eight out of ten easily. So, I think it's the role, the traditional position of the women, having to stay home. It's their way of knowing the world. It probably will change and maybe has changed.

CLARE: What if I pushed you and suggested that it's not just for the reasons you've said, but that in a sense women, and I'll risk a wild generalisation of my own, which may or may not be particularly popular, but women are in a sense more reflective about certain aspects of life, and feelings, indeed, relationships. They are in touch to a greater extent with some of the elements that literature is in touch with than are men.

THEROUX: Possibly, possibly. But I also think it's in the nature of the way men are raised – to be competitors, to be, I don't know, gladiators, warriors. To worry about their manhood. Why do women kiss each other and men not? Why do you see women, they say goodbye and there's a little smooch on the cheek and off they go. And men hold back. Isn't that interesting. I've often thought – isn't it a sign that women are easy in their sexuality and men are not? And it's in the nature of maleness to be defensive. You know, not to praise.

CLARE: And would you see yourself as a competitive male?

THEROUX: I've wondered about that but I don't think I am because I don't think that it's helpful. It may be in the nature of some writers to be competitive, but I don't see that it's a competition. I'd say that I'm writing my books, my books aren't like anybody else's books. Sometimes critics lump you. They say, you know, that I'm an Anglo-American writer. I lived in foreign countries and therefore I'm like, you know, somebody else, Graham Greene, V. S. Naipaul, or I don't know, Salman Rushdie. And I think, I'm not at all like that. I say what the hell, you know, there's no contest here. I've often found literary prizegiving weird. Weird for the way that Iris Murdoch is up there, her book is up there with Doris Lessing, Salman Rushdie and somebody else. What is the connection? There's none, none. All you could compare is one Iris Murdoch novel with another or one of mine with another. And so the idea of competitiveness in writing, I don't get it at all, I don't get it. I don't see that writing has anything to do with sexuality, with gender, except in so far as when I was raised, a writer was judged by how much money they made, so money comes into it, in so far as money is an aspect of machismo. But that's something you want to leave well behind, I think.

CLARE: And has writing changed you then, over the years? You have spoken of its mainsprings – disjunction, loneliness, a certain detachment, and you've been writing now for what, 20, 30 years?

THEROUX: Well, I've been publishing for 30 years and writing probably for 35 or 40.

CLARE: Now, if there's some therapeutic element to the process of creative writing, then, here you are, 20, 30 years on, so has it changed you? Are you different as a result of that?

THEROUX: No, I think I'm more myself. I don't think it's therapeutic. It's not therapy, writing, it's a way of seeing the world. I suppose it's a way of becoming the person that I am. Maybe there's a, a connection between writing and scientology. In scientology you're taught, as I understand it, that if you buy the E Meter, it costs a lot of money, and you train it on your engrams which are in your mind. You rid yourself of these engrams which are negative aspects, I guess, of your mind, and you become clear. Well, that's not therapy. That's a way of becoming clear, and you realise that, as I understand scientology, that you achieve this level, you become clear, and you just become more yourself and you rid yourself of these bad vibrations. Probably writing is like that. It's like the E Meter, ridding yourself of the engrams. In other words, it's not therapeutic but you're like a person who's puzzling over aspects of your existence, of your past, of the world. And you begin to understand them. That's different from being therapeutic. That's different from having a problem that you're solving. You're not curing yourself of a condition. In a way, you're processing experience.

CLARE: Yes, I suppose I was using therapy somewhat loosely. It wasn't so much curing yourself of a condition as enabling you. For example, if we take what you started out with, the notion of being incomplete, I think you once said, writers are incomplete, that in the writing process, you become more complete.

THEROUX: That might be truer to say. I think I've even suggested that there is a sense of incompleteness but it might be a way of dealing with the world. That maybe there's a sense of curiosity about the world but I'm not a politician, I'm not a general, I'm not an active person, I'm not ordering troops around, but it's a way perhaps of dealing with the world in that way. In other words, it's not an active physical thing but it's an imaginative recreation of the world. It's having another chance to imaginatively recreate a possible, I want to say violent, experience, but if I do, then you will pounce on it, and you'll say I have a problem with violence or something like that. But I think what I mean to say is – you see a lot of dissonance in the world, there is a lot of dissonance and you say, 'Why is this happening? Why is this person doing that, I wonder?' and it has an echo in my own experience. And so I think, God, war, pain, agony, laughter, what is the source of all this, what is the source of love, what is the source of romance? I used to look at women on the train and think, God, what a lovely face, and then I'd think, becoming very self-conscious, why is that woman lovely? And I would study the woman's face – I even read a book on beauty one time, just to find out what is it about symmetry, what about the length of a woman's nose, lip, chin, the symmetry of her eyes? Why am I looking at this woman, why do I find this woman attractive? I used to be fascinated by it. I guess the aspects of sexual attraction fascinated me. I didn't want to know too much but I wanted to know something. Why that one and not that one? And also, why do ugly people frighten me? Why am I being nice to this person and being rude about that person? These things are, I suppose, questions that have their answer in writing, that I'm working it out with a pencil, aren't I?

CLARE: I read a lot about you. I'd never met you before, and I was a little uneasy about coming to this interview in a way that I wasn't about a lot of others, because what I read about you seemed to suggest someone who was, edgy and difficult. You heard my introduction where I referred to some of the things other people have said about you in terms of being 'in your face' and raspy and difficult, and I've quoted your brother. But you're not like that. I thought that maybe what I'm reading is the way you come across to certain people when you want to, or it is an aspect of yourself. After all, your writing is preoccupied with, for example, duality and what people are externally and internally, and secret lives and other selves. And am I now encountering this myself? Or is this just another example of what I've seen so often before, of people represented in the media and elsewhere quite differently to how they are? Or is it that you have changed over the years and that what I'm encountering is a different Paul Theroux to the person who was written about maybe five, ten years ago? I'm saying, you're not how I expected you to be.

THEROUX: You're surprised that I'm a lovable, hobbit-like creature.

CLARE: No, I'm surprised that you said such critical things about interviewers and being interviewed that I think, well, what's he going to be like when I meet him?

THEROUX: And you were apprehensive. But I wasn't apprehensive in the least. I was sort of looking forward to talking to you because I've heard you on the radio and I was thinking, now I have you all to myself, this is going to be an interesting conversation. Also, what will I learn from it, I was thinking. You introduced me by quoting, 'You'll either love him or hate him' but you didn't quote the end of it which is something like, when someone says you'll either love him or hate him, 'I think I'll hate him.'

CLARE: And I could have said that, I'll be honest, yes.

THEROUX: When people talk about colourful characters you think, oh God, not another colourful character. But the strange thing about writing is, and I suppose being reviewed, is that you develop a public image and mine is that of a difficult person, a cantankerous traveller, a grumpy man, someone who's always poking fun, looking for trouble. This isn't true at all. What I've tried to do in my life, in writing, is arrive at something resembling the truth and if I go to a place, I don't want to be told what it's like, I don't want someone nudging me and saying, 'Hey, look at that. Did you see that back there? Did you notice that?' I want to reach my own conclusions and write about every place as if it's never been written about before and not be influenced by other people. To see it as it is, because in all true writing there's a kind of prophecy and writing that's accurate about a place, when you're writing the truth, with a kind of wit I suppose, always seems prescient and, and the prescience in writing interests me a lot. The way you can write – I wrote a book about China and afterwards people said, 'You're so awful about the Chinese, terrible about the Chinese. You don't like the Chinese government and yet they're reforming.' This was 1988. Then 1989 rolled round, Tiananmen Square, and people were saying, you know, they're really similar to those people who were shooting the students. People turned against the Chinese and said, 'They're awful, they're all murderers.' Well, they're not. It's just that the police are trigger happy and the government is repressive and paranoid and they worry about people knowing too much. I think in writing that's what I've tried to do, but I have a reputation for being difficult.

CLARE: Yes, does that puzzle you?

THEROUX: Yes, it does, it does puzzle me and I don't understand it. Sometimes, I try to account for it a lot. Sometimes I think in the States it's easy, or in Germany, in that people who are literal minded, who have no sense of irony, find irony aggressive and they're bewildered by it. The English shouldn't. The Irish shouldn't. They're always kind of ironising. And irony and that kind of wit in literature is the very stuff of the national literature of Britain, Ireland, and of other places too, France. So when an American says, 'Oh, you're grumpy,' I say, 'Well, you're just being literal minded, you don't understand that this is called irony, it's called irony.' I think actually it's simple. I think people read a lot less than they're given credit for. We think of people as natural readers. Actually, very few people read. Very few people are intrepid readers. Reading requires a lot of intellectual strength, a great risk. You've got to pay money. You've got to buy books. You've got to go to the library. It is an effort. I think most people don't do it. Look at the number of novels that are sold, not many. It is much easier to say, 'Oh, he's grumpy, you know, I'm not going to read him.' People think of excuses not to do it.

CLARE: And then when your older brother made some pretty critical remarks about you, they were seized upon. Now what you said about the critics I can buy and the sense in which irony is misread I can buy. But then there's your brother who said some pretty harsh things.

THEROUX: Oh yes, yes.

CLARE: 'No one I have ever met in my life is a worse, almost pathologically unsympathetic listener' – now that rather intrigued me since I've never actually seen anyone described that way before and I wanted to meet one. So what's that about?

THEROUX: Well, you started this session on the couch asking about my family and I think that has its roots in a lost childhood. That has its roots in the family. That is my brother's way of speaking to the family. For the record, this is a very long, seven-page attack on me written by my older brother, the occasion of which was a book that I published. So he attacked me. It was very interesting since it happened so rarely in literature that one brother attacks another. Very common for brothers to be rivals, rarer for sisters to be rivals, but brothers: Thomas and Heinrich Mann, Stanislaus and James Joyce, William James and Henry James, Lawrence and Gerald Durrell, you name it, the Shaffer twins, Lytton Strachey and his brother, lots of them. Sibling rivalry in literature is more common than anyone would think. But those were secret things. There are letters, there are comments, there are snide remarks. It's not a brother like mine who lashed out and wrote a 5,000-word attack on me. That's a letter to the family. I've said that to people. That's a letter to the family, that's to my mother, that's to the other siblings. He's not writing for the world. He doesn't want to be asked, what, 'So I guess you hate your brother, heh?' He doesn't want to be asked. He was saying, he is saying, 'Choose me, choose me. What about me?' And I think that's really interesting. It's a bit unfortunate. My mother is an elderly woman and, you know, that shook her. It wasn't a happy experience for her but I saw it as a memo to the family, 'Choose me. Why do you spend so much time thinking about Paul? You read about his books, you laugh at his jokes.' This is a cry from a person who may be, as you might say, bi-polar, who has his excitable moments and his gloomy moments, someone who I believe was somewhat taken advantage of by a magazine editor who said, 'You know, OK, write it, attack him.' And the man even suggested that I might want to review a book of his. Not at all, not at all, I don't want to write a letter to the family.

CLARE: If that is a public letter to the family, then can I ask you whether, subsequent to that, you and your brother have had the usual kind of brotherly contact since? Once that's done publicly, what happens then?

THEROUX: That's right. Someone said, 'What's the next family holiday?' I think it was something like 'I don't want to be present for their Thanksgiving dinner.' Well, of course, there wasn't one, there's not a lot you can say. I saw it actually in a violent sense, an act of destruction. It's kind of symbolic fratricide, isn't it. And so, in that sense it's rather sad, but because fratricide isn't to be recommended. I mean, I know a little bit about the human heart and that's something that's very worrying. So you're asking did I have a heart to heart with him?

CLARE: Yes, because we talked about that extended family of yours, the seven of you, I wondered whether you get together or whether you see each other much and, of course, in this case, if you do, what would happen when you next meet this brother?

THEROUX: No, I haven't spoken to him. And it would be very hard, I think, it would be very awkward for him. But, on the other hand, he's on reasonably good terms, it's important that he remain on good terms with the family and with my mother. I'm happy to take a back seat to that.

CLARE: Do you see much of the rest of your family?

THEROUX: Yes, quite a lot, quite a lot, quite a lot.

CLARE: Is your mother still in Massachusetts?

THEROUX: Yes, and I see my mother fairly regularly. What I would like to do, I'd love to write about that but in a way it's opening a wound.

CLARE: Would you love to write about that more than heal it, more than make some effort to . . .

THEROUX: Yes, I would much rather write about it, would much rather make it a subject than healing. What is healing it anyway? What is healing it? You know, when people talk about time healing things, that we go and, as in Hawaii, just make friends – have a drink, have a coconut. Good, we'll sit down, eat a banana, we shake hands and off we go and everything's fine. They're not fine. They're not fine.

CLARE: Yes, fair enough, I accept that. I'm not naive enough to think that if you and your brother met something is undone or some wound is erased, but I suppose it's rather like a broken limb if it's put together again. There's always the weak point in it, there's always the scar, but there's other aspects of the relationship between you and your brother that, that could be sustained that now are completely damaged. They're finished, they're frozen. You and he will not meet again, presumably?

THEROUX: It's pretty unlikely that ...

CLARE: And none of this will be spoken about. I'm interested that you will use it in an artistic way, but in an actual practical situation you feel there's no point in that, there's nothing to be gained?

THEROUX: I don't think it would do much good. And also I do feel that in my life I've dealt with issues like this as a writer, and what interested me about it was that two years ago my father passed away, maybe it had something to do with that, I thought, would my brother have done that three years ago, probably not? It made me very interested about his life.

CLARE: But if you met him, why wouldn't you ask him all these things?

THEROUX: Oh I would, I would, if I had the chance I would. I would say, 'What's wrong?'

CLARE: Yes, that's what I meant about you meeting him. I didn't mean your Hawaiian therapy vision. I meant that kind of exchange.

THEROUX: Yes, in Malawi they used to say, 'Sorry, sorry, doesn't heal the wound' – just saying sorry. But my question would be, 'What's wrong?' Not what's wrong with me, because obviously I'm not his problem, definitely not, definitely not. I would say, 'What is it in your life?' I don't think he'd give the answer to the

question, but I would wonder, 'What is it in your life that made
you do that?'

CLARE: And that's what you will write?

THEROUX: Can't write it, it's too hurtful.

CLARE: But that's what you would write?

THEROUX: That's what I would write. I would want to reconstruct
his life. I would want to look into it. I would want to try to
understand it, yes. In fact, I do. Sometimes I find myself
animadverting on my brother's life, and thinking again, like
people look at a big family and saying that it must be, it's just
one big nest of love. And I'd think no, that it's a basket of crabs,
it's people clambering around, and I would say, 'What is it? Why
did he do it?' It's got nothing to do with me.

CLARE: Right, but bear with me. I don't subscribe to this nostalgic
Pollyanna view of large families. I have one and much of what
you're saying I'm reflecting on and I've no doubt when they
hear this, my children will too. I'm saying you're an articulate
man and I don't know your brother, but I suspect he can cope
with much of this, but your first instinct, in other words, wasn't
to lift the phone, dial him and say, 'What's with you, what's
wrong, what's all this about?'

THEROUX: No, it certainly wasn't to lift the phone, it was probably
to burn his house down. No, when I say, 'Burn his house down,'
I'm just joking, of course, but it would be to write a withering
reply. And, actually to tell you the truth, what I wanted to do
most of all was to point out how ungrammatical and illogical and
contradictory a lot of the piece was and how, when he was a
younger man, he was a very, very funny guy and a lot of things
that he wrote were very, very funny. And it was to point out
that this isn't very funny, it's not very well written, it's not well
argued. He's trying to hurt me. But this doesn't hurt, you know,
this is just raving. And also I felt this is hurting him. But it
wasn't to make peace, no, not at all, because I think I was
curious about a motive but it wasn't to ring him up and say,
'What's it all about?' It would be first to point out how
incoherent a lot of it was and how much harm it would probably
do him. And then I created in my mind, an ingenious reply to
this whole thing, which if I were ever asked I would repeat and

then I decided not to because I thought it's too weird, but it was one of those things, a clever reply, I thought of a clever reply and then I thought when people ask me about it, I just said, 'Well, if your brother attacks you in print and says your book is junk and you're a terrible person, the family hates you, you're a terrible person, you're a bad writer, you're a bad father, a bad husband, you're a bad person all the way through, and your books are junk, what should you think except this is not a valentine?'

CLARE: And the impact on the rest of the family, given your suggestion that this was a letter to the family, my next question is then how was it received by the family?

THEROUX: Well, with shock and horror. And they found it hard to deal with because, obviously, if he was going to write that about me it's possible that he might take it in his head to write about someone else and I think that it did create a problem. And, in fact, it had precisely the reaction that I suppose he wanted, which is that you make a fuss and you frighten people. It's a bit like raving. It's an unfortunate thing but it did interest me, objectively it interested me. I could have done without it, I suppose, the way we can always do without that kind of disruption. And also people get a glimpse at a truly unholy side of family life. It's something that I would like to have some control over. I want to do the writing about it and I'd like to have the last word and I realise that I can't, you know, I can't. This is too bad. Since I'm on the couch I can tell you, one of the things that I thought was, when I was growing up, there was a family that lived about five doors down with a terribly dissolute son. He's dead now but he was an old drunken man called George Cannal and George Cannal was someone we used to watch walking down the street, drunkenly. George Cannal, even the name, George Cannal, sounds terrible, and I was thinking of writing something, *The Private Life of George Cannal*, but it would be my brother, and I would just identify with this man, but I would write about, explore his life, look at his life. And I used to fantasise about this, a novel, *The Private Life of George Cannal*. And then he'd open it and realise it's him, it's him. So, I can't do it though.

CLARE: When you said your first impulse was to burn his house down, and then we laughed, but in fact you are quite a violent person.

THEROUX: No, I don't think so. Why do you think so? Because I said that in a joking way.

CLARE: No, not because you said it in a joking way. I'm struck by a recurrent theme in your writing, this duality, is this public or personal, and some of the impulses you seem to hint at, that seethe around inside, are violent impulses, destructive, and I wondered whether that's what people pick up, that there's something about Paul Theroux, that suggests to them that behind this façade is someone quite aggressive, quite dangerous?

THEROUX: I don't feel aggressive in the least and, as a matter of fact, aggression is something I've generally avoided in my life. Last night I was walking down the street in Notting Hill and I looked up ahead and I saw three young men walking toward me. They were about 50 yards down the road and I found myself immediately crossing the street and walking down the empty sidewalk to the corner. And then I thought, in my early life, it actually brought back, because I hadn't been to that part of London before, it was midnight, and it vividly brought back to me when I was growing up, when I was eight years old, nine years old, walking down the street, if I saw someone ahead of me the idea, if you're alone and you meet three people, especially if they are your age or a bit older, they will say something or do something, they'll push you, and so avoiding that is something I've always sought. And I realised, here I am, 56 years old, and 49 years ago, I remember doing that and that was my *modus operandi*, walking down the street, avoid trouble, take the path of least resistance, just avoid them. If I were an aggressive person, I think that I'd walk toward them and say, 'Well, what are you going to do about it?' But the idea of creating an occasion for aggression is something I've seriously tried to avoid in my life. I don't feel aggressive as a writer. I feel at peace. I feel in fact that writing creates a sense of peace within me and, that after a day of writing, I feel I have a song in my heart, and I feel as if I've earned the right to go swimming, to take a bike ride, to walk, to smell the flowers. A good day's work puts me in a wonderful mood, but then the next day I feel as if I'm sitting down again and I'm solving another problem. But I feel a great joy after a day of writing. I don't say that I find it easy, as a matter of fact, I find writing rather difficult to do, but it is a great way of easing the passage of time and actually makes me happy.

CLARE: You said or maybe a character in *My Other Life* said it, 'I think my writing comes out of a horror of death and attempts to put off the big day, and writing is after all a way of creating the grave,' and then there's a nice little piece of irony, 'Americans care immensely about longevity.' Well, maybe we all do.

THEROUX: I think I said that.

CLARE: You said that?

THEROUX: Yes, but I think about death and dying quite a lot I suppose because I have no faith. Because being raised in religion you think about redemption and you think about the hereafter. The idea of an afterlife is very strong in Catholicism. I don't feel that there is an afterlife, or at least I don't know. I suspect there isn't much there. But I feel if death is extinction then the idea of living is very strong and death concentrates the mind a lot on living. But the other side of that is, of course, is beyond the pleasure principle and is a kind of horror. Looking at my own work, trying to look at it objectively, I've sometimes felt that I'm writing about death, I'm writing about a fear of death, I'm writing about dying. A writer is probably the last person you should ask to do self-analysis of their own living.

CLARE: Because?

THEROUX: Because I don't think they see it. I think that, unfortunately, the writer has to spend so much time with his or her book that they have no perspective on it. A book is written over a period of say a year or two, written, read, perhaps over a day or two. So the impression that the reader has is different from the writer. I wish I could be my own reader. I wish I could be the first reader of something that I wrote. I wish, you know, maybe under LSD or something like that, I could read it, say, *The Mosquito Coast*, a novel, particularly a novel, that I would see something in it. To come to it fresh the way I read a book by V. S. Pritchett when he died, out of a sense of piety.

CLARE: You're living where now?

THEROUX: I live in Hawaii for about half the year and the rest of the time near, not too far, from where I grew up in Massachusetts.

CLARE: Do you think of where you grew up in Massachusetts as home? Do you have a notion of home?

THEROUX: Yeah, I have a very strong notion of home. Not a house and a street and a town, but a notion of smells, sounds, seasons. I have a sense of time and the world, let's say, of the sound of cars, the sound of bees buzzing, a certain kind of weed, certain kind of flowers, certain kind of trees, the look of certain weeks and months of the year. The ways trees change. I have a very strong sense of that.

CLARE: Associated with Boston?

THEROUX: Yes, outside of Boston. The way a savage, or I shouldn't say savage, the way, the way a person living in a jungle, someone who knows nothing of books but sniffs something and says, 'It's going to rain,' sees a tree, there's a kind of tree where I grew up, it's a tree that has a different colour almost every week from May to October or November, it goes from very green and reddens though the summer and you could tell almost what week or month it is by looking at the leaves, you can tell whether it's May 31st or June 30th. I have a very strong sense of all of that.

CLARE: And do you have a sense of exile? You lived in England for 17 or 18 years.

THEROUX: Eighteen years, yes, 18 years. And it's a feeling that I never had here. There was a sycamore tree in the back garden. I looked at it, probably every day for 15 years when we lived in this house and a sycamore tree does a lot of different things throughout the year, produces little seeds and things spinning down and leaves and whatnot, and fuzz and fur, but even so, 15 years wasn't enough, I needed to grow up with that tree. I didn't have any sense of belonging here. I always felt like the man who fell to earth. I looked like everyone else but inside me I am not. I've different sympathies and people have been very kind to me but they don't know me.

CLARE: Is that why you did it though? So many writers move away, they spend a period in exile, away, living in some other land sometimes not far away from where they were born, sometimes a continent away? Was there something deliberate about being away from the United States, being away in England?

THEROUX: Yes, yes, very much so. I left the States in 1963, which was a very violent time in our history and a very disturbed time. I needed perspective. I needed to get away from my family. I needed to be in a place where people were not going to ask me what I was doing, what I was writing, how I was going to make a living. 'Well, what are you going to do with your life? Well, then what will you do?' – the questions to which I had no answer. That's a worry to me. My advice to anyone who wants to write, or to make a life, is get away from anyone who is going to ask you that sort of question, the questions that you can't answer. Go away, go to Africa, go to South America, go to a Pacific Island, live. And don't think about that. So I needed to get away. Why did I come here? I was married to an English woman and we were married you know, 23 years, but her desire was to work, to have a job, to have a life, you know, not to be baking cookies, and so we began to live here and I realised, this is a very, very good place to live for a writer, people are kind, they understand writing, they read, money is not very impor- tant. You are not measured by your salary, you weren't, in the 1970s. I never remember anyone making a killing, making a lot of money, that didn't matter. The mind was more important. So that's a good thing, when you are judged by the quality of your writing and how hard you are working but not really whether you are driving a big car or something.

CLARE: And you were a family man in your own right during those years. You had two sons. As a matter of interest, would you have liked yourself to have had a large family?

THEROUX: Yes, yes, strangely enough because I felt I understood a lot of the tensions, a lot of the dynamics of a large family and I think that I would have been more aware of them than my parents and I could have avoided a lot of conflict in a larger family. Also, it's wonderful watching children grow up, seeing them interact with each other, I would like to have had more children. I don't know whether I could have handled seven but I think it would have been very pleasant. Both my parents were the eldest children of large families, but they grew up in the Depression. They had, they knew, hard times. I think my large family, I may be flattering myself, but I think it would have been slightly different. I think I would have understood sibling rivalry somewhat and I might have been prepared for some of that. But that's just fantasy. It didn't happen and I'm not going to go to Albania and buy a pair of twins and take them home and raise them. It's not on the cards. I felt lucky in being a writer in raising a family in that I was home. I was home when the children went to school. I was home when they came home from school. Often I made tea for them, I watched television with them. I loved hearing them laugh and doing something, just being there. I spent a lot of time with them, I felt very lucky that I was able to by being home.

CLARE: And your relationship with them now? They're in their twenties.

THEROUX: I think I've a good relationship with them. They confide in me up to a point and they have their own lives. I understand that with a father who writes they're in danger of being overwhelmed and they don't want to be overwhelmed, so I understand when they want to be on their own, they want to do things that they don't tell me. They don't want my solutions. They don't want to say, 'Dad, I'm thinking of writing a novel, how do I go about it?' They've never said that. They wouldn't say that. They're more likely to say, as my son said to me not too long ago, 'I've finished a novel.' I didn't even know he was writing one!

CLARE: Have you read it?

THEROUX: Yes, I have. It's marvellous and it's different from anything that I would write, so that's another mark in his favour, I think. You're a celebrity in your own right. You've been on radio a lot. You're a celebrated doctor, psychiatrist. I would have thought that if any of your children wanted to go to medical school, they'd think, 'I wonder if I will be on the radio? I wonder if people will know my name? I wonder if I will be a household word?' I would have thought, the danger of over-whelming a child with celebrity is really pretty tough, it's pretty tough, and I would like to think that I avoided that, yes.

CLARE: We talked about what other people make of your writing, reading it and so on, when you look at what you've written do you feel, that's good, feel a sense of satisfaction?

THEROUX: No, as I said, I find that I can't read my work very easily. When I read something I've written, *The Mosquito Coast*, let's say, it's a book about jungle life, what do I look at? I read it and I see the sycamore tree outside the window. A lot of writing is just staring out the window. It's looking at a desk, it's looking at a picture on the wall. It's the experience of a season, or of a family issue. So I look at the book, and I remember the circumstances of its being written. I remember when I wrote it, I remember what was running through my mind. I remember the difficulty perhaps of writing the paragraph, I remember the variants. And so it's almost a mnemonic device for recalling experiences that are totally peripheral to the work itself. It's as though an artist, looking at a picture, doesn't see the picture, but sees the studio or sees an easel set up in a corn field and crows going overhead, or something like that, while he is painting a picture of a haystack. It's a very odd thing but I find that, I feel very separated from what's on the page and very connected with everything that went into its writing. That's why I say, in a sense, I envy the people who are reading my books because at least they're reading a whole book, they don't have to think about all the other stuff. With a travel book I think about the train, the discomfort, the food, the upset stomach I didn't mention or, with a novel, a year or two sitting in a room. Or, give the Marquis de Sade, *Justine*, and say, 'OK, Marquis, read the book.' He'll think about his prison cell, he'll think about the paper that he wrote it on, he's not going to say, this is a vivid experience in auto-eroticism. I am sure he will think of the dampness of the Bastille, I don't think that he will think about the strange sadism in the prose.

CLARE: One of the elements I think we agreed, only one for I am sure there are many others, one of the elements that has gone to make you this writer, is going back to your family, your place in it and your sense of detachment and loneliness; you referred to disfunction. That's a given, is it? That's part of you and you would identify that sense of detachment, loneliness to this day?

That's an element that even those closest to you, your wife, your children, would recognise?

THEROUX: I think so, yes, I do think so. I think there's something in this, the wound and the bow, I do think that there's something there, yes, a sense not of aggression, not cantankerous or grumpy, but of something missing that's fulfilled. It's almost as if, in writing it, you're made whole but the next day it's gone. Is it Rumpelstiltskin who spins the straw into gold but each day it is back into straw or there's something about that, that, it's not done once. And I've never understood the writer who does it once, and then goes and teaches creative writing and buys a sail boat and goes sailing. I think of it, that it's an endless task. Maybe it is the myth of Sisyphus, you know, rolling the stone up and it rolls back, rolling it up again. There's something in that, maybe it's the human condition. But I do feel there are times, sometimes you see people, a couple holding hands, and they're walking down and you see that man's not writing a book, they are happy, they are happy with each other, totally fulfilled. Is this an illusion of mine, of seeing two people completely happy, completely fulfilled? Maybe it is. The husband and wife you see in Guatemala, in Africa, in wherever, Istanbul, a man and wife, middle aged, sometimes elderly, holding hands, the woman has a handbag, the husband has a carrier bag, they're coming home from shopping, they're going home to cook a meal. I think, isn't that wonderful? I sometimes look at that. But I remember I said to my wife, my first wife, I told her this story, I said, I was just going through this, a couple holding hands, carrier bag. She said, 'I am sure they're miserable, don't kid yourself,' or something like that. It was a good remark, quite a good remark, so maybe I'm wrong.

CLARE: Paul Theroux, thank you very much indeed.

Ann Widdecombe

Ann Widdecombe came to our interview with a formidable reputation as a no-nonsense person. At the time of a row over the chaining of pregnant prisoners when she was a Home Office minister, one tabloid newspaper dubbed her 'Doris Karloff' while others made biting comments on her single status and, by implication, her unsympathetic attitudes. One MP, a woman, even suggested that she ask the Royal College of Obstetricians and Gynaecologists for private tuition on childbirth. The criticism and abuse had little effect. She is the ultimate conviction politician, with firm and seemingly unshakeable views on a plethora of issues from the violence and sex purveyed by the BBC to abortion, from capital punishment to women priests. She has not much time or patience with self-analysis, is not interested in herself, her motives, or the origins of her sense of justice, has never been seriously ill and has certainly never faced an abyss of self-doubt or demoralisation. From the opening moments I knew it was going to be tough.

There is an uncanny echo of Martin Bell's interview when, towards the end, she reprimands me by pointing out that 'it really isn't necessary to try to analyse everything to the last degree to decide who is right'. I am struck by how many people in British public life react to queries about their attitudes, motivations, the sources of their beliefs. To question or examine is quickly equated with self-indulgence or a surfeit of time. The implication is clearly that one would be better employed doing something more useful. I suppose I should not be surprised. Politicians are, for the most part, doers. Many seem impatient with doubt or uncertainty. Making one's mind up and getting on with it are so obviously the measures by which they rate each other that they appear genuinely surprised, as Ann Widdecombe is in this interview, when they encounter people who possess nothing like the same certainties and, anyway, are a little suspicious of too much confidence and too little doubt.

So making sense of Ann Widdecombe becomes a matter of seizing the occasional meagre piece of self-revelation that she lets drop and trying to detect a pattern. She does not appear to have had much sibling rivalry with her older brother and, indeed, behaves more like an only child than a younger sister which, given the gap of ten years between them, is not so surprising. The multiple school moves appear to have equipped her with a marked degree of self-reliance and confidence. Her father represented drive, ambition, the public life, while her mother sacrificed herself for her husband and two children.

Perhaps the most significant early experience is the Anglican Ann Widdecombe in a Roman Catholic school – shades of Brian Masters. Was this where she developed or at least honed her sense of justice, her ability to take and hold an unpopular position, her ability to ignore cutting remarks and personal abuse? Certainly there is nothing like a little persecution in adolescence to fuel a passionate, dogmatic belief. Otherwise hers is a sensible, solid adolescence with no rebellion – Roman history rather than the Beatles. A sense of duty – she thought briefly of being a missionary – and then she is off to university and her own ambition is now challenged and cultivated.

It is a courteous, good-humoured interview but I am aware that she is irritated by the basic premise of the series and irked by having to discuss feelings and impulses and doubts when she would much prefer a jolly good wrangle over abortion or sex on television. Occasionally I am seduced – we do discuss sex on the BBC. I, who willingly confess to having a television set and watching it, am doubtful that despite all the fuss, there is all that much sex and violence. Ann Widdecombe, who readily admits to watching hardly any and having no television set to begin with, is once again in no doubt. There is too much sex, violence and irregular living and too much of it everywhere and she is none too pleased at the amount of attention sex is getting in this interview.

So I move on, though I increasingly feel the way it must have felt
to interview another formidable woman politician with an ambitious, hard-working father and a sacrificial mother, Margaret
Thatcher. Ann Widdecombe's religious views are stated matter-of-
factly. Hers is a religion of unadorned faith. It seems eminently
practicable. It gives her strength. She prays at moments of crisis.
She believes in miracles. She regrets the fact that certainties on the
things that matter seem to hold less sway today than in former
years. She exudes impatience with my 'anchorless' position. I am
tempted to quote my heroes, Chekhov, Orwell and MacNeice, on
the merits of doubt but think the better of it and move on.

Is it my imagination or perhaps wishful thinking but as the
interview progresses I feel she relaxes? Perhaps she expects me to
be hostile and aggressive. Many media interviewers and journalists
are, and the cuttings I have read about her before the interview
contain some very personally vitriolic and insensitive remarks. In
fact, I rather admire the fact that she speaks her mind and avoids
windy blathering. We arrive at an intriguing discussion concerning
a novel she intends to write – about physical disability. She has
described her own physical appearance in less than glowing terms,
partly I suspect to take the wind out of the sails of the legion of
commentators who take such delight in commenting on the
physical appearance, style, make-up and dress sense of women in
British public life. 'Overweight', 'dumpy', 'spinster', 'ugly', are
words she has chosen for self-description. She goes further and
articulates a formidable onslaught on our current preoccupation
with physical perfection and makes an impressive argument on
behalf of all the people in our society who are physically disabled,
who are physically disfigured.

In the end I am forced to ask her why she agreed to do the
interview in the first place. She is characteristically blunt: 'I looked
forward to the duel and I think in many ways we've had one.'
Clearly she anticipated that it would be a duel and so it proved to
be. For my part I can honestly say that I had no expectations one
way or the other. But it is hard to prevent such an interview
turning into a struggle if that is how the interviewee sees it to be.
Much interviewing is understood in this way and there are
supposedly winners and losers. To keep everything under wraps

and bat away solidly for the requisite time is to win. In fairness to Ann Widdecombe, I don't feel she struggled to keep things to herself – she did not. She is as focused, uncomplicated, free of conflict and complex as she sounds.

There is an element of martyrdom about her. She is prepared to go to the stake and the Tory party whips have been warned. Her confrontation with Michael Howard is very much in character. When Ann Widdecombe believes in something she does so passionately. She will not be easily disciplined within a party structure but is a conviction politician. She speaks for the right on many issues including abortion, euthanasia and capital punishment but her remarks on personal tolerance and on prison reform suggest the need for caution before any attempt is undertaken to pigeonhole her. She takes herself for granted. She wants to get on with things.

CLARE: The only daughter of a high-ranking civil servant, Ann Widdecombe was born in 1947. Her family were staunch Anglicans. She, however, went to a strict Roman Catholic convent school in Bath, read Latin at the University of Birmingham and politics at Oxford. Following a spell in marketing with Unilever, and in financial administration at the University of London, she achieved a long-standing ambition and became a Conservative Member of Parliament in 1987 after two unsuccessful attempts.

While always regarded by the press as somewhat unusual, it is only since her attack on Michael Howard, when he was home secretary, that the former minister for prisons started to attract considerable media attention, by no means all flattering or, indeed, particularly relevant. Quite apart from the headline writers' favourite 'Doris Karloff', she's been variously described as brisk and crisp, redoubtable, fearless, a fiendish Lady Macbeth.

There is something jolly about her, but there's also something 'scarily impervious', as one of her interviewers remarked, but what above all else is most frequently mentioned is the seemingly unshakeable strength of her convictions in matters of religious faith, against abortion or for capital punishment.

Ann Widdecombe, people clearly find you rather intriguing and certainly spend some time analysing you. But what about you, are you interested in yourself?

WIDDECOMBE: Not really. I don't quite understand why people find me as intriguing as they do. They always have, ever since I started a pro-life campaign when I first came into Parliament. I've attracted what you call people's curiosity and being intrigued. I think, like most people, I don't really bother with myself at all unless I suddenly find myself doing something uncharacteristic or something that causes me to pause and think. And then, of course, I will start to ask myself why I am doing what I'm doing but on the whole, no, I don't spend a long time trying to analyse myself.

CLARE: And what sort of thing might be so unexpected that you yourself would stop and consider?

WIDDECOMBE: Well, I found the whole business with Michael Howard something quite unusual. I've always been a good friend to people. I have never before regarded myself as being a bad enemy which I think I certainly was from Michael Howard's point of view. I therefore spent a long time analysing what I was doing and making quite certain that I was doing it for reasons that I found acceptable. I was well aware the rest of the world would put their own construction on it. Now, that is the sort of thing which would cause me to stop and ask questions about myself but, in general, I take myself for granted.

CLARE: When you say ask questions about yourself, would it include looking a little at where your convictions, your values, your ideas have come from?

WIDDECOMBE: I don't usually go into them in that sort of depth unless invited to do so by an interviewer like yourself, or by an interviewer like the plethora of journalists that come to see me from time to time and then I will do. To answer the question, I think that I have a very deep-rooted sense of justice and when that sense of justice is offended in any major way and there is something that I can do to put it right, then I will usually try. I find that in my constituency work occasionally I am so outraged by something, that I will go to great lengths to try and put it right, not always successfully.

CLARE: And do you know where that comes from? How far back do you go to identify this sense of justice in Ann Widdecome?

WIDDECOMBE: I don't think I do go back. I mean, I think I start from the point that we're all in it together in this life, so to speak, and we owe it to each other not to inflict unnecessary suffering on each other. Fate itself inflicts quite enough. The average person going through life will come up against all manner of sorrows and difficulties and pains and illnesses, and I just don't think it's reasonable for human beings to inflict misery on one another. I mean, one of the things that gets me most irate in my constituency is a very trivial thing, not a major thing at all, it's a very trivial thing; it's when there are people in a neighbourhood who deliberately try to make other people's lives unbearable and pick on a family and really make the lives of the family and the children difficult. That sort of thing gets me very angry indeed.

CLARE: You will agree with me, that not everybody is like you and you're not like everybody, we're all different and the extent to which you can trace back the way in which certain values take hold isn't just an academic exercise. You must wonder sometimes why other people aren't as exercised as you are say, about matters of justice. And when you said, we're all in it together and we've all had experiences, I think it's reasonable then if I were to say to you, well, have you had those kind of experiences, when you yourself personally have found yourself on the side of the offended?

WIDDECOMBE: I haven't had personal experiences of the sort that you describe. I am not able to tell you where this sense of justice comes from.

CLARE: Did you have it at school for example?

WIDDECOMBE: I can't really recall. I can't recall whether I had it there or not.

CLARE: Or growing up?

WIDDECOMBE: I don't know. I've had it since I've had responsibility for other people, I know that.

CLARE: Do you remember much about growing up?

WIDDECOMBE: Yes I remember a great deal about growing up largely because my childhood was extremely varied. We moved about a great deal, I went to six schools by the time I was eleven.

CLARE: Why was that? I'd read that about you.

WIDDECOMBE: Why did we move about? Because my father was in what was then called the Admiralty and we used to move every three years or so, including overseas.

CLARE: And how did you cope with that? Was that something you enjoyed?

WIDDECOMBE: I did enjoy it and I took it utterly for granted and indeed, even to the extent that when we first settled for five years, I was almost personally offended by this and I wanted to know, well, where was the move, when were we going to do something different. So I obviously did enjoy it. I certainly took it for granted. Now, I think that I had too little understanding of the impact on the rest of the family. For example, when I went to Singapore when I was a young child with my parents, my brother did not, he remained at school in England. When I subsequently became a boarder at Bath Convent, I was there with girls who only saw their parents about once a year because they were left behind in England. Whereas I always went with them, I seemed to be the lucky one.

CLARE: You always went with your parents?

WIDDECOMBE: Well, I was young at the time that they were overseas.

CLARE: And your brother, how did he cope with that?

WIDDECOMBE: He's coped remarkably well. He's an extremely successful canon of the Church of England.

CLARE: But you say that you looked forward to the moves? Does that mean you were quite a self-reliant person even then?

WIDDECOMBE: I don't know. I know that I enjoyed moves, I was always terribly eager for a new school to see what that would be like. I was always interested in where we were going, and what the house would be like, and what the garden would be like, and what friends there would be around. I certainly preferred moving to such an extent that, in those days, I used to pity people who were stuck in the same house from the age of nought to 18.

CLARE: How did your mother cope with it?

WIDDECOMBE: Oh, she took it utterly for granted as well. She knew very well when she married that she would be moving around.

She was an extremely effective organiser and manager of the home and our moves were always extremely smooth.

CLARE: Were you, are you like her?

WIDDECOMBE: No, I don't think I am. My mother is not ambitious in the sense that I became ambitious. She has lived an entirely sacrificial lifestyle. She brought us up. Her first business was my father's welfare and our welfare and that is a pattern I admire and, had I decided to marry and have children, I hope it is a pattern I would have followed. It's a hypothesis, I don't know.

CLARE: You sound doubtful that you would?

WIDDECOMBE: As I say, it's a hypothesis. I don't know. I don't know what I would have done. I think if I had married at 22 and had children, I would have had a very different attitude because I was then very much caught up in the 1970s and equal opportunities, women going out to work and all the rest of it. I have since revised those views somewhat. It's just a product of age.

CLARE: In what way have you revised them?

WIDDECOMBE: I now think that it is probably better, where possible, and it's not always possible, but it is probably better where possible that, certainly when children are young, they have full-time mothers. I am aware that that view is not universally held and I'm aware that it's not a terribly popular one but it is the view I have come to.

CLARE: You would have had a full-time mother?

WIDDECOMBE: I did have a full-time mother.

CLARE: She gave herself entirely?

WIDDECOMBE: Yes, and one way of illustrating that is that when I was in my teens and at home in the holidays, one of the happiest sounds was the door opening and shutting as my mother came in from delivering my father to the station. Now, if in fact it had been the door opening and shutting as my mother went to work and I'd been thrown back on my own resources all day at home, I think that would have been very, very, a poor second best.

CLARE: And, of course, you know, because you hinted at the kind of political incorrectness that some of this might be seen as, you know that critics would say, 'Well, that's fine, but you didn't follow your mother, you didn't do what she did, you're a woman of the 1990s, you're out carving your own career.'

WIDDECOMBE: Yes, I am, very much so. That's why I said I'm not like her.

CLARE: You're not like her, no. What about your father?

WIDDECOMBE: My father was certainly very ambitious and had a lot of drive and a tremendous amount of interest in his work. He was a senior civil servant. I think I have some characteristics of my father but I've also got some of my mother. My mother is exceptionally kind and caring about other people and I think that some of that comes out in me.

CLARE: And your father was ambitious?

WIDDECOMBE: Yes.

CLARE: For himself?

WIDDECOMBE: He was ambitious to achieve things. I think it is always difficult to say. When I'm asked this question I never know exactly what the answer is. People say, 'Are you ambitious for yourself?' and I say, 'Well, I can only actually do the things I want to do if I can get on and get into a position to be able to do them.' So, from that point of view, yes, I'm ambitious for myself but I think it would not be worth having at all if all one was concerned about was one's own advancement. It wouldn't be worth having. There's got to be a cause. There's got to be a distant banner to which you're rallying.

CLARE: But I'm struck by the fact that your brother who's ten years older, he's a canon, you're the politician and I wondered was your father ambitious for you? Was he ambitious for your brother?

WIDDECOMBE: He was ambitious for both of us but it was always the view at home that we chose what we would do. There was never any undue pressure. We were always encouraged. If, for example, I had said, what might I have said, I want to go into outer space, I think the reaction would have been to say, 'Well, then you need A Level physics and chemistry, my dear, not Latin and Greek.' It wouldn't have been, 'Nonsense, don't talk such rot!' I think that they were very supportive but they never put on undue pressure and my brother and I chose our own ways. In fact, our professions are remarkably similar.

CLARE: What did you want to do when you were growing up?

WIDDECOMBE: Initially, I wanted to teach, then I wanted to be a missionary, then I wanted to teach, and then from the age of about 15, 16, possibly a bit earlier, I wanted to be a politician.

CLARE: You were in a number of schools. In one of the schools, you were a Protestant in a Catholic school?

WIDDECOMBE: That was throughout my senior education, yes. That was a stable period. I only went to one school for my senior education.

CLARE: And, that was chosen because?

WIDDECOMBE: It was chosen for its academic value and for its discipline, two things which my parents were looking for.

CLARE: You said somewhere that it was a strong Anglican family but they were content to see you in a Catholic school?

WIDDECOMBE: Oh very. My mother was the daughter of a Roman Catholic. There were a wide range of traditions in the family and there had been a Baptist tradition and there had been a strong Anglican tradition. My uncle, for example, was a vicar and we had lay readers in the family. So it was a mixed tradition.

CLARE: Was your mother a Roman Catholic?

WIDDECOMBE: No, my mother was not a Roman Catholic, my mother was an Anglican.

CLARE: And what was it like being an Anglican in a Roman Catholic school?

WIDDECOMBE: Oh, I think it taught me a very great deal, not in the religious front but in a different way. It's very difficult to remember this now but it was an age in which there was a lot of intolerance between the two denominations. It was still the case that Roman Catholics could not go into Anglican churches without special permission. Anglicans took a very severe view of some Roman Catholic practices. There was a lot of antagonism between the two churches, which seems incredible now but was very much the fact then. And, therefore, if you were in a minority, as I was in that school and what is more, a practising member of that minority because of my brother and my strong Anglican traditions, I had to stand up for myself very, very early.

CLARE: When you say a minority, were you a minority of one?

WIDDECOMBE: Oh no, certainly not, no.

CLARE: There were others?

WIDDECOMBE: There were quite a number of us.

CLARE: But it was still quite a minority?

WIDDECOMBE: We were a minority but there were a number of us, both day girls and boarders.

CLARE: And what kind of form would this kind of intolerance take?

WIDDECOMBE: Oh, for example, we weren't allowed to go to church, to our own church, on Sundays. It was before Vatican II.

CLARE: So they wouldn't let you go?

WIDDECOMBE: We weren't allowed to go to church on Sundays. As soon as I got into the fourth form, when we were allowed out for two hours on our own on a Sunday, I used to go but that was out of my own time. Prior to that, that wouldn't have been allowed.

CLARE: And the girls themselves, how did they behave towards you?

WIDDECOMBE: Oh, the girls actually were vastly more tolerant than we were being taught to be by our elders. I certainly never had any persecution on that score from other girls, no, never.

CLARE: What qualities do you think it brought out in you?

WIDDECOMBE: It taught me to stand up for myself. It taught me to take an unpopular minority position if I had to, and it taught me how to do it without antagonising everybody around me. It would have been profoundly unwise to have actually antagonised the nuns, which I managed not to do, most of the time anyway, I managed not to do that.

CLARE: Yes, they can be tough. Were there some tough ones?

WIDDECOMBE: They were very good. I am still in contact with some of them and have a tremendous respect and affection for them and for that period in my life. But yes, they were very tough and very demanding and we were very, very strictly disciplined. It was a very, very disciplined school in the 1960s when everybody else was into Beatles and mini skirts.

CLARE: And what happened to your exposure to the Beatles and the mini skirts?

WIDDECOMBE: The Beatles never did inspire me very much, I regret to say, because I know they've inspired just about everybody else. As far as mini skirts went, I first ventured into a mini skirt at Birmingham University. I didn't do at school. We would not have been allowed to.

CLARE: And put it this way, would it have been the sort of school that you'd send your own child to?

WIDDECOMBE: I think the answer to that is at that time, yes, that would have been appropriate. Now, I don't think it would be appropriate. I think in the event that I had a child and was looking for a school, I would certainly be choosing a single-sex Catholic school but there, I think, the similarity ends. On the whole, I prefer a slightly more tolerant way of bringing children up and disciplining them.

CLARE: And you'd pick single-sex because?

WIDDECOMBE: Less distractions.

CLARE: You weren't distracted?

WIDDECOMBE: I wasn't distracted at all.

CLARE: What was for you the equivalent of what the Beatles and mini skirts and so on were for your contemporaries in other schools?

WIDDECOMBE: Oh, I was terribly keen on Roman history. I really liked Roman history. I read Roman history until it came out of my ears and enjoyed it. It wasn't for a swotting point of view, I just enjoyed doing it. And I had great fun with that. As far as other things went, I just enjoyed reading in general and whatever else it is that girls of that age do, other than the Beatles.

CLARE: But you were a serious person.

WIDDECOMBE: I was a moderately serious person. It's very easy to caricature somebody who doesn't like pop music, and at that time I didn't, as a very serious person. I could sometimes be quite jolly!

CLARE: So, when you went to Birmingham, was that a great change, to go from such a school into an open campus?

WIDDECOMBE: Yes, it was, but again I took it for granted because my life had been one of continual change and I took it very much for granted. I took what I'd suddenly found myself in as being something utterly normal and to be expected. And so, yes, it was a big change. I think the real change came when I went to Oxford and where I then met people who had very, very high aspirations. That was the difference between Birmingham and Oxford. At Birmingham, people talked about going into teaching or whatever it might be, going into the Civil Service. At

Oxford, people would talk about becoming the head of the Civil Service, editing *The Times*, not going into journalism, getting into the cabinet, not just going into Parliament. Now, a lot of that was just youthful nonsense and never materialised but there was a different attitude, a very, very strikingly different attitude, and I did notice that at the time and was quite surprised by it.

CLARE: Intimidated?

WIDDECOMBE: No, but I was certainly surprised, certainly surprised. It wasn't until that moment something that I had been used to. People would play down their abilities rather than play up.

CLARE: You say that mini skirts, the Beatles, didn't figure much and the opposite sex wasn't a distraction in school. What about a distraction in university? What about the social life there?

WIDDECOMBE: Yes, the social life certainly at Oxford was very much a part of the political life. It went hand in hand with it. I certainly enjoyed Oxford from all sorts of points of view. Everybody's got memories of Oxford – commemoration balls, punting down the river, long sunny days with tea on the lawn. Oxford has all sorts of sentimental connotations, I think, for most people who've been there and certainly the social life was quite a major feature.

CLARE: You said somewhere, I can't remember where, that you did have a romantic relationship at Oxford but you said it didn't survive into the real world.

WIDDECOMBE: I think I said it didn't translate to the real world.

CLARE: That's it, yes, and I was intrigued by that because of the notion that whatever it was, it wasn't real.

WIDDECOMBE: I didn't necessarily say that it wasn't real but that it was in a particular context. The man concerned was a fellow officer of the Oxford Union. We had politics in common. We had quite a lot of Oxford activities in common. The real world was different and it didn't survive transition. I don't think that makes it unreal but it wasn't something that was destined to last. He is now extremely happily married, extremely successful. I am very happily unmarried and moderately successful and I think we are both glad that things went the way it did.

CLARE: I was rather intrigued by the fact that when you've talked about personal matters, or sexual matters, you tend to say things like, that sex in contemporary society is overrated, and I wondered why you say that?

WIDDECOMBE: Because it screams at you from everywhere. If you go into the average newsagent, even the most mainstream of women's magazines are screaming, absolutely screaming, some item on sex at you from the cover. It is now the case that you can hardly read a contemporary book without there being some very explicit passage in it. I think we have got the whole thing out of proportion and I think it is something that wasn't the case, for example, in the 1950s and even in the early 1960s. And OK, that is the way society is. I'm not even going to make a value judgement on it, but what I am going to say is I think we've got it out of proportion.

CLARE: But, of course, occasionally you do make a value judgement. You said, for example, that you don't have television. That is fair enough, I know several people who don't but you went on to say why should you pay for sex and filthy language and so on? And again, that somewhat intrigues me because, well, with respect, I do watch occasionally television, and it struck me that that's not quite how the good old BBC comes across to me and I was rather intrigued. I wondered why you have a tendency to sort of hive off sexuality where others might say, 'Well, it's there but there's lots of other things there as well'?

WIDDECOMBE: I'm afraid that, with all due respect to the surroundings in which we find ourselves at the moment, I think that the media have been a tremendously corrupting force. I think that the eternal diet that is turned out, not only of sex but of violence, of irregular living, of contempt of authority, all these things stand out. There are plenty of programmes before the nine o'clock watershed that, were I a parent, I would be profoundly uneasy about exposing a child to. Now, that is my view. I don't seek to inflict that on anybody else, but people do tend to get terribly uptight when I say I won't have a television because of it. But I won't because I would have to pay a licence. Why should I pay for a programme to be made when I object to it?

CLARE: One of the reasons I'm doing this interview, is because you are a politician. When you say you don't want to do anything about it, that's fair enough. But as a politician, as someone who does do things, you do things, you influence policy and you change things and so on, your views in many ways are much more interesting than mine. I'm hardly likely to change very much, but you could find yourself in a position of being in charge of broadcasting in Britain. So, in that sense, your views are of particular interest. In that sense, indeed, how your views develop are of interest. Would you agree with that?

WIDDECOMBE: That is perfectly fair, that were I to be in charge of broadcasting I think it would be vastly more interesting that I do not have a television. As it happens, I don't seek to dictate to other people whether they have a television or not. I have a very strong view on some of the stuff that comes out. I personally wouldn't like to be responsible for it. There's a lot of other very worthy material that comes out.

CLARE: I often wonder whether the reason that there was that great explosion in the 1960s was that if sex was overrated in the 60s, it was somewhat underrated in previous years. I'm thinking of my own parents' attitudes to sexuality. They lived perfectly reasonable lives but it wasn't something they talked about. My mother would be very embarrassed if sexuality was discussed in the way it is now on radio. And so there was a sort of reaction. And that's what interests me about you, that you come out of that period as I do, but with somewhat different views.

WIDDECOMBE: I think it is just historically a fact that the pendulum always swings violently, it never seems to settle comfortably in the middle. It always swings violently. I'm quite happy to believe that the 1960s were a reaction to the 1950s. What I am addressing is the situation I find myself in, not the situation that prevailed before.

CLARE: Is there any side of you which envies a certain kind of freedom about sexuality?

WIDDECOMBE: No, absolutely not. There is no side of me which has the remotest interest actually. The only time I discuss these things is when people like you ask me.

CLARE: That's true and of course people like me will ask you, because you do hold a firm view on sexuality. It's not as if you're neutral on it. You're actually quite firm. You feel there's far too much, it's too explicit.

WIDDECOMBE: Too much emphasis, too much emphasis.

CLARE: That's right. But you will agree Ann, that that will cause people like me to ask you questions about it. If you, I don't know, if you were an expert in finance, I certainly wouldn't interview you, but others would, others would.

WIDDECOMBE: But you see, Professor, what I haven't said is that you shouldn't ask me these questions. What I've said is I only address them when people like you ask me these questions. Very often I think what happens is: people ask me these questions and I answer and then the people out there get the idea that this is what is preoccupying me and that I'm spending too much time on this or too much time on that. And I certainly get a lot of reaction like that, not about this particular issue that we've been discussing, but sometimes if I'm addressing something in particular and being asked questions on it, everybody will think that I do nothing else for 24 hours a day except worry about that.

CLARE: Yes, I'm not sure they will, I think it's perceived that the media are much more curious about these things than you are, but I take your point, I think that's fair. And, of course, I find myself in a sense in a similar dilemma because it is only one aspect of you, it's an interesting aspect of you though, because of your firm religious convictions, and also because you have found yourself, interestingly enough, in one or two situations already in your political life which caused your views on men and women and relationships to loom up again in the most extraordinary ways.

WIDDECOMBE: More than once or twice.

CLARE: The issue I'm thinking of is that famous controversy over the pregnant woman chained to the bed. Again, that's why people like me particularly are interested in, not just Ann Widdecombe the politician and the successful academic, going through university and so on and a person with certainly very firm convictions. But what sorts of views you have about what to me are actually much more interesting issues, and that is the way in which people relate to each other. Because putting my cards on the table, that's why I'm doing what I'm doing and I'm not doing politics which is about, it seems to me, life at a slightly different level. So that's the justification for asking, and it's the only justification.

WIDDECOMBE: No, I didn't ask you to justify it.

CLARE: No. I feel the need to.

WIDDECOMBE: We're doing a role reversal at the moment! I didn't ask you to.

CLARE: I know you've said before that you don't have to experience something to have views on something, and I think you used the analogy of, you don't have to murder somebody to understand or take a view on murder.

WIDDECOMBE: To know it's wrong.

CLARE: But that's a little different. Murdering somebody isn't part of the mainstream of life, thankfully, whereas sexuality is, sexuality is.

WIDDECOMBE: Hang on, I haven't said that all sexuality is wrong. All I have said is that we have got it entirely out of proportion as a society, that's all I've said.

CLARE: But let me stop you there, and say, but it could be said, somebody might say to you, well, you know, sex is now properly rated, it is a very . . .

WIDDECOMBE: Are we going to spend this entire interview . . .

CLARE: It is a very important issue.

WIDDECOMBE: Are we going to spend this entire interview on sex? I really think that we have it overrated. I think that it's been given a completely undue emphasis in this interview and that is my view. I have always said that I think that the way that we have emphasised it to the exclusion, I think, sometimes of looking at things in a much wider context, of emotion and intellect, not of just sheer animal instincts, I think that we have got it out of proportion. That is all. I've never said that it's wrong *per se*, never.

CLARE: Are you someone who has doubts?

WIDDECOMBE: About what?

CLARE: About anything?

WIDDECOMBE: I expect I've got doubts about some things, most people have.

CLARE: Well, about important things. Do you ever think you might be wrong?

WIDDECOMBE: No.

CLARE: Seriously wrong?

WIDDECOMBE: No, no I don't think I might be seriously wrong because those things which are very important to me I have thought through and I have come to a clear view on them. I cannot say it is beyond all possibility that I am wrong, I mean, that's how you get dictatorships. But I can say I am myself convinced that I am right and I am convinced on important things which I have thought through, as opposed to things which I am sometimes invited to comment on off the cuff. But things that I have thought through, I believe I've got right, I believe I've got right. I don't ask everybody else to share that same conviction.

CLARE: But as a politician, you then act on the things you believe are right?

WIDDECOMBE: Yes, but the distinction I am making is that if, for example, you take a different view, I regard that as your right to take that view. As far as possible I think that society should provide for people to take different views and practise different things, as far as it is possible. Now, we will all have different views as to where you have to draw the line as to what is possible and what is desirable and where social interests actually overtake the interests of the individual. We will all draw the line in different places. But I am convinced that those things which I have thought through, quite obviously if I've thought them through and come to a view, I am convinced they're right. I always when I go to the electorate, I've always put my views on conscience issues, always, even if I know some of them are unpopular. I put them to the electorate so that people know exactly what they're getting. I think that is important. There is one thing I do despise, actually, and I really do despise it, it's the havering politician who tries to have things all ways, not because he says honestly, 'Actually, I haven't made my mind up,' that's different, occasionally we don't make our minds up. But the politician who says, 'Well, actually, I think this but it's a bit unpopular so I'm going to try and dress it up and I'm going to try and present it in a different way to the electorate.' That I actually think is wrong.

CLARE: What about just ordinary people, leaving aside politicians who can't make up their minds, or find it very difficult to be certain?

WIDDECOMBE: It's up to them, up to them.

CLARE: When I was asking you about doubts, I was actually thinking of religious doubts?

WIDDECOMBE: Yes.

CLARE: Have you ever had a crisis of belief?

WIDDECOMBE: I wouldn't say there's been a crisis. I certainly went through a period of agnosticism. I always describe it this way. There was no great blinding flash in the night on either going into agnosticism or coming back from agnosticism. I've always described the descent into agnosticism as the erosion of belief, the very gradual erosion of belief. And my return to Christianity was the gradual erosion of unbelief. And in the course of those two journeys, there would have been a day when I said to you, 'Yes, I am a Christian,' and a day when I said to you, 'Well, now actually I'm not, I'm an agnostic.' So, quite clearly, there were periods in my life when I've had doubts.

CLARE: And the process of sorting out those doubts?

WIDDECOMBE: Very gradual, very gradual.

CLARE: Wouldn't that be a sort of self-analysis?

WIDDECOMBE: No, it was much more gradual than that. I can only describe it as the erosion of unbelief, the coming back from agnosticism. It was very, very slow. There was no one point when I would say that was when I decided I had it wrong.

CLARE: But you would have been thinking about it?

WIDDECOMBE: I think I was thinking about it subconsciously a great deal.

CLARE: And during that time, how did you feel?

WIDDECOMBE: Oh quite comfortable. When I was an agnostic it wasn't a situation of saying, 'Well, I just don't know.' I actually took the agnostic view which was, there is no knowledge beyond material phenomena and I actually stuck very firmly to that. And I was quite comfortable with that view which I held for some time. And slowly it was eroded.

CLARE: And could you not be comfortable with it now?

WIDDECOMBE: Oh I certainly could not be comfortable with it now.

CLARE: Because?

WIDDECOMBE: Because I have rejected it.

CLARE: And you came to reject it, you say, slowly?

WIDDECOMBE: Slowly and gradually. And as I say, there was no Damascene conversion. There was no one point that I can identify for you and say, 'At that point I changed my mind.' It didn't happen like that at all.

CLARE: But it wasn't just the change from agnosticism to belief, it was the change from agnosticism to a belief in a personal god.

WIDDECOMBE: It was the point of return when I think I made one of my greatest mistakes. I think that when I came back from agnosticism, and knew that I was coming back from it and knew that I was going to be an active Christian, I think the mistake I made at that point was to come back as an Anglican, when I was already very convinced that Rome was right, already very convinced that only Rome was actually standing up to the challenges of the modern world. I went back to the C of E purely because, I believe, of my Anglican roots. If you like, it was just something natural. I think I was wrong.

CLARE: But can I stop you there. When you say Rome was right, you make it sound like the choice between two political parties. You mean the political view of Rome. But the actual nature of belief in God is what I'm really interested in. It's a hill of beans in one sense between Rome and Canterbury, that decision, when the bigger decision is an actual belief in God, a God to whom you've described personally praying.

WIDDECOMBE: Yes, of course, I personally pray to Him. I may say I have been much misrepresented. Recently, when I was asked, when I prayed, what happened, I said, 'Well, when you pray you feel you are answered.' I found this translated across the press almost into hearing voices and all the rest of it. I was very, very badly caricatured and that was one of the many irritating things that I went through a couple of weeks ago. I do believe in a personal God and I do believe that when you pray you are personally answered. And, of course, since being a Roman Catholic, the whole company of Heaven comes into it, it isn't just a prayer to God.

CLARE: It is difficult to explain, isn't it?

431

WIDDECOMBE: Very, very.

CLARE: The psychiatrist might think of it in terms of auditory hallucinations, hearing voices saying, 'Ann, do this!'

WIDDECOMBE: Oh, I certainly don't do that. It would be much clearer if I did, wouldn't it?

CLARE: It would be much clearer, yes, and indeed some might see this interview as a total failure because you haven't said so! You are a person of certainties, and you've got clear views on life and politics and society. In addition, though, you do have a personal relationship, as you see it, with God, who helps you do what you do. Now I'm interested in this psychologically, you understand, because of course that gives you enormous strength. It's not just Ann Widdecombe who feels that X, Y or Z is the way forward, there's a sense in which God is on your side?

WIDDECOMBE: Yes, but be careful. There is a huge danger I think about any politician, I'm not thinking of anyone particularly, but anybody in general, claiming a monopoly of Christian wisdom. I was very perturbed just before the last election when I thought that effectively, he was fairly careful in his wording, but effectively that was what Tony Blair was trying to do at one point and claim for one party a monopoly of Christian virtue. Now, I think you have to be very careful when you say, 'God is on my side.' I much prefer to say, 'I am on God's side.' I think that's certainly better. You have to be very, very careful that you are not excluding people who are equally close to God who have come to a different view.

CLARE: But I was raising it in the context of actual individual decisions. You, very honestly, I thought, revealed the extent to which, when you were pondering what you were going to do about Michael Howard, you prayed. Now, allowing for the way in which the media will misrepresent this, it was a hostage to fortune to an extent, because what you were clearly saying was that God guided you.

WIDDECOMBE: Yes, I feel he does. I feel that when I pray about any one of a number of matters he guides me. It would be quite pointless praying for guidance if one didn't think one was going to get it.

CLARE: The problem is of course, only you can know that.

432

WIDDECOMBE: That's true.

CLARE: So if I'm judging your decisions or your judgements I can't, for the life of me, take that on board. I've got to take it that this is what Ann wants to do and she does it.

WIDDECOMBE: No, that's fair enough. But I was asked had I prayed about it, had I consulted a priest about it and I was truthful and said yes to both things.

CLARE: When you were praying, was it a prayer in the nature of 'Oh God, take this away from me, I don't want to do it'?

WIDDECOMBE: Oh, there was certainly a very strong element of that around, yes. I didn't want to do it.

CLARE: Would there have been an element that you most certainly did want to do it?

WIDDECOMBE: There was a very strong conviction that I was going to have to do it, and a very strong conviction that it was the right thing to do. It was a very momentous thing to do, not just in my own terms, but much more so in terms of the effect on Michael. It was a very momentous thing to do.

CLARE: Why do Christians drag in God at such moments? Why can't you then decide that you will have to do this on your own initiative?

WIDDECOMBE: If I did something without reference to God, I would never myself be certain that I was doing the right thing. We don't drag God into it. As I say, I responded to direct questions: Had I prayed? Yes I had. Had I consulted a priest? Yes I had. I was answering questions truthfully. It is then very easy to caricature it as somebody saying they're on a divine mission. I never claimed that at all.

CLARE: No, no, and I understand that. I don't come from that tradition so you wouldn't expect me to do that. I am sufficiently aware of the nature of religious belief to know that that's not the way it works but I do feel always uneasy when I see, even as carefully argued as you've argued it, a relationship between religion and politics. You warned me, I notice, but of course, you're the politician. No point in warning me, it's you that needs to be warned.

WIDDECOMBE: Which is why I don't ever claim a monopoly of Christian virtue. Nobody's ever heard me do it. Nobody has. I have always said there is a case to be made for Christianity in capitalism, there's a case to be made for Christianity in socialism, and indeed for any woolly old thing in between. But nobody has ever heard me claim that there is only one possible solution politically which is compatible with Christian factors. Nobody's ever heard me say that. That was why I issued the warning.

CLARE: Your faith is in a God who guides and helps and intervenes?

WIDDECOMBE: And intervenes.

CLARE: To the extent that there would be evidence of God's presence?

WIDDECOMBE: I do believe in, in miracles. There has been one, I'm not prepared to give details but there has been one within my own family. I do believe in miracles. I do believe in an actively intervening God.

CLARE: One within your close family?

WIDDECOMBE: Yes. I do believe in an actively intervening God.

CLARE: Can I just stop you? You say you wouldn't talk about it but ...

WIDDECOMBE: I'm not going to give details, no, because it was not for me. It was not my miracle, it was somebody else's.

CLARE: But it has affected your belief

WIDDECOMBE: It was certainly a factor yes, and certainly it is one of a number of things that makes me believe that yes, there is active intervention. Again, if there weren't, I wouldn't pray. If I'm in a situation of danger or something like that, there would be no point in praying unless you believed in active intervention, no point at all. Waste of time.

CLARE: You're very logical on so many things. If I were to, I won't, but if I were to discuss capital punishment with you I've no doubt we'd be discussing the evidence of whether it's a deterrent or whether it isn't, and the problem of convicting innocent people and executing them and so on. So I'll spare you that and you'll spare me that. But none the less, you'd act in those instances in terms of evidence that we would then argue about. But in terms of this, and it really does interest me, there is no way, you'll say to me, 'I came back to knowing God after a thoughtful search.'

WIDDECOMBE: Yup!

CLARE: But there's no evidence that you can give me as to how that came about. This is Ann Widdecombe for once not being quote – logical – unquote.

WIDDECOMBE: Well, to a lot of people I've noticed religion never does appear particularly logical. I can only tell you the processes that I went through. I cannot dream them up.

CLARE: But it's not logic, it's faith.

WIDDECOMBE: In order to satisfy your . . .

CLARE: I'm saying, isn't it faith?

WIDDECOMBE: I believe the Creed's a statement of fact.

CLARE: But it opens with the words: 'I believe.'

WIDDECOMBE: Exactly. But I actually divide Christians up into two groups, if you like, on this. There are some who will say that it's a statement of belief and there are some who will say it is a statement of fact. Now when I say 'I believe', I am actually iterating in my view what is a statement of fact.

CLARE: Absolute fact?

WIDDECOMBE: Absolute fact.

CLARE: Your life then has a number of rock-hard certainties in it, political certainties, religious certainties?

WIDDECOMBE: Oh yes, oh yes, absolutely.

CLARE: Personal certainties?

WIDDECOMBE: Absolutely.

CLARE: Does it surprise you that I'm surprised?

WIDDECOMBE: Yes.

CLARE: Why?

WIDDECOMBE: Is your life sort of completely anchorless?

CLARE: No, no. Don't do that to me! We're not talking about extremes.

WIDDECOMBE: You said a number of certainties, you didn't say all certainties, you said there are a number of certainties. I can't believe your life doesn't have a number of certainties, of course it does.

CLARE: No, but on the major issues of life, you are much more certain.

WIDDECOMBE: On those issues which I . . .

CLARE: For instance, the purpose of life. You know what that is, you've got a religious conviction. Politically, you've got convictions. On many of the issues of modern life and living, how people bring up their children, what kind of schools they should go to, whether they should be single sex, and so on. You have got very certain convictions.

WIDDECOMBE: Now I think actually what you have done there is to distort what I said and I think this is important, this is very important. You have just said to me I've got very strong views on what sort of schools people should send their children to. No, I gave you a very strong view on the sort of school that, had I a child, I would send my child to.

CLARE: Fair enough.

WIDDECOMBE: It doesn't invalidate other people's choices.

CLARE: No, fair enough, I did extend that. It's your basic political and religious convictions that I'm struck by. You summed it up very nicely for me in the discussion on religion. You say Christians divide into those for whom it's a matter of faith and those for whom it's a matter of fact. And, I don't think it would surprise me if I'd been asked to guess which you would have been. You are a person of conviction.

WIDDECOMBE: Yes.

CLARE: And that's all I asked you. When I said to you, 'Are you surprised I'm surprised?' You said, 'Well, don't you have convictions?' Yes, I have some, but on the biggest questions of life I'm ...

WIDDECOMBE: But those are the very questions on which we must have convictions. Those are the very questions on which it is most dangerous to be rudderless.

CLARE: You mean you can't have doubts about whether there is a God?

WIDDECOMBE: I think it is better that you do not have doubts. That it is most important that you resolve it.

CLARE: I didn't say whether it was better. Oh Ann, I think it would be much preferable if I had no doubts about the meaning of existence and the purpose of this journey through life, but the fact is I do and the question of why, whether it is better or not, shouldn't enter into it. Surely the question is whether it is true?

WIDDECOMBE: Well, I have no doubts. You obviously have some. I don't, you do. That's a fact. Why are we spending an hour discussing it?

CLARE: Oh, because it's all part of an image of you. You were very intrigued that at the very outset I said to you, are you as intrigued as other people about yourself, and you said no. But one of the things I believe people are rather intrigued about in relation to you, I may be wrong about this, is that you have got a series of very firm convictions. You're not unique in this. There are a number of other people I can think of in British politics in post-war years ...

WIDDECOMBE: I'm very relieved to hear it!

CLARE: Yes, I'm not so relieved to hear it. I suppose I'm always a little wary of people who have firm convictions on things and the question I asked you, whether you had any profound doubts, you say not really.

WIDDECOMBE: I think that's actually rather a sad feature of the age as well. I think a lot of people these days suspect certainty, are slightly nervous in the presence of strong conviction whereas a few centuries ago the opposite would have been true. People would have expected you to know your mind and to have had strong convictions. My line is that this is something that everybody comes to, either their convictions or their doubts on their own, and that actually, there's nothing spectacular either in somebody having a conviction or in not having a conviction. It is just the way it happens to be. I happen to be a person of conviction.

CLARE: But why do you say, 'It's the way it happens to be'?

WIDDECOMBE: It is the way it happens to be. Look ...

CLARE: You mean the way that you and I have the same or different views on something is just a matter of chance?

WIDDECOMBE: Oh, I certainly think chance, but also approach to things. But chance plays a very wide part. I think that some people, for example, could never imagine going through life without a partner. Some people actually prefer to go through life on their own. Some people have no strong view either way, they'll just take it as chance, whatever happens to come. And I think that you can apply that to all sorts of things.

CLARE: Which are you?

WIDDECOMBE: In that particular analysis, I'm the chance person. I've never been anti-marriage, I'm never particularly given it a priority. It's been a mixture of choice and chance that it hasn't happened.

CLARE: Would you have liked it to happen?

WIDDECOMBE: No, not actively.

CLARE: Would you like it to happen?

WIDDECOMBE: No, oh no, not now.

CLARE: Why not?

WIDDECOMBE: Good heavens no, not now. No, no. I'm nearly 50 and I'm very set in my ways and I would be a most uncomfortable companion I can assure you.

CLARE: Why? You might be a very stimulating companion?

WIDDECOMBE: You've actually I think brought out some of the reasons why. Great convictions. No, no, certainly not now.

CLARE: You had a nice phrase which I, I read to my wife. You said about the relief of not being married, you said the relief that there was no somebody there demanding his supper or wondering where on earth I'd put his clean socks.

WIDDECOMBE: I think that sums it up?

CLARE: Do you think so?

WIDDECOMBE: Yes, I do. Not because I think marriage is about clean socks, just in case anybody takes that too literally. But it is about mutual demands, demands on each other and I have now got into a pattern whereby I'm relieved to be on my own, whereby there comes a time when I can go home and shut the door on the world and I am absolutely alone and I value that tremendously.

CLARE: What are the disadvantages?

WIDDECOMBE: I suppose the disadvantages are that when things are hard, you are managing alone, and that's just something that you have to face up to.

CLARE: You've mentioned one of the demands of marriage, which is, or of a personal relationship, which is to take account of the other person. Does that mean that, I've got to choose my words carefully, does that mean that the danger of a person who is not in that kind of relationship is that they can become selfish?

WIDDECOMBE: You mean am I selfish? I may well be in as much as

438

I've got into a pattern of doing things in a certain way which I like to do but, on the other hand, the whole of my working day is spent in the service of other people so that's the antidote to it.

CLARE: But could you conceive of a situation where I might meet you in a year or two's time and you might say, 'You know I was quite wrong about that. I met somebody and ...'

WIDDECOMBE: Oh gracious no, no, no.

CLARE: Does that mean you don't think that you'd be attractive to somebody?

WIDDECOMBE: No, I haven't really bothered to work that one out. Though, bless my soul, if I believe all the press says the answer to that is probably no.

CLARE: But you don't believe all that?

WIDDECOMBE: Well, I haven't really bothered to work that out, that was a rather frivolous aside. I haven't bothered to work that out. I am just now, having spent decades on my own, managing things the way I like to manage them, having now got the sort of job which is an 18-hour-a-day job, and a seven-day-a-week job, and having got something, which as far as I'm concerned is utterly fulfilling, which is the public service side, which I think is a part of politics that people too greatly underestimate. I am not looking for any additional dimensions. That's all I'm saying.

CLARE: I wasn't suggesting you were looking. I was wondering whether you anticipated that as a possibility. In other words, how open is your future? We talked about this issue of chance. Of course, chance is a strange thing. It can throw up things quite unexpectedly and one of the things, of course, it often does do to people is, just after they've enunciated some position that they've adopted, that they're not going to do this or they'll never do that, lo and behold something happens. I've certainly had that happen to me.

WIDDECOMBE: My future is open in as much as I could walk down and walk outside Broadcasting House and have a heart attack and that would be that. I mean one's future is always open. You can never say with total certainty that this is what will happen.

CLARE: But politics would be your whole life?

WIDDECOMBE: Certainly I do not wish to be engaged in any other profession other than politics.

CLARE: So what do you say to those people who feel that in that tremendous battle with Michael Howard, your political future could well have been closed off?

WIDDECOMBE: Oh, that was a price that I knew that I would have to pay right from the start. I'm aware that this will be mammothly open to misinterpretation, but I felt that in a way I was being brought to the time of trial. That if I let that weigh with me, that if I let my own political future weigh with me over an issue which I did consider to be mammothly important in all sorts of different ways, then really it wouldn't be worth having as a political future. As I've said, to look at self-advancement in its own right, it isn't worth fourpence three farthings, it really isn't.

CLARE: But, before we began, you and I were discussing the politicians I've interviewed in this series over the years, and I was struck by how many of them in a sense are very much their own people. They are individual politicians and hence I doubt will ever hold real power. Politics is full of shabby and odd things happening and behind-doors deals. For people with very firm convictions it can be a very painful process. It often means they will be successful as individual politicians but not in the team, not in the cabinet, not in government?

WIDDECOMBE: It's actually very hard to level that against me, when I was in the team for six and a half years.

CLARE: I was suggesting it as a result of what happened then. Obviously things had gone quite well up to then. You didn't have that kind of conflict of conscience until then.

WIDDECOMBE: No, I managed to play perfectly well as a team player up to then although I admit it's unlikely I could play perfectly well as a team player again.

CLARE: But did it disappoint you, for example, that you felt so strongly about what you did and had to do, that you were alone in a way?

WIDDECOMBE: Oh absolutely.

CLARE: You would have got support I'm sure in the tea room and so on and people said nice things to you, but in the end it didn't move other politicians to feel that something has to be done about this?

WIDDECOMBE: No, let me make it very clear. One or two colleagues did very kindly come out in support. I actually said to them, 'No, you know, this is something that I want to do alone. It is something that it is much better that I do alone without embroiling other people in.'

CLARE: But isn't politics always about embroiling other people?

WIDDECOMBE: No, it's not always about embroiling other people.

CLARE: Very often, then, very often.

WIDDECOMBE: It can often be about embroiling other people but not always, not invariably. I think there are some things about which you say, 'I don't actually want to get anybody else caught up in this. This is something which I feel I've got to do.' What I said was very straightforward: I'm going to make my doubts and my reservations known. It is then entirely up to my colleagues whether they take those into account or not and if they want to say no, they're not going to take those into account, that's up to them. I did my duty at the point that I made my doubts and reservations known. I didn't have to go any further.

CLARE: But does it affect your judgement of your colleagues that they didn't. You felt so strongly, this is something you said was massively important. You prayed to God about it. You sought religious advice. You knew it put your political career on the line. It did have the unfortunate connotations of an individual vendetta because it was you against him. They listened. You did your bit. People used words like 'courageous', 'indomitable' etc. and other words. And then that was that.

WIDDECOMBE: Oh yes, that was that.

CLARE: This is the arena in which your life is pitched. Does it not affect your perception of your colleagues?

WIDDECOMBE: I think every time you take a stand on something, and I have taken a number of stands in my time, then quite obviously the way that you look at your fellow MPs is going to be somewhat coloured by whether they share that stand, whether they actively oppose that stand, whether they just shrug neutrally. It would be somewhat coloured. But politics is a great kaleidoscope of changing alliances and people that you can be bitterly opposed to one day are people with whom you can be allied the next. And therefore the fact that there were some

441

colleagues who thought that I was quite bonkers and there were other colleagues who gave me a lot of support but made sure it was all extremely *sotto voce*, and behind closed doors, that is something that I would expect and I have no doubt that there will be other issues when some of those colleagues and I will shift positions.

CLARE: You would expect them to think you were bonkers?

WIDDECOMBE: I would expect some of them to think I'm bonkers because I'm afraid there are some politicians who believe that you should never, ever, ever, under any circumstances, do anything to rock the boat, and you should always put yourself first and I actually went against both those two great criteria.

CLARE: Are they more inclined to think you're bonkers if you're a woman?

WIDDECOMBE: No, I think this is twaddle. I'm actually rather sick of the self-pitying attitude of women in Parliament who believe that every time somebody thinks that they're not doing the right thing that it's all because they're a woman. That's rot. I've never regarded myself as a woman MP in that sense. I'm an MP who happens to be a woman and I see myself on an exact par with the men. I got there by exactly the same route as they did, by a process of selection and election and no, I don't feel that there is any particular persecution because you're female, I think that's just rot.

CLARE: But you feel more sympathetic to the men in Parliament than to many of the women?

WIDDECOMBE: I certainly get on well with the men in Parliament and the truth is that over, for example, something like the pregnant prisoner controversy, my worst problems were caused by the women, not by the men.

CLARE: Just why should that surprise you?

WIDDECOMBE: I'm not saying it surprises me, I'm just saying it's a fact.

CLARE: Yes, but I wouldn't have thought my sex is notable for its considerable concern for pregnant women prisoners. My sex isn't the sex that gets pregnant.

WIDDECOMBE: Well, that at least must be one thing that we both totally agree on! That is a fact, not a statement of belief, you're quite right. But give science time and you never know. But, I actually find it very easy to sympathise and empathise with the men in Parliament, I've never had a problem on that score.

CLARE: But on that particular issue, since you raised it, the pregnant woman issue, is it sentimental then to anticipate that more women in Parliament might actually elevate some of the more feminine concerns, say, of a pregnant woman prisoner?

WIDDECOMBE: Hang on, they weren't just elevating feminine concerns, as you put it. There was a huge attack on my own childlessness, and that came from women, it did not come from the men. In fact the men registered distaste and a lot of Labour men did so afterwards to me in private.

CLARE: Yes, though would that not have been related to the fact that they might have expected that a woman, and you've explained why they were perhaps wrong, but they might have expected that a woman, childless or otherwise, a woman might have been more sensitive to the needs of a pregnant woman prisoner than men?

WIDDECOMBE: First of all, I think there is a huge presumption there that I was insensitive to the needs, whereas what I was trying to do throughout was to point out that we didn't have a policy of chaining people in childbirth, we didn't have a policy of chaining people in labour. But yes, there was a policy that people were secured between prison and hospital and in hospital, only so long as it wasn't affecting the medical treatment. Now I kept making ...

CLARE: But it's not done now, is it?

WIDDECOMBE: No we changed the policy.

CLARE: But you didn't press to change the policy?

WIDDECOMBE: I defended the policy as it was my ministerial duty to do at the time.

CLARE: But that's the following orders argument isn't it?

WIDDECOMBE: That's not the following orders argument at all. The fact is that if you are a member of the government there are certain conventions and ministers of state do not change policy. My secretary of state, who was then Michael Howard, has been in this instance unfairly criticised for leaving me to it. In fact, he was up in the air, in an aeroplane, but uncontactable and could not change the policy up in the air in an aeroplane when he didn't even know what was happening back in London.

CLARE: But you mean if you'd had a firm conviction that pregnant women prisoners shouldn't be shackled, you would have postponed doing anything about it until Michael Howard got off the plane?

WIDDECOMBE: I mean the fact is that secretaries of state change policy, um, and no change of policy is just done at the dispatch box by a minister under pressure. Those are facts of life. Had we actually had a policy of chaining women in childbirth, I would have changed it long before, long before the controversy happened. The controversy was over a completely different policy, which has been massively misunderstood which was not that we chained women in labour, we did not chain women in labour. What we did was to secure women who had arrived at hospital for treatment until such time as it was medically desirable not to do so. That was the policy. Now that policy was subsequently relaxed, in my view quite rightly, but that was the policy.

CLARE: You say you were attacked by many women about your childlessness?

WIDDECOMBE: Yes, I certainly was.

CLARE: How did you feel about that?

WIDDECOMBE: Well, I think my main reaction was distaste. Nothing more than that, just distaste.

CLARE: You did understand, I presume, why some of it might have been angled in that way?

WIDDECOMBE: I understood well enough why it might have been angled in that way, I understand why people do a lot of things that I don't approve of.

CLARE: Being childless isn't a particularly painful thing for you?

WIDDECOMBE: I have long since got past the stage where political comment, whether in or outside the House or in the media or elsewhere, actually hurts.

CLARE: Is that right?

WIDDECOMBE: I think that if I'd had all that to cope with the day after I got into Parliament, it would have done massive damage, but you become inured by degrees. I've now been in Parliament ten years, I'm utterly used to it. I've been a minister for six and a half years, even more used to it. It is now the case that it has lost its power completely to hurt. I can't remember when I was last actually damaged in my feelings by anything that was said in the press and media, or in Parliament.

CLARE: Are you easily hurt outside of those considerations, press, media and Parliament?

WIDDECOMBE: Outside press, media and Parliament? Yes. I think that if friends betray, which mercifully is extremely rare, but if friends are ever treacherous, that hurts, yes. And therefore I don't betray.

CLARE: The extent to which you've developed this extra skin layer of immunity – how's that done?

WIDDECOMBE: I don't know, it just happens. It's something that happens. If it doesn't happen, I think you'd tend to stay out of the limelight and not be very controversial and not take tough stands.

CLARE: You come across as a person very much in control of feelings.

WIDDECOMBE: It's not a question of being in control of it. Genuinely, it no longer hurts. As I say, if I'd had it all the day after I got into Parliament, I think it would have done because I wouldn't have become inured, I wouldn't have got used to it.

CLARE: Take other feelings. Are you someone, for instance, who blows your top or loses your temper?

WIDDECOMBE: Mercifully not often. When I do it's fairly spectacular, but mercifully not often.

CLARE: Is it fairly spectacular?

WIDDECOMBE: On the rare occasions when it happens it can be spectacular.

CLARE: So you keep those sort of feelings under a tight rein?

WIDDECOMBE: I think it's better to do so. I think it's much better to do so. I don't actually have much respect for people who shout and therefore I wouldn't respect myself if I shouted.

CLARE: Let me ask you, is it a question of keeping emotions under a tight rein or, by and large, the emotions aren't there, except on those times when they suddenly rise volcanically to the surface? Do you see the difference? Some people have to constantly stay in touch with their feelings and keep them under control because they're temperamental. I suppose I'd be one of them. Whereas others are really fairly phlegmatic people.

WIDDECOMBE: I don't explode easily, it's quite true. I'm not fighting against explosion all the time, I don't explode easily. I think one of the things I have to battle against is probably sometimes being almost too, you call it phlegmatic, not exploding enough. Sometimes I think to myself, hang on, you know, you really should be angry about this.

CLARE: Are you someone who doesn't express other feelings easily?

WIDDECOMBE: Like what?

CLARE: Affection?

WIDDECOMBE: Oh no. I think I'm quite an affectionate friend.

CLARE: I felt in some of the things I read about you that you're a bit suspicious about the later twentieth-century emphasis on feelings.

WIDDECOMBE: Oh I am. I mean the idea that everything has to be guided by feelings and nothing by thought and conviction, I think is a load of old nonsense. But I'm certainly not suspicious of feelings as such and I take great care of my friends' feelings.

CLARE: So it's a matter of balance?

WIDDECOMBE: Yes.

CLARE: And you feel a balance is out of synch?

WIDDECOMBE: I feel that there is an over-emphasis, with due respect to you, on close analysis, on having to rationalise everything, on digging deep into why people do things which come quite naturally to them. If those things are harmless to themselves and to other people, I say let them get on with it.

CLARE: But is there then a place for analysis?

WIDDECOMBE: Oh there has to be a place for analysis. You are not a prisons minister without coming to the view that analysis is very necessary, not only in terms of individuals but in terms of groups.

CLARE: How much did that change you, your experience as a prisons minister?

WIDDECOMBE: It reinforced some convictions which I had, such as the huge part that idleness plays in crime, by which I don't mean unemployment, but I mean idleness in terms of unstructured, chaotic, disorganised days. That was very much re-emphasised. I think what it probably did was to convince me in certain thoughts which I had always had but hadn't really had the experience to base the convictions on.

CLARE: Did it change you in any way?

WIDDECOMBE: I don't think so. Others may be a better judge of that. I don't think so.

CLARE: There was nothing you saw in your time as prisons minister that . . .

WIDDECOMBE: Yes, there was plenty I saw.

CLARE: That significantly affected a conviction?

WIDDECOMBE: I'm much more intolerant now of what I call the Colonel Blimp tendency to think there is a quick and easy solution to everything and that all you've got to do is make life sufficiently hard for people and they automatically change. I never did hold to that view but I am much less tolerant of it now and actually tend to get very impatient of it when it's expressed.

CLARE: Do you think there is a role in the prisons, particularly with, for example, quite serious and repetitive offenders, do you think there is a role for the sort of analysis that we are talking about, trying to make sense of why somebody continually does something pretty terrible?

WIDDECOMBE: Oh yes. I think that one of the biggest steps forward that we've taken in recent years is offending behaviour courses, is making prisoners confront their own behaviour, the reasons why they do it, the effects that it has on other people. I think that is one of the most significant things we've done and it's something which I do sincerely hope never goes down the tube because of resources.

CLARE: But one of them did. I am thinking of the unit run by Bob Johnson in Parkhurst. It went down the tube.

WIDDECOMBE: Oh, there were plenty more that were actually being expanded and built on. I'm never going to say that because one particular thing is stopped in one prison, what I'm saying is that I hope that in general we always give emphasis to offending behaviour courses. Not each individual course in every single prison, I'm not saying that at all. That's like saying that you must keep every school open. I wouldn't say that but what I would say is that all schools should be good schools and I think that our offending behaviour courses must increase both in terms of volume and in terms of quality.

CLARE: What if I said to you that far from it being a modern propensity, this endless self-analysis, that in many ways you could say of human beings that they don't analyse enough, that they don't examine their motives for doing X, Y and Z enough, and that were they to, they might become more humble and they might become more cautious.

WIDDECOMBE: I think they'd waste a phenomenal amount of time, quite honestly.

CLARE: Would that be such a bad thing, in view of the sorts of things that people do who don't think too deeply about things? Then we spend an awful lot of time undoing them.

WIDDECOMBE: What you actually heard me say was that if it's harmless to themselves and other people, let them get on with it and don't bother analysing it.

CLARE: Ah, but that's very dismissive. I'm not talking about harmless.

WIDDECOMBE: Where it's harmful I think that is different.

CLARE: But that's an interesting split, harmless or harmful. I was thinking of more a good, bad split, valuable or not valuable. Harmless makes it sound like an interesting diversion. It's a bit like some people's view of art, that it's a harmless diversion and it keeps people off the streets. But I was thinking of it more positively than that. That actually in the exploration of what we are about, lies the possibility that we would become, with or without a personal God, we would become somewhat more humble, and therefore less dangerous.

WIDDECOMBE: I think some analysis just goes on subconsciously anyway. Whether it is when you are gathering your thoughts before general confession in church, or whether it is when you're asking yourself why you are doing something that you are doing, or whether it is when your wife says to you, 'I do wish you wouldn't do that because actually it is very harmful.' I think some sort of analysis like that is going on all the time. What I am saying is that I think you can overdo it. I think you can try to rationalise away everything. Life really isn't like that. We do have instincts as well as thoughts and we do all come to different views. And it really isn't necessary to try to analyse everything to the last degree to decide who is right. Some things in this life will be important. We will differ in our views of what is important. Some things are important. Those things which are important to you, yes, of course you must jolly well make sure that you know why you are doing them and you know why they are ruling passions. But other things that are not important, don't waste time on.

CLARE: And do you feel you know why so many things are so important to you?

WIDDECOMBE: Well, I know the things that I consider important. For example . . .

CLARE: No, no, but do you know why you consider them important?

WIDDECOMBE: My pro-life campaign I actually believe concerns one of the most fundamental issues, not just of the decade but of the entire millennium. Where does life begin and the protection of life. Now, to me, that is tremendously important. There are other things, quite obviously, Almighty God, it goes without saying, is tremendously important. But other things, do I have a television, do I like this particular book, you know, these sorts of things, this is not important.

CLARE: The issue of abortion is an interesting one because there one can take a position and argue it but how you see your opponent is very important. One of the things I'm struck by in the abortion–anti-abortion debate is that it isn't just that people disagree but that they each see the other in a certain way. For instance, if you insist that abortion is murder, then does that mean that people who hold a different view of when life begins or who see a collision of rights between mother and child are murderers?

WIDDECOMBE: Certainly upholding killing. Well, no, murder has a particular connotation, murder is a criminal killing. Now if abortion is legal then perforce it is not a criminal killing but they are still certainly upholding killing. I have always said that. I have never used a term like 'murderers' because actually I don't

449

think it improves debate but I have never hesitated to use the word 'killing'.

CLARE: But would that be the only reason you wouldn't use the term, because it wouldn't improve the debate? Do you actually think that that's what they are?

WIDDECOMBE: No, I've just explained, murder has a criminal dimension. I have said ...

CLARE: The deliberate destruction of human life.

WIDDECOMBE: I have certainly called it the deliberate destruction of human life. That is what I believe it to be.

CLARE: But then aren't they murderers?

WIDDECOMBE: No, Professor Clare, you are a very clever man and you can understand that murder has a connotation of criminality. If abortion is lawful perforce, it is not criminal. It doesn't alter the fact that in my view it is still killing.

CLARE: And your views of those who oppose you would be like your views of people who oppose you politically on other things, that they are mistaken but you can respect their position?

WIDDECOMBE: I don't actually respect the anti-life position. I never have respected it. I respect the individual, I don't respect his position. There are some positions I respect even though I don't share them and I can do that quite easily and understand why the individual's arrived at that view. I respect the individual, that is an individual soul, but I don't respect the conclusion, no, not in the least.

CLARE: But isn't it an important issue, the extent to which we do respect an individual who holds different views?

WIDDECOMBE: Oh it's crucial. It is absolutely crucial that we recognise that we are all equal in the sight of God, we are all working towards the same salvation, or should be. And it is quite wrong that we should write off an individual because of his views. But it is equally right that if those views are so wrong that we believe that they are harmful and damaging to life itself, then we should fight those views hand, tooth and nail.

CLARE: I come from a Roman Catholic background, you from an Anglican background. Just listening to you and thinking about this, my question is: do you think a firm religious upbringing actually enables people to stand out against, say, a given conventional wisdom. Do you think it does?

WIDDECOMBE: I think there are a lot of people who've had firm religious upbringings who actually take the quiet route and don't stand out, no matter what they may think privately. I have always taken the view, not something I've come to, something which comes quite naturally to me, which is if I believe something I will speak it, on the whole. There are always exceptions to that, but on the whole.

CLARE: And if you were to put your finger on what it is that identifies you as different to the large number of other people who do what you say and I agree with you, I take your point, what is it, that's what intrigues me? That must intrigue you to an extent when you think about it?

WIDDECOMBE: I truthfully don't know. When I said right at the beginning of this interview that I take myself for granted, I'm afraid that is very much the case.

CLARE: And so you wouldn't do what I might do and that is, look back to your parents, the kind of emphasis that they had and the values that they had that you identified with. In other words, you wouldn't do what in a sense politically you're doing which is, by trying to create a different political society, to try and engender change. You came out of an environment, you must believe that it had some kind of role, otherwise why would you bother changing it?

WIDDECOMBE: That presupposes that I want change. If I want change in myself, that would only be because there was something I didn't like, something I felt was wrong.

CLARE: Is there?

WIDDECOMBE: Oh well, there's always something. If you think I come without original sin, certainly not. Of course there are things wrong.

CLARE: But none sufficiently large to change?

WIDDECOMBE: Not in terms of views held, which is what we've been talking about.

CLARE: What aspect of yourself, quite apart from your convictions, if you had the ability and the choice, would you wish to change?

WIDDECOMBE: Oh, greater patience.

CLARE: Greater?

WIDDECOMBE: Patience. I am a pretty impatient soul.

CLARE: Are you?

WIDDECOMBE: Greater patience.

CLARE: You've been very patient today. But you are impatient?

WIDDECOMBE: It's enforced impatience.

CLARE: Is it, is it a struggle?

WIDDECOMBE: Yes it is, yes. Yes, when people are asking me questions which, with all due respect, I might wish to dismiss and can't but must answer them properly, I can get quite impatient, yes.

CLARE: Why did you agree to this interview?

WIDDECOMBE: Why did I agree to come along?

CLARE: Yes, because this isn't your cup of tea.

WIDDECOMBE: No, I looked forward to the duel and I think in many ways we've had one.

CLARE: That's what appealed?

WIDDECOMBE: Yup, we've had a duel.

CLARE: That's true, yes indeed. Because you're religious, the question I normally ask people, do they think about death, I won't even demean the conversation by asking you that! But is it something that again you're phlegmatic about, that if it happens, it happens?

WIDDECOMBE: I'd rather it didn't happen too soon.

CLARE: There are things you want to do?

WIDDECOMBE: There are things I want to do. There are lots of things I want to do.

CLARE: What do you want to do?

WIDDECOMBE: I want to write a novel. I'm just beginning to do so.

CLARE: A novel!

WIDDECOMBE: Yes, a novel. I'm sorry that you're so surprised by this.

CLARE: A political novel?

WIDDECOMBE: A political dimension but it's not about politics, no.

CLARE: But it will draw on your experiences?

WIDDECOMBE: It will certainly draw on my experience but essentially it's about handicap, which I think is one of the big issues in society today.

CLARE: Why do you want to write a novel about handicap?

WIDDECOMBE: Partly as a result of the work I've done on pro-life but also because of other observations I've made. I think we have physical perfection out of all proportion in the same way that I've said we've got a lot of other things out of all proportion. And that we spend far too much time worshipping the norm of physical perfection. And I think that is actually having a much greater impact than we realise on people who are disabled, people who are disfigured, people who are odd in some sort of way. I think it is particularly obscene, and I think I use the word advisedly, when you have already beautiful women having operations in order to make themselves even more beautiful. We've just got the whole thing out of proportion. You've got young girls with slimmer's disease because they've got some view of the perfect figure, and it's dangerous. It's dangerous in a very much wider way.

CLARE: But apropos of that and relating it to you personally, I was quite upset to see you do that to yourself. You described yourself as overweight, ugly, having crooked teeth, a spinster – at 49! Were you doing something mocking there, taking a caricature and trumping it?

WIDDECOMBE: No, I was meeting the press on its own ground and quite obviously was trying to ...

CLARE: But you're none of those things.

WIDDECOMBE: Well, I don't know about that. I'm certainly overweight. What the press was trying to do was to use these things in a way to hurt. And what I was effectively turning round and saying was, 'Yes, all those things are true, so what, so what?' You know, so what?

CLARE: But you know they're not true?

WIDDECOMBE: Well, hang on, I mean they were very specific. The press said I was overweight, I am. That I have crooked teeth which I do, etc., etc., etc. But what does that matter?

CLARE: Well, you used one word that I think is of some importance. You used the word ugly.

WIDDECOMBE: Because that was what was said.

CLARE: Yes, but you don't believe that?

WIDDECOMBE: Whether I believe it or not I'd say, so what, so what?

CLARE: But you don't?

WIDDECOMBE: Well, there is this in it – that somebody should not be afraid to be ugly if what you're actually talking about is purely the physical presentation and not what goes on inside. Somebody should not be afraid of that because there are lots of ugly people. There are people severely disfigured, there are people mammothly disabled. Now, when I was growing up and when you were growing up because you point out we were contemporaries, there were an awful lot of people around who were war disabled, war disfigured, we took them for granted. You still had a lot of children suffering from polio, we took that for granted. None of those things are good things but what we didn't shy away from was the absence of physical perfection in those people. They were still people. We are now at the stage where we routinely abort children for hare lip and club foot. Whatever sort of a state have we got into? And that was what I was really defying when I made those comments.

CLARE: And you're going to write a novel pulling some of those issues into it?

WIDDECOMBE: Pulling some of those themes together.

CLARE: That seems an interesting other road taken in the sense that politics is one area, a novel and fiction is another. Is that related to a feeling that for the moment your political career is on hold?

WIDDECOMBE: Well, certainly there is a hole caused by the very simple fact of not being a minister. There is a hole there, which needs to be filled by something. Now, obviously, I will have much more time for my constituents, much more time for my family, much more time for myself. I've got all of that, and I want to devote some of that time, not all of it, but some of that time to doing something which I've always wanted to do, which is to write.

CLARE: Do you think it's likely that you will reveal a good deal of yourself in your novel?

WIDDECOMBE: Oh no, it's not going to be autobiographical. I'm absolutely determined on that, totally determined on that.

CLARE: Even though ...

WIDDECOMBE: If I wanted to write an autobiography, I'd write an autobiography.

CLARE: Even though what drives it is related to an empathy that you have with other people.

WIDDECOMBE: No, I think what drives it is a very strong view that any minute now we're going to get quite a major euthanasia debate in this country and whatever happens I think that we've got to be alert to the way that we have started to put physical perfection above spiritual perfection and above the individual.

CLARE: So it will be a political novel.

WIDDECOMBE: There will be, as I said, a political dimension. There will be a philosophical dimension. There will be, if you like, a religious dimension.

CLARE: Have you ever had a serious illness?

WIDDECOMBE: Never.

CLARE: So you've never been on the edge either of physical dissolution or mental dissolution?

WIDDECOMBE: Never, I'm very pleased to say.

CLARE: You're not someone who gets depressed?

WIDDECOMBE: No.

CLARE: So you're an optimistic person?

WIDDECOMBE: Oh, I don't sort of bubble over with the joys of life believing that everything is going to be all right. I'm not optimistic in that sense.

CLARE: Are you pessimistic in that sense?

WIDDECOMBE: I'm accepting, I take things very much for granted. As I say, I don't stop and analyse every last thing and whatever comes I have to deal with it, when it comes.

CLARE: So when you think of the life that you've got, what are you particularly grateful for?

WIDDECOMBE: Oh, I'm grateful for a huge number of things. I'm very grateful for the stability and happiness of my childhood. I would put that right at the top. And when I see so many people who don't have stable and happy childhoods, I think it's a massive tragedy because it's the foundation on which the rest of your life is built.

CLARE: Do you think you would have made a good mother?

WIDDECOMBE: What a very good question, I don't know the answer to it. I don't know the answer to it. And given that I don't know the answer perhaps it's as well I never tried!

CLARE: Ann Widdecombe, thank you very much indeed.

like someone
cuts not of
I steat bloodip manoy

People are
hard 2 find
the scenes but that
set right